The Slaves of the Churches

The Slaves of the Churches

A History

MARY E. SOMMAR

OXFORD
UNIVERSITY PRESS

OXFORD
UNIVERSITY PRESS

Oxford University Press is a department of the University of Oxford. It furthers
the University's objective of excellence in research, scholarship, and education
by publishing worldwide. Oxford is a registered trade mark of Oxford University
Press in the UK and certain other countries.

Published in the United States of America by Oxford University Press
198 Madison Avenue, New York, NY 10016, United States of America.

© Oxford University Press 2020

Library of Congress Cataloging-in-Publication Data
Names: Sommar, Mary E., 1953– author.
Title: The slaves of the churches : a history / Mary E. Sommar.
Description: New York, NY, United States of America :
Oxford University Press, 2020. |
Includes bibliographical references and index.
Identifiers: LCCN 2020007944 (print) | LCCN 2020007945 (ebook) |
ISBN 9780190073268 (hardback) | ISBN 9780190073282 (epub)
Subjects: LCSH: Slavery and the church—History—to 1500. |
Slavery—Religious aspects.
Classification: LCC HT913 .S66 2020 (print) |
LCC HT913 (ebook) | DDC 306.3/62—dc23
LC record available at https://lccn.loc.gov/2020007944
LC ebook record available at https://lccn.loc.gov/2020007945

1 3 5 7 9 8 6 4 2
Printed by Sheridan Books, Inc., United States of America

With love and gratitude to those unnamed ancestors who were among the subjects of this book.

Contents

Acknowledgments

Every work of scholarship owes a great deal to the efforts and experience of others. Some of that debt is acknowledged in the footnotes. And the rest, here. I am very thankful to many colleagues, friends, and family, especially David Collins, Gottfried and Margaret Heller, Richard Helmholz, Kathryn Kleinhans, Kathy Kremer, Tonya Johnson, Barbara Jones, Peter Landau, John McLarnon, Clarence Maxwell, Hermann Nehlsen, Kenneth Pennington, Ashley Sherman, Harald Siems, Albert Sommar, Charley Sommar, Loree Strickler, Paul Stuehrenberg, and Anders Winroth, without whose assistance and encouragement this book would never have been possible. In addition, thanks are due to the students in my Global Slavery seminar for their insightful and probing questions as well as to the library staffs of Yale University and Millersville University for their invaluable assistance. And, lastly, I owe a great debt of gratitude to the staff at the Oxford University Press, especially Cynthia Read, Hannah Campeanu, and Rick Stinson for turning my scribblings into something that can be shared with others.

One more acknowledgement must be made. An overwhelming anguish about the legacy of slavery is flooding our cities as this book goes to press. While a scholar must maintain a certain objectivity and distance from her work if an historical study is to have any significance, this does not mean that, when the work is done, she will not weep.

Abbreviations

ANF	*Ante-Nicene Fathers* (New York 1885)
CHC	*The Cambridge History of Christianity* (Cambridge 2006–)
CWHS	*The Cambridge World History of Slavery*, vol. 1: *The Ancient Mediterranean World*, ed. K. Bradley and P. Cartledge (Cambridge 2011)
DDC	*Dictionnaire de droit canonique*
EOMIA	*Ecclesia Occidentalis Monumenta Iuris Antiquissima,* ed. C. H. Turner (London 1907–)
HMCL	*History of Medieval Canon Law*, ed. W. Hartmann and K. Pennington (Washington, DC 1999–)
MGH	*Monumenta Germaniae Historica*
MIC	*Monumenta Iuris Canonici*
NPNF	*Nicene and Post-Nicene Fathers* (New York 1890–1900, 2nd series 1991)
PG	J.-P. Migne, *Patrologia graeca*
PL	J.-P. Migne, *Patrologia latina*
RSV	Revised Standard Version
ZRG.KA	*Zeitschrift der Savigny-Stiftung für Rechtsgeschichte. Kanonistische Abteilung*

1

Introduction

A number of years ago, I realized that the medieval European church had owned large numbers of slaves, a realization I found quite shocking. So I began to try to understand this issue in light of the canon law that is my scholarly home turf. Several exploratory conference papers and articles received an enthusiastic welcome from my colleagues, and I decided to turn the project into a book about the canon law that regulated ecclesiastical slaveholding over the long term. Then, in 2016, the Jesuits at Georgetown University in Washington, DC, announced that they were in the process of coming to terms with their slave-owning history, particularly the sale of some 272 poor souls South to Louisiana in 1838. The story was in the national news for several weeks.[1] And I realized the timeliness of my question about those who were known as *servi ecclesiarum*, the slaves of the churches.

More than fifty years ago, David Brion Davis looked at the "institutional continuity between ancient and modern slavery" in an effort to "problematize" slavery as a focus of academic inquiry.[2] In other words, he tried to figure out a way to define just what was meant by the word "slavery." There are many different ways that human beings throughout history have dominated other humans and forced them to do their bidding. But dispassionate scholarly inquiry requires a clearly defined object and clearly defined rules for investigation. This helps us to avoid the temptation to impose modern ideas of morality on our historical subjects, judging the ancients according to standards of which they could not possibly have been aware. Instead, we can analyze their behavior based on what we are able to learn of their own standards. The present work is an attempt to understand just what those standards were in connection with ecclesiastical servile dependents and to find out how these standards came to be.

---

[1] Craig Steven Wilder, *Ebony and Ivy: Race, Slavery, and the Troubled History of America's Universities* (New York 2013), provides a detailed picture of how slavery contributed to the success of many of the best American universities.

[2] David Brion Davis, *The Problem of Slavery in Western Culture* (Ithaca 1966) 31. Also see his *Slavery and Human Progress* (New York 1984).

The Slaves of the Churches. Mary E. Sommar, Oxford University Press (2020). © Oxford University Press.
DOI: 10.1093/oso/9780190073268.001.0001

This is not a comprehensive account of the church's views on slavery. Over the years, a number of scholars have attempted to do that, with varying success.[3] The general consensus of the best work in this area is that, overall, the position of most Christian churches concerning slavery did not change much over the centuries from ancient Rome until the nineteenth century; that of Roman Catholic canon law, not until the latter half of the twentieth.[4] The results here say nothing to challenge that. Neither does this study aim to describe in any detail how ecclesiastical institutions managed their affairs, their agricultural estates, or their domestic arrangements. These factors varied a great deal chronologically and, even more so, geographically. A comprehensive account would be unwieldy, and anything less would lead to conclusions that were valid only in connection with a particular sample population. This sort of analysis must await later investigations. The focus of the present inquiry is fairly narrow and thus able to be very clear: What were the church's regulations concerning its own unfree dependents? The temporal boundaries extend from the very beginning of Christianity, when norms for the behavior of the fledgling church were vague and varied, to the end of the medieval period, when secular as well as ecclesiastical jurisprudence became an international theoretical discipline. Eventually church law was relegated to the domain of the theologians.

This study also makes no attempt to evaluate how well the churches in various regions and in various centuries held to their regulations. For one thing, there is simply too much data from these fourteen centuries for such a global analysis to be practical—or comprehensible. And, more importantly, the available data does not generally document how well people broke or kept the rules except when there was a large scandal. Court records, especially from the early periods, are notoriously incomplete. Any analysis would be skewed in favor of sensational cases and would mislead us about the real picture. Again, these questions must be left for later investigation. This study traces the church's own norms concerning ecclesiastical unfree dependents and the evolution of these norms over time, with attention to how they were affected by the social, economic, political, and legal developments of the

---

[3] Several works stand out here for their scholarliness and impartiality: John T. Noonan Jr., *A Church That Can and Cannot Change* (Notre Dame, IN 2005); John Francis Maxwell, *Slavery and the Catholic Church* (Chichester 1975); and Rayford W. Logan, "The Attitude of the Church toward Slavery Prior to 1500," *Journal of Negro History* 17 (1932) 466–80. Also see Charles Verlinden, *L'esclavage dans l'Europe médiéval* (Bruges 1955) and Patricia Gravatt, *L'Église et l'esclavage* (Paris 2003).

[4] It should be noted that when I speak of "the church," I am usually referring to the Roman Catholic Church since this study ends more than a hundred years before Martin Luther's protests.

larger society. A few scholars studying the history of canon law have looked at some issues where slavery was a factor.[5] However, very little attention has been directed at the relevant ecclesiastical norms of the earlier centuries, and nothing, to my knowledge, has focused on the regulation of ecclesiastical servile dependents.

Theories about Slavery

Slavery as an institution, or as a phenomenon, has been found in just about every human society. Despite countless negative judgements of slavery that range from regretting slavery as an unfortunate situation to condemning it as outright evil, slavery has persisted, even where it has been expressly forbidden by legal or moral sanctions. In many societies, there were few sources of protection for the downtrodden, and few safe alternatives for those who were enslaved. Even if individual slaves were eventually set free, society rarely provided options that did not depend on the support of the former master, support that usually required the former slave to perform services in return. Thus, the economic and social realities often kept people in perpetual servitude of one kind or another. The enormous social as well as economic benefits to the slave owner resulted in a disinclination for even the kindhearted to find alternatives.

Popular understanding of the history of slavery and the Christian church frequently claims that the teachings of Christianity have always condemned slavery and were instrumental in its eventual abolition in Western society. But these claims fly in the face of the evidence. While Christian charity may have influenced how some people regarded slaves and what they thought about the practice of slavery, for most of its history the churches as well as individual church leaders had slaves and other unfree dependents, often in vast numbers. The Roman Catholic Church did not condemn slavery outright until the late twentieth century.

Although prejudice and personal domination are clearly evident in the behavior of many who controlled unfree dependents throughout history, for slave owners, slavery was often an economic issue, albeit one with enormous social consequences. And though we like to think of religious groups

---

[5] Generally, these studies have looked only at the twelfth- and thirteenth-century "classical" period of canon law and have concentrated on slavery as it affected marriage or clerical ordination.

as being concerned with "higher things," neither religious institutions nor the individuals who are a part of them are exempt from life's economic realities. The scholarship about ecclesiastical economic resources reveals three points of view. Some scholars have condemned how the institutional church and its personnel have dealt with these resources, especially concerning the accumulation of wealth. Others have taken a more defensive position, high-mindedly arguing the need to "preserve the patrimony" at all costs and dismissing what they viewed as the naiveté of those who praise the virtue of poverty. A third way of approaching the question of ecclesiastical wealth is more useful.[6] It recognizes that the church and the clergy have often accumulated material resources in quantities greater, often much, much greater, than that needed for basic sustenance. But it also acknowledges that the institutional church has always been run by human beings with human weaknesses. And the slave owners among them were seldom motivated to choose against slavery. Writing twenty-five years ago, David Pelteret cautioned, "A distinction must be drawn between the Church as an organization which followed a set of *administrative* principles and the Church as a collection of individual Christians who followed a set of *moral* principles."[7] Sometimes administrative efficiency challenges one's loyalty to high moral standards.

The literature on the history of slavery is vast. And no one study could hope to encompass all of the insights that this literature has provided. However, it may be useful here to consider some of the recent scholarship about slavery in general.[8] Along with Davis's insights, the work of Joseph

---

[6] The most helpful of these is John Gilchrist's classic study of how the church tried to regulate economic behavior in medieval Christendom, providing an invaluable overview of the laws concerning what he called "The Paradox of Spiritual and Economic Well-Being," *The Church and Economic Activity in the Middle Ages* (London 1969) v. Also helpful is Daniel K. Finn, *Christian Economic Ethics: History and Implications* (Minneapolis 2013).

[7] David Pelteret, *Slavery in Early Medieval England* (Woodbridge 1995) 255. Emphasis his.

[8] Recently a number of scholars have given a lot of thought to the difficulties of analyzing the phenomenon of slavery on a large scale. See, e.g., Damian Alan Page, "Slavery as a Global and Globalizing Phenomenon," *Journal of Global Slavery* 1 (2016) 1–4; Kostas Vlassopoulos, "Does Slavery Have a History? The Consequences of a Global Approach," *Journal of Global Slavery* 1 (2016) 5–27; Jeffrey Fynn-Paul, "Empire, Monotheism and Slavery in the Greater Mediterranean Region from Antiquity to the Early Modern Era," *Past and Present* 205 (2009) 3–39; and the essays in *Slavery across Time and Space: Studies in Slavery in Medieval Europe and Africa*, ed. P. Hernaes and T. Iversen (Trondheim 2002).

Other scholars have tried to describe slavery from various theoretical perspectives. Along with the sociological perspectives of Orlando Patterson and others, there are some who have considered slavery from a philosophical point of view. A good summary of philosophical considerations can be found in Marcus Bull, "Slavery and the Multiple Self," *New Left Review* 213 (1998) 94–131. Others have considered slavery as a purely economic phenomenon. The work of Stanley Engerman has been

C. Miller and of Orlando Patterson has informed my approach to the problem at hand.

Miller's approach considered slavery neither as an "institution" nor as a moral problem.[9] Slavery is, among other things, a way for people to increase their power: economic power, political power, social status, and so forth. "Slaving," according to Miller, is a strategy employed by many people in many societies throughout history as a way to solve the problems particular to their own situations. I have found this insight to be most helpful, as it encourages us to look at each society from its own perspective and not in the light of how it anticipated the model found in the nineteenth-century New World. Thus, in this study we shall look at various societies in turn to see what choices those people made about the use and management of labor. We shall also look at the extent to which the church shared the choices made by the society as a whole. And we shall find that the church generally followed the choices made by the larger society. However, over time the church's behavior was likewise influenced by a few specifically ecclesiastical laws and customs.

Also very important to my understanding has been the work of Orlando Patterson. He focused on the "natal alienation" that characterizes the slave state.[10] He argued that economic factors are far less important in the master-slave relationship than is the "relation of domination" that robs the slave of his social existence, family, gods, and personal honor. The power that the slave has thus lost becomes part of the power of the master, enhancing not only his economic status and his social position, but also his own sense of self. Understanding these "invisible" components of the slaving relationship helps one to understand why people in master-slave relationships so often act against moral norms or against what seems to be common sense.

---

very influential, for example, "Some Considerations Relating to Property Rights in Man," *Journal of Economic History* 33 (1973) 43–65; and that of Pierre Dockès, *Medieval Slavery and Liberation*, trans. A. Goldhammer (Chicago 1982), originally published as *La Libération médiévale* (Paris 1979). See also Evsey D. Domar, "The Causes of Slavery or Serfdom: A Hypothesis," *Journal of Economic History* 30 (1970) 18–32; and the essays in *Terms of Labor: Slavery, Serfdom, and Freedom*, ed. S. Engerman (Stanford 1999). The appendix provides a bibliographic summary of works about medieval servitude in particular.

[9] Joseph C. Miller, *The Problem of Slavery as History: A Global Approach* (New Haven 2012).

[10] *Slavery and Social Death: A Comparative Study* (Cambridge, MA 1982) is Patterson's classic work. His essay "Revisiting Slavery, Property and Social Death," in *On Human Bondage: After Slavery and Social Death*, ed. J. Bodel and W. Scheidel (Chichester 2017) 265–92, explained in more detail how all theoretical explanations of property inherently depend on the relationships among various persons. In slavery, said Patterson, the relational aspects supersede all others.

Sampling and Other Methodological Considerations

Choosing the data to be included in this study was a complicated task. However, concentration on the central question of the church's regulations concerning ecclesiastical unfree dependents indicated how to proceed. Rather arbitrary lines were drawn to distinguish temporally those social groupings that seem to have shared a particular set of norms. The earliest Christian communities of the New Testament era have been treated separately from the later, post-Constantinian church. The year 500 CE was chosen as an arbitrary dividing line between Roman imperial societies and Germanic kingdoms. A new era began when Charlemagne's empire dominated Continental politics and the bishop of Rome began to emerge as a dominant ecclesiastical figure. The penultimate chapter looks at the society of the later medieval period that evolved from the Carolingian world's decline, a period that resembles our modern conception of the "Middle Ages" in many ways. Geographic sampling changes over the centuries as well. Over time, the eastern portions of the old Roman Empire became less and less involved with the canon law developments in the western church, while the British Isles slowly began to engage more deeply with the mainstream church on the Continent.

The sampling of historical texts used to study these disparate periods varies as well. There is relatively little available from the first Christian centuries. But many more written materials have survived from the later centuries, their number increasing exponentially as time went on. This has resulted in the need continually to narrow the scope over time in order to make the analysis manageable and the results comprehensible as well as valid. The final choice was to present a fuller analysis of those normative texts that turned out to have been influential on the long-term traditions of the canon law of the western European church, while noting ideas and customs that were common for a time, and then later faded away. Of course, it is an absolute principle that teleological analysis is categorically to be avoided. Such intrinsic bias in favor of what we now think important can blind an investigator to what really happened. Yet, after having looked at vast amounts of data, it does not violate this principle to omit from the final presentation of the results an extensive consideration of those items that proved irrelevant to the question in the long run.

In preparing this study of the church's official teachings about its unfree dependents, all "general" canonical texts were analyzed. And in order to understand these in more depth, a good deal of canonical material that had only local validity was also examined. This included all of the canons of the "ecumenical" councils over the two-thousand-year history of the Catholic Church as well as all of the local synodal material up until the end of the ninth century. From this point on there was an enormous increase in the number of local synodal texts as well as episcopal *acta*, so a random, but geographically and temporally balanced, sample was examined. There was also a complete survey of the normative canonical material from the twelfth- and thirteenth-century "classical" period of the canon law as well as a random sample of the numerous earlier collections that had prepared their way.

In addition, a broad and large random sample of the letters, charters, sermons, royal proclamations, and so on that are available from the various societies in question was studied in order to get to know both the people who established the norms and those for whom these norms were intended. These texts provide examples of acceptance of as well as deviations from the canonical principles. In the earliest centuries, there was no central organization of the Christian leaders, and there remain relatively few documents about what they thought. Thus, the data sample is able be essentially all-inclusive. However, once Constantine incorporated the church into the workings of his empire, the volume of Christian texts—on all subjects—increased rapidly. Forced to be selective, while we look at all of the normative material, practical considerations force us to limit discussion to only a sample of the ancillary evidence. This sample represents the most influential Christian thinkers and leaders of the day in the various regions of the Late Empire.

The focus then narrows to the "Germanic kingdoms" of western Europe, where it is possible to present the results of a relatively complete consideration of all of the available normative evidence. The Germanic ruling classes had not been used to depending on the written word, and by that time, eastern norms had become less influential in the West. Most of our discussion concentrates on the Visigoths and the Franks. The other societies surrounding the Gothic and Frankish "core" kingdoms did not produce much in those centuries that sheds light on our question. The Carolingian Empire is the subject of the next chapter, with a brief look at the British Isles, where the Christian church was now beginning to provide a united and influential canon legal point of view about ecclesiastical unfree dependents. A complete survey of the records of church councils and synods from the Continent as well as from the Isles during this period and a fairly complete survey of the insular penitential literature from this period provided the theoretical

perspective. A large sampling of the registers of imperial and episcopal correspondence as well as the records of ecclesiastical estates provided the context
needed for interpretation.

Little material relevant to our inquiry has been preserved from the unsettled post-Carolingian period. But from the late eleventh century on, there is
an increasing flood of evidence from secular as well as ecclesiastical sources.
The number of local, episcopal synods increased dramatically, and it is simply
not possible to consider all of these documents. Episcopal correspondence
flourished even more. Cherry-picking from widely known texts or oft-cited
examples is not likely to produce an accurate assessment. So instead, given
that the end purpose is to understand the "official" church norms for dealing
with its own unfree dependents, it was necessary to narrow the focus even
more in order to permit a complete examination of the large body of canon
law that emerged from the professional legal scholars in the twelfth and thirteenth centuries. A large, random, yet balanced sampling of legal commentary, locally valid proclamations and enactments (lay and ecclesiastical),
personal correspondence, estate records, and so forth provided a number of
illustrative examples from different points of view.

Finally, a few points about the interpretation and presentation of this information. First of all, we need to recognize how much some words changed
their meaning over time. The Latin words *servus* and *mancipium* were originally used to refer to chattel slaves, that is, humans who were possessions of
their masters in the same way as any livestock. In later centuries these terms
were often used to refer to all unfree persons, even though later medieval
servi frequently lived in circumstances that gave them considerable independence if not legal liberty.[11] And a number of more specific terms were used
in everyday life. However, the old language of the canon law texts was not
changed to reflect the changes in society. The church law continued to use
the vocabulary of Roman law. This vocabulary confusion may well have contributed to how people understood these canonical texts in later centuries.
Even now we often cannot tell the exact circumstances of the unfree persons
referred to in many of those texts. Their word choices simply do not permit
us to distinguish between chattel slaves and other persons whose legal and
practical freedom was limited to a greater or lesser extent. It should also be
noted that all translations herein are the author's, unless specifically stated
otherwise.

---

[11] A short glossary of Latin terms is available in the back matter.

We also need to acknowledge that legal documents have long been disparaged as being unrepresentative of what was actually going on in the society in question. And, to some extent, this is a fair assessment. However, the same applies to letters, treatises, and other documents, especially in connection with something as difficult as slavery. Writers generally write what they want people to believe that the author thinks. Legal texts reveal what the lawmakers wanted to be on record as having approved, not necessarily what the lawmakers really thought, nor what was actually going on in the society. Historians need to balance the testimony of evidence from a number of sources to find out what actually happened in the past.[12] In addition, the historian of the canon law, like the scholar of constitutional law, needs to balance an understanding of the intent of the original authors of the ancient texts with a sensitivity to these normative texts' meaning to later centuries. Sensitivity to the original as well as to the later understanding of religious and legal texts is not the only thing to be borne in mind. A writer needs to be sensitive to the thoughts of the readers, for example, in the choice of gendered language. I have chosen to use the male pronoun as the default, not as "masculine by preference," but merely because choosing one pronoun is easier, and the masculine applied to more cases here. Finally, especially when discussing a topic as sensitive as slavery, historian and reader alike need to remain sensitive to the changing attitudes toward this subject over the centuries.

Overview of Subsequent Chapters

We begin with a consideration of the role that slavery played in the Roman and Jewish societies of the first century of the Common Era. Slavery was a normal part of the economic structure, but both traditions cautioned against slave ownership's inherent dangers of cruelty and mistreatment. Then the New Testament is examined as a source of social data and of legal norms concerning slavery. The New Testament is examined separately from other texts of the first centuries of the Christian era because of the much greater influence that the Scriptures had on the thinking of later centuries. Next, the non-scriptural texts from these first centuries of Christianity show that the earliest church leaders owned slaves and that they behaved very much

---

[12] For an interesting discussion about this, see Conrad Leyser, "Introduction: The Transformation of Law in the Late and Post-Roman World," *Early Medieval Europe* 27 (2019) 5–11.

like their non-Christian counterparts, accepting the normality of slavery, if sometimes concerned about possible abuses. And data from this era suggests that the fledgling Christian churches as corporate bodies may have owned a few slaves. There was also concern that the property of a given church and the property of the bishop, the local leader, might not be sufficiently distinguished. After Constantine legalized the practice of Christianity in the fourth century, the church and its leaders behaved in much the same way as did other elites of this society, seeing slave ownership as normal and necessary, but, like the ancient Stoics, urging virtuous behavior toward one's unfree dependents.

With the arrival of the northern Germanic peoples in what had been the Western Roman Empire, although a few new customs arose concerning the treatment of slaves, not much changed concerning church ownership of human resources. One interesting new development concerned the subsequent condition of slaves who had been given their freedom in a ceremony called *manumissio in ecclesia*. This was presided over by a local bishop empowered to act as a magistrate in charge of the legal proceedings. In some Germanic kingdoms, such newly freed persons became bound to the local church where the ceremony had taken place. And, although not the property of the church as chattel, they had numerous obligations to that church, and these obligations usually continued for their descendants.

Charlemagne's empire was a time of legal reform and centralization along with cultural and social expansion. Edicts and statutes from Charlemagne and his descendants showed considerable concern with ecclesiastical property, including slaves and other sorts of unfree dependents. One can see the evolution and consolidation of earlier regional customs into a sort of standard point of view on the subject: slaves and other unfree laborers were a normal and necessary part of any large establishment, and church property was to be inviolate—except when the needs of the king required otherwise. The principle of the inalienability of ecclesiastical property had begun in the earliest days of the church as a way to ensure that the relatives of a deceased bishop would not claim more than their due. This property belonged to God, and the clergy were merely the stewards of the resources that the church needed to do God's work in the world. But by the ninth century, the inalienability principle was often used as a tool for protecting church power and influence, leading to an amalgamation of donated properties that enriched ecclesiastical institutions to such an extent that their leaders became the equals of the great lords and magnates of the empire. Although changes in estate management procedures may have produced some amelioration of slaves' harsh conditions, the outsized growth of church estates resulted in increasingly impersonal administration of their workforce. In addition, the everlasting bondage of ecclesiastical servile and freed dependents continued. A ninth-century law discussing the marriage of slaves might have been a harbinger of change. Logic suggests that if slaves could enter into a marriage contract, they would first have to be seen as legal persons capable of doing such a thing. However, legal recognition of their personhood was not yet forthcoming.

The penultimate chapter looks at the later medieval period, often seen as the "classical" era of ecclesiastical law. This explores, among other things, the ramifications of the church's interest in regulating the marriages of its unfree people as well as the church's legislative efforts to protect ecclesiastical property. As European society emerged from the difficult period that followed on the collapse of the Carolingian Empire in the early tenth century, there was a new focus on the study of law, both the rediscovered Roman legal scholarship of antiquity as well as the accumulated canon law of the previous thousand years. A twelfth-century legal genius, Master Gratian of Bologna, analyzed the laws concerning ecclesiastically dependent unfree persons and concluded that, in the end, once a person became a *servus* of the church, it was nearly impossible for him or his descendants to break free. Subsequent commentary elaborated on the details of how the church should manage its unfree laborers. But the principle of inalienability kept all church property, including human beings, under tight control. At the same time, these unfree persons were now able to contract marriages and to enjoy certain, if limited, individual rights.

There were no particularly significant changes in the canon law concerning slavery from the later thirteenth century to the modern period. Also, the beginnings of what modern scholars have termed "the Atlantic World" and the transatlantic slave trade changed the nature of how slavery was viewed, both by those who made use of it in these later centuries and by the modern scholars who study these questions. Thus, this study concludes with the late medieval period as a natural breaking-off point from both legal and economic historical considerations.

The institutional church has always been managed by human beings with human weaknesses. And the slave owners among them were seldom motivated to choose against exploiting the unfree persons under their control. This study is an examination of the institutional church and its personnel over the first thirteen or so centuries of western Christianity to see how they sought to regulate their affairs in connection with their unfree dependents.

2

The New Testament and Slavery

Pre-Christian Greco-Roman Attitudes and Law

If this is to be a fairly thorough investigation of the church's thinking and actions concerning ecclesiastical servile dependents, we need to start at the very beginning. And before we can comment on the early Christian church's views about slavery, it is only fair for us to survey the attitudes about slavery in the environment that gave rise to the first Christians. This means that we need to understand the social, philosophical, and legal issues relating to unfree persons in the Roman Principate, particularly in the eastern Mediterranean. We also need to understand how the ideas and customs concerning slavery found in the Jewish community of the first century agreed with or differed from those of the wider Greco-Roman culture. Not only was Jesus of Nazareth himself a Jew, as were his first disciples, but also for more than a century, many of the early Christians identified themselves as Jewish as well.[1]

Ancient Rome was one of the few true "slave societies" that have existed in human history, comparable really only to the slave society of the American South.[2] The gulf between slave and free is made explicit in a text from Emperor Justinian's sixth-century CE compendium of Roman law that states: "All persons are either free or slaves."[3] In Rome there was a vast divide

---

[1] Joel Marcus, "Jewish Christianity" (CHC 1.87–102), provides an overview of this issue.

[2] Moses I. Finley, *Ancient Slavery and Modern Ideology*, 2nd ed. (Princeton 1998) 77. There is a vast literature on slavery in ancient Rome. In addition to Finley's classic work, some of the most helpful recent studies include *The Cambridge World History of Slavery*, vol. 1: *The Ancient Mediterranean World*, ed. K. Bradley and P. Cartledge (Cambridge 2011) (CWHS); Keith R. Bradley, *Slaves and Masters in the Roman Empire: A Study in Social Control* (New York 1987); Peter Garnsey, *Ideas of Slavery from Aristotle to Augustine* (Cambridge 1996); Gloria Vivenza, "Roman Thought on Economics and Justice," trans. D. Stewart, in *Ancient and Medieval Economic Ideas and Concepts of Social Justice*, ed. S. T. Lowrey and B. Gordon (Leiden 1998) 269–328; Alan Watson, *Roman Slave Law* (Baltimore 1987); and *Corpus der Römischen Rechtsquellen zur antiken Sklaverei*, 10 vols., ed. T. J. Chiusi et al. (Stuttgart 1999–). W. W. Buckland, *Roman Law of Slavery: The Condition of the Slave in Private Law from Augustus to Justinian* (Cambridge 1908), although from an earlier historiographic era, provides useful reference collections organized by topic. The comprehensive literature on slavery in the New Testament era is mentioned in the next section.

[3] *Institutiones Justiniani* 1.3.pr. Attributed to the second-century jurist Gaius.

The Slaves of the Churches. Mary E. Sommar, Oxford University Press (2020). © Oxford University Press.
DOI: 10.1093/oso/9780190073268.001.0001

between slave and free—a divide so vast that in law slaves were frequently categorized as "things" rather than as "persons."[4] In fact, in many documents, slaves were listed along with the cattle and durable goods. Slaves were "tools with voices."[5] Yet, as we find in all legal systems, there were paradoxes in the Roman slave law, revealing that the Romans were sometimes conflicted about slavery. As Watson pointed out, slavery is the only principle in Roman law that was admitted to be "against nature."[6] But as the second-century legal scholar Gaius said, slavery was an institution that was recognized by all cultures, despite the fact that, against nature, it involved the subjection of one person to another.[7]

Despite the emphasis on the impersonal status of slaves, in a number of situations the personhood of the slave was implicitly acknowledged, as in the many discussions of whether or not it should be permissible to separate slave mothers from their children.[8] The great second-century jurist Ulpian came right out and said, in a discussion of who had the right to the "fruits" of another's slave, "A human being cannot be included in the fruits of another human being."[9] This is a particularly interesting passage because it explicitly differentiates between the offspring of a human slave and the offspring of a cow, or a goat, or some other such animal, which were always seen as the "fruits" of the cattle. Ulpian was not alone in his views. Centuries earlier Aristotle, in his discussion of the natural inferiority of slaves, had acknowledged that even then there were some who disagreed with his ideas about some persons being "natural slaves." He said that those who disagreed with him "maintained that for one man to be another's man is contrary to nature, because it is only convention that makes the one a slave and the other a freeman and there is no difference between them by nature, and that therefore it is unjust, for it is based on force."[10] Nonetheless, Aristotle's opinion

---

[4] See Watson, *Roman Slave Law* 46–66 for a discussion of this question, especially as it applied to agreements of purchase and the theft of a slave as property.

[5] Varro, *De Agri Cultura* 1.17.1.

[6] Watson, *Roman Slave Law* 7. Also see *Corpus der römischen Rechtsquellen zur antiken Sklaverei*, ed. J. M. Rainer, vol. 1, *Die Begründung des Sklavinstatus nach Ius gentium und Ius civile*, ed. H. Wieling (Stuttgart 1999).

[7] *Institutiones Justiniani* 1.3.2.

[8] See Watson, *Roman Slave Law* 67–104 for a comprehensive treatment of this and other issues of slave personhood.

[9] *Digestum Justiniani* 7.1.68.pr. Also see Watson, *Roman Slave Law* 103.

[10] Aristotle, *Politics* I.2.3 (1253b), trans. John T. Fitzgerald, "The Stoics and the Early Christians on the Treatment of Slaves," in *Stoicism in Early Christianity*, ed. T. Rasimus et al. (Grand Rapids, MI 2010) 141–75, here 152. A good summary of Aristotle on slavery can be found in Garnsey, *Ideas of Slavery*.

that some people were born to be slaves prevailed, although in later centuries the Stoic philosophers rejected many of his ideas about slavery. Another example of the way that slaves were treated sometimes as things and sometimes as persons is the fact that a slave was held responsible (like any other person) for the crimes he or she committed, and could even be put to death by the state if, for example, the slave had not defended his or her master's life.[11]

Another paradoxical aspect of Roman slavery was the frequency with which the Romans freed their slaves. Manumission was very common in Rome, and there were numerous laws detailing the various procedures for how this should be done and about the different possibilities for the future life of the now freed slave. There were actually a number of laws limiting manumission because of a concern that too many freed slaves would create an urban underclass that might cause problems for the society. We shall examine this in more depth later when we discuss the practice of *manumissio in ecclesia*, setting slaves free in a church ceremony.

Despite these few instances where a slave was recognized as a human being, no matter how well a Roman family treated their slaves, no matter if slaveholders acknowledged the personhood of their slaves, they were still slaves and legally were the property of their owners. Good treatment was limited and often short-lived, frequently serving more as a reminder of the slaves' dependent status than providing relief from it. Slaves were property and were commonly considered to be fungible goods.[12] Although there are accounts of slaveholders dealing with their slaves as human beings, most of the positive reaction of the slaveholder was based on what the slave did, rather than who he or she was. A slave might be valued for being a good teacher, or a good physician, a good domestic worker or a good commercial agent, or even for being a good sexual partner. But there is a conspicuous lack of data showing that slaves were praised for their deeper personal qualities, as one finds in praise of friends or relatives. Seneca the Younger, writing to Lucilius, said that although slaves can be their owner's friends, "good material" needs someone to craft it into something usable.[13] A slave was raw

---

[11] Watson, *Roman Slave Law* (134–37) has provided a translation of Ulpian's second-century discussion of the *senatus consultum Silianum* (*Digestum Justiniani* 29.5.1), which held that all slaves who lived under the same roof where their master was murdered were to be tortured and then put to death, based on the logic that slaves should protect their masters from harm. Also see Buckland, *Roman Law of Slavery* 90–97.

[12] See Jonathan Edmondson, "Slavery and the Roman Family," in CWHS 337–61. Also: Sandra R. Joshel, "Slaves and Roman Literary Culture," in CWHS 214–40.

[13] Seneca, Ep. 47. See also William Chester Jordan, *From Servitude to Freedom: Manumission in the Sénonais in the Thirteenth Century* (Philadelphia 1986) 229.

material, like a piece of wood, that could be formed into whatever the owner needed. A slave's individuality was not important. As property, a slave could be treated with the same lack of restraint that was permitted in dealing with a cow, a fence, or any other possession.[14]

There is a story about a certain Vedius Pollio, a friend of Caesar Augustus, who fed his misbehaving slaves' flesh to the moray eels that he kept in a fishpond in his garden. He thought that a diet of human flesh would make the eels, a delicacy in ancient Rome, taste better. It seems that there was a dinner party where a slave boy broke a crystal cup. His punishment was to become fodder for the eels, but the emperor was present and he intervened and rebuked Vedius Pollio.[15] Not all slave owners were so cruel—in fact, it is because people were so horrified by Vedius Pollio's behavior that we know about the story—but his behavior was well within the law. During the Republic and early Principate, the law held that a master could do pretty much whatever he wanted to do with his slaves without outside interference. The legal classification of slaves as property and not as persons also provided certain business advantages. As property, a slave had no legal standing, and thus there were limits on any contracts that a slave entered into on behalf of his owner.[16] This often ended up being to the benefit of the slaveholder, who limited his own liability by having a slave act on his behalf. However, this inability to enter into contracts also meant that slaves could not marry, could not inherit, could not own anything, and could not go to court (to sue someone) if they were wronged.

Despite these restrictions many Roman slaves prospered to a certain extent. Slaves were allowed control—not ownership, but control—over a certain amount of money. The amount of this *peculium*, which technically belonged to the master, varied widely. A slave could use it for business purposes, his own or his master's, and many slaves were quite successful at business. In fact, many slaves were slave owners themselves. This kind of business success, especially the "ownership" of other slaves, really enhanced a master's status and thus such activities were encouraged.

The general philosophical outlook of the Greco-Roman world said that some people were superior and others inferior. In the *Politics*, Aristotle

---

[14] Over time there were laws restricting the overly cruel punishment of slaves. See Watson, *Roman Slave Law* 115–33.

[15] Seneca, *De Ira* 3.40.2.

[16] See Watson, *Roman Slave Law* 90–114. Also see Vivenza, "Roman Thought" 290–300. Buckland, *Roman Law of Slavery* treats these issues extensively in I.131–396.

had said that while sometimes individuals might be caught up in inappropriate enslavement, for the most part "natural" slaves were those people
who were deficient in reasoning capacity—more so even than women—
and thus needed others, their betters, to make decisions for them and to
tell them what to do.[17] However, Page DuBois has pointed out that this was
a very minor point for Aristotle. The ancients, she said, were much more
interested in owning these slaves than in dominating their psyches.[18] Or,
as Thomas Wiedemann put it: "They were not so much thinking *about*
slavery as using the concept 'slavery' to think *with*."[19] Later, the Stoics, no
longer particularly supportive of this idea of natural slavery, spoke more
about the "slavery of the soul," a sort of "moral slavery" that was present in
those who were not virtuous and wise and that bore no relationship to the
less important legal slavery that is the subject of our discussion.[20] Since
legal slave status was beyond the control of the affected individual in most
cases, there was no point in worrying about it, according to the Stoic point
of view. The idea of psychological or spiritual slavery was very influential on St. Paul and other early Christian thinkers. The idea that the legal
status of one's body in this world was less important than the status of one's
soul in the next became a fundamental teaching of the Christian church
that continued for centuries. We will discuss it in connection with Pauline
thought, and again in later chapters.[21] Despite these insights, in Rome, as
in most slaveholding societies, the ideas that slaves were somehow inferior
to their owners persisted. Cicero, for example, despite his Stoic ideals, was
very clear that slaves were those who needed to be ruled by others: "The
master's restraint of his slaves is like the restraint exercised by the best
part of the mind, the reason, over its own evil and weak elements [the
passions]."[22]

---

[17] Aristotle, *The Politics*, Book I. Plato said that those deficient in reason benefited from having
a master. However, as Fitzgerald ("Stoics" 147) pointed out, Aristotle had even less respect for
"barbarians" (*Nicomachean Ethics* 7.5.6). Thornton Lockwood Jr., "Is Natural Slavery Beneficial?,"
Journal of the History of Philosophy 45 (2007) 207–21, is a thoughtful and sensitive consideration of
the Aristotelian position.

[18] Page DuBois, *Slaves and Other Objects* (Chicago 2008) 189–205. Owning nice things—slaves or
anything else—enhances the status of their owner and helps determine their identity.

[19] Thomas Wiedemann, "The Regularity of Manumission at Rome," *Classical Quarterly* 35 (1987)
162–75; quoted in Peter Hunt, "Slaves in Greek Literary Culture," in CWHS 23.

[20] Garnsey, *Ideas of Slavery* 128–52 provides a brief summary of the most trenchant passages on
slavery from Stoic writers.

[21] For a detailed analysis of the Christian-Stoic connection, see Runar M. Thorsteinsson, *Roman
Christianity and Roman Stoicism: A Comparative Study of Ancient Morality* (Oxford 2010).

[22] Cicero, *De re publica*, quoted in Augustine, *Contra Julianum* 4.12.61.

There were any number of theories presented for the inherent inferiority of slaves. But a great variety of people found themselves in this position—from every imaginable ethnic group, including some freeborn Romans, and displaying skills ranging from mining salt to practicing medicine to engaging in international commerce. Thus, it was hard for the Romans to come up with a consistently satisfactory explanation for this inferiority. And these explanations all seem to be reducible to the belief that a person of honor would never stoop to serve another person, would never submit himself to the will of another. A "real man" would never take orders from another person to do things, particularly distasteful things, simply because that other person wanted them done. It was one thing to be compensated for your expertise in certain specialized areas. In these cases, the remuneration could be seen as a gift in gratitude for a favor, a *beneficium*.[23] But it was quite another to accept a position where you were subservient to another and, ignoring your own will, had to obey the instructions of another person, no matter how odious—even against your own beliefs or self-interest.[24]

So, the logic ran, since no real man would submit himself to another in this way, then someone who did this, who was obedient, i.e., submitted his will to that of another person, must somehow be less than a real man. Thus Plato's and Aristotle's and Cicero's points of view.[25] The Romans really seem to have believed that slaves were inferior beings for the simple reason that if the slaves had not been inferior, they would never have submitted themselves to their masters.[26] There are a few weaknesses inherent in this idea—besides its circular logic—for example, the fact that people could move either into or out of slave status for various reasons, and that, in many cases, slaves who were set free went on to become full Roman citizens. If slaves were fundamentally inferior, this would of course not have been possible. But the social fiction of inferiority continued.

What slaves thought about themselves is, of course, another story. The surprising thing is that most of the data we have suggests that the slaves in ancient Rome seem to have accepted the institution of slavery without

---

[23] Vivenza, "Roman Thought" 312–13.

[24] Vivenza, "Roman Thought" 294–96.

[25] See A. H. M. Jones, "Slavery in the Ancient World," in *Economic History Review* 2nd Ser. 9 (1956) 185–89. Also available in *Slavery in Classical Antiquity*, ed. M. Finley #1. Also note that this distinction holds true only for men. Women were frequently expected to be subservient, in one way or another, regardless of their legal status.

[26] Granted, this is a sort of backward kind of logic, but it is logical. If only those people who X will do Y, then someone who does Y must also X.

question, even if they felt that they as individuals really did not belong to this inferior group, that they somehow had been inappropriately categorized. Although there were a number of slave revolts in ancient Rome, these revolts did not have as their aim the hope of overthrowing the system, of abolishing slavery altogether. They were in protest against particular circumstances that the rebelling slaves found intolerable.[27] And although there was also a large population of former slaves in Roman society who had little reason to fear the consequences of openly discussing the evils of slavery, texts expressing abolitionist views are conspicuously absent. Some recent work suggests that the reason that we have not found evidence of slaves objecting to the general idea of slavery is that we simply have not looked at the right data. But there is almost no textual data available that was written from the slaves' own point of view.[28] Although some of the ancient fables might be read as "encoded" stories of the cruelty and untrustworthiness that slaves experienced in their relationships with their masters, to date there is, regrettably, so little of this kind of data available that it is much too early for us to form any detailed conclusions about it. Also these literary sources don't really express abolitionist sentiments, just protest against poor treatment. Still, the historian cannot help but wonder if the fact that our data about Greco-Roman slaves' thoughts about slavery is so overwhelmingly from the slaveholders' point of view does not somehow render at least some of our conclusions unreliable.

There are two additional points that must be taken into consideration about the slaves' own perceptions of their status. First is the fact that many persons sold themselves into slavery when faced by dire financial emergencies: they would rather have been slaves than free and desperately, starving, poor.[29] True, many poor people lived in dread of slavery, in dread of losing their honor. And there are a number of reports of those who actively sought death in preference to enslavement, as did the heroes of Masada. But there were also many people who accepted the system of slavery as being useful to them, as providing them some benefit in exchange for abdicating, at least

---

[27] Especially the conditions in the Sicilian mines, where, it was generally acknowledged, slaves were sent to die. See Keith Bradley, "Resisting Slavery at Rome," in CWHS 362–84.

[28] See Clarice J. Martin, "The Eyes Have It: Slaves in the Communities of Christ-Believers," in *Christian Origins*, vol. 1 of *A People's History of Early Christianity* (Minneapolis 2005) 221–39. Also see Bradley, *Slaves and Masters*; J. Albert Harrill, *Slaves in the New Testament: Literary, Social, and Moral Dimensions* (Minneapolis 2006); and Robert Knapp, *Invisible Romans* (Cambridge, MA 2011).

[29] J. Albert Harrill, in *The Manumission of Slaves in Early Christianity* (Tübingen 1995) 30–31, argued that self-sale does not support the idea that slavery was viewed as not being so bad. He pointed out that in Rome self-sale usually was for a specific term and that indentured servitude is not at all the same condition as permanent chattel slavery.

temporarily, their self-determination. The other and perhaps more critical point is that many slaves owned slaves themselves. These slave's slaves were known as *servi vicarii* and their owners as *servi ordinarii*.[30] It is bad historical methodology to try to guess the psychological motivation of these slave slaveholders. They probably derived a lot of the same benefits as did free slaveholders. And they may have found some amelioration of their own dishonorable situation in the pseudo-honor of owning these *vicarii*. But the very fact that the *servi ordinarii* seem to have participated in this system in a voluntary way shows that these slaves did not reject the system, i.e., that they apparently did not fundamentally disagree with the idea of slavery as such, however much they may have deplored their own slave status. There seems to have been a disconnect in their minds between the advantages of being a slaveholder and the disadvantages of their own position as slaves, owned by another. Keith Bradley suggested that this may have been in part because the diversity and limited mobility of the slave population did not allow these slaves to form a common identity.[31] While individual *servi ordinarii* may have seen their own dependent situation as intolerable and unjust, there is no evidence available that suggests that any made the connection that they were in fact doing this same injustice to others.[32] However, until we have more data from the slaves' point of view, the most we can say is that the institution continued throughout the Roman Empire and the succeeding European societies for more than a thousand years without any general outcry for abolition, not even on the part of former slaves.

The traditional view of the Romans about how one became a slave helps to explain this idea that there was an entire class of inherently inferior nonpersons whom it was acceptable to exploit in every possible way. According to ancient tradition, in the earliest days of the Roman Republic the slaves were prisoners of war, whose lives had been spared on the battlefield.[33] The logic was that the prisoner-of-war slave had "as good as" died in the battle and that the captor who had preserved his physical life then owned

---

[30] See Jean Andreau and Marion Descat, *Esclave en Grèce et à Rome* (Paris 2006), trans. M. Leopold, *The Slave in Greece and Rome* (Madison, WI 2011) 107.

[31] Bradley, "Resisting Slavery," also suggested that these slave slaveholders were "the ultimate symbol of the structural centrality of slavery in Roman society." This practice has been noted in other societies as well.

[32] And indeed, this disconnect on the part of *servi ordinarii* may well be similar to the disconnect on the part of the average slaveholder concerning the humanity of their *servi*. The fact that I own you constitutes, in itself, proof that you are so dissimilar to me as to be nonhuman and thus not deserving of treatment as a human.

[33] *Digestum Justiniani* 1.5.4.2; *Institutiones Justiniani* 1.3.3.

that life. A good Roman was supposed to commit suicide before accepting dishonor. Thus, a slave was someone who should have died, but who was still around due to his inferior nature. The slave was dead in terms of the society, even if his body was still moving. Orlando Patterson's famous phrase "social death" sums it up very well.[34] A prisoner of war became a slave and was dead to his old preslavery life. Now his body lived only through the master's will.

Of course, there were other ways of becoming a slave. In the Republic and again to some extent in the Late Empire prisoners of war made up the majority of new slaves. But during the Principate, it seems that most slaves were born into slavery, the child of a slave mother and her master or a slave father.[35] Also there was the practice of selling oneself or one's children. Some slaves were foundlings who had been set out to die of exposure. The law held that anyone who rescued such children had the right to their servitude. And slavery was a common punishment instead of— again—putting someone to death. However, none of these other options for enslavement do anything to refute the argument of a slave's inherent inferiority. The claim that slaves were deficient in reasoning capacity or in moral character are also just variations on the basic theme that a slave was someone who deserved this fate.

Although masters and mistresses faced few limitations on how they treated their *servi*, owners were often exhorted to be kind to their slaves. There were several reasons why kindness was recommended: cruelty to slaves was bad for the master's/mistress's soul or psyche and cruelty to slaves led to uprisings, which were bad for society as a whole. Also, contented slaves were generally better workers. Additionally, in one of these paradoxes that we see with the Roman institution of slavery, some people advocated treating one's slaves well because a slave was a fellow human being, a very unfortunate fellow human whose misfortune was due to some inherent inferiority or was punishment for some evil. Seneca the Younger wrote that you should follow the golden rule with slaves, treating them as you would wish to be treated by your betters.[36] As Epictetus, the Stoic philosopher, had said: slaves "are brethren by nature . . . the offspring of Zeus."[37]

---

[34] Orlando Patterson, *Slavery and Social Death* (Cambridge, MA 1982).
[35] See, e.g., Walter Scheidel, "The Roman Slave Supply," in CWHS 286–310. Also note that at different times, the details of parentage and an infant's freedom varied. See Watson, *Roman Slave Law* 9–17.
[36] Seneca, Ep. 47.
[37] Epictetus, *Discourses* 1.13.

Keith Bradley saw the paradoxes in the Romans' treatment of their slaves as simply a balancing act in the search for social control.[38] On the one hand, slaves had to be compelled to do what their masters wanted, and force was often needed to keep them under control. But the slaves' fear of violence at their master's hand had to be measured against positive incentives to do their work well. Good treatment of slaves, along with the possibility of eventual manumission, kept them happy and productive and reduced the likelihood that they would begin to exercise violence against the slaveholder. This fear of slaves can be seen in the *senatus consultum Silanianum* of 10 CE that called for the execution of all slaves living in a household whose master had been murdered, a strong motivation for slaves in the household to come to their master's aid. In this same vein, Seneca the Younger, writing to the young Nero, told him about the Senate's decision that Roman slaves not be required to wear distinctive clothing lest they find out how numerous they were and rise up against their owners.[39]

Given the main question of this study, we should also consider any temple slaves in the Greco-Roman culture of the first century. And indeed, there were many. In ancient Rome, there were three different categories of slave owners: private individuals, the emperor, and the city. Most slave owners were private individuals whose slaves belonged to them as did their houses, cattle, and furniture. In the later Roman centuries, there were also "imperial slaves" who received special treatment, both positive and negative, because of their owner's exalted position. While officially owned by the emperor, imperial slaves often had duties that were very similar to those of the "public slaves." Those slaves who were owned by the city, Rome or any other city, were known as public slaves. Their duties varied widely, from relatively menial tasks to such exalted positions as collecting municipal revenues or processing legal documents.[40] Public slaves also filled positions in the various temples and assisted priests in their cultic functions. In ancient Greece as well, many of the public slaves also served as temple slaves, often referred to as sacred slaves. Such

---

[38] Bradley, *Slaves and Masters.*

[39] Seneca, *De Clementia* 1.24.1. Keith R. Bradley, "Roman Slavery and Roman Law," *Historical Reflections / Réflexions Historiques* 15 (1988) 477–95, pointed out that there were, indeed, a number of external indications of a person's slave status, not the least of which was the slave collar. However, our point here is that slaveholders feared the possibility that slaves might be empowered to rise up.

[40] See Andreau and Descat, *Slave in Greece and Rome* 118.

sacred slaves were very common in Greco-Roman society. Their duties ranged from menial domestic or agricultural tasks to assisting the priests in religious rituals. The god's temple was his or her residence, in a sense. So the god's slaves, including the temple personnel, served the deity as slaves served any other master—that is, in any way that the master saw fit. And some sacred slaves worked the lands whose revenues supported the temple's functions.[41] The slaves of a given temple were often very numerous. Strabo, a first-century BCE Roman scholar, claimed that one temple in Cappadocia (modern Turkey) had more than six thousand slaves.[42] But we should note Thompson's insight that sacred slaves did not always fit the category of chattel, such as the cat-keepers of the Egyptian goddess Bastet or the sacred prostitutes serving Aphrodite in Corinth.[43] Thus, the answer to our question is yes, the religious institutions in the ancient world owned slaves, a lot of slaves.

In sum: first-century Roman society, especially in Italy, was a slave-dependent society, including numerous temple slaves. With the enslaved population ranging from 10 to 30 percent of the overall inhabitants of the territories that made up the empire, managing the resultant tensions was a difficult task.[44] On the one hand, slaves were the property of their owners and could be forced to do the owner's bidding. Slaves were not only an important labor resource, but also a type of luxury goods that enhanced their owner's status. At that time a society without slavery was virtually unknown. On the other hand, slaves were human beings who were capable of resistance and whose degradation caused a certain discomfort to the more sensitive members of society. The great monument of Roman civilization, the Roman law, expressed their paradoxical way of dealing with the issue of slavery. Acknowledging that slavery was against the "law of nature," the Roman law admitted that, "contrary to nature," slavery was a part of all human societies, tacitly acknowledging that slavery existed because of the mess that humans had made of things.

[41] Peter Cohee, "Temple Slaves in Ancient Greece and Rome," *Macmillan Encyclopedia of World Slavery* (New York 1998) II 888–89.

[42] Strabo, *Geographica* 12.2.3, 6. On this see Walter Scheidel, "The Roman Slave Supply," CWHS.287–336, here 292.

[43] Dorothy J. Thompson, "Slavery in the Hellenistic World," in CWHS 194–213, here 200–202.

[44] For an extended, up-to-date discussion of these numbers see Scheidel, "The Roman Slave Supply," and also Neville Morley, "Slavery under the Principate," in CWHS 265–86.

Slavery in Jewish Law and Culture

Although much of the recent scholarship about slavery in first-century Palestine emphasizes that the Greco-Roman view of slavery seems to have predominated, there were a few features of the ancient Hebrew tradition that still mattered, and the rabbis debated these ideas at great length.[45] The story of Moses freeing the Hebrew slaves from Pharaoh's domination and leading them out of Egypt is one of the most essential components of Jewish identity. And this continuing consciousness of their own ancestors' slave past may well help account for the relatively few differences that did exist in the ancient Jewish traditions about slavery.

Most of the laws found in the Hebrew scriptures about slavery are generally similar to the laws of other cultures in the Ancient Near East.[46] Long before the time of Moses, slaves were a normal component of the lives of the patriarchs. Jacob's fourteen-year service in the household of Laban was the bride price for Laban's daughters.[47] But there is no mention of this as having been shameful. Indeed, Jacob willingly entered into the agreement, complaining only when Laban switched daughters after the first term of seven years was up and then willingly entered into a second such agreement for the other daughter. The complaint was only that Jacob felt cheated, not that he had a problem with servitude. This story is especially interesting as it shows that service was not about personal status but about one person doing the bidding of another. Laban said to Jacob that as a kinsman, Jacob should not serve him for nothing.[48] The word used here, עֶבֶד ('eved), is the same word that was commonly used to describe a chattel slave.[49] So it seems that

---

[45] The literature on Jewish slavery practices is somewhat limited. The best recent treatment can be found in Catherine Hezser, *Jewish Slavery in Antiquity* (Oxford 2005), most of which she summarized in "Slavery and the Jews," in CWHS 438–55; also see Calum Carmichael's somewhat more speculative *The Spirit of Biblical Law* (Athens, GA 1995). Garnsey, *Ideas of Slavery*, also provides a nice summary of this issue.

For a summary of Jewish slave law both before and after the first century of the Common Era see David M. Cobin, "A Brief Look at the Jewish Law of Manumission," *Chicago-Kent Law Review* 70 (1995) 1339–48.

An interesting account of the rabbinical debate about one aspect of Hebrew slave law can be found in David Henske, "The Hebrew Slave in Tannaitic Law: History and Exegesis," in *Studies in Jewish Law in Honor of Professor Aaron Kirchenbaum*, ed. A. Edrei (Tel Aviv 2001) 1–29.

[46] See, e.g., Daniel Snell, "Slavery in the Ancient Near East," in CWHS 4–21; Bernard Jackson, "Biblical Laws of Slavery: A Comparative Approach," in *Slavery and Other Forms of Unfree Labour*, ed. L. Archer (London 1988) 86–101. Also, Carmichael, *Spirit of Biblical Law* 28, 49–63.

[47] Gen. 29:13–30.

[48] Gen. 29:15.

[49] Indeed, *'eved* and *'avad* occur nearly one thousand times in the Hebrew scriptures (according to Strong's *Concordance of the Bible*), and these are the terms used in the Exodus story as well. Snell

the only difference between Jacob and Laban's other slaves was that Jacob had volunteered for seven years of servitude in return for payment, i.e., a wife; the others may not have had this relatively advantageous arrangement with their master.

Slavery came again to the next generation of that family when Jacob's son Joseph became the slave of an Egyptian. In time, Joseph's relatives joined him in Egypt, apparently as free landholders. But later pharaohs began to oppress these and other immigrants to the relatively prosperous land of Egypt. The book of Exodus is the story of the return of Abraham's descendants, along with a lot of others who wanted to escape Egyptian oppression, to the land that was eventually called Israel. The Hebrew scriptures from that point on recorded that God said that these Israelites were his slaves because he had freed them from the land of Egypt, in other words, because God had purchased the right to their services. The legal codes that purport to be from that era, although they reached their final form much later, frequently provided for good treatment of slaves as well as of orphans and widows and the poor, explicitly recalling the Hebrews' own oppression in Egypt. However, as Catherine Hezser pointed out, these texts do not allow us to conclude that Israelite slave owners actually followed these ideals.[50] Still, the Passover feast, the ritual commemoration of the Exodus events and of freedom and a time when slaves joined their masters at table, became a central religious observance of the Jewish faith after the Romans destroyed the Temple in 70 CE. Whether or not the first-century Palestinian Jews obeyed the Torah prescriptions exactly, they could not escape the traditions reminding them of their own slavery—first at the hand of the Egyptians and then again as a result of later conquest, even if they did not equate their ancestors' slavery with that of their own household staff. Regrettably though, beyond the symbolism of slavery as a part of the Jews' history, the available sources do not allow us to know much about actual behaviors.

In the various reform texts from the seventh century BCE and later there were frequent exhortations to treat one's slaves with justice and mercy. For example, Deuteronomy forbade a master to have sexual relations with a newly captured female slave for at least thirty days because she needed the

("Slavery in the Ancient Near East" 18) pointed out that *'eved* also meant, more universally, "worker," and argued that the worker's status vis-à-vis freedom was another issue.

[50] Hezser, *Jewish Slavery in Antiquity* 363–76; "Slavery and the Jews" 371–76.

time to adjust to her new situation.[51] At the same time, a need to control slaves through the use of force was also acknowledged.[52] By the time of the exiles' return from Babylon in circa 538 BCE, Jewish slavery practices generally resembled those of their neighbors and later those of the Greeks and the Romans. However, some things that the Romans practiced regularly, like selling one's children, were in theory frowned upon by the Jews, as was killing one's slave.[53]

Jewish law provided that slaves who were themselves Jews should be enslaved for no more than a period of six years, and there were a number of other limitations on their servitude, although there is evidence that these prescriptions were not always obeyed.[54] Gentiles, that is, outsiders or foreigners, i.e. inferior people, could be enslaved for life.[55] However, given the need for ritual purity in all members of the household, many slaves were, if not fully Judaized, at least ritually cleansed, even circumcised, and many became fully Jewish after manumission.[56]

Given the overall question of this study of ecclesiastical persons or institutions who were slaveholders, we need to ask if first-century Jewish religious leaders had slaves. There is little data about temple slaves in ancient Israel, except to say that there were such and that they resided away from the general slave population.[57] State slaves were a different and separate group from the temple slaves. Usually state slaves were prisoners of war who were the property of the king. Other state slaves were Israelites who had been called up as corvée labor for a particular project, such as building the Jerusalem Temple. It is interesting that these do not seem to have been set apart, as were the permanent temple slaves. Perhaps this is because the corvée laborers were working on the Temple before it was used for its sacred purposes and thus they had not been touched by

---

[51] Deut. 21:10–13.

[52] E.g., Ben Sira's second-century maxim: "Fodder and a stick and burdens for a donkey; bread and discipline and work for a slave." Quoted in Jennifer Glancy, *Slavery as a Moral Problem: In the Early Church and Today* (Minneapolis 2011) 7–8.

[53] See Hezser, "Slavery and the Jews."

[54] Exod. 21:1–7; Lev. 25:40–41; Deut. 15:12–18. See Cobin, "Brief Look" and also Hezser, "Slavery and the Jews" 443–44.

[55] See Snell, "Slavery in the Ancient Near East" 18 and Hezser, *Jewish Slavery in Antiquity* 29–31.

[56] Hezser, *Jewish Slavery in Antiquity* 29–36. Some of the impetus for waiting until manumission for a full conversion seems to have been that the rabbis frowned upon having Jewish slaves. After the destruction of the Second Temple, this changed, as it was too dangerous to have non-Jews living in your household. Cobin, "Brief Look" 1343.

[57] John Byron, *Slavery Metaphors in Early Judaism and Pauline Christianity* (Tübingen 2005) 45.

holiness. Most of the available evidence for Roman era Palestine suggests that the Jewish religious leaders did keep slaves, as befitted their individual circumstances. Herod the Great and the other Hasmoneans, as Roman client kings, presided over immense households with hundreds of slaves, some for domestic operations and others simply as enhancements to their royal prestige. The New Testament and also the writings of Josephus frequently referred to the slaves of the high priest in first-century Jerusalem, a relatively large household. And even some of the poor rabbis of the Roman period seem to have had a few slaves, if only to bolster their honor and position in society.[58]

One of the most influential Jewish writers of the first century CE, Philo of Alexandria exemplifies how both the Stoic and the Aristotelian ideas about slavery were largely compatible with the traditional Jewish views on this subject.[59] In some ways Philo seems to have thought that the Stoics' idea of spiritual slavery was a concept that applied especially to the Jews, who had been set free from bodily slavery in Egypt to become slaves of God. When he spoke of non-Jews, Philo took a more Aristotelian view, saying that God had made them to be inferior and that they were more suited to slavery than their superiors, the Jews, God's chosen. However, the fact that Romans like Cicero saw Jews to be natural slaves was a different story.[60] Along with Josephus, Philo believed that Jewish enslavement by the Romans was punishment for sin.

Thus, it is clear that, despite the Exodus tradition, for the most part first-century Jews happily followed Greco-Roman ideas and customs concerning their slaves. Although some pious Jews may have treated their slaves somewhat better than did the general population, there is nothing in the sources from that era suggesting that the rabbis or other Jewish leaders were opposed to the practice of slavery overall. Indeed, many of them were slave owners themselves. Some Jews, the Essenes, did reject slavery, but they were extremists who practiced radical asceticism. Still, despite the overall similarities with Greco-Roman customs, the Jews' behavior toward their slaves was influenced by long religious traditions.[61]

---

[58] Hezser, *Jewish Slavery in Antiquity* 174–78, 296. Some sources suggest that pious students, although free, out of humility performed tasks in their rabbi's household that traditionally had been assigned to slaves.

[59] Garnsey, *Ideas of Slavery* 157–72 presents an excellent summary of Philo on slavery. See also Hezser, *Jewish Slavery in Antiquity* 57–61.

[60] Cicero, *De provinciis consularibus* 5.10.

[61] See Hezser, *Jewish Slavery in Antiquity* 380–92 and "Slavery and the Jews" 453–54.

The New Testament and Slavery

We have seen that in the Roman Empire of the first century slavery was an ordinary part of everyday life.[62] The early Christian church, formed in this Greco-Roman cultural world, was also informed by the religious world of the ancient Jewish community. And in both Greco-Roman and Jewish cultures, slavery was simply taken for granted. True, we have seen that, at least in theory, Jewish law limited the servitude of fellow Jews, but otherwise there were few differences that set the Jews apart from their pagan neighbors in terms of how they treated those over whom they held *dominium*. It was in the midst of this slave-oriented culture that the new ideas of Christianity were born.[63]

One very common Greek word to indicate a male slave is δοῦλος. In the 124 times that the concordance to the Greek New Testament lists the word δοῦλος, not once do we find it in a situation where we can find any condemnation at all of slavery as an institution.[64] Δοῦλος is found most frequently in the gospels, especially in Matthew and Luke in the parables, where it was used in simple descriptions of everyday life because, in the gospel era, slavery was a normal, unquestioned part of life. In telling stories to illustrate his religious ideas, Jesus used scenes from everyday life that his audience could relate to. Since daily life in first-century Palestine included slaves, Jesus's stories frequently included slave characters.

---

[62] Although the provinces generally did not have the high concentration of slaves found in Rome itself and throughout Italy, it is nevertheless reasonable to assume that in Roman-ruled Palestine the population would have been at least 10 percent servile, and perhaps more in the centers of Roman activity. For more on the distribution of the slave population in this era see Morley, "Slavery under the Principate" 265–86 and Scheidel, "The Roman Slave Supply" 287–310.

[63] Given that the New Testament is a product of this slave-dependent culture, it might well be expected that these texts would have accepted the idea of slavery unquestioningly and would have said nothing at all against the custom. Yet for many moderns this comes as a bit of a surprise. Perhaps this is due to our modern disapproval of the justifications for slavery in the American South that used the Bible as a support for their position, or perhaps from a desire to believe that the first Christians, often idealized as the purest example of their faith, could never have willingly participated in something that the modern world views as so heinous. Nevertheless, in order to present a fair analysis, it is important to maintain an awareness of the widespread—and erroneous—preconceptions about early Christians and slavery that are held by many twenty-first-century Westerners, even those who strive for scholarly impartiality.

[64] New Testament concordances show that cognates of δοῦλος occur more than forty times and παῖς / παιδίσκη (boy, slave / girl, slave) and their cognates an additional thirty times or so. See Paul R. Coleman-Norton, "The Apostle Paul and the Roman Law of Slavery," in *Studies in Roman Economic and Social History in Honor of Allan Chester Johnson*, ed. P. R. Coleman-Norton (Princeton 1951) 155–56 on this as well. More recently, John M. G. Barclay's article "Paul, Philemon, and the Dilemma of Christian Slave-Ownership," *New Testament Studies* 37 (1991) 161–86, is also helpful.

Paul introduced the idea that Christians were δοῦλοι of Christ, perhaps continuing the ancient Hebrews' metaphor of God having "purchased" their freedom from Pharaoh. Paul also famously said that in Christ "there is no δοῦλος or free" (Gal. 3:28). This was not a call for the abolition of slavery. Rather, recalling the Stoics' teachings, Paul was explaining to the Christians of Galatia that for the Christian, the things of this world (slave/ free; Jew/Greek; male/female) are unimportant in the face of salvation and the world to come.[65] Although he did not call for the abolition of the institution of slavery, Paul does seem to have been in favor of the manumission of individual Christians who were slaves. He recommended to Philemon, whose slave, Onesimus, had come to know Paul, that Philemon should free Onesimus and forgive his (unspecified) transgressions. But even Paul, in this sole New Testament passage with so much as a hint that slavery might be antithetical to the Christian way of thinking, did not simply let the runaway Onesimus remain free. Paul, acting as a good Roman citizen, sent Onesimus back to his master, merely begging the master to reconsider. Advocating for the manumission of a particular individual who was unfortunately bound by the chains of slavery in no way implied rejection of this basic economic practice. Paul was no abolitionist.

Other epistles addressed to the Colossians and Ephesians sometime after Paul's death told slaves to obey their masters because that was what God wanted them to do. In other words, they upheld the social order as God's will. Epistles that were written even later (1 Titus, Timothy, and 1 Peter) said that slaves should obey their masters to prevent Christians from coming into conflict with the larger society. These texts suggest that as the nascent church moved from a charismatic movement to a recognizable community, the Christians had begun to rethink some of the questions about charism versus adaptation to their social milieu.

Since this book is a study of church law and ecclesiastical slavery in the Christian church, we should also look at the New Testament text as normative legal text to see if it can serve as a legal source about slavery in the society of the very first Christians. There are three questions about the first-century Christian communities to ask of this material. First, what does it tell us about the views about slavery in the culture that produced the texts? Second, does this material have any instructions (explicit or implicit) about issues that

---

[65] R. A. Horsley, "Paul and Slavery. A Critical Alternative," *Semeia* 83–84 (1998) 153–200 provides a nice analysis of this question.

have to do with slavery? Third, is there any information about slaveholding by religious leaders, Christian or otherwise, or about corporate slaveholding by a group of Christians in early versions of an "institutional" church?

For the most part, the gospel writers used the words δοῦλος (slave) and sometimes παῖς (boy, often used to designate a beloved slave). And, for the most part, in our texts these words were used in a very unremarkable fashion to refer to the slaves who were a normal part of everyday life in first-century Palestine. In the Synoptic Gospels and Acts, the word δοῦλος and its cognates appear at least seventy times, usually used simply to designate a character in a story that is being told. There are, however, a few things about the New Testament community that we can conclude from the use of this word. First, when the same story appears in more than one gospel account—as occurs at least eight times involving a δοῦλος—this word remained the same even though other words used to tell the story usually changed a bit. This suggests that δοῦλος was being used in these accounts in its ordinary, mundane sense of a person who is owned and controlled by another and that the word should not be understood to have carried any deeper meaning. In two different yet parallel stories, the status of the master changed from a king or ruler to an ordinary man (ἄνθρωπος).[66] However, the underlings remained δοῦλοι. Thus, the royal δοῦλοι in these stories must have been actual slaves and not just abject royal subjects referred to metaphorically as "slaves." The ordinary man in the one version could not have had free persons in subjection to him in the way that a king, in the other version, might have had. In another story a master sold the wife and children along with his misbehaving δοῦλος, clearly showing that the entire family were chattel.[67] Also, in the Gospel of Luke (17:7–8), Jesus explained the duties of the faithful to God by analogy with a δοῦλος in a small household who had been working in the fields all day, yet was still expected to prepare and serve the master's supper before his own. This is not a very kind way to treat a tired man, but that is the way of servitude. It does not seem to have occurred to Jesus—or at least not to the author of this text—that the servant might have been relieved of his cooking duties out of consideration for his tiredness. Recent scholarship has addressed the fact that Jesus and the gospel writers accepted without comment the lack of consideration shown to slaves and the frequent violence

---

[66] Matt. 22 / Luke 14 and Matt. 24 / Luke 12.
[67] Matt. 18.

used to control them.[68] Their acceptance of behavior toward slaves that was not acceptable toward others reinforces the idea that Jesus and his followers did not question the prevailing ideas about slavery as a normal part of their society.[69] There are also a number of episodes in the life of Jesus and the apostles related in this Synoptic material where slaves were part of the story. Most famously, there is a scene in all three gospels where Peter cut off the ear of "the high priest's slave" at the time of Jesus's arrest. And the stories in the Acts of the Apostles clearly show that there were many slaves and slaveholders in the fledgling Christian community.

The word δοῦλος actually referred to the total submission of one person to another and did not particularly refer to any particular tasks or duties of the subservient one. The act of waiting on another person was διακονία. And the difference between these two terms can be seen in a story about Jesus and his disciples that occurs in Matthew's and Mark's Gospels.[70] Jesus told the disciples that someone would be great among them must be a διάκονος to his fellows, but that someone who would be first among them must be their δοῦλος. Serving one's fellows would gain their love and respect—in itself a radical notion in the culture of first-century Palestine—but true leadership required complete subjection to the needs of those being led.

This introduces a theme that would characterize Christian thought from that time on. Even today, the Roman pontiff is called "the slave of the slaves of God" (*servus servorum Dei*).[71] And this idea echoes the prayer that Jesus reportedly said in the Garden of Gethsemane as he awaited his arrest: "Let not my will, but your [God's] will be done."[72] Recall that losing one's will to the control of another was the essential characteristic of a slave in the Greco-Roman world. In the process of enslavement, a person's ability to exercise their own will was taken away without their consent. In the ancient Eastern

---

[68] See, especially, Jennifer Glancy, who has pointed out that in the gospel story about the healing of the centurion's servant, the miracle is seen as something good for the slaveholder, with no mention of the slave's point of view. Glancy (*Slavery in Early Christianity* (Oxford 2002) 102–29 and *Slavery as a Moral Problem* 10. Also see Mary Ann Beavis, "Ancient Slavery as an Interpretive Context for the New Testament Servant Parables with Special Reference to the Unjust Steward (Luke 16:1–8)," *Journal of Biblical Literature* 111 (1992) 37–54. Also see Chris de Wet, *The Unbound God: Slavery and the Formation of Early Christian Thought* (New York 2018).

[69] However, Glancy optimistically suggested that unquestioning acceptance of a behavior does not necessarily mean approval (*Slavery as a Moral Problem* 22–23).

[70] Matt. 20:26–28; Mark 9:35.

[71] See I. A. H. Combes, *The Metaphor of Slavery in the Writings of the Early Church, Journal for the Study of the New Testament* Supplement Series 156 (Sheffield, UK 1980) 100–101, on use of "slave" as an honorific title for clerics.

[72] Matt. 26:39, 42; Mark 14:36; Luke 22:42.

religions and the mystery religions of the first century, δουλεία was the word used to describe the relationship of a believer to his or her god. Following this line of thought, voluntarily ceding control of one's will to God, or to a superior standing in God's place, became the supreme act of Christian heroism. On a par with physical martyrdom, this death of the will and giving up control of one's life to God was to be the foundational act of the monastic life.

In the Fourth Gospel, the word δοῦλος occurs mostly in the unremarkable sense. However, the author of this gospel had Jesus talk about slavery in a metaphysical sense at the Last Supper. Jesus said that the disciples were no longer his δοῦλοι, but his φίλοι, his friends (15:15). In an earlier discourse, Jesus referred to the δοῦλοι of sin as well (8:34), a metaphor that would be taken up and expanded upon by Paul. The Fourth Gospel's description of the Jewish high priest's household is a bit longer than that found in the Synoptic Gospels. And even more than in the three earlier texts, it is very clear here that this high priest had a large number of slaves in his household.[73] For our purposes, in a study about slaves owned by the church and ecclesiastical personnel, this is interesting because it is clear evidence that a high-ranking Jewish religious official had a staff of slaves commensurate with his position in society. And there is nothing in the gospel text that even hints of disapproval about this. The slaves were mentioned merely as other characters in the story. While the early Christian community may have disapproved of a lot of things that the high priest had done, owning slaves was not one of them.

Paul talked a good deal about slavery in the metaphysical sense, but he also mentioned the everyday situations of slavery that were so common in the greater Roman world, especially in the letter to Philemon about his slave Onesimus that we looked at above. For our purposes, the great debates about the precise relationship of Paul to Onesimus, or to Philemon, and about the situation between Onesimus and his sometime master, Philemon, are not very helpful. What is useful for our purposes is the fact that Onesimus's status as a slave was never questioned. And although Paul urged Philemon to free Onesimus, Paul did not hesitate to send Onesimus back to his master, as Roman law prescribed. This tells us two things about Paul: first of all, that he was a man of his time, who apparently did not see slavery as a moral problem in and of itself; and second, that Paul thought it appropriate to obey the Roman law regarding slaveholders and their property. Perhaps the most

---

[73] John 18:18 and 18:26 mentioned the δοῦλοι gathered around the fire in the high priest's courtyard. And 18:17 mentioned the high priest's παιδίσκη (housemaid).

concise non-theological discussion of this question can be found in Paul R. Coleman-Norton's classic article from 1951 in which he pointed out that there was nothing in Paul's cultural world that would have led him to think of abolishing slavery. He also noted that Paul avoided pointed sociopolitical condemnation. Paul, like the Stoics, taught that inner liberty of the soul was what really mattered, and since these first Christians expected Jesus to return again any day, there was no need to reform the current social order.[74] Worldly status, said Paul, had no importance in the spiritual world.[75] Slave or free, male or female, Jew or Gentile, none of these would matter in the world to come.[76] Even more pertinent to our inquiry is that Philemon was apparently considered a leader in his local Christian community, given the fact that he was corresponding with an apostle. So this letter also provides evidence of a Christian leader who was a slaveholder.[77] Note that Philemon's status as a slaveholder was not called into question. The only question was about the fate of one particular slave, Onesimus.

Paul's metaphysical discussions of slavery occurred in several forms. He referred often to himself as δοῦλος of Christ.[78] And he exhorted his readers to abandon their slavery to sin in order to embrace, in their freedom, slavery to Christ or to righteousness.[79] This metaphor was not unique to Paul, however. The Q source (a resource believed to have been used by the authors of Matthew's and Luke's Gospels) used similar imagery when Jesus told his followers that they had to choose between serving (δοῦλεύειν) God or "Mammon."[80] And in later texts, other New Testament writers also used the term δοῦλος of Christ.[81] The origin of Paul's conception of Christians as δοῦλοι of Christ has been the subject of much discussion.[82] Many scholars have contended that this recalls the old custom of referring to Moses and King David and others as slaves of God. Others have said that this conclusion isn't

---

[74] See Coleman-Norton, "The Apostle Paul" on this.

[75] 1 Cor. 7:17–24, 12:13; Gal. 3:28.

[76] A good discussion of these sorts of ethnic and social divisions in the community can be found in David E. Aune, "Human Rights and Early Christianity," in *Christianity and Human Rights: An Introduction*, ed. J. Witte Jr. and F. S. Alexander (Cambridge 2010) 81–98.

[77] Glancy, *Slavery in Early Christianity* 91–92.

[78] E.g., Rom. 1:1; Gal. 1:10; Phil. 1:1.

[79] E.g., Rom. 6:6, 16–22; 1 Cor. 7:21–23.

[80] Matt. 6:24; Luke 16:13.

[81] E.g., Acts 4:29, 16:17; Col. 4:12; Eph. 6:6; 2 Tim. 2:24. Also Titus, 1 James, 2 Peter, Jude, and Revelations all used this phrase in the first verse of their first chapters.

[82] Two recent summaries of these discussions of the slavery metaphor in early Christianity, including surveys of older literature on the subject, can be found in John Byron, *Slavery Metaphors* and in Combes, *The Metaphor of Slavery*.

a very good fit with the rest of Paul's Christology. Still others have suggested that it was a parallel to the Exodus: just as the god of Abraham demanded that the Israelites serve him in return for their freedom from slavery in Egypt, Christ demanded service from Christians whom he had freed from slavery to sin. But this metaphor of slavery was also used throughout the Ancient Near East in various religious situations and was frequently de rigueur in reference to a monarch; the phrase "slave of God" was regularly used as an honorific in both Christian and earlier cultures.[83] Paul said that Jesus himself had taken on the form of a δοῦλος of God—i.e., a human being—in order to show his readers the proper way to behave. In all of these passages, Paul's knowledge of Roman law concerning slavery is apparent and what he said about it suggests that he had great respect for the law. But this theological material is not very helpful for our purposes right now.[84]

The non-Pauline epistles can also provide us with some data about the early Christian community and slavery. First of all, we consider the letters to the Ephesians and Colossians, likely written in the late first century by disciples of Paul.[85] On our topic they said pretty much the same thing: slaves should obey their masters with good will and masters should treat their slaves well. The reason offered for this command was that God would reward them all in heaven, where legal slavery or freedom is irrelevant.[86] As Eduard Lohse noted, observing the customs of the generally accepted social order was seen to be one way to express their allegiance to the lordship of Christ.[87] For example, the letter to the people of Ephesus says:

Δοῦλοι, be obedient to those who are your earthly masters, with fear and trembling, in singleness of heart, as to Christ; not just for appearances' sake, as the people-pleasers do, but as δοῦλοι of Christ, doing the will of God from the heart, rendering service with a good will to the Lord and not to men, knowing that whatever good anyone does, he will receive the same again from the Lord, whether he is a δοῦλος or free. Masters, do the same to them, and forbear threatening, knowing that he who is

---

[83] There are also a number of New Testament passages where a slave to sin, etc., is contrasted with a "son" or "heir," especially of God. E.g., John 8:34–35 and Gal. 4:1–7.

[84] The idea of pious Christians as "slaves of God" is fascinating and well worth investigating further. However, such an investigation is beyond the boundaries of the present study.

[85] Wayne A. Meeks, *The First Urban Christians*, 2nd ed. (New Haven 2003) 8.

[86] Eph. 6; Col. 3.

[87] Eduard Löhse, *Colossians and Philemon*, trans. W. R. Poehlmann and R. J. Karies, Hermeneia (Philadelphia 1971) 158. On this also see Martin, "The Eyes Have It" 221–39.

both their master and yours is in heaven, and that there is no partiality with him.[88]

This text, as well as its companion in the letter to the Colossians, obviously provided norms for behavior in the Christian community. It is not technically correct, when speaking of the first century, to categorize biblical texts as "canon law." But Scripture and other such texts have always been normative for the Christian community. And these particular texts from Ephesians and Colossians were clearly regulatory in nature, with punishment, albeit in the afterlife, provided for violations. Slaves were to carry out the commands of their masters, whether Christian or pagan, and Christian masters were to treat their slaves properly. Slaveholders were described in a way that suggested that God had put them, accountable to the Deity themselves, in charge of the lesser slaves here on earth. This echoes the Aristotelian idea that slaves were inferior to their masters.[89] However, as Jennifer Glancy pointed out, we do not know exactly what was meant by treating one's slaves properly. Roman notions about the "proper" treatment of slaves encompassed actions that would horrify many in our century.[90] The Romans regularly depended on severe beatings to force obedience and viewed torture as the only reliable way to extract evidence from a slave.[91] Even Jesus seems to have thought it proper for a master to demand that an exhausted slave prepare and serve dinner before taking time for himself. In these letters to Ephesus and Corinth, the command for slaves to be obedient is clear, although their masters' responsibilities cannot be determined with any precision. The masters were exhorted merely not to do anything that God would punish them for doing, without providing clear guidelines. If these texts were used as behavioral norms, it seems that the limits on the slaves' behavior were much more clearly defined than were any limitations on the behavior of their owners. And, indeed, this imbalance accords well with what we know of first-century attitudes concerning the roles of slaves and their masters.

---

[88] Eph. 6:5–9. Translation adapted from the Revised Standard Version (RSV).

[89] Harrill, *Manumission* 85–117, discussed the idea that a Christian slaveholder functioned as God's *villicus*, or unfree overseer. All Christians are slaves of God, but human slaveholders rank higher than their slaves. He found a number of analogies to Varro's *Columella* and other Greco-Roman manuals for how to run an agricultural estate in these epistles, as well as in other similar "household codes" written by early Christians, including the *Didache*, and the Epistle of Barnabas, which will be discussed in the next chapter.

[90] Glancy, *Slavery in Early Christianity* 143–45.

[91] See Kenneth J. Pennington, "Torture and Fear: Enemies of Justice," *Rivista internazionale di diritto commune* 19 (2008) 1–39.

The texts known as the Pastoral Epistles, 1 and 2 Timothy, and Titus, come from the second century and probably reflect the views of another community of the Pauline tradition.[92] In these later texts, the earlier explanation for why one should perform the duties of one's station, whether obeying a master's orders, or treating one's slaves justly, is different and no longer had to do with divine reward or punishment. Now the faithful were exhorted to perform their duties in order that they not scandalize their non-Christian neighbors:

> Let all those who are under the yoke borne by the δοῦλοι regard their masters as worthy of all honor, so that the name of God and the Teaching may not be defamed. Those who have believing masters must not be disrespectful on the ground that they are brethren; rather they must serve all the better since those who benefit by their service are believers and beloved.[93]

The first letter of Peter told slaves to be submissive to their masters, as wives were to be submissive to their husbands. Christians should obey the government as well: "Be subject, for the Lord's sake to every human institution. . . ."[94] But in addition to reinforcing the social hierarchy, 1 Peter, written in the early second century, attempted to comfort the suffering slaves by suggesting that they think of their suffering at the hands of their masters as a way to meditate on the sufferings of Christ.[95] Why these texts exhorted the faithful to adhere to Greco-Roman norms has been debated endlessly. It may well be that the later epistles included their sections on slaves' duties of obedience because some people had gotten the wrong idea from Paul's "neither slave nor free." Paul had definitely not advocated the abolition of this most important institution in the Greco-Roman social order. And the later writers of New Testament texts seem to have been concerned lest anyone think that the abolition of slavery was part of the Christian "party platform." However, the debates need not concern us here. For our purposes it is clear that a century after Jesus lived, the vulnerable Christian community found it advisable to refrain from provoking their pagan neighbors by dealing with their slaves

---

[92] Meeks, *The First Urban Christians* 9.
  Katherine A. Shaner's recent work *Enslaved Leadership in Early Christianity* (Oxford 2018) offers an intriguing perspective on the ideas about slavery found in 1 Timothy.

[93] 1 Tim. 6:1–2. Translation modified from the RSV. See also Titus 2:9–10.

[94] 1 Pet. 2:13.

[95] 1 Pet. 2:18. Knapp, *Invisible Romans* 128 noted that this is the only place in the New Testament that seems really to have understood the slaves' perspective. Also see John G. Nordling, "A More Positive View of Slavery: Establishing Servile Identity in the Christian Assemblies," *Bulletin for Biblical Research* 19 (2009) 63–84, especially 69–72.

differently than those neighbors did and that Christian leaders exhorted the faithful to follow this strategy.

So how well do these New Testament texts answer our questions? First, how much do these texts tell us about the early church's ideas about slavery? It is clear from all of the New Testament that the earliest Christians thought about slavery very much in the same way that the larger society did: slavery was a normal, if unfortunate, part of the economy and culture. The gospels did not ever record Jesus reproaching slave owners for owning slaves. And in at least one place (Luke 17) Jesus's words suggest that slaves did not merit much courtesy or consideration. The Pauline letter to Philemon explicitly reinforced Roman norms, and the later epistles took care that any overenthusiastic interpretation of Galatians 1:28, "In Christ there is neither slave nor free," be squelched. Many of the individuals mentioned as members of the earliest Christian communities were either slaves or slaveholders, and this status went unremarked in the New Testament, except as necessary to make some other point. For example, in one story Rhoda, a παιδίσκη (slave girl), had trouble persuading her mistress that Peter was at the door. Peter had apparently just escaped from prison.[96] The author's point was that since it was only a silly and unimportant slave girl who answered Peter's knock at the door, the others did not realize that he was actually there.[97]

Second, are any norms articulated? Yes. Paul's letter to Philemon provided a strong example of obeying Roman slavery laws. Ephesians and Colossians said explicitly that slaves were to serve their masters humbly and with good grace and that masters were to treat their slaves decently. Any metaphorical use of slavery versus freedom that was intended to make a theological point was not meant to be interpreted as instructions to overthrow the fundamental economic and social relationships of slavery. These norms clearly supported the idea of slavery as a fundamental part of society. And the later epistles reiterated the commands for Christians to follow the established social order.

Finally, what do our texts tell us about religious leaders as slaveholders? In his classic study of Pauline Christianity, *The First Urban Christians*, Wayne Meeks discussed the data we have about slaves and slaveholders in the New Testament, especially in the Pauline Christian community.[98] Most telling is the number of times these texts referred to so-and-so's "household" or so-and-so's "people."

---

[96] Acts 12:13–16.

[97] Harrill, *Manumission* 59 66 presented an interesting analysis of this episode as an illustration of a stock comic character in the literature of this period.

[98] *The First Urban Christians* 51–73.

Both of these terms were commonly used to refer both to the members of the nuclear or extended biological family and also to the unfree staff. Meeks concluded that the earliest Christian communities represented a cross section of Roman society, except for the extreme elite and those suffering the extremes of servitude, such as gang laborers and galley slaves. But there is also a long history of disagreement in the scholarship on this issue. For our purposes, however, it is useful to realize that slaveholders, as well as slaves, were an ordinary component of the Christian community. And there are indications that persons of wealth—who would certainly have been significant slaveholders— often assumed positions of leadership in this earliest stage of the church. For example, Gaius, Crispus, and Stephanus, men of Corinth, all provided financial and other resources to the Christians (1 Cor. 1:14, 16:15; Rom. 16:23) and Paul exhorted his readers to give them due recognition for their efforts. It is worth noting, in this same vein, that Crispus had a good deal of status in the local religious community by means of his office as *archisynagogos*.[99] From a theological point of view, the fact that slaveholders caused their household slaves to be baptized "raises uncomfortable questions about the social dynamics within Pauline churches."[100] However, in answer to our question about New Testament evidence concerning early Christian leaders as slaveholders, it is clear that there were many and that they behaved toward their slaves as did any other member of their society. Generally, the New Testament texts upheld the social norms concerning slaveholder behavior, and the first letter to Timothy required evidence that a man be able to control his household, including, one presumes, his slaves, for him to be considered a suitable candidate for a position of church leadership.[101]

In short, the New Testament provides no evidence to suggest that the earliest Christian communities condemned slavery per se. Rather, it is clear that they saw servile status as a normal part of the social order. The only norms for the governance of the master-slave relationship were that a slave was to be obedient and that masters were to treat their slaves well, without any definition of what constituted good treatment. And finally, there is a good deal of evidence that early Christian leaders regularly owned slaves, as was customary for anyone with a respected position in that society. There were no specific norms for the behavior of Christian leaders, other than those that applied to the entire community regarding the master-slave relationship.

---

[99] See the discussion in Meeks, *The First Urban Christians* 57–58.
[100] Glancy, *Slavery in Early Christianity* 39–70.
[101] 1 Tim. 3:4–5. See Glancy, *Slavery in Early Christianity* 145–46.

3

Slavery in the Early Church

Callistus: A Slave's Rise to Power

Callistus was a slave belonging to Carpophorus, a Christian and a member of the *familia caesaris* around the year 200 CE.[1] As a member of the emperor's household, Carpophorus was, if not a slave himself, then someone who had recently been set free but was still required to perform certain duties for the emperor. The slave Callistus was assigned to run a financial operation, a sort of bank, for his master. But the business failed and the investors or depositors, most of whom may well have been Christians, lost a lot of money. Callistus panicked and ran away, giving rise to accusations of embezzlement. However, after considerable effort, Carpophorus got him back and put him to work in the *pistrinum*, a treadmill where slaves were used to provide power instead of donkeys. The people who had lost their money managed to persuade Carpophorus to release Callistus from the treadmill, hoping that he would be able to help them to recover their financial losses. But Callistus apparently

---

[1] The life of Pope Callistus I (r. 217–222) is one of the most detailed records we have of the Christian slave experience in the pre-Constantinian era. The following account is taken from Hippolytus, *Refutatio omnium haeresium* IX.11–12, ed. M. Marcovich (Berlin 1986). English trans., ANF 5. This work, although written in the early third century, was lost to the West until it was discovered in a manuscript from a monastery on Mount Athos in 1841. Given that Hippolytus wrote this to refute what he saw as Callistus's heresy, his presentation of Callistus's character should not be accepted without question, and I have omitted some of the more lurid details. Jennifer Glancy, *Slavery as a Moral Problem: In the Early Church and Today* (Minneapolis 2011) 68–70), pointed out that Hippolytus's account painted Callistus as a stereotypical dishonest and rascally slave. However, this does not mean that the basic outlines of his life story were not fairly accurately represented. Indeed, if Hippolytus had completely fabricated, and not merely exaggerated, these stories about his enemy, contemporaries would have been less likely to have accepted Hippolytus's arguments.

For more information about Callistus's life and the conflict with Hippolytus see J. N. D. Kelly and M. Walsh, *The Oxford Dictionary of Popes*, rev. ed. (Oxford 2010) 9–11; Henneke Gülzow, *Christentum und Sklaverei in den ersten drei Jahrhunderten* (Bonn 1969) 142–76; as well as the somewhat outdated J. J. von Döllinger, *Hippolytus und Kallistus* (Regensberg 1853), Eng. trans., A. Plummer (Edinburgh 1876).

Major scholarly treatments of the principal figures from this era of church history include Johannes Quasten, *Patrology*, 4 vols. (Utrecht 1950); Karl Baus, *From the Apostolic Community to Constantine* (New York 1980); Henry Chadwick, *The Church in Ancient Society: From Galilee to Gregory the Great* (Oxford 2001); and Hubertus R. Drobner, *The Fathers of the Church: A Comprehensive Introduction*, trans. Siegfried S. Schatzmann (Peabody, MA 2006).

The Slaves of the Churches. Mary E. Sommar, Oxford University Press (2020). © Oxford University Press.
DOI: 10.1093/oso/9780190073268.001.0001

did not have their money, nor did he know how to get it for them. And, in an attempt to raise funds or to get away or at least to redirect his accusers' attention, he managed to get himself arrested for causing a commotion in a Jewish synagogue.[2] Whereupon, the Roman authorities sentenced Callistus to work as a slave in the Sardinian mines—as good as a death sentence.

Not long after that, a woman named Marcia, who was the concubine of the pagan Emperor Commodus but seems to have been a Christian, convinced her lover to release the Christians who were slaves in the Sardinian mines.[3] She asked the bishop of Rome, at the time a man named Victor, to provide her with a list of those to be released and set free. Victor's list did not include the name "Callistus." Nevertheless, Callistus managed somehow to convince the authorities at the mines to let him go free with the others. Upon hearing that Callistus was free, Victor paid him (paid him off?) to leave Rome and live in Antium, a town not very far from the capital. However, Victor's successor, Zephyrinus, apparently thinking that a clever fellow like Callistus might be useful, called him back to Rome, where Callistus soon acquired a good deal of influence in church affairs. When Zephyrinus died, Callistus succeeded him as Roman bishop. Callistus's papacy was characterized by steering a middle way through thorny doctrinal questions and by a remarkable sensitivity to the problems of ordinary as well as notorious sinners. And both of these areas gave rise to controversy.

It is, however, because of these controversies that we know so much about Callistus's life, something unusual in the history of this period. Callistus's great enemy was a priest named Hippolytus, who wrote a long and vitriolic condemnation of Callistus's teachings, including an account of his life that was presumably intended to undermine any respect that might have accrued to Callistus as bishop of Rome.[4] Although the details of the Trinitarian theology that were at the center of the arguments are beyond the scope of this investigation, we should note that Callistus managed to steer a middle way

---

[2] The suggestion that he was trying to force Jewish moneylenders to return money he had lost to them that we find in Döllinger, *Hippolytus und Kallistus* and Gülzow, *Christentum und Sklaverei* seems to reflect a later view of the role of the Jews in a community than what was likely in the second century. However, it is not improbable that Callistus approached the synagogue in order to meet with people with whom he had had business dealings.

[3] Commodus does not seem to have had much animosity toward Christians. The slave who managed his three-hundred-member harem, Hyacinthus, was also a Christian. John Julius Norwich, *Absolute Monarchies: A History of the Papacy* (New York 2011).

[4] Scholars are not in full agreement about Hippolytus's life story either. Most likely he was a priest at Rome who died in the 250s. However, some accounts list him as an antipope who, after reconciling with Callistus's successor, Pontian, then accompanied Pontian to the Sardinian mines, where they both died.

between two points of view that were later both dismissed as heretical. By not taking sides in the controversy, Callistus drew to himself a lot of invective, but also managed to steer the Roman church in what eventually proved to be a helpful direction.

The other accusation that was leveled against Callistus, by Hippolytus and others, was that he was lax in enforcing church discipline—in other words that he showed exceptional mercy and understanding toward sinners. The most egregious instance of Callistus's laxity, according to Hippolytus, was the fact that he did not require sinful clergy to step down from their priestly or episcopal offices, leaving judgment and punishment for their offenses to God. In addition, Callistus allowed Christian women to pair with men of low status, including slaves. Although such a marriage would not have been permitted by Roman law at that time, it was customary for elite men to take female concubines (like Commodus and Marcia) and not unheard of for elite women to take male concubines. The partners in these relationships behaved as though they were married, but did not have all of the benefits or the obligations of a legal marriage. Couples where both were slaves could not legally marry, but often lived in marriage-like relationships known as *contubernia*. Callistus seems to have been saying that it was preferable for a Christian woman to have a Christian man as her mate, even if it could not legally be a marriage. And, as Gaudemet pointed out, Callistus's recognition of such a union as though it were a marriage is one of the earliest indicators we have of the church developing a set of legal norms that did not always follow those of society.[5] Since we do not have Callistus's thoughts on any of these matters, we can only speculate based on the scarce evidence of his actions.[6] However, it does not require much imagination to think that someone who had found himself in as many predicaments as Callistus had done might have developed a real sympathy for those whose circumstances led them to exhibit less than desirable behavior.

The *Liber Pontificalis* recorded that Callistus served as bishop of Rome from sometime in 217 until October 14, 222. During this time, he built a basilica and a cemetery and ordained sixteen priests and four deacons and

---

[5] See Jean Gaudemet, "La Décision de Callixte en matière de mariage," in *Studi in onore di Ugo Enrico Paoli* (Florence 1956) 333–44. Also see James Brundage, *Sex, Law, and Christian Society in Medieval Europe* (Chicago 1987) 70–75, about the acceptance of concubinage by the early church.

[6] The only letters attributed to Callistus have been shown to have been the work of the Pseudo-Isidorean workshop several centuries later. This was a group of disgruntled churchmen who fabricated allegedly ancient legal documents for their own eighth- or ninth-century purposes. See chapter 6, note 68.

took part in the ordination of eight bishops.[7] In addition, we know from Hippolytus and other early authors that Callistus was engaged in a number of theological and legal disputes. In other words, he seems to have been a busy and productive bishop, who led the growing Roman Christian community through what was a relatively peaceful time in its history. There were no major anti-Christian persecutions from the Roman authorities during this period, and even the doctrinal controversies that caused conflict within the Christian community were not particularly heated at this time.

Callistus's exceptional good luck seems to have held out even after his death. It appears that he was killed in a street riot in Rome, perhaps caused by the locals' unhappiness at the rapid growth of the Christian community.[8] However, as a result of this violent death, his name was included on the list of martyrs and thus Callistus has been regarded as a saint, with a feast day on October 14.[9]

The point of telling this story in so much detail is that it is one of the few detailed stories we have about slavery and the early Christian leadership. There is no evidence here that either ordinary Christians or the leaders of the fledgling church condemned slavery. In fact, the evidence suggests the contrary. Marcia was a devout woman (despite her position as the emperor's mistress) who simply wanted to do something nice for her fellow Christians. Often, in the records about the early Christians, we read of pious men and women like Marcia who arranged for slaves to be freed. However, this was simply a charitable act bringing comfort to the suffering, in no way an attempt to abolish slavery.

Far from condemning slavery, this story shows several examples of good Christians who not only accepted slavery as a normal part of economic life, but also seem to have agreed with the prevailing custom of treating slaves rather harshly when it seemed appropriate. Carpophorus, Callistus's master, was a Christian and either a slave or a freedman himself. Yet he did not hesitate to punish Callistus very cruelly, by sending him to the *pistrinum*, where he was put to work like a mule or a donkey at the mill. Bishop Victor's

---

[7] *Liber Pontificalis* I.7, ed. L. Duchesne (1886–1892), Engl. trans. R. Davis, *The Book of Pontiffs*, 3rd ed. (Liverpool 2010). At this time the Roman church had forty-six elders, seven deacons, seven subdeacons, forty-two acolytes, and fifty-two lesser clerics. Eamon Duffy, *Saints and Sinners: A History of the Popes*, 3rd ed. (New Haven 2006).

[8] So many ordinations in only five years would definitely support this idea.

[9] According to the *Acta Sanctorum*, reproduced in PG 10.109–26. Henry Palmer Chapman suggested that the fact that Callistus is the earliest bishop of Rome to be listed in the fourth-century *Depositio Martirum* is in itself "good evidence" that Callistus actually died a martyr. "Pope Callistus," *The Catholic Encyclopedia* (Appleton, WI 1913), archived at NewAdvent.com.

omission of Callistus from the list of those to be freed and his subsequent efforts to keep Callistus out of Rome suggest that he may have deliberately tried to keep Callistus enslaved in the mines. At the very least, it is clear that Victor had no trouble at all with the idea of slavery, especially in regard to someone he didn't like. And finally, Callistus himself, who certainly had good reason to deplore the practice of slaveholding, does not seem to have inveighed against it after he gained his freedom.

On the other hand, although we can assume that Callistus's release from the mines also resulted in his becoming a freedman, his former slave status does not seem to have impeded his rise to considerable influence and power in the Roman church. There were no formal barriers to freedmen becoming wealthy or gaining power and prestige, but the third-century Roman aristocracy often looked down upon someone who had once held servile status. That Callistus could become the overseer of the Roman church suggests that Christian aristocrats in Rome were willing to accept St. Paul's assertion that "there is no slave or free"—at least in spiritual matters.[10]

As we saw in our discussion of the New Testament, and shall see in more detail later, slavery was a normal economic, legal, and social condition that seems to have remained relatively unaffected by the rise of Christianity in the Roman Empire. Most especially we shall look at how the church authorities used the economic tool of slavery in their personal and professional situations. Our task here is to examine how the Christian leadership dealt with the slaves in their households and with those owned corporately by the Christian community. Their challenge was how to balance the religious requirement that all be treated as equals before God with the economic requirement that the institutions of servitude remain strong.

Non-Biblical Texts

We have already examined those texts that were eventually accorded special status and included in what was believed to be the divinely inspired New Testament. But there were a number of other texts written by the leaders of

---

[10] There was also a freedman's cult of the emperor Augustus where the priests were former slaves. Henrik Mouritsen, *The Freedman in the Roman World* (Cambridge 2011) 249–54. On the question of Roman freedmen, also see Robert Knapp, *Invisible Romans* (Cambridge, MA 2011) 170–95 and Keith R. Bradley, *Slaves and Masters in the Roman Empire: A Study in Social Control* (New York 1987) 81–86.

the new Christian community that, although they were not included in the eventual canon of the Christian scriptures, exerted a great deal of influence when they were written and continued to do so in later centuries. We shall examine them in roughly chronological order, asking the same questions we asked of the New Testament texts. First: what does the text tell us about the views about slavery in the culture that produced the texts? We have looked at the Roman, secular culture, but did the evolving Christian culture hold different views? Second: remembering that canon law was not yet a coherent body of norms or documents, does this proto-canonical material have any instructions (explicit or implicit) about issues related to slavery? Third: is there anything in these texts that can tell us about slaveholding by religious leaders or by the Christian community as a body?

As we have seen, in general, Christians were exhorted to be good citizens of the empire in everything that did not go against their Christian beliefs. The earliest non-scriptural Christian text that is important for us to consider is a letter from the church at Rome to the Christians in Corinth, written in the last decade of the first century CE.[11] The text is known as "I Clement," but for centuries there has been disagreement about which Clement: was he the traditional bishop of Rome at the end of the century, or a freedman who lived in the household of an imperial cousin, or a man who worked with the apostle Paul? Or perhaps the text was written by someone else who wasn't even called Clement but attributed the work to a Clement whose name carried special significance to the writer or to the recipients. At any rate, this rather long document is concerned with disagreements within the Corinthian community that had come to the attention of the Roman Christians. After lengthy exhortations to reconcile in Christian unity and to obey the church authorities, the author also called upon the Christians of Corinth to obey "our rulers and governors on earth" whose sovereign power comes from God.[12] Tellingly, there are also prayers that God would direct these rulers toward "peace and gentleness," and that God would "deliver us [the Christians] from those who hate us unjustly."[13] This suggests that, at least in Rome, where the persecutions of Nero in the sixties and of Domitian in the early nineties had not faded from memory, the leaders of the Christian community were concerned that their flock do nothing to provoke their non-Christian neighbors'

---

[11] On this text attributed to an unknown Clement see *The Apostolic Fathers: Greek Texts and English Translations*, ed., trans., Michael W. Holmes, 3rd ed. (Grand Rapids, MI 2007) 33–165.

[12] I Clement, 60–61.

[13] I Clement, 60.

hostility. A generation or so later, in a letter addressed to a certain Diognetus, a pagan who seems to have wanted to know more about the new faith, the author explained that the Christians were good residents of the empire, saying that the Christians "follow the local customs" and "participate in everything as citizens" even though they must "endure everything as foreigners" because "their citizenship is in Heaven." But still, "they obey the established laws."[14] Here the emphasis does not seem to be so much on avoiding any situation that might antagonize their neighbors. Rather, it argued that Christians were normal people who were loyal to the emperor and happened to have different religious beliefs. Although these letters clearly expressed the Christians' desire not to deviate from social norms that did not violate their religious beliefs, neither text tells us anything about the Christians' relationships with their own households.

There are a couple of texts written by Jewish Christians at the end of the first century that discuss how Christians were to treat their slaves. Not surprisingly, they are rather similar to what we saw in the "household codes" found in the New Testament, especially in the letters to the Ephesians and to the Colossians.[15] A document commonly known as the *Didache* or *The Teaching of the Lord to the Gentiles by the Twelve Apostles* was probably written at about the turn of the second century. It said:

> You shall not give orders to your male or female slave (who hopes in the same God as you) when you are angry, lest they cease to fear the God who is over you both. For he comes to call not with regard to reputation but those whom the Spirit has prepared. And you slaves be submissive to you masters in respect and fear as to a symbol of God.[16]

Here we see the same ideas as those found in the New Testament texts. Slaves should obey their masters, and masters should treat their slaves well, because the Spirit was not concerned with earthly status. However, here there seems to be an assumption that this applied only to those slaves "who hope in the same God." Was it acceptable to mistreat non-Christian slaves?

---

[14] Mathetes, Ep. to Diognetus 5, in *Apostolic Fathers* 334–69.

[15] J. Albert Harrill, *Slaves in the New Testament: Literary, Social, and Moral Dimensions* (Minneapolis 2006) 88–89, provides an interesting comparison of these canonical texts with roughly contemporary non-canonical passages.

[16] *Didache* 4. Translation adapted from *Apostolic Fathers* 334–69.

A letter attributed to Barnabas, Paul's companion, is very similar to the *Didache*, and for a while the early church included it in the scriptures attributed to the early church leaders.[17] Modern analysis shows that this letter was probably written sometime between 70 and 130 CE.[18] In a closing section that lists detailed moral instructions for living in the "Way of Light" in "the last days" before the Second Coming of Jesus, it said:

> Be submissive to masters in respect and fear, as to a symbol of God. You must not give orders to your male or female slaves (who hope in the same God as you) when angry, lest they cease to fear the same God who is over you both, because he came to call those whom the Spirit has prepared, without regard to reputation.[19]

While scholars are still debating which document was written first, it is clear from these passages that the author of the one text had read the other. Here again we see that slaves were to obey their masters, and masters were to treat the slaves well and that status differences are not important to God. But the question also arises about whether the need for good treatment is limited to Christian slaves. However, in many situations this question of whether or not a Christian could treat non-Christian slaves badly would have been moot. Especially in these earliest decades, when householders became Christian they often required that all members of their household embrace the new faith as well.

Texts from this era written by Gentile Christians show a slightly different attitude toward slavery from that shown in Barnabas and in the *Didache*. Perhaps because they were not influenced by the ancient Jewish traditions concerning the treatment of unfree dependents, Gentile writers placed less emphasis on the idea that master and slave would face God in the same way on the day of judgment.

Ignatius, bishop of Antioch in the first two decades of the second century, wrote to Polycarp, the leader of the Christian community at Smyrna:

---

[17] For a while there were two kinds of Scripture, the gospels and epistles, seen as the inspired word of God and also later writings that were "almost as holy" but not quite at the same level.

[18] See *Apostolic Fathers* 370–79.

[19] Letter of Barnabas 19, trans. adapted from *Apostolic Fathers* 380–441.

Do not treat slaves, whether male or female, contemptuously, but neither
let them become conceited; instead, let them serve all the more faithfully
to the glory of God, so that they may obtain from God a better freedom.[20]

This is a bit different from the previous texts. It does say that slaveholders
should treat their slaves well and that slaves should obey their masters.
But here, in a letter directed more toward his colleague than to the entire Christian community of Smyrna, Ignatius seems to be telling Bishop
Polycarp that slaveholders should make sure that their slaves remained
humble—servile—for the good of their souls. In this letter, Ignatius also
wrote that slaves should not be freed with church funds. While freeing one's
slaves was a laudable act, the church should not be expected to use its limited resources to pay the expenses associated with manumission, as had frequently been the practice in the synagogues.[21] Since Ignatius also wrote a
letter to the church at Smyrna, where Polycarp was bishop, it is likely that
this letter addressed just to Polycarp was a somewhat less public document
and thus that the views on slavery implied here are indicative of Ignatius's
real attitudes.[22] In other words, it was all very well to have Christian charity
toward one's slaves—whether the slaves were Christian or not was not mentioned. But that charity did not entitle these slaves to become uppity. Indeed,
it suggested that it was the slaveholder's Christian duty to help slaves save
their souls by letting them know their place because God would reward servile docility. This passage clearly reflects a view of slavery well in line with the
mainstream Roman elite culture.

Ignatius's letter to Polycarp is perhaps the best illustration from this era
showing that the early Christian leaders—who remained very much members
of the greater Greco-Roman society—embraced the values and attitudes toward slavery and slaves that were customary in their socioeconomic milieu.
In this environment, slaves were not accorded the respect that their upper-
class owners enjoyed in everyday life, no matter the protestations of equality
for everyone "in Christ." Ignatius wrote a number of these letters during the
course of his very public journey to Rome, where he was eventually fed to

---

[20] Ignatius of Antioch, Letter to Polycarp 4, trans. adapted from *Apostolic Fathers* 263–717.

[21] Chadwick, *Church in Ancient Society* 81. Also see J. Albert Harrill, "Ignatius ad Polycarp. 4.3 and
the Corporate Manumission of Christian Slaves," *Journal of Early Christian Studies* 1 (1993) 107–42.

[22] In William R. Schoedel's extensive commentary on this letter in *Ignatious of Antioch: A
Commentary on the Letters of Ignatius of Antioch*, ed. H. Koester, *Hermeneia* (Philadelphia 1985)
257–81, he described the text as consisting mostly of advice to Bishop Polycarp, with only the final
two chapters addressed to the Smyrna community.

the lions. All along the way, he met with groups of Christians and, excited about his coming opportunity to die a martyr's death, urged them to persevere in the faith. The seven letters from Ignatius to various Christian communities that have been preserved for us are primarily exhortations to remain faithful and reminders about how to lead a good Christian life, and they also provide details about how the Christian community should be organized.[23] The letters show that proper hierarchy was very important to Ignatius, as was the dignity of the episcopal office. Thus, it should come as no surprise that Ignatius was also concerned that the proper hierarchical relationships be respected in domestic matters as well.

Polycarp, the recipient of this letter, followed Ignatius to a martyr's death some years later. The account of these events reports that it was his slaves' betrayal of him to the Roman authorities that had led to his death.[24] These slaves were captured where Bishop Polycarp was living and were tortured until one of them confessed that their master was a Christian: "The very persons who betrayed him were of his own household." The idea that the Romans thought that torturing slaves was the best way to get information on the Christians sounds to the modern reader like anti-Roman propaganda. However, as mentioned in the previous chapter, ancient Roman law required that slaves be tortured for their evidence to be legally admissible. And the Christian account of Polycarp's death does not show any surprise or dismay that his slaves had been tortured, only disappointment that they had betrayed him. The Christian who wrote the *Martyrdom of Polycarp* seems to have accepted this kind of cruelty to slaves as a matter of course.

To put this story in context, we have a Roman perspective on this question of torturing Christians' slaves as well. Gaius Plinius Caecilius Secundus, better known to us as Pliny the Younger, enjoyed a rather extensive correspondence with Emperor Trajan over a number of years, during which Pliny slowly advanced in his career as an imperial official. The letters reveal what seems to have been a genuine cordiality between these two men and a lively exchange of ideas on justice and good governance, as well as personal and official news from Pliny to his superior. Pliny was a thoughtful and a practical man, with a keen sense of fairness as well as a knowledge of law. And in his answers, the emperor appears to have been of similar mind. In 111 or 112 CE,

---

[23] As well as the letters to Polycarp and to the church at Smyrna, there are letters to the churches of Ephesus, Magnesia, Tralles, Rome, and Philadelphia.

[24] *Martyrdom of Polycarp* 6–7, *Apostolic Fathers* 306–33.

while Pliny was the governor of Bithynia/Pontus on the Black Sea in what is now northern Turkey, he wrote the emperor for advice on what to do with some Christians who had been handed over to him by the locals. Pliny was reluctant to treat them harshly since they did not seem to have done anything very terrible, and Trajan's reply called for a sort of "don't ask, don't tell" policy concerning Christians: they should be punished only if they failed to sacrifice to the gods. The most interesting passage for our investigation is toward the end of the letter where Pliny said:

> Since it was really necessary to be sure that [we had] the credible truth, we tortured two female slaves who were said to be ministers. But nothing was found except [that they believed] an enormous and distorted superstition. So I adjourned the proceedings in order to turn to you for advice.[25]

We can learn a couple of things from this passage. First of all, it is interesting to learn that there were two "ministers," perhaps deaconesses, in the church at Bithynia/Pontus who were slaves.[26] This would support our earlier conclusion about Callistus not having been impeded by the so-called stain of slavery in his rise to high office in the Roman church. But, more to the present point, this also provides independent evidence that the Romans did indeed torture slaves to get information about Christians. In this case, the slaves were not being tortured so that they would inform on their masters, but rather so that they would give more and better information about the Christian community as a whole. Torture would compel them—so it was believed—to tell the truth about their religion. Perhaps the most surprising thing about this letter for the modern reader is that it was not until he got confirming evidence by means of torture that Pliny was sure enough about his data to refer the problem to the emperor. And thus, it is clear that Ignatius's seeming indifference to the practice of slave torture was simply a reflection of the prevailing social attitudes.

---

[25] Pliny the Younger, Epistle X.96.8–9. Available at TheLatinLibrary.com. See also the extensive commentary in A. N. Sherwin-White, *The Letters of Pliny: A Historical and Social Commentary* (Oxford 1966) 691–710.

[26] See J. Albert Harrill, "Servile Functionaries of Priestly Leaders: Roman Domestic Religion, Narrative Intertextuality, and Pliny's Reference to Slave Christian Ministrae (Ep. 10,96,8)," *Zeitschrift für die Neutestamentliche Wissenschaft und die Kunde der älteren Kirche* 97 (2006) 111–30. He suggested that the use of the word *ministrae* (female ministers) may not have held the same meaning for a Roman official as the Christian word διακόνισσαι (*diakonissai*, deaconesses).

In summary, these other texts from the earliest decades of Christianity support the conclusions arrived at from an examination of the New Testament on the questions of slavery. It was to be expected that those who could afford it, including Christian bishops, would have slaves to wait on them. Those who were unfortunate enough to be slaves were expected to be obedient. While slave owners were exhorted to treat their slaves well, the limits of acceptable behavior toward a slave extended so far as to include torture as the only reliable way of obtaining legal evidence from a servile witness. Early texts from Jewish Christians had called upon the common beliefs of Christian masters and their slaves as a motive for kind treatment of those slaves. But later, Gentile texts ignored the obligations of any such bond between co-religionists. Yet at the same time, present or former slavery was not an impediment to exercising a leadership position in the Christian community. Finally, Ignatius's letter to Bishop Polycarp told him to treat his slaves in a way that might have been expected of any Roman slave owner. Not only were the Christian moral teachings about slaves unexceptional, but also the fact that the bishop of Smyrna was a slave owner seems to have been unexceptional as well.

The Post-Apostolic Generations

As time passed, the Christians no longer waited for Jesus's imminent return, and they settled down to living in this world for the long term. The religion was attracting more and more followers and also, from time to time in the late second and third centuries, more organized negative attention from the Roman authorities. The great majority of the texts from this era were concerned with apologetics and the defense of Christianity as well as advice about how to deal with the challenges of the persecutions. A number of these later texts also provide evidence of Christian leaders as slaveholders and of the problems faced by those whose slaves were forced under torture to testify against them as Polycarp's slaves had done.

In about 177 CE, Athenagoras, a sophisticated Greek, wrote a long defense against the exaggerated accusations that had been made against Christians to Emperor Marcus Aurelius and his son Commodus. In this work Athenagoras said:

We have slaves, some more and some fewer, by whom we could not help being seen; but even of these, not one has been found to invent even such things against us. For when they know that we cannot endure even to see a man put to death, though justly, who among them can accuse us of murder or cannibalism?[27]

Athenagoras was arguing that the Romans had accused Christians of atrocities for which there was no evidence, not even from slaves put to torture. Perhaps the most interesting thing about this passage, for our purposes, is the casual statement, "some more and some fewer." Athenagoras did not say, "Some Christians have slaves." Rather, this sentence suggests that it was assumed that nearly everyone would have had slaves, and that Athenagoras was merely acknowledging that some were not as well to do as others. This also shows that a number of Christians were persons of means, since they were able to afford a large number of slaves. The slaves referred to here were apparently not Christians themselves, because if they had been, the question of cannibalism would not have arisen since Christian slaves could have been expected to understand what the Eucharistic consumption of "the body and blood of Christ" really meant. But, the underlying assumption in this passage, that non-Christian slaves would readily have testified against their masters, suggests that at least some of these Christian slaveholders likely did not treat their slaves well enough to prevent such testimony. In other words, there was a normal Roman master-slave relationship, apparently undiminished by any Christian sensibilities on the part of the masters. And, indeed, most of the texts from the late second and third centuries do show these Christians to have been like their predecessors in past generations, little different from the rest of the imperial population when it came to their slaves.

Another late second-century Christian, Tertullian, the son of a North African pagan Roman centurion, also addressed the problems of slaves betraying their Christian masters. But in *Ad Nationes*, a work that reveals his legal background, Tertullian also questioned the reliability of evidence obtained from rumors and gossip, reported by enemies of those accused but without any hard proof. Admitting that disgruntled domestics or those whose "righteous indignation burst asunder all ties of domestic fidelity" might well inform on their masters, he pointed out the lack of hard evidence: "Who ever came upon a half-consumed corpse among us?"[28] Clearly, he did not think

---

[27] Athenagoras, *Legatio pro Christianis*, Eng. trans. ANF 2.
[28] Tertullian, *Ad Nationes* I.7, PL 1.638–39, Eng. trans. ANF 3.

very highly of slaves in general. And he challenged the Romans' acceptance of their testimony, which he believed was tainted and without corroborating evidence.

Tertullian was aware of the problems faced by Christian slaves, even if he was not very sympathetic toward them. In *De Patientia*, written about 203, he pointed out that a person might well learn a lot from slaves about patience and might see this as a model for Christians' behavior toward their Master in heaven. One could learn about this virtue, he added, from observing cattle.[29] It is nice that he realized how trying a slave's life might be, but any tenderness or sympathy he may have felt is certainly tempered by his categorizing these unfortunates with the farm animals. Yet, although Tertullian offered no solutions for the dilemmas faced by Christian slaves who served pagan masters, he did draw attention to the problem. In *De Idolatria*, written in 211 shortly before he left mainstream Christianity because its practices were not rigorous enough for his tastes, Tertullian discussed another difficulty for slaves. He wrote that anyone who even handed the wine to someone to be used for a pagan sacrifice, or uttered so much as a single word in connection with the ritual, should be guilty of idolatry.[30] A Christian slave could be compelled by his or her non-Christian owner to aid in pagan ceremonial activities. But this, said Tertullian, was a situation in which the slave was morally bound to disobey. The earlier injunctions to Christian slaves to obey their masters as representatives of God's authority were not to be heeded if such obedience caused the slave to do something sinful. Many of the duties of Roman slaves, especially those of prostitutes and gladiators, were inherently sinful acts according to Christian teachings. And while the vetting process for potential converts called for the rejection of servile persons in situations involving major moral transgressions, a strict constructionist like Tertullian had no mercy even for those forced against their will to do things only peripherally connected to forbidden acts.

Some Christian slaves owned by Christians were forced to sacrifice to the pagan gods in order to save the family in times of persecution. Bishop Cyprian of Carthage wrote that some Christian householders offered sacrifice to the gods themselves in order to spare their *familia* (household), including the slave members of the household.[31] In other situations Christian

---

[29] Tertullian, *De Patientia* 4, PL 1.1365–66, ANF 3.
[30] Tertullian, *De Idolatria* 17, PL 1.765, ANF 3.
[31] Cyprian of Carthage, Ep. 55, *Corpus Christianorum 3B* (Turnholt 1994).

masters ordered their slaves to sacrifice on behalf of the *familia*. However, according to Peter, the circa 300 CE bishop of Alexandria, the cowardly solution of avoiding the sin of idolatry by ordering one's slave to endanger his soul by sacrificing to pagan gods was a very grave sin—much graver than the sin committed by the slave who had been forced to sacrifice on the owner's behalf.[32] For Cyprian as well, the sin of forcing someone to commit the sin of sacrifice against their will was far worse than the sin of sacrificing against one's will, no matter what Tertullian had said.

Christians were eager to ransom those taken captive, a practice that had long been seen as a virtue by the Romans. This does not refer to those who had long been captive and living as slaves—unless they were members of one's family, and so on, who had at long last been discovered. Marcia's rescue of the Christians in the Sardinian mines was not a general feeling of pity for slaves, but of pity only for those unfortunates who were members of her own religious group. What ransoming captives meant was rescuing people who were about to begin the transition from full personhood to slavery. Someone paying a ransom hoped that the person could be liberated before succumbing to this cruel fate. Gregory "Thaumaturgus" (Wonder-Worker), the late third-century bishop of Neocaesarea, wrote a strong condemnation of those who recaptured runaway captives, in accordance with Roman law.[33] But, once enslaved, their new status was usually accepted. Dionysius, bishop of Alexandria 248–264/65, while he wrote about rescuing those carried off by the "Saracens," also spoke very matter-of-factly about his relationship with his own servile domestics.[34]

The transition period that captives faced was seen as a particularly difficult time. A good example of this can be seen in the work of Clement, a teacher in Alexandria who died around 215 CE. In his *Stromata* he referred to the ancient Hebrew custom of allowing captive women to mourn the loss of their families before they were expected to fully assume their new servile role.[35] Clement used this ancient custom as a justification for saying that Christian men should abstain from any sexual relationship with a new female captive in order to give her time to adjust to her new situation. If after a cooling-off period the master still desired the slave, he could have relations with

---

[32] Peter of Alexandria, *Penitential Canons* 6, 7, ANF 6.

[33] Gregory Thaumaturgus, *Canonical Epistle* 6, ANF 6.

[34] Dionysius of Alexandria, *The Letters and Other Remains of Dionysius of Alexandria*, ed. C. L. Feltroe (Cambridge 1904). Re: Saracens, Ep. 3, ANF 6; re: his own slaves, Ep. 10, ANF 6.

[35] Clement of Alexandria, *Stromata* 2.18, PG 9 and ANF 2.

her. However, unlike a Roman master, a Christian should not subsequently cast her off or sell her when he no longer wanted her. Instead he should set her free. Admittedly, Clement's concern was more for the master's spiritual well-being than the slave woman's, spiritual or physical. Unlike Tertullian, Clement recognized that a sexual relationship between a Christian master and his slave woman was likely inevitable, and did not condemn either of them very severely for what he apparently viewed as a relatively minor transgression. But the establishment of a waiting period did emphasize the liminal nature of the first weeks or months in her new servile status. She needed time to adjust to her new servile situation, including the fact that she was no longer free to reject what might be unwelcome sexual advances.

This culturally perceived difference between captives and slaves can also be seen in the writings of Cicero, a pre-Christian Roman who owned a great number of slaves. He praised the rescue of captives as a civic contribution like giving alms to the poor. Both, he said, were preferable to the custom of making a civic contribution by spending one's money on public spectacles.[36] Centuries later, Lactantius, a Christian scholar who ended his days as tutor to the Christian Emperor Constantine's son, wrote his masterpiece, *Divinarum institutionum*, not long after the height of the Diocletian persecutions. In this comprehensive apology for Christianity, he wrote of the desirability of ransoming captives, quoting Cicero to support his argument and adding that it was incumbent upon "the just," i.e., Christians, to do so since even the "unjust," i.e., pagan Romans, were so highly praised for this virtuous practice.[37] Earlier in this same treatise Lactantius also said that slavery was one of the many evils that had come into the world when humans were overcome by cupidity and abandoned justice, reflecting the prevailing Roman ideas that were eventually expressed in Justinian's *Institutes*: "Slavery is part of human law, because it goes against the law of nature to subject one person to another."[38] Granted, the principal purpose of Lactantius's treatise was to show the Romans that the Christian belief system was superior in every way to Greco-Roman religious and philosophical traditions. Yet Lactantius's argument, that Christian society was just and equitable where pagan society was not, did not turn to ideas on slavery as a way of demonstrating these differences. On the contrary, Lactantius was trying to explain to the Romans

---

[36] Cicero, *De Officiis* 2.63.
[37] Lactantius, *Divinarum Institutionum* 6.12, PL 6.679, Eng. trans. W. Fletcher in ANF 7.176–77.
[38] Lactantius, *Divinarum Institutionum* 5; *Institutiones Justiniani* 1.3.2.

that on the questions of captives and slavery the Christians' ideas were not much different from their traditional, i.e., pagan, ideas, even though the Christians were urged to respect the dignity of all persons.[39]

The redemption of captives was also a concern of Cyprian, bishop of Carthage 248–258, especially when those captives were Christians. He wrote to the bishops of Numidia, sending them one hundred thousand sesterces (at least half a million modern US dollars) collected by the Carthaginian Christian community for the ransom of those who had been captured by the "barbarians."[40] Other letters address the problems of those Christians, including some bishops, who had been condemned to the mines. There was, however, no talk of redemption of these slave prisoners. There was little chance that they would have the kind of luck enjoyed by Callistus a generation earlier. Instead they were exhorted to give thanks to God for this opportunity for martyrdom, since a sentence to labor in the mines was actually a sentence to suffer a slow but certain death. Cyprian asked them to pray for him and for the rest of the Christian community who were not quite so close to heaven.[41] This does not mean that Cyprian abandoned them to their fate. As was also the custom with Christians awaiting martyrdom in local prisons, along with his spiritual advice Cyprian sent gifts to ease their sufferings. We know this from the thank-you letters written in reply.[42] There were also Christians from the royal household, the *familia caesaris*, who had been sent in chains to agricultural labor gangs, also as good as a death sentence. And here again Cyprian seems to have thought that speedy martyrdom was preferable to survival in servitude.[43] Cyprian apparently saw the plight of those recently captured by the "barbarians" as fundamentally different from that of those legally consigned to forced labor because of their religion.

Ransoming captives was not merely a good pious Christian act. It was also a way of continuing in the long held Roman tradition that the wealthy should use a portion of their fortunes for the public good. Ransoming captives was a way of doing public works that did not offend Christian sensibilities, as

---

[39] For more on Lactantius see Thomas Hughson, S.J., "Social Justice in Lactantius's *Divine Institutes*: An Exploration," in *Reading Patristic Texts on Social Ethics*, ed. J. Leemans et al. (Washington, DC 2011) 185–207.

[40] Cyprian of Carthage, Ep. 62, ed. G. F. Diercks, *Corpus Christianorum 3C* (Turnholt 1996). Note: Emperor Decius died fighting the Goths in 251.

[41] Cyprian of Carthage, Ep. 76.7.

[42] Cyprian of Carthage, Eps. 77, 78, 79. In addition to spiritual gratitude, the letters referred to "your continued gifts" (77) and said, "We have received a sum under the name of an offering, together with your letter" (79).

[43] Cyprian of Carthage, Ep. 80.

did other pursuits like holding public games.[44] The only difference between Christian and traditional Roman practices concerning the plight of
captives that we have seen was in Clement of Alexandria's *Stromata*, where
he addressed the question of how to cope with the situation of one's own
captives. Clement wrote that a new slave woman was to be shielded from
having to perform her expected sexual duties until she had had time to adjust to her new situation. Clement also forbade discarding a slave woman
of whom a Christian master had grown tired, recommending that instead
she be given her freedom. Cyprian's letters also suggest that the context of
one's loss of freedom was important. Someone carried off to the mines or to a
chain gang as a consequence of their Christian belief was considered to be a
martyr-in-waiting and thus ineligible for rescue or for special considerations
as they adjusted to the new circumstances.

There are several other issues concerning Christians and unfree persons
that appear in the writings of this era. A number of people seem to have been
ready to sell themselves into bondage for pious or charitable purposes—a
sort of martyrdom perhaps.[45] However, this seems to have had less to do with
slavery per se than with slavery as an opportunity for self-sacrifice. So we
cannot really conclude very much about our questions from this practice.

Although there is a striking absence of blatant antislavery material from
this period, there are a number of texts that warn Christians of the moral
dangers inherent in great wealth and in exploiting or in owning too many
slaves. Gregory Thaumaturgus pointed out that a slave who went to bed
hungry could sleep better than a rich man whose sleep was troubled by the
lust for wealth. He said further that owning many slaves, simply for ostentation, made a person a slave to their desires.[46] A number of Christian thinkers
discussed the idea that, while a couple of slaves to help in running one's affairs might not be objectionable, the common Roman practice of owning
excessive numbers of slaves merely as a way to display one's wealth and to
obtain influence was inherently problematic. Clement of Alexandria, whom
we discussed earlier in connection with the state of a recent captive, also
discussed the moral problems of such excess. His *Paedagogus* ([Christ], *The
Educator*) is a guide to living according to Christian principles. Two of the
most important Christian virtues, continence and frugality, directly affected

[44] See Peter Brown, *Through the Eye of a Needle: Wealth, the Fall of Rome, and the Making of
Christianity in the West, 350–550 AD* (Princeton 2012) especially 395–96.

[45] E.g., in I Clement 55.

[46] Gregory Thaumaturgus, *On Ecclesiastes* 5 and 2, ANF 6.

the question of owning slaves. Continence required the Christian slave owner to control his lust for his female slaves. And frugality required that he abstain from ostentatious displays. Why did a person need many cupbearers when they could drink all they need from one cup, he asked. And he wondered why it was necessary to have several people to pour bathwater over a person who was completely capable of washing themselves.[47] Clement's clever mockery of those who depended on large numbers of slaves to perform simple tasks was a powerful critique of Roman ostentation. In the *Stromata* he referred to the temptations offered by one's "children, wife, household [i.e., slaves], and possessions."[48] But the problem he was concerned about was living to excess. Having children and a wife was not inherently sinful; neither were possessions nor slaves. Rapaciousness was the problem. Clement's ideas were like those of the pagan Stoics who also advocated avoiding excess and ostentation.

In sum, the Christian writers of the period between the mid-second century and the end of the third generally exhorted their readers to lead virtuous lives as much as possible within the norms of Roman society. This included disciplining one's slaves when it was necessary to do so. Most of the differences between Christian and Roman practices shown in these Christian texts concerned the problems associated with sacrificing to the Roman gods. Christians who forced their Christian slaves to sacrifice on behalf of the household committed an extremely grave sin, although Christian teachings exhorted the slaves who were obliged to do this to disobey this or any order that was inherently sinful, no matter the consequences to their personal safety. Christian writers' negative comments about those who owned large numbers of slaves were not abolitionist. They were exhortations against greed and excess.

Proto-Canon Law and Slavery

Thus far in this chapter we have examined various texts from the second and third centuries to see what we could learn about the prevailing views of slavery in the Christian culture as well as in the broader Roman culture, especially as these views were expressed in explicit instructions to Christians

---

[47] Clement of Alexandria, *Paedagogus* 3, PG 9.
[48] Clement of Alexandria, *Stromata* 7, PG 9.

about how to behave in situations involving their own and others' slaves. But we have largely ignored the clergy and the institutional church, who are the focus of this study, except to say that Christian leaders clearly had slaves and treated them like everyone else did. We still need to look at the earliest texts that seem to have be written as guidelines for how the Christian community as a whole—as opposed to individual Christians—should conduct its affairs.[49]

We have not yet seen any explicit evidence of corporate slave ownership by the fledgling church. Despite the troubles faced by the monotheistic Christians, the local churches generally seem to have been accepted in Roman society as being analogous to the burial societies that were so common at that time. And regardless of the legal difficulties faced by individual Christians, they seem to have owned some property in common. As we saw earlier, Callistus worked for a while as manager of the cemeteries belonging to the Roman church. Also, as did other fraternal organizations, the churches often owned a meeting place.[50] A half-century after Callistus, Emperor Gallienus (260–268) not only halted persecutions initiated by his predecessor, Decius, but also issued a decree that restored the Christians' places of worship and forbade anyone to harass them in such places.[51] This recognition of church property, both cemeteries and houses of worship, is strong evidence that the Christian community probably did engage in legal activity as a corporate body. There seems to have been no reason why they could not also have purchased slaves to service their land and buildings. However, any records of their corporate ownership of servile persons remain unrecovered.

Our task in examining these proto-canonical texts is twofold. Were there any discussions of *servi* owned by the Christian community as a whole? And what can we discover about the norms and the behavior of Christian leaders toward their *servi*, whose duties would presumably have had something to do with a leader's work in service of his flock?

For most of Christian history, the councils and synods of the church, the meetings where bishops convened to discuss pressing issues of their day, were perhaps the most influential sources of church law. But in the first three centuries of Christianity, although dozens of these meetings occurred, they

---

[49] Joseph G. Mueller discussed family law in general, as seen in some of the ancient Roman Christian texts, in "Marriage and Family Law in the Ancient Church Order Literature," *Journal of Legal History* 40 (2019) 203–21.

[50] Othmar Heggelbacher, *Geschichte des Frühchristlichen Kirchenrechts* (Freiburg 1974) 209–18.

[51] Eusebius, *Historia ecclesiae* 7.

were concerned primarily with heresies, heretics, and an occasional misbehaving cleric; they did not say very much about institutional housekeeping.[52]
Still, there are some documents concerned with church order that were seen
as authoritative, even if they were not the product of a synod of bishops. We
have already looked at the early second-century *Didache* that called for the
same obedience from slaves and good treatment from their masters that were
found in some of the later New Testament documents. More than a century
after the *Didache*, the Syrian *Didascalia Apostolorum* continued this idea,
listing "the rich who act badly towards their [slaves]" among those from
whom a bishop should not accept alms.[53] The *Didascalia* was concerned
not only with good stewardship of the resources given to the church, but
also with the sources of such funds. And this suggests that they saw these
donations, this church property, as having some kind of sacral status. Tainted
money could not be permitted to become part of this treasure lest its im-
purity offend God. In later centuries we shall see evidence that church property, including slaves, as well as liturgical vessels, and so on, were sometimes
regarded as something set apart from normal treatment. However, for now it
is sufficient to recognize that excessively harsh treatment of one's slaves was
considered to be a sin of such magnitude that it made any donation to the
church unacceptable.

Another influential text from the early church is the circa 215 *Apostolic
Tradition*, commonly thought to have been produced by Hippolytus of
Rome.[54] In the story about Callistus, we encountered Hippolytus as a sort of
villain who tried to discredit the hero of the story. However, that characteriza-
tion does not do justice to a man who was one of the most respected and pro-
lific Christian scholars of his time. Although his origins and eventual fate are
not fully known, Hippolytus did live in Rome for nearly fifty years. During at
least some of the time that Callistus was bishop of Rome, Hippolytus seems to
have been the leader of a schismatic group of Roman Christians, earning him
the title of antipope in a number of later records. Much of his work, written in
Greek, has been lost or, like the *Apostolic Tradition*, has been preserved only

---

[52] For details about these earliest councils, Charles Joseph Hefele, *A History of the Councils of the
Church*, rev. ed., vol. 1, trans. W. R. Clark (Edinburgh 1894), is still exceptionally helpful.

[53] *The Didascalia Apostolorum*, ed. E. Tidner (Berlin 1963), Eng. trans. Margaret Dunlop Gibson
(London 1903).

[54] *The Treatise on the Apostolic Tradition of St. Hippolytus of Rome, Bishop and Martyr*, ed., trans.,
Gregory Dix (1937), 3rd rev. ed., ed. Henry Chadwick (Oxford 1995).

in in Arabic, Coptic, or Latin translation, and there has been a lot of controversy about its attribution.

The *Apostolic Tradition* contains some interesting material that sheds light
on the Christians' view of slavery. *Apostolic Tradition* section II, devoted to
explaining who could or could not be accepted into the Christian community, listed a number of forbidden occupations that were typically filled by
slaves.[55] Gladiators, procurers, and prostitutes were not welcome converts
because of their inherently unclean activities. Charioteers and actors were
also excluded for their association with the worship of Roman deities, as
were magicians and astrologers. A concubine was acceptable as long as she
was loyal to one man. A man who kept a concubine was required to marry
her in order to be accepted, but a woman who kept a servile lover was required to desist.[56] A teacher was urged to change occupations because he
taught "worldly knowledge," but could be accepted if he had "no other trade."
A soldier, who would not have been servile, was eligible for Baptism only
if he renounced executions and refused to take oaths, but after conversion,
one was not allowed to join the military as a new recruit. These regulations
all make it very clear that servility per se was not the problem, but rather
the sorts of tainted activities that slaves were so often assigned to perform.
Some people believed that if such slaves died still unable to satisfy their wish
to be baptized, they could still be saved by means of what was called the
"Baptism of desire," even if they had not been permitted to join the earthly
community of Christians.[57] According to the *Apostolic Tradition*, slaves
who were not associated with the forbidden occupations still did not have
a clear path to conversion. A slave whose master was a Christian could not
be accepted until he received his master's permission, including a testimo-
nial to his good character. The slave of a pagan master was told "to please

[55] II.15, 10, 20. Tatian, in his second-century *Address to the Greeks* (ch. 23) also spoke out against
the gladiatorial games where men were treated as cattle to be slaughtered in a "cannibal banquet"
(ANF 2).

For more on the question of the Romans' ideas about undesirable occupations in general see Sarah
E. Bond, *Trade and Taboo: Disreputable Professions in the Roman Mediterranean* (Ann Arbor 2016).
The Romans' concerns were not the same as the Christians'. Association with pagan rituals was not a
problem for non-Christian Romans, but rather association with death or dishonor, such as mortuary
workers.

[56] This is one of the issues about which Hippolytus chastised Callistus, who allowed a woman to
form a quasi-marriage with her unfree lover because of the Roman prohibition of a formal marriage
of this kind.

[57] Heggelbacher, *Geschichte des Frühchristlichen Kirchenrechts* 147.

his master," presumably by being rejected as a convert, so that there would "be no scandal." The concern that Christians' behavior not cause alarm among their Roman neighbors is something that we also saw in the later New Testament writings, and certainly makes a lot of sense in the context of possible persecutions arising from such alarm. But these regulations are also clearly meant to uphold the property rights of the slave owner, Christian or otherwise. While the *Apostolic Tradition* did not discuss slave ownership by the church as a group, nor by the church leadership as individuals, it does show how much slaves were a part of the community and also that their position was not completely uncontroversial. This text shows one point of view about how Christians should behave, and it does not necessarily reflect the broader church. Dix pointed out that the ancients did not hold the *Apostolic Tradition* in anywhere near as high regard as we do today.[58] Nevertheless, despite its limitations, it does at least highlight the inherent difficulties in slaves' becoming a full part of the Christian community. There was no problem with letting slaves into heaven—after all, "In Christ there is no slave or free." But there were a lot of problems with letting this generally disparaged underclass of Roman society become full and equal members of an earthly community. This may have been because the Christians did not wish to cause scandal, or it may simply have been a reflection of the Roman Christians' inherent prejudices against the servile population.

The *Apostolic Tradition* also provides evidence of the Christians' corporate ownership of land. In a section that discusses cemetery management, it gives us a hint that the reason that we have not found evidence that the churches owned slaves corporately may well be that the bishop's slaves were used for any services that were necessary in maintaining the community's property. For example, a watchman was to be provided by the bishop, and the poor were not to be charged any more than the gravedigger's fee.[59] While this does not say explicitly that either of these persons was servile, it is clear that it was the bishop's responsibility to arrange for needed personnel. The gravediggers demanded a fee and thus may not have been servile (unless the fee was to go to their master as compensation for their services), but there is no mention of a watchman's fee, suggesting that the bishop was expected to provide one of his own men—presumably one of his own slaves—for the task.

[58] Dix, *Apostolic Tradition* 524–26.
[59] Dix, *Apostolic Tradition* III.

Summary

In this chapter we have examined several questions about the Christian church in the era before Constantine's edict of toleration. First of all, we looked at the question of how Christians in general treated their slaves. Was there any discernible difference between Christian and traditional Roman attitudes toward slaves? If there was any difference with the introduction of Christianity, it was mostly in the early years when there was a greater influence from the early Jewish Christian communities, and some Christians may have treated their slaves not quite as badly as many of the Romans did. But that does not mean that Christians treated their slaves especially well. The evidence does not demonstrate Christian masters treating their slaves any better than did their contemporaries, only exhortations to do so. Generally, the Christians regarded their slaves as possessions, just as all Romans did. If the slaves were Christians, at worship they were officially equal to their masters but we did not see evidence of equality outside of the worship setting. And we must not forget that long before the arrival of Christianity, the Stoics had advocated decent treatment for slaves on the grounds of their common humanity. Like their Roman neighbors, Christians clearly regarded their slaves not only as possessions, but also as inferiors, little different from the livestock. Slave lives were cheap and their circumstances and feelings did not enter into their masters' considerations. Since Christians usually tried to convert the significant people in their lives, many if not most Christian masters persuaded their slaves to become Christians. Actually, in the era of the persecutions, it seems that some Christian masters may have forced their slaves to be baptized so the slaves could not inform against them. However, we did not find any evidence that this changed the way that their masters treated them. Some Christians forced their Christian slaves to sacrifice to the Roman gods in order to spare the household, showing as little regard for the souls of their slaves as they did for their bodies. The Christians fully accepted the fact that torture was the norm for interrogating slaves and, while rescuing those just captured before they came fully under the yoke of servitude was seen as a pious act, freeing slaves, Christian or otherwise, was not encouraged to any great extent. Thorsteinsson concluded, based on considerable evidence, that Christians generally seem to have thought that other Christians should receive privileged treatment but he found that Christian texts did not teach "unqualified universal humanity," as the Stoics' texts did, but rather favored fellow believers.[60] And when it came to Christians' actual treatment of their slaves, privileged treatment was not the case. Neither the New Testament nor the other early Christian texts contain much, if anything that called for better than usual treatment from Christian slave owners, whether or not the slave in question was a Christian.[61] The early Christians were very active in ransoming recent captives. Slavery as a punishment for being a Christian, however, was seen as desirable, as a sort of martyrdom, and some people even considered self-sale into slavery as a pious act. Much of the Christians' attitude about slaves and slavery reflect the ideals of the Stoics: treating one's slaves well as fellow human beings, rescuing captives, practicing continence and frugality. However, there is no way of distinguishing how much of this arose from the congruence in the two value systems or from the Christians' desire to be seen as good Romans by the rest of the society.

We also looked at the question of slave ownership by early Christian leaders or by the early church as a corporate body. It is clear that the prominent members of the first Christian communities, bishops and others, did own slaves. Leaders of the Christian community were usually men with some education and with some resources, and the households of such men would have been expected to include a number of servile members. There is also evidence that suggests that the bishop's slaves would have been used to perform any necessary labor for the community as a body, in its worship facilities or in its cemeteries. There was, however, no data that suggested that servile members of an episcopal household were to be treated any differently than those in an ordinary household. Further, while it is clear that the early Christian communities did own property corporately, there is no evidence that this property included servile persons. Instead, it seems likely that the bishop provided any needed personnel from his own household. And one might well conclude that they would have been chosen from his slaves, whose status would have suited them for menial labor.

Even with the sparse evidence available, it is clear that in this pre-Constantinian period the slaves of the Christians and of their leaders received treatment that was no different from that which any slave in the Empire might have expected. The Christian communities probably did not

[60] Runar M. Thorsteinsson, *Roman Christianity and Roman Stoicism: A Comparative Study of Ancient Morality* (Oxford 2010).

[61] See G. E. M. de Ste. Croix, *The Class Struggle in the Ancient Greek World from the Archaic Age to the Arab Conquests* (London 1981) 419. See also his earlier article, "Early Christian Attitudes to Property and Slavery," *Studies in Church History* 12 (1975) 1–38.

own slaves as a corporate body at this time, and they seem to have relied on the bishop's own slaves to do what was needed for the local church. At this time there was no formal church law but, as in the New Testament, in many of the non-canonical texts from these centuries we can see the foundations of later medieval laws and customs concerning ecclesiastical slave ownership.

4

Slavery in the Imperial Church

In the early years of Christianity, the Roman authorities frequently ignored the fact that the Christian churches were gaining more and more adherents, power, and influence. There were occasional bouts of imperially sanctioned persecution of those who refused to honor the imperial gods. With the abdication of Diocletian in 305 CE, this changed. Even before Constantine and Licinius issued the famous toleration decrees in 313, Emperor Galerius had ceased official persecutions in 311, urging the Christians to pray for Rome. Then, especially after the enormous favor shown to the Christians by Constantine, the leaders of the Christian church could become full participants in the Roman social and economic world, and the church as an institution could enjoy full status as a legal entity.[1] Constantine's historian, Eusebius, wrote about Constantine's generosity to the Christian church: previously confiscated holdings were restored to their Christian owners, and the emperor caused many new places of worship to be built in a lavish style.[2] Many of these church buildings, as Eusebius took pains to make clear, had been owned communally. Constantine's largesse and favor resulted in the Christian community becoming the corporate owners of considerable wealth, especially in the form of real estate. The administration of this church property, the *res ecclesiae*, became a serious and complex responsibility for the bishops.

The newly powerful Christian community condemned not only pagan worship practices, but also what it saw as the most egregious behaviors of members of pagan Roman society—e.g., sexual license and the violence of gladiatorial games. However, they did not condemn everything that a modern person might object to, such as slave ownership. Patrick of Ireland,

---

[1] There are a number of excellent accounts of the history of the Christian church in this period. Henry Chadwick's *The Church in Ancient Society: From Galilee to Gregory the Great* (Oxford 2001) is both scholarly and readable, and it includes recent scholarship. For a bit more depth, see the CHC, vol. 2: *Constantine to c. 600*, ed. A. Casiday and F. W. Norris (Cambridge 2007). For a good overview of Constantine's actions, see Averil Cameron, "Constantine and the 'Peace of the Church,'" CHC 1.538–51.

[2] Eusebius, *Historia ecclesiae* 10, PG 20, trans. P. Maier, *History of the Church* (New York 2007).

The Slaves of the Churches. Mary E. Sommar, Oxford University Press (2020). © Oxford University Press.
DOI: 10.1093/oso/9780190073268.001.0001

writing to the British King Coroticus in the early fifth century, expressed his thoughts on the evils of slavery but did not condemn the institution itself. As a youth, Patrick had been kidnapped by pirates and sold into slavery, and one might well expect him to have held strong objections to the very idea of slavery.[3] But, as the son of a powerful man who owned many slaves, Patrick's complaint was limited to the enslavement of freeborn persons, especially through violent means. At around the same time, Bishop Augustine of Hippo was preaching the same message to his congregation in North Africa.

The great John Chrysostom, an early fifth-century patriarch of Constantinople, has often been praised for urging others to free their slaves and for freeing some of his own slaves as well. But there is the heart of the matter: he freed only some of his slaves. John Chrysostom shared the views of the other late antique Christian leaders, which were the views of most Romans of that time. Slavery was the result of sin: "Slavery is the result of greed, of degradation, of brutality . . . the institution was the fruit of sin."[4] But there was no problem with owning slaves to do menial work: "It is not appropriate . . . for the free man to devote himself to such works and to neglect those that are proper to free men."[5] But, like most of his contemporaries both pagan and Christian, John believed that testamentary manumission of at least some of one's slaves was a virtuous act and that slave ownership often had a negative effect on the master's spiritual well-being.

While some Christians did set their slaves free long before they died, this was more an expression of the idea of living in "holy poverty" than it was a rejection of the idea of slavery. Christian leaders of the day assumed that people of means would have a considerable number of slaves. The church fathers did not speak out advocating the end of slavery. Like the Roman Stoics, they lamented what seemed to be a necessary evil in their society and urged their followers to behave decently toward their slaves.[6] A number of modern readers have claimed that Gregory of Nyssa's *Fourth Homily on Ecclesiastes* presents an unambiguous statement of opposition to slavery. However, this

---

[3] Patricius, Ep. 10, 14, PL 3. On this story see Jennifer A. Glancy, *Slavery in Early Christianity* (Oxford 2002) 79–80.

[4] John Chrysostom, *Homily on Ephesians* 22, PG 51, trans. Chris L. De Wet, *Preaching Bondage: John Chrysostom and the Discourse of Slavery in Early Christianity* (Oakland 2015) 1.

[5] John Chrysostom, *On Vainglory and the Education of Children*, PG 51, trans. Anastasios D. Karayiannis and Sarah Drakopolou Dodd, "The Greek Christian Fathers," in *Ancient and Medieval Economic Ideas and Concepts of Social Justice*, ed. S. T. Lowry and B. Gordon (Leiden 1998) 163–208. Here, 173.

[6] See, e.g., Augustine, *On Psalm 124*, PL 37 and John Chrysostom, *In Matthew* 24 and *In the Acts of the Apostles* 32, PG 51.

reading of his sermon is not accurate. Gregory's homily was about excessive greed and arrogance, vices often typified by the ownership of large numbers of unnecessary slaves simply for ostentation. It was not at all a call for the abolition of slavery as an economic practice, as a more comprehensive examination of Gregory's writings will illustrate.

We moderns often fail to understand the depth of *Romanitas* (Romanness) that prevailed in the late imperial period. This persisted even after Emperor Theodosius I's 380 edict declaring Christianity to be the sole state religion, when most people then accepted Christian Baptism and took part in the required observances. But this conversion was only skin deep for, arguably, the majority of the population. Just as Christianity is deeply woven into the society of the modern West, so too were the ancient Greco-Roman religious traditions part of the fabric of the fourth- and fifth-century society of the later empire.[7] We moderns frequently celebrate Christmas and Easter, whether or not we believe. In the United States, Santa Claus and the Easter bunny are everywhere, secular manifestations of religious holidays. Some observant Jewish families put up a Hanukkah bush because they don't want to deprive their children of the joy that comes from a Christmas tree. "God Bless America" is a sort of unofficial national anthem. American money says, "In God we trust." And oathtaking is usually done with one hand on the Judeo-Christian Bible. Even our modern dating system is based on a Christian view of time, using the supposed date of the birth of Jesus as its reference point. Religion and social customs were mixed in the ancient world as well. Ramsay MacMullen has shown how deeply the various Mediterranean cults were woven into daily life in the Mediterranean societies of the early first millennium.[8] Along with the celebration of public holidays and sporting and theatrical events that invoked the old gods or retold their stories, "pagan" religious ideas and symbolism invaded everyday private life. Dinner parties were often held near the tombs of beloved deceased; medicine often depended on invoking the aid of the proper deity. Even the study of natural philosophy, i.e. the sciences, required familiarity with the ancient religious ideas: many natural phenomena were explained as the result of supernatural activities.

---

[7] An interesting discussion of this can be found in Thomas Hughson, S.J., "Social Justice in Lactantius's *Divine Institutes*: An Exploration," in *Reading Patristic Texts on Social Ethics*, ed. J. Leemans et al. (Washington, DC 2011) 185–207.

[8] Ramsay MacMullen, *Christianity & Paganism in the Fourth to Eighth Centuries* (New Haven 1997), especially 32–73.

Romanitas was not just about religious beliefs and customs. The Romans' self-understanding was based on their concept of how society was organized, the social order of things as well as the economic order. The use of slaves, so fundamental to the smooth functioning of the Greco-Roman socioeconomic world, did not disappear from the behavior even of pious and well-educated Christians. Slave labor was as much a part of Roman economic understanding as free enterprise is a part of the way the people of the modern Western economies understand their world.[9] It was inevitable that, despite their earnest Christian belief in the virtue of loving one's neighbor, most Christians living in these earlier societies—even prominent churchmen—would continue to assume that slavery was an unfortunate but integral part of life. These ideas were so deeply rooted in the socioeconomic systems of the first millennium of the Common Era that even when the political structures of ancient Rome crumbled in the West, Rome's successors were careful to preserve the basic social and economic relationships between the aristocracy and their labor force. The Christians' duty was to treat their slaves decently, but not at the cost of their own economic ruin. And many believed, along with Augustine, that enslavement was a punishment for sin, either the sin of a particular individual or the general sinfulness of humanity, which some call original sin.

An excellent example of the continuing *Romanitas* characteristic of the fifth-century church is Ambrose, bishop of Milan from 374 to 397.[10] Ambrose came from a senatorial family and enjoyed a superb classical education. His religious thought was formed largely by the teachings of the great theologians in Constantinople and Asia Minor. Ambrose held a very Stoic attitude toward slavery, tempered by a Christian understanding of the Hebrew scriptures: "*Natura* [nature, i.e., birth] does not make someone a slave but foolishness does."[11] Not even a sale, he said, can make a man a slave. "Neither

---

[9] A good discussion of the ingrained societal habit of slave owning can be found in Jennifer A. Glancy, "Christian Slavery in Late Antiquity," in *Human Bondage in the Cultural Contact Zone: Transdisciplinary Perspectives on Slavery and Its Discourses*, ed. R. Hormann and G. Mackenthun (Münster 2010) 63–79. This study will not address the many theories about slavery in the late antique period but simply proceed on the basis of the evidence that shows that slaves still formed a large part of the labor force in this culture. For a discussion of the scholarship on this, see Kyle Harper, *Slavery in the Late Roman World* (Cambridge 2011).

[10] There are several good biographies about Ambrose, including Neil B. McLynn, *Ambrose of Milan: Church and Court in a Christian Capital* (Berkeley 1994). Chadwick (*Church in Ancient Society* 348–78) has provided a concise account of his importance as an administrator and a bulwark of Christian orthodoxy. And Peter Garnsey, *Ideas of Slavery from Aristotle to Augustine* (Cambridge 1996) 191–205, provides a good summary of Ambrose's thoughts on slavery. Also see Richard Klein, *Die Sklaverei in der Sicht der Bischöfe Ambrosius und Augustinus* (Stuttgart 1988).

[11] Ambrose, Ep. 37, PL 16. Translation adapted from Garnsey, *Ideas of Slavery* 194.

does manumission set him free, but rather [wisdom]." He continued with a discussion of the story of Joseph from the Hebrew scriptures, pointing out that although Joseph had been sold into slavery, because of his wisdom he rose to hold power over those who had sold him. Slavery, said Ambrose, may be the result of sin, but it is not always the slave's own sin. Although we do not have much helpful data about Ambrose's own domestic practices, his theoretical discussions of slavery exemplify how a Christian bishop of the late imperial period continued to hold very much to the traditional Roman aristocratic ideas about the issue.

In this chapter we will look at the church's emerging body of regulations about how the servile dependents of the institutional church and of the clergy should be treated. And we will also look at a number of individual cases involving the slaves of clergy and some other prominent members of the Christian community. As in the previous chapter, we shall try to answer questions about the way slavery, particularly ecclesiastical slavery, was viewed. But the analysis now includes a consideration of whether or not the situation of ecclesiastically owned slaves was different from that of slaves with lay owners. In particular, since this is primarily a study of how the church regulated itself on this issue, we shall look at the relevant legal material to see what it had to say about church-owned slaves as well as other church property.

Councils and Synods

Perhaps the most obvious indication of the church's new status as a pillar of imperial society was the council of all Christian bishops called by Emperor Constantine himself to assemble at Nicaea (near Constantinople, on the Asian side of the Bosporus) in 325. This meeting was needed to settle issues concerning doctrine as well as procedure, or institutional housekeeping. Before that council was called, there had already been a number of local meetings of local church leaders in various cities throughout the empire, going back to the earliest years of the Christian community.[12] The meetings

---

[12] See Mark Edwards, "Synods and Councils," in CHC 2.367–85 and Kenneth Pennington, "The Growth of Church Law," in CHC 2.386–402 for useful summaries of the purposes and actions of these earliest meetings. For a more in-depth perspective see Hamilton Hess, *The Early Development of Canon Law and the Council of Serdica* (Oxford 2002) as well as Joseph Anton Fischer and Adolf Lumpe, *Die Synoden von den Anfängen bis zum Vorabend des Nicaenums* (Paderborn 1997).

were not only a way to resolve local questions, but also a way of supporting the regional Christian congregations as a community. Nicaea set an enduring precedent. From then on, the idea of holding general or ecumenical councils along with the local synods has continued to be a major component of church governance and doctrinal clarification. The proceedings of the early gatherings, both regional and general, included a good deal of material that indicates the consensus of the ecclesiastical leaders on issues of interest to our question about *servi* under the *dominium* of the institutional church and of the clergy.[13] These documents constitute the earliest "canon law." We begin our investigation of this legal material with the earliest councils held in Asia Minor, some local and some with a larger, more ecumenical focus. Then we will consider the material from local and regional synods in Gaul, Africa, and Italy to see if there were any pronounced regional differences in how to handle these questions. Regrettably, much of the material produced by these early meetings has been lost, often as a result of careful sifting done by later generations eager to substantiate their own versions of orthodoxy. But enough has been preserved for us to be able to get some idea of these late imperial bishops' thoughts on our question.

Among the canons (regulations) from the fourth- and fifth-century councils held in Asia Minor, now more commonly known as Turkey, we find discussion of three major issues connected with ecclesiastical *servi*. These are: the bishop's control over the financial resources of his church and over his own personal property; the relationship of a bishop or other clergyman to his female householders; and the necessity of respecting the rights of an individual to own property, including slaves, even when that frustrated another person's pious desires.

The earliest Christian documents that we examined in the previous chapters did not discuss in much detail the bishop's administration of ecclesiastical property. But it was clear from several sources that it was his responsibility to do so. Before being elected to the Roman episcopate, Callistus had assisted his predecessor, Zephyrinus, in the management of church property,

---

[13] While there are not many comprehensive works on the history of church councils and synods, the printed editions of the conciliar proceedings provide a lot of useful information about their circumstances. Although they do not include the most recent scholarship, two classic works remain invaluable for their depth and great detail: Friedrich Maassen, *Geschichte der Quellen und der Literatur des Canonischen Rechts im Abendlande bis Zum Ausgange des Mittelalters* (Graz 1870); Karl Josef von Hefele's *Konziliengeschichte*, published in several volumes over the second half of the nineteenth century, was soon translated into English and French, and re-edited by H. Leclerq (Paris 1907–1952).

particularly the cemeteries. And the *Didascalia* discussed the bishop's stewardship of alms given to the church. By the fourth century, there seems to have been a need to make it unquestionably clear throughout the empire that bishops alone had final say over the disposition of ecclesiastical resources.

A meeting of about twenty bishops from the eastern Mediterranean region gathered at Ankara in 314 CE made it explicit in their canon 15 that the bishop alone was responsible for church property, the *res ecclesiae*, and that this property could not be sold by unauthorized persons:

> In the matter of church property that was sold by the priests during an interval when there was no bishop, there is to be a rescission of the contract and the property returned to the church. It will be up to the new bishop to decide [how to recover and dispose of said property].[14]

Similarly, in a meeting held in Gangra (now Cankiri, in northern Turkey), most likely in the early 340s, canons 7 and 8 stipulated that only the bishop or his designate had the authority to deal with property donated to the church.[15]

At a meeting held in Antioch, probably in 341, the bishops affirmed that a bishop could use church resources, but only for legitimate purposes. These purposes included care of the poor, sustenance of the bishop, and sustenance of the lower clergy.[16] No one, neither the bishop, nor his family, nor the lower clergy could dip into church funds for any other reason.[17] The early church leaders were also aware of the dangers involved in giving one person sole control over these rather substantial resources. Antioch canons 24 and 25 made it clear that the presbyters and deacons were to be informed of the way that the bishop managed the church's wealth. The bishops at Antioch also included a rather blunt reminder that God would render judgement on anyone who misappropriated church resources:

---

[14] This translation of Ankara c.15 is based on a compilation of the four Latin versions available in EOMIA II.2.90–91. A detailed consideration of Ankara is available in Fischer and Lumpe, *Synoden* 452–88.

[15] EOMIA II.2.192–95. Although not crucial to our discussion here, the exact date of this meeting has been the focus of considerable debate.

[16] Peter Brown suggested that earmarking the *res ecclesiae* for "the care of the poor" may have been an attempt to keep church property out of the hands of laypeople or of dishonest clergy. *Through the Eye of a Needle: Wealth, the Fall of Rome, and the Making of Christianity in the West, 350–550 AD* (Princeton 2012) 508.

[17] Antioch c.25, EOMIA II.2.304–11. There were a number of meetings held in this town that was so important in early ecclesiastical history. However, most scholars agree that the canons in question came from the synod of 341.

> Church property must be taken care of with all solicitude and conscientiousness [for it belongs to] God who sees all and judges all. It is to be disposed of according to the judgement and authority of the bishop who is entrusted with the souls of the people in his congregation. . . .[18]

And they continued with a more detailed consideration of the role of the lower clergy in the custody of church resources. Not only should there be no secrets about how the bishop disposed of church resources, but it was also necessary that the priests and deacons know just what was the property of the church and what was the personal property of the bishop:

> When a bishop dies, it is necessary to be sure exactly what does belong to the church, lest it go missing, and so that what proves to be the bishop's own property does not accidentally get mixed up with the property of the church.[19]

In the previous chapter in the discussion of the *Apostolic Tradition* of Hippolytus, there was a text suggesting that it was up to the bishop to provide workers, presumably slaves, to fulfill church needs. In the absence of information to the contrary, we assumed that when a bishop was required to provide laborers in the church facilities, he would provide them from among his own slaves. Now, several decades later when the church as a corporate body had considerable resources of its own, this old custom seems to have been causing problems. Were these church resources the property of the bishop or that of the community? At issue was not only the protection of the *res ecclesiae*. There was also the need to avoid the kind of scandal that would arise from the perception that the church was trying to deprive a bishop or his heirs of what was rightfully theirs. This issue of what exactly the clergy owned personally and what belonged to God but was under the bishop's oversight eventually led to another problem. How could a human being (such as a bishop) alienate property that rightfully belonged to God? Who could set ecclesiastical slaves free?

On this issue of episcopal control of ecclesiastical resources, we must also look at data from the general council held a bit later in 451 in Chalcedon, a

---

[18] C.24. Translation from a compilation of the several Latin versions of this canon in EOMIA II.2.300–305.

[19] C.24.

town not far from Constantinople. Not content with theoretical oversight of the bishop's handling of his church's resources, Chalcedon canon 26 called for the bishop to have an administrator selected from the lower clergy to aid the bishop in these matters "so that the church's administration may not go unaudited."[20] The reason given for this new regulation was to prevent the loss of the church's property and any consequent criticism of such behavior.

The foregoing analysis of these councils' discussions of episcopal responsibility for ecclesiastical property has yielded several points that are useful for our discussion of ecclesiastical *servi*. First of all, we have seen a very strong sense that control over a church's property should reside with the bishop. But also, there were some practical consequences arising from assigning sole control over corporate resources to one individual. Even the most scrupulously honest bishop might muddy the distinction between his personal property and that of the church. This would not necessarily be a problem for the church during the bishop's lifetime so long as he was able to manage the resources well, especially since he might well use his own property for the benefit of the church, as we saw had been the expectation in the third century. However, after the bishop died, it was important to be clear what went to his heirs and what remained part of the church's patrimony. Also, as time went on, there seems to have been a growing concern that not all bishops were ideally scrupulous in their management practices. Eventually, in the mid-fifth century, an administrator was assigned to aid the bishop in these duties and to keep an eye on what he was doing.

The second major issue from the councils in Asia Minor that is relevant to this study is the problem of (male) church leaders living with women in their households. Bishops were rarely married. Some were widowers. Some had avoided marriage altogether. Some had accommodating wives who agreed to enter a convent in order to allow their husbands to live continent lives. And some bishops did continue to live with their spouses, either chastely or conventionally. But wives were not the problem. The problem was the female slaves who were part of the household. A bishop was expected to preside over a household commensurate with his social standing. Such a household would ordinarily have included many slaves of both sexes who would perform the traditional duties according to their training and physical attributes. The problem in an episcopal household arose in connection with the Roman assumption that a master would have unlimited sexual access

---

[20] Chalcedon c.26, *Decrees of the Ecumenical Councils*, ed., trans. N. P. Tanner (London 1990) 100.

to the slaves of his household. And while it was assumed that a Christian master would take advantage of this privilege, the early church seems to have thought that such behavior was unseemly for a bishop. If bishops were discouraged from having wives, or at least from having sexual relations with their wives, it is clear that a sexual relationship with a woman to whom the bishop was not married would have been well outside the bounds. In addition to the question of household slave women, there was also the question of a custom that had arisen in the early church where men and women lived together in a "spiritual" relationship as a way to enjoy each other's help and companionship but avoid a sinful union. This practice soon proved to be unsatisfactory and did not endure. As an early caution against such situations, canon 19 from the Council of Ankara in 314 said that it was forbidden to "take a vow of virginity but . . . live with someone as brother and sister."[21] The entire question of episcopal sexual behavior was addressed soon thereafter at Constantine's general Council of Nicaea in 325:

> This great synod absolutely forbids a bishop, presbyter, deacon or any of the clergy to keep a woman who has been brought in to live with him, with the exception of his mother or sister or aunt, or of any person who is above suspicion.[22]

In order to remove any temptations or any possibility for scandal, bishops were encouraged to eliminate all women from their households, except for very close relatives or the kind of women who were clearly not likely to provide temptation. "Spiritual marriages" could be ended without too much difficulty for the bishops. But, given that the close relatives of a bishop were likely to be women of relatively high status who were used to having slaves to perform menial household tasks, the problem of the bishop's domestics would persist for centuries.

The third issue of interest for this study that was addressed in these councils is that of protecting a slave owner's property rights. Under Roman law a person had the right to the unimpeded enjoyment of his property, including human property. Despite a few pious expressions of regret concerning the potential cruelties of slavery, as we have seen, the very early church had been careful to uphold Roman ideas about property rights. Some New Testament

---

[21] Ankara c.19, EOMIA II.1.104–5.
[22] Trans. Tanner, *Decrees* 7–8.

texts had even quite clearly cautioned the new Christian community to avoid disrupting the social order. The church of the late empire continued in the same vein, long after the likelihood of persecution was gone.

Canon 3 from the circa 340 Council of Gangra explicitly condemned anyone who "teaches a slave to despise [or have contempt for] his master and to abandon his duties." A slave was enjoined "to serve his master in good faith and with respect."[23] The idea that a slave might have contempt for his master suggests that the canon was aimed in part at Christian slaves in the service of pagan masters who might well have earned such contempt for their ignorance of Christian ways. Since the Council of Gangra was convened in a time when Christians were still not always happily received by their pagan Roman neighbors, one might conclude that this canon was also an attempt to avoid difficulties with the larger society. But after a generation of imperial favor shown to the Christians, a more likely interpretation is that these Christian Roman aristocrats were trying to uphold a social order of which they were very much a part. We have seen that contempt for slaves, Christian or otherwise, had long been tolerated in a number of situations. It is logical, then, to enquire if there might have been additional exceptions to the ideals of Christian love in order to uphold the principle that masters held total control over their property?

A century after the meeting at Gangra, the Council of Chalcedon upheld a master's property rights in connection with his slaves: "No slave is to be taken into the monasteries to become a monk against the will of his own master."[24] There is no ambiguity about the interpretation of this canon. Even a slave's desire to embrace a life of prayer and penitence in a monastic setting could not supersede the right to property. This principle would be reaffirmed in councils and synods for more than a thousand years.

In Syria, probably in Antioch in the 380s, a compilation of earlier texts listing instructions for liturgy and regulations for the clergy was compiled by a group of unknown scholars.[25] Known as the *Apostolic Constitutions*, this compilation included a good deal of material from the *Didache*, the *Didascalia*, and the *Apostolic Traditions* that were discussed in the last chapter. There is also a section at the end of the *Apostolic Constitutions*

---

[23] Gangra c.3, EOMIA II.2.

[24] Chalcedon c.4, Eng. trans. Tanner, *Decrees* 89.

[25] Heinz Ohme, "Sources of the Greek Canon Law to the Quinisext Council (691/2); Councils and Church Fathers," in *The History of Byzantine and Eastern Canon Law to 1500* (HMCL 3.24–114) here 29–33. Also see Peter Landau, "Die Canones Apostolorum im abendländischen Kirchenrecht, insbesondere bei Gratian," in *Folia Canonica* 3 (2000) 27–42.

known as the *Canons of the Apostles*. The *Canons of the Apostles* seems to have been the last of its genre, of the pseudo-apostolic literature that claimed its authority from its supposed apostolic authorship. After this, canonical documents were usually content to admit their contemporary authorship and derived their authority from the fact that they were produced by a synod of bishops or by other authors of acknowledged status. However, the *Canons of the Apostles* were included in Emperor Justinian's *Novellae* (canons 6 and 37) in the sixth century and again at the end of the seventh century when they were included in the documents of the so-called Quinisext Council.[26] The *Canons* continued to be held as authoritative in the East, and even in the West, although Hormisdas (bishop of Rome 514–523) had declared them apocryphal, they continued to exercise influence as part of the later canon collections. These *Apostolic Canons* repeated some things that we have found of interest for our inquiry: canons 39 to 41 incorporated material from the Council of Antioch (24, 25) and from the *Didascalia* (42, 43) concerning church property and the importance of keeping it separate from the personal property of the bishop, including his slaves.[27]

Along with the *Canons of the Apostles* and their confusing provenance, there are a number of undisputed collections of canons from various councils and synods that were compiled at this time, including the collection of eastern canons translated into Latin from the original Greek that was produced by the monk Dionysius Exiguus in Rome around the year 500.[28] This collection, sometimes referred to as the *Dionysiana*, was not the official canonical text for the western church, but it was arguably the most widely used canonical collection in early medieval Europe. Another influential collection was the *Statuta Ecclesiae antiqua* compiled by an unknown scholar most likely in late fifth-century Gaul.[29] Nothing in these collections discussed ecclesiastical *servi* or freedmen directly, but they did include the standard canons about the church's concern to preserve the *res ecclesiae* and regulate the clergy's sexual behavior.[30] Other less widely circulated canon collections from about that same time include those compiled by Cresconius in southern Gaul in the

---

[26] "Quinisext" is the name given to a council held in Constantinople at the end of the seventh century. See Ohme, "Sources" 77–84.

[27] *Canons of the Apostles* XL, XVIII, EOMIA I.1. Also see Marcel Metzger, *Les constitutions apostoliques* (Paris 1985).

[28] For a discussion of Dionysius's work see Mary E. Sommar, "Dionysius Exiguus' Creative Editing," *Proceedings of the Twelfth International Congress of Medieval Canon Law: Washington D.C., 1–7 August 2004*, ed. U.-R. Blumenthal et al. (Vatican City 2008) 209–22.

[29] Edited by C. Munier in his *Concilia Galliae A.314—A.506* (Turnholt 1963) 161–88.

[30] For example, c.15 and 27.

later part of the sixth century and the *Vetus Gallica* from the earlier part of that century.[31] These collections also preserved a good representation of the canons we have discussed here in some detail.

The way that the earliest councils in Asia Minor addressed issues about church property and episcopal behavior helped set the tone for the church's economic and social policies concerning slavery for nearly two millennia. It was decreed that the church's property rights were to be both safeguarded by the bishop and, through clerical oversight of episcopal administration, also safeguarded from the bishop. And a slave owner's property rights over his slaves were sacrosanct, even in the face of a slave's desire to enter into the monastic life. A less successful precept was that females, especially slave women, were not to live in clerical households, lest this give rise to sin or scandal. Slavery was not officially seen to be objectionable, and nonclerical Christian slave owners were not forbidden to exercise their right to use a slave's body for their own pleasure. But there seems to have been a different standard for the clergy. This was not a derogation of the clergy's property rights, but rather a way to protect them from worldly temptations. Two of these principles, the protection of church resources and of private property, were firmly based on earlier Christian customs and grounded in Roman law. Also, the clergy now enjoyed a special status in society that set them above ordinary people. That sense of privilege was sometimes extended to include their possessions, including their slaves.

Imperial Legislation

With the full acceptance of the Christian church into imperial society, we find, for the first time, secular legal pronouncements about how Christian clergy were to behave in a number of circumstances. For example, in connection with the theme of clerical sexual behavior it is interesting to note a text from 320 recording Constantine's revocation of Caesar Augustus's penalties against those who lead a celibate life.[32]

---

[31] Klaus Zechiel-Eckes edited the work of Cresconius, *Die Concordia canonum des Cresconius* (Frankfurt am Main 1992) and Hubert Mordek the *Vetus gallica* collection in *Die Collectio Vetus Gallica: Die älteste systematische Kanonessammlung des Fränkischen Gallien* (Berlin 1975). For a full account of these early collections see Lotte Kéry, *Canonical Collections of the Early Middle Ages (ca. 400–1140)*, HMCL 1. Also of interest is Ralph Mathisen, "Church Councils and Local Authority: The Development of Gallic *Libri canonum* during Late Antiquity," in *Being Christian in Late Antiquity: A Festschrift for Gillian Clark*, ed. C. Harrison et al. (Oxford Scholarship Online 2014) 175–93.

[32] *Codex Theodosianus* (C.Th.) 8.16.1.

Augustus had wanted to ensure that Rome would continue for many generations. Now, in a Christian era, the idea of a celibate life was re-evaluated. The *Codex Theodosianus* is collection of imperial legislation from the time of Constantine until Theodosius II, published in 437.[33] Book XVI of this code was concerned with Christianity and the church, including institutional issues and clerical conduct. But XVI.2.8, an imperial decree of 343 about clergy tax exemptions, turns out to be the only mention of ecclesiastical *servi*. The decree said that the clergy *and their slaves* were exempt from a particular tax.[34] Not only did the clergy enjoy a special status that afforded privileged treatment, but their possessions, their slaves, did so as well. Elsewhere in the *Theodosian Code* there are several texts concerning clergy property, and an interesting commentary on clerical misdeeds in Emperor Valentinian I's (321–375) famous edict to Damasus of Rome that was meant to prevent vulnerable women from leaving bequests to the churches under the influence of predatory churchmen.[35] However, the imperial legislation reveals little new that is of interest to our inquiry other than one text that mentions a new procedure that came to be called *manumissio in ecclesia*.[36] This method of freeing slaves by means of a church ceremony was a natural extension of the Christian bishops' ability to function as civil magistrates in certain circumstances. We shall examine this in more detail later in the chapter.

The late imperial texts discussed here did not, however, really do anything to change the nature of slavery in the Roman Empire. They were just attempts to regulate the legal affairs of Christian institutions and to adapt the Roman law to accommodate certain Christian principles like monastic celibacy.[37]

---

[33] *Theodosiani Libri XVI*, ed. T. Mommsen et al. (Berlin 1950) is available at *The Roman Law Library*, www.droitromain.upmf-grenoble.fr. Also see John F. Matthews, *Laying Down the Law: A Study of the Theodosian Code* (New Haven 2000) and *The Theodosian Code: Studies in the Imperial Law of Late Antiquity*, ed. J. Harries and I. Wood (Ithaca 1993). An English translation of legislation relevant to church issues can be found in *Roman State and Christian Church: A Collection of Legal Documents*, ed. P. R. Coleman-Norton (London 1966).

[34] C.Th. 16.2.8.

[35] C.Th. 16.2.20. Interestingly, this edict was repealed a century later by Emperor Marcion. While some modern scholars have viewed this as discrimination against a woman's freedom to dispose of her wealth as she chose, it was more likely intended to protect unsuspecting widows from falling prey to the greed of unscrupulous spiritual advisers.

[36] C.Th. 4.7.1 (*Codex Justiniani* 1.13.2).

[37] On the subject of how little actually changed in Roman slave law with the advent of Christianity see Hans Langenfeld, *Christianisierungspolitik und Sklavengesetzgebung der römischen Kaiser von Konstantin bis Theodosius II* (Bonn 1977).

The Church in Gaul and Spain

The bishops who met in the early years of the fourth century at Elvira, in the southernmost part of the Iberian Peninsula, seem to have been concerned mostly with providing guidelines on how Christians should reject pagan customs, especially those concerning sexual behavior. Official toleration of Christianity had not yet taken hold. Although scholars now generally agree that only the first twenty-one of the eighty-one canons that have been attributed to this synod actually date from 305 or 306, all of these texts eventually became influential because they were repeatedly included in later collections of ecclesiastical canons.[38] A few of the Elvira canons addressed problems involving slaves.[39] Canon 5 discussed an *ancilla* who died within three days of receiving a severe beating from her furious mistress. The mistress was to be sentenced to seven years of penance if she had intended to kill the slave, or five years if the death had been unintentional. Canon 27 forbade clergy to live with women except their sisters or their daughters who had dedicated their virginity to God. Canon 41 said that the religious idols of pagan slaves were not to be tolerated unless the Christian master was afraid of being overwhelmed by his many slaves. And canon 80 reiterated the Roman principle that a freed slave and his former master retained mutual obligations, adding that this prevented the ordination of a freedman.[40] These canons show that the bishops at Elvira clearly wanted to establish the principle that the Christian community should continue in harmony with Roman culture and customs, except for when they violated specific Christian principles. The bishops were careful to uphold the Roman property laws. Thus, a freedman's obligations to his master took precedence over his own pious desires, and a woman who carelessly beat her human chattel to death received a relatively mild punishment.[41]

---

[38] Hess, *Early Development* 40–42, provided a nice summary of the arguments for this dating. Recently there have been a number of studies on this council, including Manuel Sotomayor and Teresa Berduco Villena, "Los cánones del Concilio de Elvira: Una réplica," *Augustinianum* 48 (2008) 369–434; Miguel Lázaro Sáchez, "L'état actuel de la recherche sur le Concile d'Elvire," *Revue des sciences religieuses* 82 (2008) 517–46; and Philippe Badot and Daniel De Decker, "Historicité et actualité des canons disciplinaires du Concile D'Elvire," *Augustinianum* 37 (1997) 315–25.

[39] The text of these canons can be found in *Concilios visigoticos e Hispano-Romanos*, vol. 1, ed. J. Vives et al. (Barcelona 1963). An English translation is available in Samuel Laeuchli, *Power and Sexuality: The Emergence of Canon Law at the Synod of Elvira* (Philadelphia 1972).

[40] For a fuller discussion of the relationship between a freedman and his former master see Henrik Mouritsen, *The Freedman in the Roman World* (Cambridge 2011).

[41] This last is in line with Emperor Constantine's edict of 319 (C.Th. 9.12.1) that was repeated in 329 (C.Th. 9.12.1): if your slave died after a beating, it was considered homicide only if you had killed him on purpose, or if the beating was excessive.

Although the bishops of Gaul continued to meet with considerable frequency over the next two centuries, relatively little of what has been preserved of their deliberations is of interest to this study, although the sexual morality of the clergy does seem to have often been an issue.[42] But the records from a council held in Orange in 441 include a couple of canons about slaves and the church. Canon 5 stated that fugitives (presumably fugitive slaves) who sought sanctuary in the church should be defended because of the holiness of the location where they had sought refuge.[43] However, in general, a fugitive was protected only long enough to give the bishop time to try to calm the owner down a bit so that his response would not be overly harsh.[44] Canon 6 made it clear that the church would defend its own: ecclesiastical sanctions were to be imposed on anyone who tried to impose servitude or *obsequium* (duties of a freedman to his former master) on a slave who had been freed in a church ceremony (*manumissio in ecclesia*), or who had been both freed and bequeathed to the church.[45] This canon sheds light on a curious provision concerning *servi* and their relationship to the church: if you had received your freedom by means of the *manumissio in ecclesia* ceremony, your obligations were not to your former owner, as had been the Roman custom, but rather to the church where the ceremony had taken place. The church would defend its right to your services in the same way that it would defend its rights to any property acquired through a bequest. These canons were repeated by the Second Council of Arles, which met in that city sometime between 442 and 506 (canons 32 and 33).[46] At this same council, the gathered bishops expanded the discussion of *manumissio in ecclesia* to make it clear that the Roman law of *revocare in servitutem*, whereby an *ingratus libertus* (ungrateful freedman) could be re-enslaved, definitely applied to those freed in church if their "ingratitude" had been legally proven.[47] II Arles canon 34

---

[42] E.g., in C. Andegavense (453) c.1, 4, 11; C. Turonense (461) c.4; C. Veneticum (461/91) c.11. These and following can be found in *Concilia Galliae A.314–A.506*.

[43] C. Aravsicanum, c.5. For a discussion of how Christian churches acquired the legal power to offer sanctuary see, e.g., Beatrice Caseau, "A Case Study for the Transformation of Law in Late Antiquity: The Legal Protection of Churches," in *Confrontation in Late Antiquity* ed. L. J. Hall (Cambridge 2003) 61–78.

[44] Harper, *Slavery in the Late Roman World* 256–61.

[45] C. Aravsicanum, c.6.

[46] C. Arelatense secundum, c.32, 33. Also see Hess, *Early Development* 59 for a discussion of the provenance of these texts.

[47] C. Arelatense secundum, c.34. Also C.Th. 4.10.3. On questions about later imperial manumission and the status of freedmen see Harper, *Slavery in the Late Roman World* 463–93. However, he did not address the ties between a church and those who had been given their freedom there. Also see Mouritsen, *Freedmen* 53–60.

seems to have been intended to demonstrate that the same standards of proof applied whether the ungrateful slave had been freed in church or in another setting. However, Orange canon 6 and II Arles canon 33 both seem to have been intended to make it clear that *manumissio in ecclesia* involved a transfer of rights over the slave/freedman to the church along with the granting of freedom.

We should take a closer look at this practice of *manumissio in ecclesia*. Was this indeed legally the same as the traditional Roman forms of manumission? Although the origins of the custom of manumission occurring in a church ceremony are unclear, the idea that a bishop had at least quasi-juridical authority in the local Christian community went back to the very early days of the church.[48] In the early fourth century, Emperor Constantine regularized the practice of *manumissio in ecclesia* as part of his program of showing imperial favor to the Christian community.[49] Whether this was done out of personal piety or out of a desire to woo the Christians' support—or a combination of these—has long been debated, but understanding the emperor's motivation is not essential to our analysis. In a decree from the year 316, Constantine declared that if a master declared his slave(s) free in the church, it would be as effective as were the other legal manumission formats. Five years later, in a letter to Bishop Hosius of Cordova, Constantine made it clear that this freedom was valid everywhere and not just among Christian communities.[50] The canons just discussed from the Second Council of Arles illustrate that it was a long while before *manumissio in ecclesia* was universally accepted as the equivalent of other forms of manumission under Roman law. However, it seems to have been widely practiced from the fourth century on.

---

[48] In *La manumissio in ecclesia* (Milan 1965) Fabrizio Fabrini provided an exhaustive review of the Roman law and the scholarship on this question. But it is still not fully clear exactly how this practice of having a bishop preside over manumission proceedings became accepted, although ancient traditions of freeing a slave and dedicating them to a particular deity certainly must have resonated with the people of the first centuries of the Common Era. See also Carles Buenacasa Pérez, "Un example de la caritat cristiana a l'eglesia primitiva: La manumissió dels esclaus a *Hispania* segons les fons dels segles IV–VII," *Annales del'Institut d'Estudis Gironins* 38 (1996) 1231–43; and Marcel Fournier, *Essai sur les formes et les effets de l'affranchissement dans le droit gallo-franc* (Paris 1885) 69–81.

A good summary of episcopal judicial authority and the bishop's court, or *audientia episcopalis*, can be found in Caroline Humfress, "Bishops and Law Courts in Late Antiquity: How (Not) to Make Sense of the Legal Evidence," *Journal of Early Christian Studies* 19 (2011) 375–400.

[49] *Codex Justiniani* 1.13.1, 2. Jennifer Glancy ("Slavery and the Rise of Christianity," in CWHS 456–81) emphasized that Constantine did not necessarily promote the idea of manumission, but rather merely established that Christian bishops' authority to preside over such legal proceedings was the same as that of a magistrate (477).

[50] C.Th. 4.7.1. There seems to have been a third Constantinian text about *manumissio in ecclesia*, now lost. See David Potter, *Constantine the Emperor* (Oxford 2013) 182 and Fabbrini, *Manumissio* 48–89.

Constantine's proclamations said nothing about binding the newly freed person to the church. And there do not seem to be any specific explanations in the available sources of how the idea of such a bond became so widespread, but several possibilities invite exploration. We have seen that the practice of ransoming captives destined for slavery was frequently practiced in the early church. There are no statistics available detailing how many of these captives were really set free and how many were then under obligation to the church in one way or another. However, many of the stories about the ancient saints' pious lives make it clear that at least some of those rescued were not set free to go their own way but were often required to enter a monastery or to be trained to serve as missionaries among their own people. What about the manumission of those who had been slaves for a longer period? Some scholars have suggested that this bond between the church and the freed slave was an expression of the ancient Greek practice wherein a slave who was freed in the temple then acquired obligations to the deity in whose temple the ceremony had taken place.[51] The custom seems also to have applied on occasion in the Jewish community of the Roman Empire as well.[52] *Manumissio in ecclesia*, however, resulted in obligations to the institutional church, not directly to the Christian god.

In ancient Rome, freedmen and slaves were the principal members of what was known as the *compitales* cult, whose rituals were practiced crossroads shrines. In the first century CE, this cult was transformed to include the worship of the *princeps*'s (Augustus's) personal gods and perhaps of the person of the emperor as well.[53] This was one of the first cults in which freedmen were permitted to function as priests, i.e., as public officials. And it was a place where many freedmen rose to positions of considerable public status. This practice from the early years of the Roman Empire may have been more directly connected to the association of *manumissio in ecclesia* with service to the institutional church than was the earlier custom of dedicating former slaves to a deity. In ancient Roman practice, the crossroads had been a traditional location for a manumission ceremony. The former slave was now free to go in any direction. Free service to the cult of that place would have been, among other things, a celebration of one's freedom, and somewhat different

---

[51] On this see the discussions in Fabbrini, *Manumissio* 162–93.

[52] For evidence of inscriptions about manumitted slaves of those who worshiped the "High God" (the Jewish god, but also sometimes Zeus) who then owed services "to the synagogue," see Tessa Rajak, "The Jewish Diaspora," CHC 1.53–68, here 64.

[53] On this cult see Mouritsen, *Freedmen*, 248–54.

in character from the obligations one still had to the former master. By the time that the Second Council of Arles was held in the late fifth century, service to such an imperial cult was out of the question. However, continuing obligations to the location where one had received one's freedom may have been seen, in a way, as a continuation of the ancient *compitales* cult.

On the other side of the manumission relationship, the release of the former slave owner from his obligations to the freedman might well have been an incentive for the owner to use the ecclesiastical venue to proclaim his slave's liberty. The Roman custom of mutual obligations between a freedman and his former owner was, after all, not without cost to the patron. Since the church was already charged with protecting the poor and defenseless, the church's burdens would not always have been increased by a mutual bond with a newly freed slave.[54] And in return the church stood likely to benefit greatly from the freedman's services. The former owner would not only be released from responsibility, but he might also have derived some spiritual benefit from having "donated" the freedman's services to the church. However, although this speculation may shed light on why people might have agreed to these conditions, it does not explain how the strange custom came to be, attaching a freedman to the church where the manumission ceremony took place.[55]

Another possibility for explaining this custom is that *manumissio in ecclesia* may have been seen as a sort of ecclesiastical version of the old Roman customs of either "corporate manumission" or "manumission among friends." In the last chapter, we mentioned that when Bp. Ignatius of Antioch wrote to his friend Bp. Polycarp, among other things he said that slaves should not be freed by church funds. Ignatius did not want the Christian communities to follow in an old Roman custom where a group of people would supply funds in the form of a loan to a slave for the purpose of buying his or her freedom, lest this somehow give rise to scandal.[56] This practice resulted in obligations from the former slave to those who had effected his freedom. But the church did not supply money in the case of *manumissio in ecclesia*. Harrill suggested

---

[54] A council held in Macon in 585 gave the bishop a moral responsibility for these freed slaves. Claudia Rapp, *Holy Bishops in Late Antiquity: The Nature of Christian Leadership in an Age of Transition* (Berkeley 2005) 242.

[55] Fabbrini concluded that this bond between a freedman and the church was formed not merely to increase the resources available to the church but also to provide more laborers so that the clergy would not have to do manual labor (*Manumissio* 242).

[56] On this see J. Albert Harrill, *The Manumission of Slaves in Early Christianity* (Tübingen 1995) 158–92.

that *manumissio in ecclesia* was a form of *manumissio inter amicos* (manumission among friends), a substitute for the regular Roman manumission ceremony that took place before a magistrate.[57] But while manumission *inter amicos*, like manumission *in ecclesia*, did not require any outsiders to supply funds to purchase the slave's freedom, it did not always result in obligations to those present at the ceremony, such as the members of the church where the ceremony occurred. The origins of *manumissio in ecclesia* remain unclear.

Whatever the explanation for how this custom arose, for our purposes, it is enough to recognize that having a church official preside over manumission ceremonies was indeed a way to acquire laborers for the church. And, as we shall see in subsequent chapters, the semifree status of a freedman obligated to the church where his manumission took place eventually became a permanent condition for generations of that freedman's descendants.

Africa

The custom of having church leaders gather together in councils or synods in order to hammer out solutions to various questions began very early in Roman Africa. According to Hess, it began as early as the turn of the third century.[58] However, the issues pertinent to our inquiry do not seem to have been foremost among the concerns of the earliest African church fathers. Generally speaking, the African bishops seem to have been more concerned with who held episcopal power than with what he did with that power.[59] Going along with this concern for the legitimacy of the clergy was a concern for their purity, their sexual purity as well as their purity from heretical or pagan influences. Many of the early councils discussed the need for clergy to keep "extraneous women" (including slaves) away from their houses. For example, the council in Carthage held by Bishop Grato in the 340s addressed this in their canon 3, as did the 390 council in Carthage (canon 2) and the 393 council in Hippo (canon 16).

---

[57] Harrill, *Manumission of Slaves* 189.

[58] Hess, *Early Development* 15. Also see Fischer and Lumpe, *Synoden* 160–323 for a detailed consideration of third-century African councils.

[59] This was the case because there were two schools of thought about how to handle the cases of those Christians, including clergy, who had succumbed to pagan pressures during Emperor Diocletian's vigorous persecutions at the turn of the fourth century. These two schools of thought produced rival church hierarchies in some areas. The Donatist controversy, as this often-violent rivalry was called, along with the continuing fight against paganism, were the most important issues facing the African church in the fourth century.

Later, councils in the fifth and early sixth centuries produced legislation that is directly relevant to the slavery question. Continuing to emphasize the need for proper sexual behavior on the part of clergy, they also considered the other issues we have discussed in connection with imperial legislation and the synods in Asia Minor and Gaul.[60] Records of the meetings held to consider the case of Apiarius, a problematic priest of the early fifth century, include at least six statements reaffirming the principle that church property, the *res ecclesiae*, could not be alienated except by clergy and only according to very narrow regulations.[61] Also, as late as 525, long after the arrival of the northern Vandal conquerors, bishops meeting in Carthage reiterated the long-established principle that no one could sell church property.[62] We can also see in African texts suggestions of the continuing contempt in which late Roman Christians held their unfree dependents, as well as confirmation of the idea that *liberti* (freedmen) did not enjoy full freedom from obligations to their former masters. A council in Carthage in 419 reinforced the principle that neither *servi* nor *liberti* were considered competent to bring legal charges.[63] And councils held in Carthage in 401 and 402 reaffirmed that *manumissio in ecclesia* was a valid procedure.[64]

The records from many of the numerous councils that were held in Roman Africa are confusing. It is difficult to formulate a clear picture of exactly which canons were legislated when.[65] Many canons were preserved by various scholars over the course of the late imperial era, but the content and organization of the collections vary greatly. Also, these collections were notoriously inexact in their attribution of canons. The compilers frequently attributed later canons to early councils, often repeating material, especially canons from Nicaea and other well-known councils. These misattributions may well have been no more than the result of the common practice of enhancing the provenance of an idea or a document by attributing it to something or someone of great prestige.[66] In these collections, the concerns

---

[60] Munier, *Concilia Africae A.345–A.525* (Turnhout 1974) is the most recent scholarly edition of the proceedings of the African councils.

[61] Munier, *Concilia Africae A.345–A.525*, 109–45.

[62] Munier, *Concilia Africae A.345–A.525*, 231.

[63] Carthage, 419, c.129 in *Concilia Africae*.

[64] "Reg Carthage excerpta D. Exig" #64, 82 in *Concilia Africae*.

[65] To some extent this is due to the devastation of the Vandal conquests of the fifth century and the Arab conquests in the seventh century, when many records were destroyed.

[66] See Hess, *Early Development* 50–58 on the complicated history of the African canonical texts. Also, Peter Landau, "Die Breviatio canonum des Ferrandus in der Geschichte des kanonischen Rechts," in *Ius Canonicum in Oriente et Occidente: Festschrift für Carl Gerold Fürst zum 70. Geburtstag*, ed. H. Zapp et al. (Bern 2003).

of the compilers are dominant, and we cannot be precise in our evaluation of the bishops' original concerns. Notwithstanding, certain themes appear frequently, including the necessity of clerical purity, a question that seems to have come up quite often and would have had an effect on the behavior of clergy toward any unfree female domestic personnel. Proper handling of church property was also at issue. For example, in the collection compiled by a Carthaginian deacon named Ferrandus in 523–546, of the 232 items listed, six dealt with the need for proper authorization before disposing of the *res ecclesiae.*[67]

Arguably the most influential figure in the African church of this period was Bishop Augustine of Hippo (354–430).[68] His theological and philosophical contributions to the history of Western civilization are legendary and his extraordinary pastoral abilities inspired centuries of men and women entrusted with the care of souls. However, Augustine was very much a Roman aristocrat as well, a man of his time, and his thoughts on the issue of slavery are very helpful to an understanding of ecclesiastical servitude in the late imperial period, especially in Roman Africa.[69] Augustine taught that although slavery was the unfortunate consequence of sin, one should still treat one's slaves decently.

On first consideration, his theory about slavery and sin is somewhat disappointing: all things come from God. Slavery is God's punishment for sin. A just God must punish sin, and punishments are meant to be unpleasant. Thus, since slavery is a just God's punishment for sin, it cannot be unjust, no matter how unpleasant.[70] But upon further consideration, one can see that Augustine was trying to come to terms with any philosophical or religious discomfort that at least some Roman Christians seem to have experienced in connection with the ownership of slaves. Toward the end of *The City of God*, his masterwork, Augustine discussed the origins and legitimacy of the institution of slavery.[71] He began by saying that slavery was not a part of God's original plan: in the beginning humans were given dominion over the animals, but dominion over humans was not included (Gen. 1:26). Slavery,

---

[67] *Concilia Africae A.345–A.525*, 284–313.

[68] Biographical details in this section about Augustine have been drawn largely from the classic account of Augustine's life: Peter Brown, *Augustine of Hippo* (London 1967; new ed. Berkeley 2000). Augustine's own self-reflections can be found in his *Confessions*, PL 32. The best modern English translation is that done by R. S. Pine-Coffin in 1961, which is now available as a Penguin Classics paperback.

[69] On elite bishops see Raymond Van Dam, "Bishops and Society," CHC 2.343–57.

[70] This summary is adapted from Garnsey, *Ideas of Slavery* 216–19.

[71] Augustine, *De Civitati Dei* 19.15, PL 41.

Augustine said, was introduced when Noah cursed his son Canaan for his sin: "Cursed be Canaan; a slave of slaves shall he be to his brothers" (Gen. 9:25).[72] Augustine explained that "sin had brought about the label [slave], not nature." And he continued that the traditional Roman theory that slavery began when those not killed in war were taken captive was a good illustration of his point about sin: "Even a just war is waged out of sin, as well as in order to fight against the opponent." God will humble the victors, said Augustine, to punish or to remove their sins, while enslavement (if not death) is the punishment of the vanquished. "Thus, the first cause of slavery is sin. One person is subjected to another and put in bondage. Nothing happens unless God wills it." God is not unjust, said Augustine, and God knows how to administer the proper punishment. This divine justice, continued Augustine, is why St. Paul admonished slaves to obey their masters.

While this explanation may still be somewhat unsettling to the modern reader, it does make clear how Augustine came to his conclusions. Augustine had always lived a life of relative privilege. Even during the economically difficult years of his boyhood in Thagaste (modern Souk Ahras, in Algeria) and his peripatetic student years, he was still a member of the class that did not willingly perform manual labor and would likely have enjoyed the services of at least a few slaves.[73] Augustine's financial picture seems to have improved during his time as a teacher of rhetoric in Italy, and it is likely that his household staff grew in size. In 387 Augustine was baptized a Christian and not long afterward he returned to his native Africa, where he was ordained a priest and later bishop of Hippo Regius (modern Annaba), a town about sixty miles from his birthplace. Here he spent his last thirty-five years as an influential preacher and teacher. Having presumably been served by slaves his entire life, Augustine does not seem to have been troubled by the economic realities of life in North Africa, at least not by the reality of managing the estates owned by the church of Hippo that were perhaps twenty times as extensive as those Augustine's family had ever possessed.[74] However, Augustine did take seriously the Christian—and Stoic—ideas about alleviating the plight of captives and not treating one's slaves with cruelty, as well as about the virtues of manumission. Toward the end of his life he famously

---

[72] This puzzling story about Noah's anger at his son continues to perplex scholars, but that is not relevant here.

[73] On slave owning by those considered not to be "wealthy" see Harper, *Slavery in the Late Roman World* 47–60.

[74] Brown, *Augustine of Hippo* (1967) 192.

wrote a letter describing the horrors of the slave traders who were ravaging the African countryside scooping up slaves to resupply the Europeans after their estates had been devastated by the "barbarian" raids.[75] While he may not have thought slavery was objectionable per se, the violent enslavement of free men and women definitely was.

Much of what we know about Augustine has come to us through his sermons and his correspondence. As a pastor, Augustine preached regularly to his congregation of urban homeowners and well-to-do agriculturalists, most of whom would have been served by slaves.[76] In a sermon about Jesus's Sermon on the Mount, Augustine pointed out that although even Jesus seems to have assumed that slaves sometimes deserved a beating, the severity of the punishment should be commensurate with the offense.[77]

In Hippo Regius, Augustine lived together with a monastic community of men, eschewing the luxury available in an episcopal residence.[78] In a sermon about the ascetic life, he made it clear that prospective monks should free their slaves and also donate their property to the church.[79] Renouncing earthly possessions, including one's slaves, was a common practice among those attempting to follow a life of asceticism, and Augustine's point was that monks and other clergy should aspire to live in holy poverty. Interestingly, Augustine did not recommend selling the slaves and donating the proceeds. He said clearly that the slaves should be set free and then these manumitted slaves would be taken care of by the church. It is not clear if this was because it was the church's responsibility to care for the poor or because *manumissio in ecclesia* had been the means for freeing them. Like many of his contemporaries, Augustine believed that manumission of slaves was good for the soul of their former owner.[80] Any benefits reaped by the former slaves were not the point. And, in Augustine's scheme, the slave would still have been obligated to some extent to the monastery or church in question. The story of the deacon, Heraclius, provides some helpful insight.[81] When

---

[75] Ep. 10*. The * refers to the recently discovered letters of Augustine that have been published by Johannes Divjak (Paris 1983); Eng. trans. R. B. Eno, *Saint Augustine: Letters*, vol. 6 (Washington, DC 1989).

[76] On the makeup of Augustine's congregation see Leslie Dossey, *Peasant and Empire in Christian North Africa* (Berkeley 2010) 149–53.

[77] Luke 12:47–48; Augustine, *De Sermone Domini in Monte*, PL 34.1262.

[78] This was a relatively common arrangement. Augustine would certainly have been aware of the community surrounding Ambrose in Milan and similar communities in Asia Minor.

[79] Sermon 356.3, PL 39.1576. On this, see Klein, *Die Sklaverei* 211.

[80] See Gervase Corcoran, *Saint Augustine on Slavery* (Rome 1985) 47.

[81] Sermon 356.6–7.

Heraclius joined Augustine's monastic community, his slaves came to live in the monastery along with him. Heraclius's mother held half-interest in these slaves, which would explain why they were not given their freedom as Augustine recommended. However, these slaves were eventually set free, presumably after the mother's death, and it is likely that they remained with the monastery. The point of the story is that Augustine expected sacrifices from those entering the monastic life, but not to the extent that such sacrifices violated the property rights of a third party.

We should explore in a bit more detail this idea that the monastery would take care of the manumitted slaves. As we have already seen, in the Roman Empire, newly freed slaves remained in a mutual relationship with their former owners. In order to protect the new freedman in a harsh and uncertain world, the former master was expected to look out for his former slave's interests. In return, the freedman was expected to render certain services to his patron—or, in Gaul in cases of *manumissio in ecclesia*, to the church. These obligations were not nearly so extensive as had been the burdens of servitude, but they most certainly were of considerable benefit to the patron or to the church. So then, we might also see Augustine's regulations as a way of providing benefit to the monastery. In addition, it is likely that Augustine was trying to prevent problems like those caused in Rome in the first decade of the fifth century when a wealthy young Christian couple, Melania and Pinian, announced their intention to set free thousands of their slaves before embarking on a circuit of the Mediterranean that would culminate in the foundation of a monastic establishment in Palestine. Facing an uncertain and potentially dangerous future, the slaves revolted. They were persuaded to stand down only after Pinian's brother promised to take back the slaves and behave as a proper master or patron was expected to do, that is, to feed and house them.[82] Whatever Augustine's motives were, the monastery received the services of the freedmen instead of the revenue from their sale to a new master. The slaves in question, while bound to the monastery, either as obligated freedmen or as monks themselves, were likely better off than they would have been otherwise. Despite their obligations to the monastery, they were legally free and their needs were provided for.

[82] An interesting analysis of this problem can be found in Kat Cooper, "Poverty, Obligation, and Inheritance: Roman Heiresses and the Varieties of Senatorial Christianity in Fifth-Century Rome," in *Religion, Dynasty, and Patronage in Early Christian Rome: 300–900*, ed. K. Cooper and J. Hillner (Cambridge 2007) 165–89. Also see Brown, *Eye of a Needle* 291–307 on the problems created when the wealthy renounced their wealth.

Asceticism on the part of its bishop does not mean that the church of Hippo Regius did not possess slaves. Along with the presumably unfree staff of Augustine's lightly used episcopal residence, a large part of the labor force on the considerable agricultural properties owned by this church would also have been servile. Even though this was a time when some estate records show increased reliance on a free, albeit somewhat oppressed, rural workforce, the conservative nature of the institutional church seems generally to have slowed changes in ecclesiastical property management arrangements overall.[83] As the temporary steward of the *res ecclesiae* in Hippo, Augustine would not have been free to dispose of the servile staff, stripping his church of so much of its wealth. All we can know for sure is that he preferred the simple life among his (legally) free monks and he required that new monks free their slaves because monks should practice asceticism. And we also know that, despite his theories about slavery, Augustine the bishop seems to have behaved well toward those slaves whose lives touched his.

Italy

Italian history from this period is, if anything, even more complicated than what we have seen elsewhere in the old empire. After waves of raiders swept through the peninsula in the late third and fourth centuries, the "Byzantine" Roman emperor in Constantinople tried to recover control in Italy, but this much-hated Byzantine rule soon collapsed. Unlike the other Germanic conquerors, the Lombards who arrived in Italy in the mid-sixth century did not quickly take full advantage of the administrative structure provided by the Christian church. This was partly because the bishops, especially the bishop of Rome, seem to have been associated with the old imperial regime, and thereby with the Byzantines who maintained a presence in Ravenna until the mid-eighth century although headquartered in Constantinople. Nevertheless, a number of these bishops, often members of old aristocratic families, were able to provide order and a small measure of stability for their flocks in this chaotic era.[84] Gregory I of Rome has long been admired for his ability to deploy clergy as needed when local dioceses collapsed under

---

[83] For more discussion about this situation see Corcoran, *Saint Augustine on Slavery*. Also see Cam Grey, "Slavery in the Late Roman World," CWHS 482–509.

[84] A good recent history of this period can be found in *Italy in the Early Middle Ages: 476–1000*, ed. C. LaRocca (Oxford 2002).

Lombard pressure, but a clearly defined leadership structure under the guidance of the papacy was still some time in the future.[85]

For most of this period, Italian Christians and their clergy followed the traditional Roman ways of dealing with their slaves. The old plantations run by gangs of slaves were slowly transformed into estates worked by families of tenant farmers, but these tenants were rarely free.[86] The churches continued to be major landholders and continued to follow the old Roman customs in dealing with their unfree personnel.

The data from Italian councils in this era is not abundant. But by the fifth century papal letters, called decretals, held authority equal to that of the conciliar decrees.[87] A decretal is a letter stating the bishop of Rome's response to a question, usually on a legal matter, that had been posed in a letter received from another bishop. And while the Italian canons and decretals do not provide a great deal of data about our questions of ecclesiastical servitude, they do make it clear that the Italian church shared many of the same concerns as the churches in other areas of the empire.

Around the turn of the sixth century, several synods met in Rome to consider the affair of the Roman bishop, Symmachus. The proceedings of these synods made it clear that alienation of church property was not to be undertaken lightly. Symmachus's election to the Roman episcopacy had been contested for a number of reasons, most of which are not relevant here. As is typical in political feuds, all sorts of charges were raised by his enemies, including mishandling of the *res ecclesiae*. And in response, the gathered bishops made it clear that church properties or the fruits therefrom could not be alienated except as needed to support pilgrims, needy clergy, or captives, or in order to transform the assets in question into a more usable form.[88] Apparently, Symmachus's alleged sins aside, episcopal misuse of church

---

[85] There are a number of recent, interesting studies of the Roman bishop's increasing influence, e.g., Kristina Sessa, *The Formation of Papal Authority in Late Antique Italy: Roman Bishops and the Domestic Sphere* (Cambridge 2011) and the collection of essays in Cooper and Hillner, *Religion, Dynasty, and Patronage.*

[86] Chris Wickham, "Rural Economy and Society," in LaRocca, *Italy in the Early Middle Ages* 118–43, here 129.

[87] Detlev Jasper, "The Beginning of the Decretal Tradition," in *Papal Letters in the Early Middle Ages* (HMCL 2) here 12–17. On this also see Glen Thompson, *The Earliest Papal Correspondence* (Columbia University dissertation 1990) 239.

[88] The proceedings and correspondence from these synods can be found in "Acta Synodorum Habitarum Romae," ed. T. Mommsen, MGH, *Auctores Antiquissimi* 12 (Berlin 1894) 393–460. Sessa (*Formation of Papal Authority* 225–39) argued that mishandling of the *res ecclesiae* played a greater part in the Symmachean affair than many scholars had previously recognized. See also Julia Hillner, "Families, Patronage, and the Titular Churches of Rome, c. 300–c.600," in Cooper and Hillner, *Religion, Dynasty, and Patronage* 225–61.

resources was a matter of considerable concern, as was the greed of the clergy at all levels. As late as 610, a synod in Rome still found it necessary to declare that clergy were not to engage in business activities, despite many earlier such pronouncements.[89] Although the exact details of what constituted good stewardship may have varied over time and place, a bishop was always expected to be a good steward of God's property.

While concern about ecclesiastical financial affairs seems to have been paramount in late antique Rome, there was also concern about the sexual morality of the clergy. Many priests and deacons were married and they were advised to abstain from relations before presiding over the holy mysteries. Bishop Siricius of Rome (384–399), writing to Bishop Himerius of Tarragona, said explicitly that clergy must be "without blemish" if they were to preside over the Eucharistic feast.[90] This obvious reference to ancient Hebrew laws regarding sacrificial animals makes it clear that the issue was not totally the problem of sexual misbehavior, but also of the need for ritual purity in those leading worship. Concubines were forbidden to Italian clergy, but in the Italian texts we do not see the same concern for proximity to slave women that we have seen elsewhere. Nonetheless, the need to keep the church and the clergy pure and uncorrupted was still important. Peter Brown pointed out that in the late fifth century when Gelasius I wrote decretals forbidding slaves to be ordained or to enter a monastery without their owner's consent, he was actually upholding the interests of the wealthy classes. However, Gelasius was not merely preserving private property. He was also protecting the church from the pollution of having the "unclean" members of the lowest level of society: "Nor should the dignity of the clerical ministry be tarnished by persons subject to the obligations [of slaves to their masters]."[91]

Although written somewhat later than most of the material discussed in this chapter, the well-preserved correspondence of Gregory I, bishop of Rome from 590 to 604, provides a good deal of information on how Italian churchmen of Late Antiquity viewed ecclesiastical *servi*.[92] This evidence details how the church followed many of the old Roman customs in connection with their servile dependents. Gregory, the son of an old Roman

---

[89] In the fourth century, for example, Jerome had lamented how shameful it was that clergy were amassing private fortunes, rather than caring for the poor. Jerome, Ep. 52, PL 30.

[90] Siricius, Ep. 1, PL 13.

[91] Gelasius, Ep. 14.xiv.14, PL 59, trans. Brown, *Eye of a Needle* 474.

[92] In *The Rise of Western Christendom: Triumph and Diversity AD 200–400*, 3rd ed. (Oxford 1996), Peter Brown reported that Gregory's pontificate may have produced as many as twenty thousand letters. The most recent edition of these letters is that done by D. Norberg (Turnholt 1982).

aristocratic family and prefect of Rome in 573, was reluctantly drafted into papal service as a deacon and legate to Constantinople from 579 to 585/86.[93] After a few more years in papal service in Rome, he was elected to the episcopacy in 690. As bishop of Rome at the turbulent end of the sixth century, Gregory's responsibilities included providing pastoral care for the many Christian communities ravaged by the years of war as well as administering the vast resources of the Roman see for the benefit of the church and of the needy Roman populace. He became what Peter Brown called a "managerial bishop," a job that required a firm hand.[94] This was a job for which Gregory was exceptionally well suited, given his family's holdings and his political experience in service to the Roman state and as a diplomat in Constantinople.[95]

In connection with our question, it is interesting to notice that Gregory customarily used the word *mancipia*, a word that emphasizes their lack of personal status, when referring to the ecclesiastical *servi*. Gregory was very concerned about the efficient management of the vast papal estates, those that were sublet to tenants as well as those that were managed directly by papal agents.[96] In fact, of the eighty-two letters preserved in the register of his first year in office, nineteen (23 percent) were addressed to the rectors, i.e., managers, of the papal "patrimony," especially in Sicily. In this correspondence, Gregory reminded his estate managers, mostly subdeacons, that alienation of church property, the *res ecclesiae*, was not permitted and that although the slaves and tenants on ecclesiastical estates were to be well treated, they were also to be considered as part of the *res ecclesiae*. There is a letter from July 591 that is rather startling to the modern way of thinking in that it seems to show that the bishop of Rome had little mercy when it came to unfree ecclesiastical dependents. In this letter, Gregory reminded Anthemius, his agent in Campania who was concerned about the status of certain children of

[93] There exists a vast bibliography on the life and accomplishments of Gregory I. A good, recent biography can be found in Carole Straw, *Gregory the Great* (Berkeley 1988), or in Robert Marcus, *Gregory the Great and His World* (Cambridge 1997).

[94] Brown, *Eye of a Needle* 496–97.

[95] See Christopher Hanlon, "Gregory the Great and Sicily: An Example of Continuity and Change in the Late Sixth Century," in *The Bishop of Rome in Late Antiquity*, ed. G. D. Dunn (Burlington, VT 2015) 197–216.

[96] The papal estates were indeed vast. Straw, *Gregory the Great* 22–23, claimed that the Roman see owned somewhere between 1,360 and 1,800 square miles in Italy, Sardinia, Corsica, Arica, Gaul, Dalmatia, and Sicily. On Sicily, according to Peter Brown (*Rise of Western Christendom* 190–215), the more than four hundred papal estates covered almost 5 percent of that island's land area. According to Sessa (*Formation of Papal Authority* 117–24), these Sicilian estates provided work for about one hundred thousand *coloni*, as well as uncounted slave laborers.

estate *servi*, that kindness was no excuse for ignoring the law.[97] Gregory, we must not forget, was a Roman aristocrat.

While a number of his letters did deplore the servile condition, upon closer consideration it becomes clear that Gregory's deepest concerns extended only to two very limited situations. First, he had great compassion for captives, especially those who had not yet been reduced to slavery, lest they suffer that terrible fate. Even after years of servitude, Gregory believed that justice should prevail in cases involving those wrongly in captivity. In September 595, he freed Montana and Thomas, *servi ecclesiae* whose parents' ransom had been paid by the church many years earlier, but who nonetheless still found themselves in servitude.[98] Gregory also objected vigorously to Christians coming under the domination of non-Christian masters. In April 596 he wrote to Bishop Fortunatus of Naples that slaves of Jews or pagans should be manumitted if they wanted to convert to Christianity.[99] Apparently, the property rights of those who weren't Christians were of lesser importance.

From Gregory's letters we can deduce that once people had been legitimately enslaved, their fate was sealed and they were to be treated as any other asset—unless they belonged to undesirable masters. A slave was no longer a person in the fullest sense of the word. Thus, concern was appropriate for someone in peril of becoming such a nonperson, especially under non-Christian dominion. But Gregory thought, as did many of the late antique church fathers, that slavery was the result of sin. While masters were exhorted to recognize their common humanity with their slaves, they were also expected to be completely in charge of their unfree dependents, especially since the masters were responsible for their slaves' souls.[100] Slaves were to obey their masters and would receive their freedom in heaven.[101] Runaway slaves who sought sanctuary in the church, even if they wanted to become monks, were to be returned to their masters.[102] One is reminded of the apostle Paul, another respectable Roman citizen, who did not allow the runaway Onesimus to escape his servile bonds and sent him back to his master, Philemon. The 595 Synod of Rome, over which Gregory presided,

---

[97] Ep. 1.53.

[98] Ep. 6.12.

[99] Ep. 6.29.

[100] On this see Adam Serfass, "Slavery and Pope Gregory the Great," *Journal of Early Christian Studies* 14 (2006) 77–103.

[101] Ep. 7.27.

[102] E.g., Ep. 3.2. Also see Serfass, "Slavery and Pope Gregory" 93.

was concerned that ecclesiastical *servi* would declare a desire to enter God's service as monks as a way to escape legal servitude. So anyone who "desired to change from legal servitude to the church to the service of God" should first live a while as a layman (presumably free) to see if he really was a suitable candidate.[103] While not necessarily an expression of disdain toward servile persons, the text explicitly stated a concern that people would do anything to gain their freedom. It is also important to note that this text seems to assume that a *servus ecclesiae* could be freed if he wanted to become a monk. We shall discuss this question in more depth in a later chapter.

One thing in particular stands out from Gregory's letters: he sometimes gave ecclesiastical *servi* to others as gifts. For example, in January 593, Gregory gave his *consiliarius* (adviser), Theodorus, a slave boy named Acosimus.[104] This appears to be in contravention of the principle of nonalienation of the *res ecclesiae*, which Gregory claimed to uphold.[105] In the absence of detailed evidence, we might optimistically believe that such gifts were from Gregory's personal holdings, but it also seems likely that Gregory thought that such use of church property was his episcopal prerogative. In May of that same year, Gregory directed Peter of Sicily to give a sum of money and an unnamed slave boy to Bishop Paulus of Naples in gratitude for his efforts on behalf of the Sicilian church.[106] In this case, the boy was clearly not Gregory's personal property. An argument could be made that a brother bishop or a close adviser also counted as part of the overall church and thus these gifts did not really alienate church property. They merely relocated it to another ecclesiastical location. However, this would presume a much larger view of "the church" than we have yet seen elsewhere. While Gregory upheld the nonalienability of the *res ecclesiae* in principle, on a number of occasions, his actions seem to have overstepped his authority.[107] Perhaps he felt justified in doing so because he was such a good steward. And he did acquire a lot more slaves for the church of Rome than he gave away. For example,

---

[103] Ep. 5.57.

[104] Ep. 3.18.

[105] For example, Ep. 1.39, where Gregory instructed Peter of Sicily to get back lost church property: "*Res ecclesiastici* must be returned, unless there is a good reason not to do so." And Gregory explicitly included the *mancipia* in this directive.

[106] Ep. 3.35.

[107] In order to resolve such questions, we would need to investigate the authenticity of these texts. Richard Helmholz suggested that the records of Gregory's correspondence with the church in the British Isles may have sometimes been altered so that the letters were more in conformity with Germanic practices. *The Oxford History of the Laws of England I: The Canon Law and Ecclesiastical Jurisdiction* (Oxford 2004) 8–9. If Helmholz is correct, we might well wonder how accurate our copies of Gregory's other correspondence are.

in September 595, Gregory instructed Candidus, a priest in Gaul, to purchase some seventeen- and eighteen-year-old Angles and to send them to the Roman church, making sure that the boys were baptized first lest they be killed during the journey.[108] Gregory said that the reason he wanted to buy slaves in Gaul was that he needed to use up some Gallic coins that he would not be able to spend in Rome. The slaves would most likely have been used to serve in the activities of the church in Rome.[109]

Gregory I, known as "The Great," proved to be an able administrator who took care of his church's physical as well as spiritual wealth. But his attitudes toward the church's human chattel was typical for a late Roman aristocrat. The boys discussed in the letter to Candidus were to be baptized, in case of death during the course of the perilous journey south, but concern about their physical safety or comfort was not mentioned. The ancients had called slaves "tools with voices." For Gregory they were still tools, albeit tools with souls as well as voices.[110]

The Cappadocians

Returning to Asia Minor, the ancient heart of the church and near the center of the later Roman Empire, it may be useful to look at the circle of family and friends surrounding Basil the Great, bishop of Caesarea. They were a remarkable group of men and women, noted for their intellectual activity as well as for their saintly lives.[111] Basil was the son of a wealthy family in the province of Cappadocia, on the southeastern edge of the Black Sea. His younger brother, Gregory, bishop of Nyssa, their sister, Macrina, and Basil's

---

[108] Ep. 6.10. On the papal properties in Gaul see Gregory I. Halfond, "*Patrimonium Ecclesiae Nostrae*: The Papal Estates in Merovingian Provence," *Comitatus: A Journal of Medieval and Renaissance Studies* 38 (2007) 1–18.

[109] Peter Brown (*Eye of a Needle* 468) pointed out the irony in purchasing slaves to serve the poor of Rome. However, to a Roman, the inferiority of a "barbarian" to any Roman, no matter how poor, was a given. In a different interpretation, John Moorman said that Gregory had purchased the boys and educated them in Christianity in order to send them back home as missionaries. *A History of the Church in England*, 3rd. ed. (London 1980) 12–13.

[110] For more about Gregory's attitudes about slaves see John T. Noonan Jr. *A Church that Can and Cannot Change* (Notre Dame, IN 2005) 38–40.

[111] There has been a great deal of scholarly interest in the theology of the three "Cappadocian Fathers," Basil and the two Gregorys. A recent summary of their lives as well as their thinking can be found in Patrick Whitworth, *Three Wise Men from the East: The Cappadocian Fathers and the Struggle for Orthodoxy* (Durham 2015). For an in-depth consideration of the Cappadocian fathers and their views on slavery see Richard Klein, *Die Haltung der Kappadokischen Bischöfe Basilius von Caesarea, Gregor von Nazianz und Gregor von Nyssa zur Sklaverei* (Stuttgart 2000).

great friend, Gregory of Nazianzus, were also widely known for their holiness as well as their intellectual accomplishments. They practiced asceticism and gave generously to the poor in an attempt to exemplify the Christian ideals that they preached.

Basil the Great (bishop of Caesarea from 370 to 379) met Gregory (later bishop of Nazianzus) during their school days in Caesarea. They later studied together in Athens, and both young men sought the monastic life after they had completed their education. Giving most of his property to the poor, Basil began a life of solitude in a corner of his family's estates at Annisa, where he was soon joined in the contemplative life by his mother, his sister, and his friend Gregory. But their intellectual gifts and their family backgrounds, along with their obvious personal piety, caused the young men to be called to lives of service in the church. Basil was ordained a deacon in 362 and in 365 a priest in the church of Caesarea. In 370, he became its bishop. Two years later, Basil consecrated his friend as bishop of nearby Sasima. Gregory was not happy with this appointment and never actually served as Sasima's bishop. Instead, he went on to succeed his father, another Gregory, as bishop of Nazianzus in 374, but returned to the contemplative life only a year later. His obvious talents led to his again being called out of tranquility to serve the church, this time as bishop of Constantinople. Upon his consecration in 380, Gregory found the church in Constantinople in an uproar over doctrinal controversies, and he was an ardent and effective promoter of what turned out to be the orthodox position. But once again, Gregory withdrew from public life when the political controversies became overwhelming, and in 381 he retired into solitude on his family's estates until his death a decade later. Basil's younger brother, Gregory, had joined him and Gregory of Nazianzus in their monastic life in Annisa early in 362. And when his brother Basil called him to be bishop of Nyssa in 372, the younger Gregory also reluctantly embraced a career of service to the church. He later went on to be bishop in nearby Sebaste and died in about 395.

The Cappadocians were strongly influenced by the teachings of Gregory Thaumaturgus, who was discussed in the previous chapter.[112] The "Wonder Worker" had written strongly against excessive displays of wealth and against using slaves as status symbols, saying that such behavior made the slave owner himself a slave to his own desires. However, Gregory Thaumaturgus

---

[112] Whitworth, *Three Wise Men* 13–14.

had also thought that owning a few slaves to help with running one's household and business affairs was not objectionable.

Basil, although well known for his dedication to the poor and his concern for the redistribution of wealth, shared the attitudes of his contemporaries when it came to the personality of slaves. In this same vein, he held the standard late Roman Christian views on slavery: although slavery was not a natural or desirable state, one's inner state was more important—and moreover, all men were slaves before God.

While there does not seem to be much evidence about Basil's own actions as a slave owner or about his dealings with the slaves who were a part of his church's patrimony, we can deduce what his attitudes must have been from what little evidence is available. In 369 Basil wrote to his longtime friend, Sophronius, asking him to use his influential government position to help Gregory of Nazianzus deal with the affairs of Caesarius, Gregory's deceased brother. Basil explained that the problems had arisen because the executors of Caesarius's estate had been "slaves and men of no better character than slaves."[113] Clearly, this son of a wealthy aristocrat did not hold a very high opinion of servile persons.

Gregory of Nazianzus, while not from quite the same kind of aristocratic background as Basil and Gregory of Nyssa, did belong to a family of considerable wealth. And, as one would expect from someone from this sector of society, he owned a considerable number of slaves even after his retirement into a life of solitude and contemplation. Gregory wrote a detailed will, likely in order to avoid difficulties for his own estate like those that had resulted from his brother's mismanaged affairs. In Gregory's will, there is a good deal of evidence about his ownership of slaves. In fact, he left the bulk of his estate to a former slave, "Gregorius, who was a slave of my household [and] whom I manumitted long ago, is to be heir of the entirety of all my possessions, both moveable and fixed, wherever my possessions are."[114] After gaining his freedom, this Gregorius had gone on to become a monk and a deacon, his new, free name having likely been chosen out of respect to his mentor and former owner.[115] Gregory of Nazianzus apparently did not let Gregorius's former status get in the way of their close personal relationship, and in his

---

[113] Ep. 33(32), PG 37. English trans. NPNF 2.

[114] PG 37. An English translation is appended to Raymond Van Dam, "Self-Representation in the Will of Gregory of Nazianzus," *Journal of Theological Studies* n.s. 46 (1995) 118–48. Note: here, for simplicity's sake, I list the PG references for the Cappadocians' work. More recent editions of some of these texts are listed in Johannes Quasten, *Patrology*, vol. 3 (Washington, DC 1950).

[115] Van Dam, "Self-Representation" 128.

will Gregory explained that he had "designated him as heir so that he might completely preserve everything for the church." Such close relationships between former slave and master were not uncommon in late Roman society. Gregorius was to enjoy Gregory's legacy as long as he lived, and then "restore all my possessions, both moveable and fixed, to the holy Catholic church of Nazianzus, exempting nothing at all, except whatever I specifically leave someone in this my will as a legacy or a trust." So, Gregorius's enjoyment of Gregory's wealth was limited. In fact, one could interpret this as a commission from a patron to his client, his freedman who owed him certain services. And the final service was the duty to ensure that no scandal arose about Gregory's handling of his own and his church's resources. Giving everything in the end to the church precluded any possibility of charges being made that Gregory or his heirs had misappropriated church property. Gregorius's task was to be sure that Gregory's affairs were in order and his reputation untarnished. And he was given fifty gold coins to keep for his own in return for this faithful service.

While Gregory of Nazianzus clearly enjoyed a life of ease, he does not seem to have abused the privilege. And his will called for a number of his slaves to be set free and given small bequests, but he is not unique in this. As we have seen, a Roman gentleman of leisure was expected to show kindness to favorite slaves and freedmen and was also expected to live a virtuous life without excesses. Whitworth pointed out that it was exactly the great wealth that Gregory and Basil enjoyed that gave them the freedom to disdain wealth.[116] Those who do not understand real need can easily talk about the benefits of the simple life. Neither of these men suffered lives of real poverty, instead keeping for themselves sufficient resources to ensure a relative comfort in which to enjoy their asceticism—in Gregory's case at least, this included a number of estates. Basil and Gregory of Nazianzus both seem to have tried to put their Christian and Stoic beliefs into practice, treating their servile dependents with kindness, but not too much.

The youngest of the three Cappadocian fathers was Gregory of Nyssa. He followed a path somewhat different from the one taken by his elder brother, Basil, and their friend, Gregory of Nazianzus. The younger Gregory did not travel to be educated and, as a young man, he married a woman named Theosebia. When Basil consecrated him bishop of Nyssa in 372, Gregory accepted the challenge, but remained in Nyssa for only a short time. He

---

[116] *Three Wise Men* 137.

was forced to leave in the face of opposition from ecclesiastical enemies.[117] Like the other Cappadocians, Gregory of Nyssa argued strongly against the excesses of the rich, and he preached about the Christian's duty to care for the poor. Also, his experience of family life gave him more intimate insight into the difficulties faced by his flock, and he often wrote about the pain caused by the bonds of human love.

Gregory of Nyssa has often been hailed as the only one of the early church teachers to speak out against slavery because of what he said in his *Fourth Homily on Ecclesiastes*. However, a closer reading of this text shows that such a conclusion is not accurate. Gregory's essential assumptions about slavery were no different from those of his contemporaries. The sermon is about Ecclesiastes 2:7–11, a poetic description of how a rich man who lived to excess realized the emptiness of his life, repeating the phrase "all is vanity." The poet's list of this wealth begins with slaves and slave girls and cattle and sheep. Gregory of Nyssa argued that someone who boasts about owning a lot of slaves (among other things) "turns the property of God into his own property . . . [causing him to] overstep his own nature through pride."[118] This overturns God's law for humanity, Gregory continued, and by giving some people dominion over other human beings, ignores God's command that humans shall have dominion over things and creatures that do not have reason.[119] Owning other human beings is also illogical, said Gregory: "By dividing the human species in two with 'slavery' and 'ownership,' you have caused it to be enslaved to itself and to be the owner of itself." Further: "If a human being is made in the image and likeness of God, what price do you put on God's likeness?"[120] This certainly does sound a lot like abolitionist thinking.

However, while Gregory railed against the evils of arrogance from a wealthy slave-owner, he never actually called for a change in the economic practice of using slave labor. Gregory talked about the ultimate worthlessness of a scrap of papyrus that gave one person ownership control over another, but he seems to have assumed that the economic practice of slavery

---

[117] A pro-Arian emperor, Valens, exiled Gregory in 378 because of his views on the Trinity. Eventually Gregory's "Orthodox" position became the theological standard.

[118] Gregory of Nyssa, "4th Homily on Ecclesiastes," PG 44, trans. George Hall and Rachel Moriarty in *Gregory of Nyssa Homilies on Ecclesiastes: An English Version with Supporting Studies. Proceedings of the 7th International Colloquium on Gregory of Nyssa, St. Andrews, 5–10 September 1990*, ed. S. G. Hall (Berlin 1993).

[119] See Gen. 1:26, Ps. 8:6–8.

[120] Referring to Gen. 1:26.

would continue. He went on to condemn the arrogance of all of those who exploited their wealth—in whatever form—to excess instead of using it to help the poor. Since the passage in Ecclesiastes has exactly that same theme, the ultimate meaninglessness of worldly success, it is likely that Gregory's sermon was meant merely to reinforce that theme. If he had, indeed, intended to argue for the abolition of slavery, logic would have forced him to condemn the ancient Hebrew practices as well, but he did not do so. Also, if abolition had been Gregory's intent, he would probably have repeated the theme in other exegetical or theological works. And again, he did not, although there are other works discussing the dangers of excessive wealth and the need to care for the poor as well as condemning the notion that slaves were inferior beings.[121] It is more likely that in this homily Gregory was trying to explain why "all is vanity," why riches are ultimately worthless. And an overabundance of slaves was simply a good example of excessive wealth. There is no evidence to suggest that Gregory of Nyssa disagreed with his teacher Gregory Thaumaturgus, who had said that owning a few slaves to perform certain tasks was acceptable so long as you behaved decently. In contrast, Gregory of Nyssa's pious biography of Gregory Thaumaturgus extolled the elder Gregory's preaching, listing various instances of the praiseworthy advice found in his sermons, including: "Slaves were taught to be obedient to their masters, those who ruled were urged to respect their subjects."[122] Gregory of Nyssa did not criticize his mentor's point of view. Gregory of Nyssa's beliefs, like those of his teacher, were in line with the teachings of St. Paul that true human freedom could be found in Jesus Christ. But this referred to freedom of the soul, not freedom from slavery of the body here on earth.[123]

Gregory of Nyssa also wrote a pious biography of his sister, Macrina. She was known as Macrina the Younger to distinguish her from her grandmother, Macrina the Elder, another pious woman who became known for her care of the poor. Macrina the Younger was betrothed according to her father's wishes to a young man "of good birth and remarkable steadiness."[124] However, the

---

[121] Excerpts from an earlier work, *De Hominis Opificio*, can be found in T. J. Dennis, "The Relationship between Gregory of Nyssa's Attack on Slavery in His Fourth Homily on Ecclesiastes and His Treatise *De Hominis Opificio*," *Studia patristica* 17 (1982) 1065–72. While *De Hominis Opificio* contains rather emotional condemnation of the arrogance of slave owners, Gregory said no more than that slavery is evil, as had many others before him.

[122] Gregory of Nyssa, *Life of Gregory the Wonderworker*, PG 46; English translation available at www.documentacatholica.omnia.eu.

[123] See, e.g., his treatise "On Perfection," PG 46. English translation available in *Greek Orthodox Theological Review* 29 (1994) 349–79.

[124] Gregory of Nyssa, *Life of Saint Macrina*, PG 46. English translation by W. K. Lowther Clarke (1927) at www.tertullian.org.

bridegroom died before the wedding could take place, and Macrina chose to honor her betrothal as having been equivalent to a marriage. Before long she persuaded her mother to join her in a life of renunciation and contemplation: She "persuaded her mother to give up her ordinary life and all the showy style of living and the services of domestics to which she had been accustomed before, and bring her point of view down to that of the masses, and to share the life of the maids, treating all her slave girls and menials as if they were sisters and belonged to the same rank as herself."

The entire document makes it clear that Gregory of Nyssa was extremely fond of his sister and viewed her as an inspiration and as a role model for all Christian men and women. However, Macrina and her mother still had slave girls to tend to their physical needs, as was the custom for aristocratic women who took the veil, even though they otherwise lived an essentially monastic life.[125] The important thing for Gregory was that they were not arrogant or boastful about their privilege: "Macrina drew on [her mother] to adopt her own standard of humility. She induced her to live on a footing of equality with the staff of maids, so as to share with them in the same food, the same kind of bed, and in all the necessaries of life, without any regard to differences of life."

It is important to note here that manumission of these slave girls was not mentioned. They remained slaves. While their living conditions may have been pretty much the same as their mistresses' were, they were not there voluntarily and were not free to leave. It does not seem to have dawned on Gregory of Nyssa (or his sister, for that matter) that these "maids" would have been very conscious of the difference in their legal status.

Gregory of Nyssa's *Fourth Homily on Ecclesiastes* is undoubtedly the most negative statement about slavery that we have seen thus far from a Christian leader. But his other writings clearly show a very different position; he was not an abolitionist. Gregory lived in a world where the idea of abolishing slavery was not something that could have even been imagined. What Gregory hoped for was that people would renounce excess (often typified by ownership of large numbers of slaves) and that they would treat their dependents with love and kindness and recognize that all were equal in God's

---

[125] A century later a woman named Olympias also took fifty of her household slaves with her when she entered a religious community. John Chrysostom, "Letter to Olympias," PG 52, translated in NPNF, 1.09. And see Wendy Mayer, "The Audience(s) for Patristic Social Teaching," in Leemans et al., *Reading Patristic Texts* 85–99, here 89. Also see the discussion of Caesaria, sister of Bishop Caesarius of Arles, in the next chapter.

eyes. Gregory clearly saw slave ownership as normal, even for those who embraced the ascetic life. Gregory of Nyssa, like the other Cappadocians, was a man of his time.

Conclusions

Given the ubiquity of slaves in late antique Roman life, one might well wonder why the texts from the imperial church contain relatively few mentions of the unfree population, Christian or otherwise. But that is a very modern way of looking at these texts. The fact that slaves are mentioned relatively infrequently is actually a consequence of their being so much a part of everyday life in the late empire, for pagans and Christians alike. One would not likely comment on the lack of material concerning plumbing or parsley. Plumbing and parsley, too, were an important part of Roman life, but they were not important in differentiating Christian from non-Christian behavior. These early Christian texts were concerned with the issues of the Christian faith and with the running of the organization that presided over the practice of that faith. Only those areas of daily life that were changed or particularly affected by the Christian religion were addressed. Parsley and plumbing remained unchanged when the empire became Christian, and there was no need to mention them in these texts. Similarly, slaves were mentioned in these texts only when there was something about slaves or about how to deal with them that was particular to the Christian community.

In this chapter we have looked at church laws and imperial proclamations, along with correspondence and other evidence from major Christian figures throughout the late empire, from the Anatolian peninsula to Iberia, at the western edge of their world. And the results were pretty much the same in all instances. There were three major concerns expressed about slaves, either about slave ownership in general or about the slaves of the institutional church and its personnel, the focus of this study. First of all, the texts reaffirmed the biblical command for slaves to obey their masters and for masters to treat their slaves decently. As we saw earlier, this had also been the teaching of the pagan Stoics. Another concern expressed in many of the texts was the purity of the clergy. Especially bishops were forbidden to have contact with sexually available women, including slave girls. But it seems that the most pressing concern was about proper management of the church patrimony, including its unfree human resources. The *res ecclesiae* were considered to be inalienable.

There were some whose lot it was to be slaves, God's punishment for human sin. They were needed to do the work that was beneath the honor of their owners. Christian owners were expected to treat their slaves decently and not to indulge in excessive displays of wealth because cruelty and greed were considered bad for the soul. Although slave ownership did not disqualify a person from living in monastic asceticism, manumission of one's slaves was a virtuous act. Also, if someone did decide to set a slave free, and to do so in a church ceremony, the traditional obligations of a freedman to his former owner were transferred to the church where the ceremony took place. This was not only a way for a slave owner to increase the spiritual value of setting a slave free, but it also provided a semifree labor pool for the church. Regrettably there is as yet no clear explanation for why or how this custom arose.

Individual clergy who owned slaves—as most of them seem to have done—were not expected to follow any special regulations in connection with their slaves other than abstaining from sexual relations with their slave women. There were, however, limitations on the institutional church. The church was entrusted with God's property on earth, property that had been donated to the church for the care of the poor and for the salvation of the donor's soul. As the stewards of this property, the bishops of the church had the responsibility to ensure that no one could alienate the *res ecclesiae* arbitrarily. There are a number of sensational stories about clerical mishandling of church resources, but much of the material we have examined shows that it was sometimes a struggle for bishops to keep their own affairs separate from those of their church. One solution seems to have been to provide very stringent guidelines saying that no one could alienate any church property, except in very specific circumstances. This caution, so important if the church were to continue doing God's work in the world, resulted in a state of affairs where there was almost no way to escape ecclesiastical servitude. If an ecclesiastical slave were manumitted, he would remain obligated to the church. And the slave of a layperson, if he were set free in a church ceremony, would incur these same obligations.

We moderns are often uncomfortable with the idea that the early church, even the great "church fathers" like Augustine and the Cappadocians, accepted slavery as part of God's plan. A number of scholars have tried to argue that these men, especially Gregory of Nyssa, preached against the institution of slavery. But, as we have seen, these conclusions are the result of a mis-reading of the sources. Many people called for an end to the abuses and for kindness toward one's slaves, as well as for the freedom of recent captives. Many lauded the manumission of slaves as a virtuous act. But these were all long-standing Roman precepts. None of the early Christian evidence that we have found called for an end to the economic practice of employing slave labor. A very few ascetics did live without slaves, but there seems to be no ev-idence that they thought others should do so as well.

The story of Sidonius Apollinaris, a late fifth-century bishop in southern Gaul, provides a final example of how a highly respected and pious church of-ficial thought about slaves, including those with ecclesiastical owners. Born to a Gallo-Roman patrician family, Sidonius began his life in imperial ser-vice, rising to be the prefect of Rome in the 470s. However, a career reversal sent him back to Gaul, where he soon became the bishop of Clermont, then an important city in what is now south-central France. At that time, both the Visigoths and the Burgundians were causing difficulties for the old Roman families, and Sidonius lamented the end of the old ways.[126]

A good deal of Sidonius's extensive correspondence has been preserved, and we can see glimpses of how he viewed those of the servile classes.[127] A slave owner himself, Sidonius clearly continued to recognize the long-held stereotypes about servile character deficiencies, describing an unpopular local official as one who "swaggers like a slave" and a slave woman whose episcopal master had recently put her out of his bed as "a most shameful slave girl."[128] Sidonius thought, too, that it was appropriate for slaves to maintain a certain distance from their betters.[129] But he also thought that one should treat one's slaves well: in a letter praising his friend Eutropius, Sidonius cited his "well-fed shepherd" along with his bountiful flocks as evidence of his friend's distinction.[130] In another letter Sidonius praised Philagrius's clem-ency in dealing with his household, adding that he himself was "not tortured if [his own] household slaves were not tortured."[131] However, Sidonius made it clear that good slaves were evidence of the master's goodness—in other

---

[126] Jill Harries, *Sidonius Apollinaris and the Fall of Rome* (Oxford 1994).

[127] A standard edition of Sidonius's writings is the facing page Latin-English edi-tion: *Sidonius: Poems and Letters*, trans. W. B. Anderson, 2 vols., Loeb Classical Library (Cambridge, MA 1936).

[128] Ep. 2.1 and 9.6.

[129] Ep. 4.8.

[130] Ep. 1.6.

[131] Ep. 7.14—certainly an odd way of putting it.

words, not evidence of the slaves' own inherent qualities. In a letter about how "illustrious" a certain Vettius was, Sidonius began with the fact that his *servi* were good workers, compliant, friendly, and obedient.[132] The slaves' excellence was attributed to Vettius' own good qualities rather than to the slaves.'

Along with these typical Roman attitudes toward servile persons, Sidonius also exhibited charity toward them that was probably more than what would have been expected of the average Roman. For example, in a letter to a certain Pudens, Sidonius wrote that the daughter of his own former nurse, a freedwoman, had run off with the unfree son of Pudens's nurse. Sidonius asked that Pudens "release the *stuprator* (rapist, fornicator) from his hereditary position of unfree laborer and tenant farmer to that of a free *plebian*, becoming his patron instead of his master."[133] Since a union between a free woman and an unfree man was not acceptable, Sidonius was seeking the only remedy he knew of that would preserve the woman's reputation and the legitimacy of any children that would ensue from the union.

In another letter, to Bishop Lupus of Troyes, Sidonius wrote concerning the plight of a woman who had been captured by a band of outlaws and sold as a slave many years previously. Her family eventually tracked her down, but not before she had died a slave. Her last owner, an acquaintance of Sidonius, had purchased the woman in a public sale from a certain Prudens, another acquaintance of Sidonius, who lived in Troyes. But now the woman's family was threatening to bring criminal charges against the woman's final owner. Sidonius's letter was an appeal to Lupus, as the local bishop, to try to sort out this matter and protect any wronged or innocent parties, "to worm from them the whole story of this outrage."[134] Sidonius asked Lupus "to relieve the distress of the one party and the danger of the other by compounding some innocuous remedy." Sidonius spoke charitably not only of the captive woman and her family, but also of those duped by her captors.

Sidonius's concern for unfortunates of any sort was exemplary, but, as Harries noted, it also served to enhance his own power and political position.[135] Yet more than mere personal gain seems to have motivated Sidonius; he seems to have been genuinely concerned about those on the margins of society. Writing of a Jewish merchant called Gozolas, Sidonius said that he

[132] Ep. 4.9.
[133] Ep. 5.19.
[134] EP. 6.4, trans. Anderson.
[135] *Sidonius Apollinarus* 209–12.

was "a man whom I, too, should like as a person, if I did not despise his religious faith."[136] In another letter he wrote of "your Gozolas—and God grant that he may be mine also."[137] Whether or not Sidonius was writing about Gozolas's potential conversion to Christianity, it is clear that he could see beyond the Jew's outsider status, just as he seems to have had genuine compassion for the unfortunates in the slaves' stories. What is particularly interesting for our purposes here is that Sidonius's attitudes toward the unfree persons and other unfortunate outsiders in these stories is somewhat changed from the attitudes that we saw in the writings of earlier Romans, even Christian Romans.

Sidonius does not seem to have written anything explicit about his thoughts on slavery per se. And the examples we have seen show him to have been a Roman through and through, who upheld Roman law and custom. But, at the same time, he was a compassionate man who took seriously the Christian precept to love one's neighbors, no matter their station in life. Slaves were a normal part of society, but as fellow humans, they deserved compassion. While Sidonius still apparently saw himself as a Roman aristocrat, his letters reveal a softening of his heart that allowed him to see the humanity of these people who were in trouble, even if they had been touched by servitude.

In Sidonius's time, the Roman Empire in the West was beginning to buckle under the weight of new Germanic rulers. In the next chapters we shall look at ecclesiastical *servi* in the European world after the power of the Roman Empire had faded.

---

[136] Ep. 3.4, trans. Anderson.
[137] Ep. 4.5, trans. Anderson.

5

Ecclesiastical Slavery in the
Germanic Kingdoms

Transitions

Once Constantine moved his capital from Italy to Constantinople, the New Rome, the eastern and western provinces began to grow further and further apart. After a largely disastrous attempt in the sixth century to regain territories lost to Germanic rule, the imperial court in Constantinople focused on consolidating and securing the territories where they did exercise real control. And the eastern and western lands continued to grow ever more distant from one another. Europe experienced great political and social upheaval between the end of the fifth century and the emergence of the familiar political units of France, England, and the Holy Roman Empire by the late eleventh century. The people of this era had only a brief respite during the eighth and ninth centuries when the Carolingians' hegemony over most of continental Christendom provided relative calm to those who did not challenge their power. But even this period was fraught with internal power struggles as well as difficulties along the borders of Charlemagne's empire. The following chapters will not attempt to chronicle these events, but merely provide background information pertinent to our study of ecclesiastical servitude.[1]

---

[1] A number of excellent general histories of this period have been published recently, including Averil Cameron, *The Mediterranean World in Late Antiquity, AD 395–700*, 2nd ed. (New York 2012); Chris Wickham, *The Inheritance of Rome: Illuminating the Dark Ages 400–1000* (New York 2009) and his *Framing the Early Middle Ages: Europe and the Mediterranean, 400–800* (Oxford 2005); *The Long Morning of Medieval Europe: New Directions in Early Medieval Studies*, ed. J. Davis and M. McCormick (Burlington, VT 2008); Peter Heather, *Empires and Barbarians: The Fall of Rome and the Birth of Europe* (Oxford 2010); Walter Goffart, *Barbarian Tides: The Migration Age and the Later Roman Empire* (Philadelphia 2006); and *The Early Middle Ages*, ed. R. McKitterick (Oxford 2001). Herwig Wolfram's *Das Reich und die Germanen* (Berlin 1990), trans. T. Dunlap *as The Roman Empire and Its Germanic Peoples* (Berkeley 1997) remains well worth reading, despite the fact that the scholarship has grown a great deal from the foundational insights he provided. A good cross section of the scholarship about the Merovingian era and the complexities surrounding the ethnicity of the Goths and others can be found in the articles assembled by Thomas F. X. Noble in *From Roman Provinces to Medieval Kingdoms* (New York 2006).

The Slaves of the Churches. Mary E. Sommar, Oxford University Press (2020). © Oxford University Press.
DOI: 10.1093/oso/9780190073268.001.0001

Historians who study the late antique / early medieval period use archaeological, art historical, and economic data, along with historical texts, to help them understand exactly what happened and why during these centuries that used to be called the Dark Ages. Recent scholars have acknowledged that "darkness" did not characterize this era at all. These centuries were illuminated by the brilliant minds of those who were able to forge a new vision of the world by combining what they saw as the most essential features of Greco-Roman traditions with the fresh, new perspectives on life and society that the conquerors had brought with them. Any perceived darkness was due to the fact that the relative paucity of written records from these centuries challenged the historians' traditional methodology. But in recent years scholars have demonstrated that this was a time when enormous and enduring transitions were occurring, transitions that eventually set the stage for the emergence of modern Western society.

Traditionally, the major political events relevant to the present chapter were said to have begun with the official end of Roman rule in the western provinces in 476 when Romulus Augustulus, the last western Roman emperor, was deposed by a military commander named Odoacer. In a break with precedent, Odoacer took the throne for himself instead of installing a puppet Roman on the western imperial throne. However, this event was actually part of the centuries-long military struggle for control in the Roman Empire. Most scholars now see a more significant political break as having taken place in 493 when Theodoric, a Gothic king, replaced Odoacer and established the kingdom of the East Goths or Ostrogoths.[2] By this time it was clear that the Roman Empire centered in Constantinople no longer held majority sway in the West. And despite the reluctance of many in the western lands to abandon the *Romanitas* of their ancestors, social, political, and economic changes were already well underway. The new rulers were mostly Christian, but they belonged to cultures that had been converted by a follower of the priest Arius and were unaware that Roman Christianity had officially rejected many of Arius's teachings at the Council of Nicaea in 325. During the centuries after their conversion, they had often been at war with the empire and thus were separated from the Christian mainstream. The new rulers were considered heretics by their Roman subjects because they followed these "Arian" teachings.

---

[2] See Wickham, *Inheritance of Rome* 97–100 for further discussion of this point.

The Goths swept through the Adriatic coast and Italy during the late fourth and fifth centuries. In time, they settled down somewhat and established a kingdom in the southern part of Gaul, extending westward into the Iberian Peninsula. These West Goths, or Visigoths, although they were slowly pushed out of Gaul, continued to rule over a relatively stable kingdom in modern Spain until the Arab conquests of the early eighth century. In 589 King Reccared converted to Roman Christianity, having seen the advantages that removing the stigma of heresy would provide when dealing with his Hispano-Roman subjects.

At first, there were a number of different groups holding sway in Gaul, including the Burgundians, who ruled in what is now the southeastern part of France, and the Franks, whose homelands clustered around the modern borders of Belgium and the Netherlands. Over the course of the fifth to seventh centuries, the Franks, first ruled by the Merovingian dynasty and later by the Carolingians, gradually extended their control. They absorbed the kingdom of the Burgundians in 534. They also pushed the Visigoths into Iberia. The success of the Franks was due in no small part to their conversion to Roman Christianity, which was the religion of their subject Roman populations. Eventually, the Franks expanded the limits of Christian Europe northward all the way to the Baltic coast and eastward as far as the Oder River. Divided in the ninth century into the kingdoms of West Francia and East Francia, roughly the same as modern France and Germany, the Carolingians endured almost until the end of the millennium. Then, exhausted by, among other things, the incursions of the Scandinavians into their lands, the descendants of Charlemagne succumbed to new dynastic houses that controlled the emerging polities of France and the largely German "Holy Roman Empire."

In Italy, the Ostrogoths lasted only until 554 when the Eastern Roman Empire regained control of the peninsula. However, these Byzantines, as the later Roman Empire of Constantinople is known, were not able to retain control in Italy very long. Their return was not universally welcomed and they soon were forced to retreat to Ravenna, whence they struggled to retain influence. In 568 the pagan Lombards arrived, setting off a new period of instability. The bishops of Rome, notably Gregory I (590–604), continued to enjoy considerable secular political power until the Lombard threat increased in the early eighth century. But by the 770s, the Lombard kingdom was absorbed into the Carolingian Frankish Empire.

In this chapter, we shall concentrate on the church of the sixth and seventh centuries in greater Gaul and on the Iberian Peninsula and on how both ecclesiastical and political leaders viewed the question of ecclesiastical servitude. In the next chapter, we will examine the question in the Carolingian era and take a brief look at the emerging Christian legal consciousness in the British Isles. Given Charlemagne's alliance with the bishop of Rome, an alliance forged for both military and political advantages, it is no great surprise that the newly crowned "Holy Roman Emperor" showed great concern for ecclesiastical matters, including an attempt to regularize and unify such policies throughout an empire that extended across Europe. But Charlemagne's hegemony did not penetrate completely into the areas of culture and custom. Many people still clung to the old ways and beliefs. Nevertheless, the influence of the Carolingians was strong, even beyond their borders. For example, most of the law codes attributed to the various cultures on the borders of Carolingian Gaul seem to have been composed under the influence, if not the direction of those Franks who eventually came to function in many ways as the successors to the Roman emperors in the West.

In recent decades there has been a wealth of scholarship trying to answer the question of how the Roman slave system was transformed into the varieties of labor arrangements that characterized the later medieval period.[3] The organization of agricultural labor, in particular, seems to have encompassed a number of different statuses, ranging from traditional chattel slavery to peasants who were legally free but who labored under such a burden of obligation to their landlords that it is hard to see how their lives were much different. There were many semifree statuses as well, varying greatly over time and place, in what Alice Rio has called "a sliding scale" of relationships between masters and lords and their dependents.[4] An example of this can be

---

[3] Alice Rio's recent study of late Roman and medieval European slavery, *Slavery after Rome* (Oxford 2017), promises to set a new standard in this area. But Marc Bloch's classic, *Slavery and Serfdom in the Middle Ages* (Paris 1966), trans. W. R. Beer (Berkeley 1975), remains foundational to an understanding of these questions. See also Hans-Werner Goetz, "Serfdom and the Beginnings of a 'Seigneurial System' in the Carolingian Period, a Survey of the Evidence," *Early Medieval Europe* 2 (1993) 29–51 and Ross Samson, "Rural Slavery, Inscriptions, Archeology, and Marx: A Response to Ramsay MacMullen's 'Late Roman Slavery,'" *Historia* 38 (1989) 99–110. Important longer works focusing on various different regions include Pierre Bonnassie, *From Slavery to Feudalism in South-Western Europe*, trans. J. Birrell (Cambridge 1991); Pierre Dockès, *Medieval Slavery and Liberation*, trans. A. Goldhammer (Chicago 1982); Steven A. Epstein, *Speaking of Slavery* (Ithaca 2001); and Paul Freedman, *The Origins of Peasant Servitude in Medieval Catalonia* (Cambridge 1991).

[4] Alice Rio, "'Half-Free' Categories in the Early Middle Ages: Fine Status Distinctions before Professional Lawyers," in *Legalism: Rules and Categories*, ed. P. Dresch and J. Scheele (Oxford 2015) 129–52.

seen in a document drawn up in Paris in 508. It details what King Clovis gave to his daughter, Theudechild, as her portion of the family wealth. In the catalog of the various *villae*, or agricultural establishments, it lists everything of value in each *villa*, including the agricultural workers who lived there. Clovis seems to have considered these workers to be assets that he could pass down to his daughter. While all of these workers were called *coloni*, or tenant farmers, only some were listed as *servi*, or slaves, as well. Clovis did not see all of these *coloni* as slave labor. The text also indicates that each *villa* was expected to pay its lord a particular *annona*, or yearly payment, regardless of the legal status of the tenants, although the amounts varied from place to place.[5] In addition there were domestic workers who were listed as *servi* or were referred to by other terms that suggested unfree status.

Except in those cases where differences in the ecclesiastically controlled laborers' legal status made a recognizable difference in how they were treated by their masters, these questions are not especially pertinent to our study. The mechanisms of social or economic change are not our focus.[6] We shall simply take it that over time there were changes in society and in the way that the labor force was managed. In the present discussion we are concerned with those laborers of any kind whose legal status was not clearly defined as free and who were dependent on ecclesiastical masters.

Caesarius of Arles

Caesarius was bishop of Arles, a city in Provence in southern Gaul, from 502 to 542.[7] Born to a noble family in Chalon-sur-Saône about the year

---

[5] Deed of Gift from Clovis I to his daughter, Theudechild, Paris, October, 508. MGH, *Diplomata regum Frankorum: Die Urkunden der Merovinger*, vol. 1, ed. T. Kölzer (Hanover 2001) 18–26.

[6] For an excellent and detailed discussion of this question in the early medieval period see Wickham, *Framing* 258–302. Also see the appendix for an overview of recent scholarship.

[7] This summary of Caesarius's life story has been put together based largely on the hagiographically enhanced *Vita Caesarii*, written by his friends Bishop Firminus of Uzès, Bishop Cyprianus of Toulon, Bishop Viventius, the priest Messianus, and the deacon Stephanus. Data is also available in Caesarius's *Testament*, in his *Regula ad Virgines*, and in his correspondence and collected sermons: *Caesarii Arelatensis Opera Varia*, ed. D. Germani Morin (Bruges 1942); also, in PL 67 and in English translation, *Caesarius of Arles: Life, Testament, Letters*, trans. William E. Klingshirn (Liverpool 1994). William E. Klingshirn's *Caesarius of Arles: The Making of a Christian Community in Late Antique Gaul* (Cambridge 1994) provides a splendid modern analysis of Caesarius's role in the Gallic church of this era. More recently, the February 2018 issue of *Early Medieval Europe* (vol. 26) was dedicated to "The World of Caesarius of Arles." See also Allen E. Jones, *Social Mobility in Late Antique Gaul: Strategies and Opportunities for the Non-elite* (Cambridge 2009) 38–44 and Peter Brown, *The Rise of Western Christendom*, 2nd ed. (Oxford 2003) 150–54.

470, Caesarius received the kind of training in the classics and in the art of rhetoric that was customary for the sons of such families. He began his career as a cleric at the local church. Two years later, drawn to the asceticism of the monastic life, he left Chalon. The *Life of Caesarius*, written by several of his friends a few years after Caesarius died, illustrated this renunciation of worldly luxuries by recording that he left home and traveled to the monastery of Lérins "accompanied by only one slave."[8] Around 495, Caesarius left the monastery and went to Arles, where he quickly ascended the clerical *cursus honorum*, becoming the city's bishop in 502. Although only a generation or so had passed since Sidonius Apollinaris's episcopacy, Caesarius's experiences reveal a very different world.

The early sixth century was a period of great turmoil in southern Gaul.[9] When Caesarius arrived in Arles, the city was still adjusting to the Visigoths, who had gained control of that region in 476 after decades of conflict. But Visigothic control over Provence was ended by the victory in 507 of the Frankish forces under Clovis, allied with the Burgundians, whom the Visigoths had displaced three decades earlier. Then, in 508, the city of Arles suffered greatly under a siege mounted by the Ostrogoths, who may have been responding to the recent defeat of their fellow Goths. The Ostrogoths ousted the Burgundians and the Franks and established Arles as their new capital in that region. This was the beginning of a relatively peaceful interlude that lasted nearly three decades. However, by the late 530s, the Franks were back in control in Arles.

Caesarius's role in this last change was the subject of much discussion. His biographers firmly defended Caesarius's loyalty to his city, saying that he had "prayed constantly for all."[10] But the Arian Goths claimed that Caesarius had betrayed the city to his Frankish co-religionists. The Franks had forged an agreement with the Byzantine Emperor Justinian's generals, who were attempting to reconquer Rome's lost territories. It is the duty of hagiographers to paint their subjects in the best possible light, and there is certainly an argument to be made that Caesarius may have felt a certain affiliation with the Roman Christian Franks under Clovis. On the other hand,

---

[8] *Vita Caesarii* 1.5. It was customary to bring slaves along when entering this monastery, as it was in the establishments of Macrina and Olympias discussed in the previous chapter. See Peter Brown, *Through the Eye of a Needle: Wealth, the Fall of Rome, and the Making of Christianity in the West, 350–550 AD* (Princeton 2012) 421.

[9] Details of this can be found in Wolfram, *Das Reich* 248–65 and Klingshirn, *Caesarius of Arles* 111–12, 256–59.

[10] *Vita Caesarii* 2.32.

as Wolfram pointed out, under Arian Visigothic kings the Roman Christian bishops enjoyed a certain independence and power that the Visigothic rulers did not permit to their Visigothic, Arian bishops.[11] So Caesarius may well have been innocent of the charges. With the change to a Roman Christian regime, he stood to lose a lot of his independence and influence. Similar charges were brought against Bishop Caesarius in 505 when the Visigothic King Alaric exiled him to Bordeaux for allegedly having plotted to deliver the city of Arles to the Burgundians, allies of the Franks. This earlier episode is a bit murky because Caesarius's detractor was a certain Licinianus, whom historians suspect of having invented the charges out of spite and in a grab for political power. In 506, Alaric seems to have had a change of heart and soon after Caesarius returned from his short exile, the king had him call together the local bishops for a church council held in the city of Agde. Whatever Caesarius's actions may have been in these cases, it is clear that he was an important figure in the political sphere under both the Gothic and the Frankish regimes.[12]

The long years of war had resulted in many people being taken as captives on all sides, Roman Christians like Caesarius, Arian Christians from among the Visigoths and Ostrogoths and many others, Christian and pagan alike. Caesarius was apparently very concerned about the fates of all of these new captives who were destined for slavery.[13] As we saw in previous chapters, the Roman aristocratic tradition—as well as the Christian church—saw it as a virtuous act to rescue captives from becoming enslaved. And Caesarius, a good Roman as well as a good Christian, tried to redeem as many of these poor souls as he could.[14] He also sent out the clergy under his control to assist him in aiding these unfortunates: "He directed abbots, deacons, and other clergy to go out to redeem the suffering [captives]."[15]

Considerable financial resources were required in order to effect so many ransoms. But, as we have seen, church property was not to be alienated for

---

[11] Wolfram, *Das Reich* 210. On non-Roman bishops see Ralph Mathisen, "Barbarian Bishops and the Churches 'in barbarici gentibus' during Late Antiquity," *Speculum* 72 (1997) 664–97.

[12] An interesting discussion of the problems faced by the bishops of this era as they tried to balance their duties as Christian leaders with the expectations of their Germanic secular lords can be found in Gregory I. Halfond, "The Endorsement of Royal-Episcopal Collaboration in the Fredegar Chronica," *Traditio* 70 (2015) 1–28.

[13] *Vita Caesarii* 1.21. Also see Klingshirn, *Caesarius of Arles* 94–95 and Eberhard Bruck, "Caesarius of Arles and the Lex Romana Visigothorum," in *Studi in onore di Vincenzo Arangio-Ruiz nel XLV anno del suo insegnamento* (Naples 1953) 1.200–217.

[14] *Vita Caesarii* 1.15, 1.23, 1.27, 1.32, and *passim*.

[15] *Vita Caesarii* 1.23.

any but the gravest of reasons. Although the redemption of captives had often been listed among the permissible uses of ecclesiastical resources, this idea was not universally accepted.[16] But Caesarius believed that the relief of so much suffering more than justified the loss of church resources: "I do not believe that the God who gave himself for the redemption of humankind is opposed to his servant giving [church resources] for the redemption [of captives]."[17] He went so far as to have the silver trim chipped away from the church building so that it could be sold to provide ransom money.[18] This attitude brought him into conflict with other ecclesiastical officials, as we shall discuss in more detail later. It is, however, important to note that this rescue activity was only in aid of those who had not yet completed the transition into enslavement. Caesarius, as a man of his time, did not have any problem with ownership of those already enslaved.

Caesarius's *Vita* also praised his care for the poor.[19] Slaves were not included in this group either. It was assumed that slave owners would have a vested interest in taking reasonably good care of such valuable property. Charity was for the nonservile population who had no patrons and no resources of their own and had nowhere else to turn. There are two stories in the *Vita* about Caesarius healing someone's slave, but in neither case was the question of manumission discussed.[20]

Caesarius was a slave owner himself. Like all aristocrats, he was expected to have personal attendants like the anonymous slave who accompanied him from his parents' home when he first entered monastic life and the slaves who carried the sedan chair he relied on for travel in his later years.[21] His last will and testament mentioned two slaves for whom Caesarius seems to have felt some affection: "I hereby confirm the gifts that have been bestowed upon my slave, Briciano. Agritia, my own dear slave girl, should cheerfully serve the monastery where Caesaria is abbess."[22] The other household slaves he commended to his episcopal successor.[23] Briciano and Agritia seem clearly

---

[16] For a helpful discussion of this question see Claudia Rapp, *Holy Bishops in Late Antiquity: The Nature of Christian Leadership in an Age of Transition* (Berkeley 2005) 228–32.

[17] *Vita Caesarii* 1.22.

[18] *Vita Caesarii* 1.23.

[19] *Vita Caesarii* 1.15.

[20] *Vita Caesarii* 1.37, 2.15.

[21] *Vita Caesarii* 2.34.

[22] *Testament.* The abbess of this house, St. John's, may have been Caesarius's sister, sometimes referred to as Caesaria the Elder, who had helped her brother establish this convent. Or it may have been another Caesaria, who is sometimes referred to as Caesaria the Younger.

[23] *Testament.*

to have been Caesarius's to dispose of. It is not clear whether the other slaves were Caesarius's personal property or were part of the *res ecclesiae*. However, the fact that they were given to the care of Caesarius's successor suggests that they belonged to the church.

Records show that slave ownership continued to be common for bishops in the post-Roman era. For example, the *Testamentum* of Bishop Bertram of Le Mans, who was related to the Merovingian royals, detailed the numerous properties that he owned personally, including the slaves (*mancipii*) needed to run them.[24] In Visigothic Iberia, Braulio of Zaragoza's *Vita of Amelian the Confessor* reported that even though he was a hermit, Amelian lived with the help of his agricultural slaves. In fact, Amelian had originally purchased Braulio as a slave and then set him free to follow the monastic life, serving his former master no longer as a slave but as a pupil.[25] And the *Vita* of Fructuosus of Braga, bishop of Dumio, reported that he had been "betrayed by his own slaves."[26]

Caesarius apparently treated his slaves relatively well for a late Roman aristocrat. His *Vita* said that he took pains to limit the punishment of his slaves to what was proper—only thirty-nine lashes, the same as for his nonservile dependents.[27] This punishment may sound severe to a modern reader, but the authors of the *Vita* must have thought that this equal treatment of free and unfree workers would show that Caesarius had been kind toward his slaves. In his sermons Caesarius exhorted his people to be aware of their duty to support the salvation of their slaves and other dependents, reminding them: "Although in their present corporeal condition, [your] slaves are subject to you, the chains of slavery are not everlasting.[28]

Perhaps most of all, Caesarius was known for his personal holiness and for his austerity. And while a lot of this reputation may well have been influenced by his hagiographers' need to establish a spiritual foundation for Caesarius's worldly power, there is plenty of independent evidence to confirm his good character.[29] Caesarius's will made it clear that he did not have any share in his family's wealth, and it detailed the modest possessions he had remaining to

[24] PL 80.387–410; also see Wickham, *Framing* 186–87.

[25] PL 80.699–714.

[26] PL 87.437–70. For more about this see Jones, *Social Mobility* 71–78.

[27] *Vita Caesarii* 1.18.

[28] *Vita Caesarii* 1.47. On Caesarius's sermons see Igor Filippov, "Legal Frameworks in the Sermons of Caesarius of Arles," *Medieval Sermon Studies* 58 (2014) 65–83 and Leandro Navarra, "Motivi sociale e di costume nei sermoni al popolo di Cesario di Arles," *Benedictina* 28 (1981) 229–60.

[29] On holiness as a requirement for authority see Rapp, *Holy Bishops* 2005.

bequeath to his heirs: the two personal slaves and a few articles of clothing.[30] This is a great deal less than was frequently the case with his fellow bishops. For example, Remigius of Reims, whose hagiographer called him an ascetic as well, had more than two dozen properties (including the slaves needed to work them) to bequeath to various people at his death in 533.[31] Ironically, it was Caesarius's relative poverty that had resulted in his being condemned for not using his own resources but instead using the property of the church to ransom captives. Some local church leaders went so far as to try to get the Ostrogothic authorities to arrest him in around 511 on the charge of having violated the Roman church law forbidding the alienation of church property, even though Roman church law did not necessarily apply in Provence at that time. In self-defense, Caesarius went to the royal court in Ravenna, where King Theodoric saw that Caesarius was only a penurious holy man and sent him home with lavish gifts—which Caesarius immediately used to ransom more captives.[32]

Caesarius also founded a monastery for women, just outside the city of Arles. His *Regula ad virgines* (*Rule for Nuns*) detailed two main concerns for the community. First, the nuns should renounce all worldly possessions and not own any individual property, not even their own clothing or their slaves.[33] "No one may have her own slaves, except the abbess," who would presumably use them to aid her in fulfilling her obligation to care for the other nuns' well-being.[34] Upon entering the convent, a woman's worldly possessions were to be given to the abbess for the good of the community.[35] Owning things, said Caesarius, contradicted the New Testament's prescriptions for living the best life possible.[36] But, as we saw in the previous chapter, late Roman aristocratic women often brought their *ancillae* with them into the convent. The custom of nuns retaining slaves for domestic duties was also documented in Gregory of Tours's *Historia Francorum*, where he told of Radegund, a Frankish noblewoman who founded a convent in Poitier, using Caesarius's *Rule*.[37]

---

[30] *Testament.*

[31] Klingshirn, *Caesarius of Arles* 89.

[32] Klingshirn, *Caesarius of Arles* 114–26.

[33] *Regula ad virgines* 15, 27, PL 67.1103–21.

[34] *Regula ad virgines* 4.

[35] *Regula ad virgines* 19. On this Rule, see Maureen Tilley, "Caesarius' Rule for Unruly Nuns: Permitted and Prohibited Textiles in the Monastery of St. John's," *Early Medieval Europe* 26 (2018) 83–89.

[36] Found in Matt. 19 and Luke 14. *Regula ad virgines* 4.

[37] Gregory of Tours, *Historia francorum* 10.16, ed. W. Arndt and B. Kutsch, MGH, *Scriptores rerum Merovingicarum*, vol. 1 (Hanover 1885), Eng. trans. L. Thorpe (London 1974). See also Venantius's *Life of Radegund* 24, PL 88.502. More information can be found in Klingshirn's translation of Caesarius's *Testament* 76 n. 29.

Radegund employed slaves to perform menial chores. However, these slaves were no longer the property of their former mistresses; Radegund's slaves belonged to the community. We saw in the last chapter how Augustine dealt with a similar situation, but it is difficult to make comparisons, given the incomplete nature of the data available.

Another concern addressed in Caesarius's *Rule* was that the nuns should be left undisturbed and that outsiders not be permitted inside the monastery. Neither men nor women, not even the nuns' family members, were allowed into the private areas of the convent except for someone performing sacramental duties, or workmen (including their slaves) who were doing building maintenance. High-ranking clergy, especially travelers, could be given accommodations, but socializing was not permitted. It is indicative of the way that people of this culture viewed their unfree dependents that the convent slaves were not mentioned in the rather exhaustive treatment of this question. We know that there were slaves in the convent, and we have no reason to assume that they all took the veil. But they were not mentioned in this context.[38] Probably the workmen's slaves were mentioned because they posed as big a threat to the nuns' chastity as did their owners.

As bishop of Arles, the most important city in the region, Caesarius exerted considerable influence, and presided over a number of church synods in the first three decades of the sixth century. After the Frankish conquest, Caesarius's influence was reduced when Arles was no longer the capital city, but he still continued to attend these meetings for at least another decade.[39] We shall look at the relevant legislation in some detail later. Here it is sufficient merely to recognize the substantial role that Caesarius played in shaping ecclesiastical policies in southern Gaul from the beginning of the sixth century onward.

Caesarius died on August 27, 542, the anniversary of the death of St. Augustine, one of his great heroes.[40]

Although the *Life* of Caesarius of Arles was clearly composed as hagiography and not as a modern data-driven historical analysis, it is useful for the information it provides about what the Christian clergy in early sixth-century Gaul thought was desirable in a bishop. With the addition of Caesarius's correspondence and other writings, we have enough information to conclude

---

[38] *Regula ad virgines* 33–37.
[39] Klingshirn, *Caesarius of Arles* 137–45.
[40] *Vita Caesarii* 34. See Brown, *Eye of a Needle* 151.

that he is a reasonably good example of a western church leader of his era and of the problems that such a person faced. The story of Caesarius of Arles is also a useful example of how the Roman educated classes tried to cope with life under their new Germanic overlords, and it documents the slowness of the transition from Roman culture to early medieval culture in very clear ways. Caesarius was born to a minor aristocratic family who were still able to live largely as they had long been accustomed. He was a complex character. Caesarius's *Vita* strove to paint him as an exemplar of the Christian ideal, charitable and ascetic. However, as Chris Wickham pointed out, later Roman aristocrats were drawn to careers in church administration because of the opportunities for power that were presented to someone charged with the management of the by now considerable ecclesiastical wealth.[41]

The fact that Caesarius's tenure in Arles lasted through Gothic as well as Frankish secular political regimes is an example of how the church tried to continue on its way, even in the face of changing political climates. As later Gothic and the Frankish legal texts made clear, the Goths' and the Franks' attitudes toward servile persons and toward ecclesiastical property and personnel were different from the attitudes of the majority of the late Roman aristocracy. However, in the texts written by Caesarius and his contemporaries, no great differences from the opinions of the churchmen of the previous century can be detected. While it is very likely that the legal texts reflected the ideas that rulers of that time and of later centuries wanted to preserve, it is also likely that in the early days of Frankish and Gothic hegemony in Provence, the Roman Christian community continued in their late Roman attitudes toward their slaves and toward ecclesiastical property, unaffected by the customs of these newly arrived rulers, whether Arian Christian, Roman Christian, or pagan. Along with his personal holiness and charity, Caesarius was a man of his time, and he never relinquished his family's ideas about property and the ownership of slaves.

In this study we have been following the development of canonical prohibitions on the alienation of church property, the *res ecclesiae*, over the early centuries of the church.[42] It was forbidden either to sell church property or to give it away, in all but a few exceptional circumstances. And this policy was

---

[41] Wickham, *Inheritance of Rome* 106. Also see Ralph Mathisen, *Roman Aristocrats in Barbarian Gaul: Strategies for Survival in an Age of Transition* (Austin 2011).

[42] A. H. M. Jones's 1960 article "Church Finance in the Fifth and Sixth Centuries," *Journal of Theological Studies* 11: 84–94, provides useful insights about this question in the centuries being discussed here.

taken very seriously in Caesarius's time. A late fifth-century Roman prefect had said, "It is wrongful and sacrilegious that the goods which a man has, for the sake of the poor, bestowed on the venerable church on behalf of his own salvation or the eternal rest of the souls of his family should be transferred to another by those particularly entrusted with preserving it."[43] And we have seen how people reacted when Caesarius sold the *res ecclesiae* to ransom captives. But there is also a great deal of evidence to show that Caesarius took very seriously his duties as steward of the church's wealth.

Perhaps Caesarius's *Testament* shows most clearly his concern with the canonical principle of the nonalienability of ecclesiastical property. As Gregory of Nazianzus had done, to be sure that there was no suggestion that he used his position to enrich his family, Caesarius said specifically that one reason he had made the will was so that "none of my relatives would presume to take anything away from the church where I presided, except those things which I have bequeathed to them."[44]

His correspondence with the bishop of Rome, at that time the most prestigious and arguably the most influential bishop in the West, also shows this concern for church order. It also illustrates Caesarius's resistance to some of the Romans' ideas when they came into conflict with his own. The letters reveal the kinds of discussions that were taking place in an effort to establish in which precise circumstances it was permissible to alienate church property.

When Caesarius was in Rome in 513, he presented the Roman bishop, Symmachus (498–514), with a petition listing several violations of church law that caused him considerable concern. Among these was the fact that there were some people in the church in Gaul who were alienating ecclesiastical properties. He urged Symmachus to use his influence to see to it that the *res ecclesiae* be kept intact, except as needed for the use of the church or the care of the poor, or in order to endow a monastery. Caesarius's petition followed the canons passed by the recent council held in Agde, over which he had presided, except for the monastic endowment exception. But, since Caesarius had used church resources for this purpose himself, this additional exception was important to him.[45] Symmachus, who had experienced difficulties about his own treatment of the *res ecclesiae*, replied with a somewhat more conservative position, saying that the *res ecclesiae* could not be

[43] Quoted in Klingshirn, *Caesarius of Arles* 114.
[44] *Testament.*
[45] Caesarius, Epistola 7a.

alienated except in "convincing necessity" and then only for so long as the recipients might live.[46] This neatly avoided the question of monastic endowment (since it might be argued that a monastery as a corporate body does not die, but only individual members of the community).

The following year, Symmachus's successor, Hormisdas (514–523), wrote Caesarius in reply to his petition for immunity from local episcopal control for the convent that he had built near Arles. Caesarius had also asked that the nuns be allowed to keep the funds that he had given them from the sale of some church property. Hormisdas agreed to the petition for perpetual immunity and also agreed to the idea that the nuns should keep Caesarius's gift. However, Hormisdas made it clear that this was a one-time exception to the principle of nonalienation of church property since this was a donation "made by love." And he cautioned Caesarius that such alienation of ecclesiastical estates should not happen in the future.[47]

Caesarius seems to have played a major role in the formation of the early sixth-century synodal legislation and secular laws, including those concerned with the treatment of the *res ecclesiae*. And, although Caesarius clearly seems to have been a good Christian man, it is important to remember that he was a late Roman aristocrat's son with great ambition and great talent, as well as the shrewdness to use the one in pursuit of the other.[48]

Secular Law

At first glance it is hard to see many patterns in the forest of conciliar canons that were produced by the bishops of Gaul and Iberia in the sixth through the eighth centuries.[49] However, if we preface our consideration of the canon law with a thorough look at the secular law, the regional attitudes and concerns become a bit clearer in relief, as it were.[50]

[46] Caesarius, Epistola 7b.

[47] Caesarius, Epistola 18.

[48] See Lucy Grig, "Caesarius of Arles and the Campaign against Popular Culture in Late Antiquity," *Early Medieval Europe* 26 (2018) 61–81, for an analysis of the values that Caesarius stressed in his sermons.

[49] This section and the following section on canon law include expanded and updated versions of ideas first published in Mary E. Sommar, "Ecclesiastical *Servi* in the Frankish and Visigothic Kingdoms," *ZSR.KA* 96 (2010) 57–79.

[50] Among the numerous books and articles on the questions of slavery and law in these cultures, I have found the following particularly helpful: Hermann Nehlsen, *Sklavenrecht zwischen Antike und Mittelalter: Germanisches und römisches Recht in den germanischen Rechtsaufzeichnungen* (Göttingen 1972); Patrick Wormald, "*Lex Scripta* and *Verbum Regis*: Legislation and Germanic Kingship from Euric to Cnut," in *Early Medieval Kingship*, ed. P. H. Sawyer and I. N. Wood (Leeds 1977) 105–38; Ian

We shall look first at various Frankish laws, which show a number of common features and evolutionary patterns. These laws of the Burgundians, the Salian Franks, the Ripuarians, the Alamans, and the Bavarians were all in one way or another influenced by the power of the Merovingian rulers, but they display regional differences.[51] The Frankish ecclesiastical regulations reflect the influences both of the ancient Frankish traditions and of the Roman Christian church. We shall also look at the laws in the Gothic societies. The Ostrogoths do not seem to have given any special notice to unfree persons in ecclesiastical *dominium*, although several of their legal texts do make it possible to speculate about the situation of such persons. The Visigoths included quite a number of laws about the church *servi*, in their secular decrees as well as in their synodal canons. The Lombard laws made it clear that, while there was no preferential treatment of ecclesiastical personnel, this did not mean that transactions involving the *res ecclesiae*, including ecclesiastical *servi*, were not to be honored.

The current scholarship about these secular legal traditions is not at all comprehensive. This situation, along with the relative paucity of reliable evidence, makes it probable that any attempt to produce a systematic and comprehensive analysis of the law and social customs regarding ecclesiastical slaveholding at this time would likely produce results that would lead to an inaccurate understanding of the events on the part of the modern reader and would certainly be unfair to those who produced these laws. But we can certainly get a snapshot view of what some people were thinking in those centuries.

Another methodological issue must be addressed here as well. At the time of this writing, the scholarship has not yet reached consensus on the extent to which any law—especially the Germanic laws of the early medieval period— represents the actual practice of a society.[52] However, while acknowledging

Wood, *The Merovingian Kingdoms, 450–471* (London 1994); Harald Siems, *Handel und Wucher im Spiegel Frümittelalterlicher Rechtsquellen* (Hanover 1992); Roger Collins, "Law and Ethnic Identity in the Western Kingdoms in the Fifth and Sixth Centuries," in *Medieval Europeans: Studies in Ethnic Identity and National Perspectives in Medieval Europe*, ed. A. P. Smyth (Basingstoke 1998) 1–23; P. S. Barnwell, "Emperors, Jurists, and Kings," *Past & Present* 168 (2000) 1–29; Hermann Nehlsen, "Die Einfluss des Alten und Neuen Testaments auf die Rechtsentwicklung in der Spätantike und im frühen Mittelalter bei den germanischen Stämmen," *in Leges—Gentes—Regna*, ed. Gerhard Dilcher and Eva-Marie Distler (Berlin 2006) 203–18; and Michael Edward Moore, *A Sacred Kingdom: Bishops and Frankish Kingship, 380–850* (Washington, DC 2011).

[51] There were local laws for many different groups that had been conquered by the Franks (Thuringians, Frisians, Saxons, etc.), but I shall concentrate on those laws that have been the most influential over time and that addressed our questions most directly.

[52] The most recent comprehensive investigation of early Germanic law is Karl Ubl, *Sinnstiftung eines Rechtsbuchs: Die* Lex Salica *im Frankenreich* (Ostfildern 2017). A useful English summary of

the boundaries imposed by this difficulty, it is not unreasonable for us to proceed based on the assumption that the particular material that was chosen
for inclusion in a given legal text, secular or ecclesiastical, can indeed reveal
a good deal about the customs and prejudices of a particular culture. At least
it can tell us what the compiler of the laws thought was important to present.
Thus, even such limited data as we are able to examine here still allows us to
reach some general conclusions about the nature of servitude and the church
in these post-Roman cultures. The data leaves one with the distinct impression that when it came to the question of ecclesiastical servitude, the Frankish
societies were more concerned with overall social rank and privileges and
with the proper sanctions for a given rank, while the Visigoths, especially
in their Iberian kingdom, may have been somewhat less concerned with the
social hierarchy and focused their legal energy on the maintenance of ecclesiastical purity and authority. In general, as was illustrated in the story of
Caesarius of Arles, the early medieval church continued the ancient concern
that two basic principles be followed in any regulations or customs that involved ecclesiastical *servi*: church resources had to be conserved; and inappropriate behavior on the part of those associated with the church was to
be avoided. Many of these early church canons about *servi ecclesiarum* continued to exercise influence for centuries, and some eventually became a
part of a twelfth-century legal text, famously known as Gratian's *Decretum*,
which, including these early canons, remained a part of church law until the
twentieth century.

Gaul: The Burgundians

The story of Caesarius of Arles began when the Burgundians were in control
of much of what is now southern and eastern France. Despite their absorp-
tion into the Merovingian Frankish kingdom in 534, after the decline of the
Carolingian Frankish kingdoms in the ninth century, Burgundy re-emerged
as a kingdom once again.[53] Here we shall focus on the laws attributed to

---

this important work can be found in Wilfried Hartmann's review essay in the *Bulletin of Medieval
Canon Law* n.s. 35 (2018) 389–400.

   Thomas Faulkner, *Law and Authority in the Early Middle Ages* (Cambridge 2016), provides an in-
depth account of Germanic law, especially as it developed in later centuries. See also Collins, "Law
and Ethnic Identity" and Wormald, "*Lex Scripta.*"
   [53] See, e.g., Wolfram, *Das Reich* 248–59.

Gundobad, the former *magister militum* of the Roman army who became king (480–516) and to his son and successor, Sigismund (516–523).[54] The Burgundians made no specific mention of *servi ecclesiarum* in their earliest law code, which is known as the *Liber Constitutionum*. These laws have been attributed to King Gundobad although they were promulgated by his son, Sigismund, at the beginning of the sixth century. Titles 14.5, which provided for nuns to have a share in the division of their family's inheritance, and 70.2, which discussed the principle of sanctuary, make it clear that although the Burgundian code made no special provisions for how the church was to transact its business, Christian institutions were a strong presence in that society. The circa 500 *Lex Romana Burgundionum*, often called the *Papianus*, included a chapter (3.1) on their customs for *manumissio in ecclesia*. Slaves were set free by means of a ceremony in which the bishop or other church official inscribed their names in a special record, a *tabula*.[55] Yet, in contrast to some of the other codes, the *Lex Romana Burgundionum* did not specify any enduring relationship with the church after such a ceremony.[56] Although the Burgundian kingdom came under the control of the Merovingian Franks during the 520s and 530s, there is evidence that the *Liber Constitutionum* was still consulted as late as the ninth century. This makes sense, given that the Burgundian traditions were preserved to the extent that Burgundy eventually reappeared after the fall of the Carolingians.

The Salian Franks

There were a number of different groups of people who were included among the Franks. But it was Clovis, from the family who called themselves the Merovingians, who consolidated Frankish control over much of Gaul in the

---

[54] *Leges Burgundionum*, ed. L. R. de Salis, MGH, *Leges nationum Germanicarum*, vol. 2 (Hanover 1892). The standard English translation is K. F. Drew, *The Burgundian Code* (Philadelphia 1949).

[55] Collins ("Law and Ethnic Identity") suggested that the traditional interpretation of the role of the *Lex Romana Burgundionum*, as law intended only for the Roman subjects of the Burgundian rulers, presumes much too complicated a governing philosophy. Rather, this should be seen as a compilation of legal texts made for private use.

[56] *Lex Romana Burgundionum* 3.1 referred explicitly to the *Codex Theodosianus* (C.Th.) 4.7.1, which also provided for manumission in front of the bishop acting in the capacity of a magistrate and stated that the person thus set free should have "full and complete freedom." *Theodosiani Libri XVI*, ed. T. Mommsen et al. (Berlin 1950) is available at the Roman Law Library www.droitromain.upmf-grenoble.fr.

Marcel Fournier's *Essai sur les formes et les effets de l'affranchissement dans le droit gallo-franc* (Paris 1885) remains useful as a compendium of the relevant legal material.

early sixth century. He established the Merovingians as a powerful dynasty that ruled over different Frankish groups as well as over the Burgundians and the indigenous Gallo-Roman population.[57] These Merovingians were part of the group known as the Salian Franks, whose territory had been in the north-western part of what is now France, Belgium, and the Netherlands. The other major Frankish groups will be discussed later.

The oldest version of the *Lex Salica* comes from the reign of King Clovis or even earlier.[58] It applied both to the Franks, the majority of whom were likely still followers of the old Germanic religious beliefs, and, at least to some extent, to the Christian Gallo-Roman conquered population, who largely still looked to the Roman law.[59] In the earliest laws, many of whose provisions clearly predate the circa 510 promulgation of the written version known to modern scholars, there is a good deal of evidence that these Merovingians, whether or not they were Christians themselves (either Arian or Roman), were well aware of the religious institutions of the Christian Gallo-Romans. Still, as we saw with the Burgundian laws, there is nothing here in these earliest Frankish laws about *servi ecclesiarum*.[60] Clovis accepted the Roman Christian tradition, and Wolfram suggested that he may have "enjoyed a certain measure of Roman education."[61] But it is not until somewhat later that we find a more detailed consideration of the roles of those who owed various levels of obligation to the church in Frankish royal decrees. This delay may well be due to the fact that slavery does not seem to have played as great a part in the earlier Frankish economy as it did after the Franks had become more Romanized. Wood pointed out that although the Franks had household slaves, they rarely had gangs of slave laborers, as the Romans did, and Nehlsen speculated that the Franks may not have seen slaves as nonpersons as had been the Roman tradition.[62]

---

[57] See especially Wood, *Merovingian Kingdoms* 51–54, 115; and Katherine F. Drew, introduction to her translation of *The Laws of the Salian Franks* (Philadelphia 1991) 24.

[58] Ubl, *Sinnstiftungen eines Rechtsbuchs* 53–55.

[59] *Pactus Legis Salicae* and *Lex Salica*, ed. K. A. Eckhardt, MGH, *Leges nationum Germanicarum*, vol. 4 (Hanover 1962). There is also a helpful English translation by K. F. Drew in *The Laws of the Salian Franks*. For the present study, it is not necessary for us to concern ourselves with the debates about who exactly it was who issued the various parts of what has been traditionally seen as the Salic law. The rough chronological order that has been preserved despite questionable attributions will suffice for our purposes.

[60] Wormald ("*Lex Scripta*" 112) pointed out that the absence of material regulating the behavior of the church in the earliest laws should not come as a surprise. If, indeed these early "codes" were compedia of ancient custom, one would not expect to find included the kind of new regulations that became necessary only after the subjection of a largely Christian society.

[61] Wolfram, *Das Reich* 198.

[62] Wood, *Merovingian Kingdoms* 107; Nehlsen, *Sklavenrecht* 266.

An example of the Frankish view of slaves as fully human can be seen in a decree attributed to King Clovis on the occasion of the 511 church council in Orleans. This decree promised the king's protection for ecclesiastical personnel, explicitly listing the *servi ecclesiarum* among those who were to receive this protection.[63] In this decree church slaves were clearly seen as persons. But soon the idea that ecclesiastical and royal slaves should be given preferential treatment was questioned. Chapter 6 of the *Pactus pro tenore pacis*, from the era of King Childebert I (511–558) began, "If slaves of the church or of the fisc or of anybody else are accused by someone of a crime [they all receive the same treatment]."[64] In other words, slaves of the church or of the fisc (i.e., of the ruling house) were to receive the same treatment as any other slave. A later decree from King Childebert II, proclaimed at Cologne in 595/96, repeated this explicitly: "If a *servus ecclesiae* or a *servus* of the fisc commits theft, he is to be punished the same as the *servi* of the other Franks."[65] However, this equality was also extended to nonhuman assets, e.g., in chapter 21 of Chlothar II's decree of 614 that called for equal treatment of pigs, whether they were foraging in church-held forests or in forests held by others.[66] Despite such egalitarian statements, it seems that the belongings of the king and of the church continued to receive special protections and their *servi* received special treatment in the Frankish laws. For example, Chlothar II's Edict of 614, chapter 7, stated that those under the protection of

---

[63] *Chlodowici regis ad episcopos epistola*, MGH, *Leges: Capitularia regum Francorum*, vol. 1, ed. A. Boretius (Hanover 1883) 1. In his notes to the 511 Council of Orleans, Friedrich Maassen said that this letter is found only in some of the manuscripts of the canons of the council, albeit the oldest. He concluded that it was probably genuine. *Concilia Aevi Merovingici*, ed. F. Maassen, MGH, *Concilia*, vol. 1 (Hanover 1893) 1.

[64] *Capitularia regum Francorum* 1.3.3–7. This was incorporated into a later version of the Salic law as Title 87. Nehlsen, *Sklavenrecht* 334–41 suggested that these procedures included torture, as had been standard practice in Rome. However, for our purposes, what is relevant is that ecclesiastical *servi* were not to receive preferential treatment. Per Nehlsen (*Sklavenrecht*), this was an attempt by the Franks to replace the old Roman custom of torturing slaves with a Frankish custom, in this case, casting lots.

[65] *Capitularia regum Francorum* 1.7.15–17, c.13. This was incorporated into the Salic law as Capitulary VI.3.

A later document that claimed to be the "Interpretation" of the *Pactus pro tenore pacis* said: "The law makes no distinction between ecclesiastical slaves or slaves held by benefice holders and the slaves of other persons." Drew, who included it as Capitulary VII.7 of her English translation of the Salian legal texts, pointed out that this capitulary, which was not included in Eckhardt's 1962 edition for the MGH, had been included in his earlier work, *Pactus Legis Salicae* II.2, found in *Kapitularien und 70 Titel-Text* (Göttingen 1956) 450–56. Since the more recent MGH editor excluded this text, I shall mention it only in passing in this note.

[66] *Capitularia regum Francorum* 1.9.20–23; *Leges nationem Germanicarum* 4.1.269; 4.2.187.

the church could not be adjudicated unless their bishop or his representative was present.[67]

The Ripuarians

The early seventh-century *Lex Ribuaria*, the law for the northeastern regions of Francia or Austrasia (centered in the Rhineland), contained a good deal of material about persons who were under obligation to the church.[68] First, there were church *servi* and *ancillae*, whose only difference from other *servi* and *ancillae* seems to have been that the church's slaves could not be set free unless a replacement was provided to the church in their stead.[69] This apparent fungibility of slaves suggests that the Ripuarian Franks had adapted somewhat to the ancient Roman ideas about the non-personhood of a slave. In addition to slaves, there were other groups who were under ecclesiastical obligations, illustrating the complexity of free and semifree statuses that characterized medieval non-elites. One group, whose status suggests that they enjoyed only partial freedom, were the "church's men" or "church's women" (*homo/mulier ecclesiasticus/a*) who were usually mentioned in tandem with the "king's men and women" (*homo/femina regius/a*).[70] Many of the Ripuarian laws give the impression that these were ecclesiastical or royal retainers who commanded a somewhat lower *wergild*, that is, compensatory payment for loss of life, or were liable for different financial penalties than were ordinary free Franks.[71] However, their status becomes clearer in Title 61, whose main concerns were the *tabularii* and the status of children from mixed unions.

In late imperial Rome, a *tabularius* was someone who held a position of some responsibility in the record-keeping department of a government official or institution. This position was normally held by a freedman in the first several years after his manumission, and there were possibilities of

---

[67] *Capitularia regum Francorum* 1.9.20–23. Also see the proceedings of the 614 Council of Paris, ed. C. de Clerq in *Concilia Gallia A.511—A.695* 148 (Turnhout 1963).

[68] *Lex Ribvaria* (hereafter *L.Rib.*), ed. F. Beyerle and R. Buchner, MGH, *Leges nationem Germanicarum*, vol. 3.2 (Hanover 1954). There is also a useful English translation by T. J. Rivers, *Laws of the Salian and Ripuarian Franks* (New York 1986).

[69] *L.Rib.* 61.3.

[70] This does not seem to have been the same office as the *sagibaron* mentioned in the *Lex Salica* because of the large differences in their *wergild*.

[71] Re: *wergild* see, e.g., *L.Rib.* 9, 10, 11, 14, 15. Re: other penalties see *L.Rib.* 19–23.

advancement to a level of considerable power in, especially, the imperial service.[72] Although it is not entirely clear what the Ripuarian law meant by a *tabularius/tabularia*, they seem to have been former slaves who had been given their freedom through a ceremony based on the old Roman custom of *manumissio in ecclesia*, wherein the former slave's name was "written on the tablets according to the Roman law, by which the church lives."[73] In Anglo-Saxon England, the names of those manumitted in church were written on the flyleaves of Gospel books. However, as we saw earlier, the Burgundians recorded these transactions on a *tabula*. The Ripuarian law also called for their names to be written on a *tabula* and then referred to such a person as a *tabularius/tabularia*. They were then expected to manumit their own slaves using this same procedure, and there were monetary penalties for noncompliance.[74] The law also said that the offspring of a *tabularius* would also remain *tabularii* and, along with their parents, would live under the protection of the church, subject to the bishop's jurisdiction. Further, the church would hold ultimate control of their financial resources. Whether or not a *tabularius/tabularia* performed record-keeping duties in this circumstance is not clear, but it seems unlikely given the number of people who apparently held this status. In ancient Rome, they had all been male, but the Ripuarian law included both genders in this category. Nevertheless, it is clear that the Ripuarian *tabularii/ae* were not the same as other freedmen or freedwomen. Unlike the earlier Frankish and Burgundian laws about those who received their freedom in the old Roman process, where slaves were simply manumitted before a public authority who happened to be a bishop, or in a church manumission ceremony, the Ripuarian laws made it clear that *tabularii/ae* and their descendants would remain perpetually in a relationship of mutual obligation with the church. Title 61 of the *Lex Ribuaria* continued with several chapters stipulating the status of the offspring of various mixed marriages: free Ripuarians, slaves, *tabularii*, and also the *homines/ ancillae* of the king or of the church.[75] The general principle, found in 61.15,

---

[72] See P. R. C. Weaver, *Familia Caesaris: A Social Study of the Emperor's Freedmen and Slaves* (Cambridge 1972), especially 243–50. Also see *C.Th.* 8.2.0: *tabularii* in public service or in the imperial household were generally expected not to be servile, although this did not apply to those in private households.

[73] *L.Rib.* 61.1.

[74] *L.Rib* 61(58).1.

[75] The *L.Rib.* apparently used the words *femina, mulier,* and *ancilla* interchangeably to indicate female persons.

was that the children took the status of the lower-status parent.[76] The details of the provisions of Title 61 make it clear that the status of a *tabularius* or a *homo ecclesiasticus* or *regius* was higher than that of a *servus*, although not at the same level as that of a free Ripuarian. From Title 61 and the earlier titles concerning *wergild* and other penalties, we can roughly estimate that the Ribuarian society's ranking was as follows: first, king; then bishop (*wergild* of 900 solidi), free-born priest (600), free Frank (200), other Germanic free man (Burgundian, Alaman, Frisian, Bavarian, or Saxon—160), then next a Roman or a *homo ecclesiasticus* or *homo regius* (100), then *tabularius*, and lastly *servus* (36).[77] Women's ranking was more complicated, but one can assume that the same hierarchy applied.[78]

The fact that a king's man or a *homo ecclesiasticus* merited the same *wergild* as a free-born Roman does not permit us to conclude that such persons were considered free. The *homo regius* was not a free Ripuarian, but rather a person (unfree or semifree) who took his relatively high status from his master, and it is likely that the high worth assigned a *homo ecclesiasticus* was analogous. Although bishops in this society were often Romans, the *wergild* of a bishop was higher than that of any nonroyal person, even a free-born Ripuarian Frank. Just as the situation of the *tabularii* is not completely clear, neither is it clear how one received the status of a *homo ecclesiasticus*. It is tempting to speculate that a *homo ecclesiasticus* could have been the descendant of a former slave whose manumission in the church—or you might say, manumission to the church—resulted in his becoming a *tabularius*. Or perhaps a *homo ecclesiasticus* was equivalent to what was called a *colonus* (tenant farmer) in some other societies like the Bavarians and the Alamans. For the present, the relative positions of these categories of ecclesiastical obligatories remain a bit muddled. But, whatever was meant by a *homo ecclesiasticus* as opposed to a *servus ecclesiae*, it is clear that there were various levels of servitude and obligation to ecclesiastical authorities. And the idea that church freedmen (or women) retained perpetual obligations to the church eventually became a lasting feature of church law.

[76] Beyerle, *L.Rib.* (160 n. 15) considered this title to be original to the Ripuarian law, but Wood (*Merovingian Kingdoms* 116 n. 1) suggested it may actually have been taken from a law proclaimed by King Clovis II (sometime after 614) or from a decree (c.7) of the Council of Macon in 585.

[77] *Wergild* for a *tabularius*, unknown, but less than a *homo regius/ecclesiasticus* and more than a *servus*.

[78] The *wergild* for a woman depended on the likelihood of her producing children.

The Alamans

In the early seventh century, as Merovingian hegemony extended eastward beyond Austrasia to Alamannia and Bavaria, the Frankish legal ideas spread as well. The Burgundians had been permitted to retain their own time-honored and apparently workable laws, but the Alamans and the Bavarians refashioned their customs into laws that strongly resemble those of the Franks. Around 625, Chlothar II's laws for the Alamans were proclaimed in the presence of "33 dukes and 33 bishops and 45 counts."[79] This earliest version, which came to be known as the *Pactus Legis Alamannorum*, like the other "first-generation" legal compendia did not contain any explicit provisions for *servi ecclesiarum*. But Title 19.1, declaring that church property could be defended in the same way as private property, recognized the right of the institutional church to hold property. As can also be seen in other societies, in the later revised and expanded version of these laws a considerable number dealt with ecclesiastical affairs, including the various categories of unfree persons who were associated with the church.[80]

The somewhat later *Lex Alamannorum* made clear the inalienability of church property, the severity of penalties for desecration of the sacred, and the inviolability of sanctuary.[81] Killing a *servus ecclesiae* incurred the same penalty as did killing a *servus* of the king, forty-five solidi, which was three times the usual amount for killing a slave.[82] The same threefold penalty also applied to someone who harbored a fugitive *servus*, *ancilla*, or *mancipium* of the church or committed any other kind of legal infraction against the church.[83] Yet killing a "*liberum ecclesiae*, whom they call a *colonum*, . . . [was compensated] as for other Alamans."[84] It is interesting that the death of a *colonus ecclesiae*, in this society a legally free tenant farmer whose landlord was the church, was not seen to cause as great a loss to the church as the loss of a *servus ecclesiae*. While both the slave and the tenant farmer may well have

---

[79] *Leges Alamannorum* (hereafter *L.Al.*), ed. K. Lehmann, rev. K. A. Eckhardt, MGH, *Leges nationum Germanaicarum*, vol. 5.1 (Hanover 1966). There is a useful, if flawed, English translation as well: *Laws of the Alamans and Bavarians*, trans. T. J. Ryan (Philadelphia 1977).

[80] Although the received text likely originated in the early eighth century, it has been included in this analysis because it is clearly an expanded version of the 625 text.

[81] *L.Al.* 1–22. The *Lex Alamannorum* was compiled a good deal later than the *Pactus*, perhaps even as late as the eighth century.

[82] *L.Al.* 7.

[83] *L.Al.* 20.

[84] *L.Al.* 8.1. A *liberus ecclesiae* may have been equivalent to the *homo ecclesiasticus* mentioned in the Ripuarian law or to a *tabularius*.

done the same work for their ecclesiastical lords, a tenant could be replaced with no major financial outlay while, with the loss of a slave, the church suffered not only the loss of his labor, but also the loss of his person, which was the property of the church. The worth of a *servus ecclesiae* was equal to that of a royal slave, and a *colonus ecclesiae* had to render tribute to the church "the same as a *colonus regis*" or pay the same heavy fine.[85] Although the *colonus* was not church property, his tribute was. The obligations, in kind or in days' labor, of *servi* and *ancillae* were also stipulated, clearly differentiating them from the *coloni*.[86] This nuanced differentiation between property and, as it were, staff is an illustration of the sophistication of early medieval legal thinking.

An interesting provision of Alamannic law concerns a woman who married an ecclesiastical slave.[87] If she had previously been a slave herself and had been manumitted, either in church or by a secular declaration, she would become permanently an *ancilla* of the church. But if a woman who had always been free married a *servus ecclesiae*, she and her family had three years in which they might buy her freedom. If this happened, any children of the marriage would remain as slaves of their father's church. (The woman's resulting marital status was not mentioned, but her manumission may have voided the marriage as well.) This different treatment for those who voluntarily embraced ecclesiastical servitude can also be seen in the situation of one who voluntarily gave himself as part of a "donation" to the church and who might then receive as a "benefice" the usufruct of this property—including himself—for the duration of his life.[88]

Thus, even without complete clarity concerning the definitions of some of the various statuses, we can say with some confidence that the Alamannic society had a status structure somewhat similar to that found with the Ripuarian Franks. However, here there is no mention of any special status associated with having been freed *in ecclesia*, as we saw with the Ripuarians' *tabularii*. When *manumissio in ecclesia* was mentioned in the Alamannic laws, it was always mentioned in parallel with the other type

---

[85] *L.Al.* 22.

[86] *L.Al.* 21, 22.

[87] *L.Al.* 17.

[88] *L.Al.* 2. Note: This provision applies to property, including the ownership of one's own self. It is a clear statement of the idea that a free person's property was seen to include his own person. *L.Al.* 1 also explicitly mentioned someone "giving his property [and/or] himself to the church." This documents the fact that self-enslavement was still occurring, arguably with some frequency. We shall discuss this practice in more detail in chapter 7.

of manumission, by means of a charter. *Manumissio in ecclesia* does not appear necessarily to have attached any particular obligations to the one being set free.[89] This conclusion is supported by the fact that the law seems to have seen no great loss to the church from the loss of the services of a *liberus ecclesiae* tenant farmer.

The Bavarians

The Bavarian code was much shorter and also somewhat simpler than that of the Alamans.[90] While the extant versions of this code all date from the mid or late eighth century, it is appropriate to include the *Lex Baiuvariorum* in this chapter because the ancient customs reflected in the written text stemmed from a society that was very closely allied with, occasionally subject to, the Merovingian Franks and because the prologue of the Bavarian code explicitly placed itself in the Frankish tradition.[91] Title 1, concerned with ecclesiastical matters, provided for the customary inalienability of church property, for sanctuary, and for the more severe penalties that were incurred for crimes against ecclesiastical persons or property.[92] There was also a requirement for clerical chastity, resembling that found in the church canons and in the Visigothic laws, but not in the other Frankish codes.[93]

The obligations of *servi* and *coloni ecclesiae* that were detailed in *Lex Baiuvariorum* 1.13 are roughly similar to those found in the Alamannic laws. However, 9.2, which appears to have been a later addition, said that the reason for assessing harsher penalties for theft from a church, or from the duke's *curte* (home farm, as opposed to one worked by a tenant), or from

---

[89] Although this accords with the practices found in Roman law, it is impossible to say if the Alamannic laws intended to follow the Roman custom, or if it was an independent custom. It may be that the special position of the *tabularii* was unique to Ripuarian society.

[90] *Lex Baiuvariorum* (hereafter *L.Bav.*), ed. E. von Schwind and E. Heymann, MGH, *Leges nationem Germanicarum*, vol. 5.2 (Hanover 1926). A useful, if flawed, English translation is available in Ryan, *Laws of the Alamans*.

[91] See Wood, *Merovingian Kingdoms* 116–17; Carl I. Hammer, *From Ducatus to Regnum: Ruling Bavaria under the Merovingians and Early Carolingians* (Turnhout 2007) 146–50; and Peter Landau, *Die Lex Baiuvariorum: Bayerische Entstehungszeit, Entstehungsort und Charakter von Bayerns ältester Rechts- und Geschichtsquelle* (Munich 2004). Also helpful for the wealth of detail it provides is Carl I. Hammer, *A Large-Scale Slave Society of the Early Middle Ages* (Burlington, VT 2002).

[92] *L.Bav* 1.10 states that someone who killed a bishop could be enslaved to the church, along with his wife and children until he paid the required *wergild* to the king or to the people or to the bishop's family.

[93] *L.Bav.* 1.12.

a workshop or a mill, was that "these are public buildings and are always open."[94] Thus, it seems that for the later Bavarians it was not merely the exalted nature of the one being offended against, but also the practical need to protect the accessibility of public places, that called for greater penalties. Overall, the classifications of *servi, coloni,* and *liberti ecclesiae* in the Bavarian laws seem to have been somewhat less complicated than what we have seen with the Alamans or the Ripuarian Franks. And there was no mention of *tabularii* or of *homines* or *feminae ecclesiastici/ae*. Further, the relatively short *Lex Baiuvariorum*, which seems to have been mostly concerned with the proper consequences of wrongdoing, did not discuss procedural issues.

The *Formulae Andegavensis* is one of the many collections of sample documents that were compiled in the Middle Ages for use in legal situations. This one is from Angers, a city not far from Paris, probably from the late sixth century.[95] Although these written documents may not perfectly reflect the customs of the nonliterate members of this society, they are extremely useful in helping modern scholars understand how everyday people thought business ought to be conducted. A number of these texts contain information that is relevant to the present discussion. Two items in the *Formulae Andegavensis* samples dealt with the manumission of a slave who would then be under the protection of a church. It is clear that some services would have been due this church from the newly freed person, but there was no mention of the phrase *manumissio in ecclesia*.[96] However, it is only logical to assume that the services due the church seen in these two documents from Angers are examples of how this community dealt with a law about *manumissio in ecclesia* that demanded certain obligations toward that church from the person who had been set free. Thus, the lack of specificity about the venue of the manumission ceremony suggests that such events must usually have taken place in a church. Other texts in the *Andegavensis* collection included material about the apparently rather common practice of self-sale, including the sale of half of one's freedom to someone else for a certain period of time.[97] In general,

---

[94] This was probably added to *L.Bav.* at a later date because it contradicts the provisions of Titles 1 and 2. For a further discussion of peasant societies at this time see Wickham, *Framing*, especially 442–590.

[95] *Formulae Merowingici et Karolini Aevi,* ed. K. Zeimer, MGH, *Leges,* vol. 5 (Hanover 1886). There is also an excellent, scholarly translation in Alice Rio, *The Formularies of Angers and Marculf: Two Merovingian Legal Handbooks* (Liverpool 2008).

[96] *Formulae Andegavensis* 20, 23.

[97] *Formulae Andegavensis* 2, 3, 19, 25 and re: half-free status, 38 and 18.

the texts in this collection confirm that there was nothing remarkable in the church owning unfree persons and that, no matter what some people might have thought about the personhood of their *servi*, they still treated them like chattel. The formulas also confirm that postmanumission obligations to the church were common.

Although it is difficult to make any definitive generalizations about the Franks' treatment of *servi ecclesiarum* based on the meager records that are available, there are a few general statements about these several early medieval societies that it does seem safe to make at this point. It was clearly considered matter-of-fact for clergy and ecclesiastical institutions to have slaves and other unfree persons under their dominion, and there were a number of various unfree statuses of such persons. The ancient *manumissio in ecclesia* was widely practiced, and some of the texts show that this procedure forged some kind of bond between the freed individual and the church where the ceremony took place. Generally, there were more severe penalties assessed for crimes committed against ecclesiastical dependents, including *servi*, just as there were for offenses committed against the church and the clergy. These penalties were often similar to those for crimes committed against the king or the duke or his belongings, suggesting that there was a similar reverence for the ecclesiastical and secular offices. It is likely that many of these customs concerning *servi ecclesiarum* were of Germanic origin.[98] The 437 Theodosian compilation of Roman law, used widely in early medieval Europe, had not included any special treatment for church slaves, except for 16.2.8, which said that clergy and their *mancipii* were free of certain taxes. And while *manumissio in ecclesia* was given an entire Title (4.7), the *Codex Theodosianus* said clearly that the person who was set free enjoyed "complete and full freedom." Of course, in Roman society there was usually a bond between a freedman and his former master, but the *Codex Theodosianus* did not call for any special obligations to the church where the manumission took place. We shall reserve discussion of the canon law of early medieval Gaul until later, after we have examined the secular laws of the Gothic and Lombard societies.

---

[98] See Nehlsen's classic monograph, *Sklavenrecht zwischen Antike und Mittelalter*, which, as the title implies, provides a more extensive consideration of how much—or how little—in these early European law codes was of Roman origin.

Italy: The Ostrogoths

The *Edictum Theodorici Regis*, promulgated some time shortly before the year 500 CE, did not contain any material that dealt explicitly with *servi ecclesiarum*.[99] The gradual separation of the Gothic peoples into the East Goths (Ostrogoths) and the West Goths (Visigoths) had begun long before the promulgation of this edict. But a few chapters of this law show similarities between Ostrogothic and Visigothic laws, evidence of how the Goths' common attitudes toward their slaves and toward the church carried over into their later legal texts.[100]

Like most slaveholding societies, the Ostrogoths viewed their slaves as inherently inferior. There are a number of chapters in these laws that dealt with how to handle the consequences of slaves' trickery and flight. But chapter 61, concerning a slave who had had sexual relations with a willing and acquiescent widow, perhaps best shows the particular disgust and contempt in which those of servile status were held in Gothic society. The text said that not only should the slave be burned alive, but the widow should also receive capital punishment as though she had committed adultery because "she did not blush to lie under servile lust."[101] This same situation was also dealt with in the edict of Emperor Constantine that referred to the ancient *Senatus Consultum Claudianum*. But the Roman law had called only for the woman's enslavement, and the language was much milder.[102] From very early on, the language of Gothic regulatory texts was exceptionally derogatory toward the unfree.

The East Goths seem to have seen the church both as an organization parallel to the secular government and as something outside the bounds of ordinary life. Capital punishment was the consequence of the violent removal of persons or anything else from "churches, i.e. religious locations."[103] This text made explicit the special nature of churches, which suggests that this might

---

[99] *Edictum Theodorici Regis* (hereafter *Ed. Theod.*), ed. F. Bluhme, MGH, *Leges*, vol. 5 (Hanover 1868) 145–79.

[100] See, e.g., the discussion in Nehlsen, *Sklavenrecht* 120–50. Paul Freedman (*Origins of Peasant Servitude* 203) suggested that the harshness of the Goths' attitudes toward slaves may explain the notorious *mal usos* (bad customs) of the later medieval relationship between Spanish lords and their dependents. See also Carlo Calisse, *A History of Italian Law* (New York 1969) 18–21 for a discussion of Ostrogothic law in general.

[101] *Ed. Theod.* 61.

[102] *C. Th.* 4.12.1 The original law on this subject, the *SC Claudianum* of 52 CE had also called for the woman to be enslaved.

[103] *Ed. Theod.* 125.

not have been automatically clear to everyone. At any rate the severity of this sort of offense was made clear, and it was to be taken very seriously. It is interesting to compare this to the regulations found in the Frankish codes. The punishment the Franks levied for such offenses was not death. Instead, the special nature of the holy things and of the church was indicated by the much higher fines that were levied for theft of ecclesiastical property and in the higher *wergild* demanded upon the death of a cleric. The Goths seem to have seen such crimes as serious because they were offenses against the sacred or because they required that the deity be placated lest his wrath be aroused. The Frankish laws seem to have been more a reflection of the fact that the church and the clergy enjoyed a high rank in that society.

The Byzantines

Ostrogothic control of Italy did not last very long after the death of Theodoric in 526. The Roman emperor's forces from Constantinople began their invasion of the Italian Peninsula in 534, and these Byzantines were then driven out by the Lombards, who first arrived in 568. The constant wars of the sixth century left society in chaos. There was effectively no more "Germanic" law in Italy at that time and the Byzantine Romans' relatively short and unpopular reign from their new capital in Ravenna does not seem to have had much effect on how the Italian church dealt with its servile dependents.[104] Nonetheless, we should look at the Byzantine legal texts to see if there is anything pertinent to our question.

At about the same time that the Byzantine forces were trying to take back control of Italy, in Constantinople there was an attempt to make Roman law more comprehensible. Under instructions from Emperor Justinian, scholars produced an analytic compendium of a thousand years' worth of material, enactments, and commentary. Not surprisingly, this *Corpus Iuris Civilis*, as it is now known, contained a great deal of material about slave ownership. However, it does not provide much new insight for our inquiry about ecclesiastical *servi*. The work is a compendium of earlier Roman law, much of which had been included in the *Theodosian Code* that we have mentioned several

---

[104] John Julius Norwich is an acknowledged master in the field of Byzantine studies. His *Short History of Byzantium* (New York 1997) is both scholarly and very readable. Also very approachable is Judith Herrin, *Byzantium: The Surprising Life of a Medieval Empire* (Princeton 2007). On slavery see Youval Rotman's *Byzantine Slavery and the Mediterranean World* (Cambridge, MA 2009).

times. However, there was an additional, later volume known as the *Novellae*, i.e., Justinian's new decrees.[105] And here there are a couple of things that are interesting for our purposes.

Novella 120 was concerned with the alienation of church property. It made clear that alienation of the *res ecclesiae* was forbidden except in specific and limited circumstances, for example for the redemption of captives (120.9–10). Not only does this decree show a good deal of agreement between the eastern and western branches of Christianity on this particular question, it also shows that in the East, Justinian thought that it was proper for an emperor to make regulations concerning the disposition of church property. *Novella* 123 suggests a bit less respect for a layman's property. It said that a *servus* who had been ordained without his master's consent would be considered a free man after a specified period. If his master did not reclaim him in time, all that the former master could hope for was some financial compensation.

Another interesting text, although not specifically about church *servi*, is Justinian's *Novella* 22.7, which says that a Christian marriage continued to be valid even after one spouse had been captured and enslaved.[106] It was not until the eleventh century that in the eastern empire a Christian marriage was required for the union of two servile persons. But, as Rotman pointed out, Justinian's law did provide an opportunity as early as the sixth century for this idea to receive consideration. Although there seems to have been some servile marriage in the West, the idea did not enter the canon law until later.

Justinian's laws were promulgated in Italy in 554. However, as far as I have been able to determine, the imperial enactments of this era seem not to have introduced any changes in the Italians' treatment of ecclesiastical *servi*.

The Lombards

When the Lombard kings issued their laws in the seventh and eighth centuries, they did not directly address ecclesiastical slaves except as part of

---

[105] The modern standard edition of the *Novellae* is the one edited by Rudolf Schoell (Berlin 1963). An English translation can be found online at http://www.uwyo.edu/lawlib/blume-justinian/ajc-edition-2/novels/index.html. A brief history of the *Novellae* can be found in Timothy G. Kearley, "The Creation and Transmission of Justinian's Novels," *Law Library Journal* 102.3 (2010) 377–97. See also Max Conrat, *Die Lex Romana Canonice Compta: Römisches Recht im frühmittelalterlichen Italien* (Amsterdam 1904).

[106] See Rotman, *Byzantine Slavery* 32–33, 141–44 for discussion.

the general property of the church. The political power of church leaders like Gregory I of Rome in the late sixth century was somewhat diminished under the Lombard laws, probably because the bishops were thought to have retained some loyalty toward the Byzantines in Ravenna and in Constantinople.[107] The newly arrived Lombards did not want to grant power to anyone whose loyalty was suspect.[108]

The earliest legal text that we have from the Lombards comes from King Rothair (636–652). He was an Arian Christian, and his edict of 643 made his Christianity very clear. It began: "*In nomine Domini . . .* In the name of the Lord, here begins the law of Rothair."[109] But his new subjects—all Roman Christians—considered him a heretic. The prologue to this rather long and inclusive edict did not mention ecclesiastical leaders at all, only secular judges.

Rothair made it clear that church buildings had a special status in Lombard society. In chapters 35–40, the section devoted to *scandalum*, i.e., disturbing the peace and similar infractions, only *scandalum* perpetrated in the king's palace in the king's presence received a more severe penalty (death) than *scandalum* perpetrated in a church. The magistrate who collected the forty-solidus penalty for *scandalum* in a church was to place the money on the altar "where the offense occurred." *Scandalum* in the city where the king was staying, but not in the king's actual presence, resulted in only a twelve- to twenty-four-solidus penalty, depending on the level of violence involved. There was no ritual prescribed for the healing of the broken peace in the king's city like the symbolic placement of money on the altar after *scandalum* in a church. For any nonecclesial *scandalum*, the money simply went to the fisc. However, the church's special status does not seem to have extended to all situations. Rothair's *Edict* also made it clear that taking sanctuary in a church was not an acceptable alternative for a fugitive slave. While the denial of sanctuary to unfree persons was not unique to Lombard society, it is

---

[107] On this see Calisse, *History of Italian Law* 72–73.

[108] In his eighth-century *History of the Lombards*, Paul the Deacon reported an interesting technique that the Lombards used to consolidate their control: they freed the slaves of those they conquered if the slaves would agree to fight for the Lombards against their former masters. Paulus Diaconus, *Historia Langobardorum* I.12–13 (Latin text archived at documentacatholicaomnia.eu). There is a very nice English translation done by W. D. Foulke: *History of the Lombards* (Philadelphia 1907). A good scholarly consideration of Paul the Deacon can be found in Walter Goffart, *The Narrators of Barbarian History* (Notre Dame, IN 1988).

[109] Lombard royal legislation can be found in *Edictum Langobardorum*, ed. F. Bluhme, MGH, *Leges*, vol. 4 (Hanover 1868) or in English translation as *The Lombard Laws*, trans., K. F. Drew (Philadelphia 1973).

unusual that Rothair called for rather severe penalties to be exacted from a bishop or priest who did not return such a fugitive. After three requests from the runaway's master, a bishop who did not voluntarily return the *servus* in question was to be compelled not only to return the fugitive, but also to provide another similar slave from his own possessions.[110] This provision shows that, unlike church buildings, the clergy did not necessarily receive special treatment. It also confirms that ecclesiastical personnel customarily held slaves.

Lastly, in Rothair's laws numbers 222 and 224 there was a detailed discussion of the various forms of manumission available in mid-seventh-century Lombard society.[111] First was the simple act of manumission, like that commonly found in ancient Rome and in the other post-Roman Germanic kingdoms, that resulted in the *servus* or *ancilla* being relieved of servile status while retaining certain obligations to the former master, including the master's right to inherit from a former *servus* who died without heirs. The burdens did not, however, pass on to later generations. There was also the possibility of a *servus* becoming both free and a "stranger" (*extraneus*) to his former master. This *extraneus* did not retain any obligations to the former master, and if such a person died without heirs, the deceased's estate reverted to the fisc. Such a manumission ceremony sometimes included a fictional sale followed by the old Roman custom of manumission at a crossroads. Or the manumission could be done simply by royal decree. The *extraneus* provision had to be stated explicitly at the time that freedom was given. Alternatively, a lightening of the servile burden could be achieved by making a *servus* a *haldius* (or *aldius*). While the details of what this status entailed are not fully clear, we do know that a *haldius* was somewhere between servile and non-*extraneus* free. Later Lombard texts show that in time, the *haldius* status was expanded to include those who were freed as non-*extraneus*. In Rothair's law there is no mention of *manumission in ecclesia*, although this practice did continue. Given the fact that the Italian bishops were thought to have retained allegiance to the emperor in Constantinople to the detriment of their new Lombard overlords, they did not possess the kind of status in Lombard society that they enjoyed in Gaul and in Visigothic territory. It is not surprising that Rothair would not have emphasized their magisterial power.

---

[110] Rothair, Law 272.

[111] See the discussion of this section in Theodore John Rivers, "*Symbola, manumissio et libertas Langobardorum*: An Interpretation of *Gaida* and *Gisil* in *Edictus Rothari* 224 and Its Relationship to the Concept of Freedom," ZSR. *Germanistische Abteilung* 95 (1978) 57–78.

King Liutprand (712–744) is the other major Lombard figure whose legal legacy is recognized today. He was a Roman Christian, as were most Lombards by his time, and his annual decrees showed the influence of this change—although he was by no means allied with the church hierarchy in the way that Visigothic and Frankish rulers were. The prologue to the laws proclaimed in the first year of Liutprand's reign announced that these were "the laws that have been instituted by this Catholic Christian prince," and Liutprand made it very clear that it was God who had made him king—no mention of bishops.

Liutprand's laws show a greater degree of Roman influence than do the laws of his predecessors. In his proclamation of 717, Liutprand added a variation of the old Roman custom of *manumissio in ecclesia* to the possible ceremonies for giving a *servus* or *ancilla* freedom. In the Lombard version of this ceremony, the owner would first hand over the slave to the king, who then handed the slave to the priest or bishop, who then walked around the altar together with the slave. The former slave was then free, and Liutprand said clearly that neither the freedman nor his children would again be servile.[112] Although in some situations masters might retain their former slaves' *mundium* (guardianship), this was not the case for manumission at the king's hand and for *manumissio in ecclesia*. *Mundium* was assigned a monetary value, and, in effect, it limited the freedom of the former slave. Slaves (and their children) freed by the king or freed in the church would be "without *mundium*"; i.e., they were legally independent of their former master.[113] In an interesting reversal of others' customs for *manumissio in ecclesia*, in 721 Liutprand repeated and clarified that a church ceremony was only for those *servi* or *ancillae* who were to be made *fulfreal*, fully free, and not for those who were to be *haldii*.[114]

Liutprand's laws also show that it was common, and apparently encouraged by the Crown, for people to give slaves to the service of the church. In 727, Liutprand said that if someone gave a female slave, an *ancilla*, to a convent, any subsequent sexual mistreatment of such a woman would incur a greater penalty than mistreatment of an ordinary *ancilla*.[115] Also, the penalties were to be paid to the woman's owner. Although nuns were regularly called *ancillae Dei*, God's slaves, when it came to violation of a nun who was

---

[112] Liutprand, Laws 9 and 10.
[113] Liutprand, Law 10.
[114] Liutprand, Law 23.
[115] Liutprand, Law 95.

a servile woman, she was still considered the property of her human master. Harsher penalties for the violation of nuns were not because of the exalted status of these ecclesiastical personnel themselves, but because of the honor due to God, their ultimate master. Yet the master who had given the woman as a nun still retained the right to collect the damages, even when their magnitude was determined by the woman's services to God. Any respect due to the church or to the clergy was not on account of their own honor, but rather on account of the honor due to God.

Liutprand's 727 proclamation also included a section about the question of when Lombard law or Roman law could or should be used.[116] More than a century after the Lombards had arrived in Italy, the need for such a legal distinction shows how tenuous was the Lombards' control over the territory that they had conquered. The Lombards had not integrated themselves into the ecclesiastical lives of their conquered peoples in Italy in the way that the Franks and Visigoths did in Gaul and in Iberia.

We have seen that in other Germanic kingdoms of this era, the clergy had a somewhat exalted status. For example, in the laws of the Ripuarian Franks, a bishop was valued more highly than anyone else outside the royal family. However, a century after their arrival, the Lombards still did not place any particular value on bishops beyond the limits of their religious duties and their practical value to God. This can be seen quite clearly in a law from 735 that amended the earlier provisions about not granting sanctuary to fugitive slaves with a provision that called for severe penalties for a lord who reclaimed such fugitives with the use of force.[117] The lord's penalty was to be paid to "the guardian of the church building" (*custode ipsius basilicae*)—no mention of that guardian being a "bishop." The Lombards' general lack of acknowledgment of any clerical claims to preferred status can also be seen in Aistulf's laws of 755, where he thought it necessary to declare that business agreements made with a bishop, an abbot, or another "guardian of the church" must actually be honored. Aistulf explicitly included slaves in the kinds of property that were bound by this law.[118]

In summary, the Lombard legal texts show clearly that the Lombard rulers considered themselves to be Christians, chosen by God to rule. But their

---

[116] On this see Brigitte Pohl-Resl, "Legal Practice and Ethnic Identity in Lombard Italy," in *Strategies of Distinction: The Construction of Ethnic Communities, 300–800*, ed. W. Pohl and H. Reimitz (Leiden 1998) 205–219.

[117] Liutprand, Law 143.

[118] Aistulf, Law 16 (VII).

concern was with the honor of God and not that of God's ecclesiastical representatives. Sanctuary was honored: one should not violate God's honor by
violence in his presence. Pious generosity toward the institutional church
was encouraged because the institutional church was the caretaker of God's
earthly property. And *manumissio in ecclesia* was a valid legal procedure.
However, unlike the Roman *manumissio in ecclesia*, where the bishop acted as
the magistrate who presided over the proceedings, in Lombard *manumissio
in ecclesia*, the king was the competent authority. He received the slave first
and then handed him or her over to the bishop for a procession around the
altar, around God's own royal throne. And there was apparently no lasting
bond between the newly freed and the church where that had taken place.

The Visigoths

The Visigoths reigned for a time in southern Gaul and then, after being
displaced by the Franks, they slowly moved into the Iberian Peninsula.[119]
Despite long struggles against the Franks along their northern border, the
Visigoths established the Kingdom of Toledo and held control in much of
what is now Spain until they were conquered by the Arabs in the early eighth
century. King Reccared's conversion from Arian to Roman Christianity in
589 completed the Visigoths' integration into the old Hispano-Roman society, whose religious attitudes had also been influenced by the Byzantine
presence in the southeastern portion of the peninsula in the sixth century.[120]

The seventh-century, often-revised *Lex Visigothorum*, also known as the
Liber Iudiciorum, was the last and most influential of the secular legal texts
from this culture. The text included fragments of an earlier code attributed
to King Euric or to Alaric's 506 CE abbreviation of Roman law.[121] There
are also a number of texts from Visigothic conciliar documents, the majority of which were produced to some extent under the direction, or one
might even say the sponsorship, of the Visigothic kings, who characteristi-
cally kept a close hand on ecclesiastical affairs.[122] A great deal of this material

---

[119] On the conquest of the Visigoths and their resurgence in Iberia, see Wolfram, *Das Reich*
260–78.

[120] On this see Judith Herrin, *The Formation of Christendom* (Princeton 1987) 220–49.

[121] *Leges Visigothorum / Liber Iudiciorum* (hereafter *L. Vis.*), ed. K. Zeumer, MGH, *Leges nationum
Germanicarum*, vol. 1 (Hanover 1902). There is a useful if flawed English translation by S. P. Scott
(Boston 1910) as well. *Codex Eurici*, ed. K. Zeumer, MGH, *Leges nationum Germanicarum*, vol. 1
(Hanover 1902); *Lex Romana Visigothorum*, ed. G. Haenel (Leipzig 1849).

[122] *Concilios Visigóticos e Hispano-Romanos*, ed. José Vives (Barcelona 1963).

dealt with issues involving unfree persons, including the treatment of *servi ecclesiarum*.[123] Among other things, these texts show us that the Visigoths, like the Ostrogoths, demonstrated an exceptionally strong revulsion against servility.[124]

The oldest remaining evidence of Visigothic legal thinking, King Euric's pre-500 CE code, is a reflection of Visigothic society when they were still in southern Gaul. In the few remaining fragments of this text there is clear evidence of a strong Christian presence in the society, including an interesting statement about the inalienability of church property: children of the clergy were not to inherit the *res ecclesiae*.[125] There is also evidence here of the low regard in which slaves were held in Gothic society: Fragment 300 has been reconstructed as saying that someone who had been enslaved who did not take advantage of an opportunity to gain his freedom should remain a slave forever "because it is unfitting that a man should be free who would willingly subject himself to servitude."[126] However, as was the case in other early laws, there was nothing in Euric's code concerning ecclesiastical *servi*.

The *Breviary of Alaric*, or the *Lex Romana Visigothorum*, was, as its title says, a collection of Roman legal texts made for the Visigoths sometime in the early sixth century, probably in southern Gaul as well.[127] There is a reasonable likelihood that Caesarius of Arles had some influence over the contents of this abbreviation of Roman law, "Alaric's Brief." Bruck pointed out that Alaric had this work compiled during the same period that he had Caesarius, newly returned from his brief exile in Bordeaux, convene the Council of Agde.[128] This council produced a great deal of legislation concerning church matters. And Caesarius, a well-educated Gallo-Roman aristocrat, would have had the sort of legal expertise that was required to compile Alaric's *Breviary*. As was

[123] Given the unusually large number of slaves in Visigothic society (see Bonnassie, *From Slavery to Feudalism* 60–130 and Nehlsen, *Sklavenrecht* 161–68), it is understandable that they would have devoted much of their regulatory energies to these questions.

[124] There is a considerable amount of recent and useful scholarly literature about the Visigoths and their laws. See, e.g., Roger Collins, *Visigothic Spain, 409–711* (Oxford 2004), especially 223–46; Wolf Liebeschuetz, "Citizen Status and Law in the Roman Empire and the Visigothic Kingdom," in *Strategies of Distinction* 131–52; P. D. King, *Law and Society in the Visigothic Kingdom* (Cambridge 1972); and Wickham, *Inheritance of Rome* 130–40.

[125] *Codicis Eurici* Fragment 306 and also Fragment 335, which is useful despite the fact that there is too much text missing to be sure of its full meaning.

[126] *Codicis Eurici* Fragment 300, ed. Zeumer 15. This was reconstructed based on *L. Vis.* V.4.10. A. Barbero and M. I. Loring ("The Catholic Visigothic Kingdom," CMH 1) suggested that the Visigoths despised their labor force so greatly that they did not even bother to respect the centuries-old divisions between *servi* and *coloni*, treating them all as slaves.

[127] For a detailed analysis see Max Conrat, *Breviarium Alaricianum: Römisches Recht im fränkischen Reich in Systematischer Darstellung* (Leipzig 1903).

[128] Bruck, "Caesarius of Arles," 1.200–217. Also see Klingshirn, *Caesarius of Arles* 95.

the norm for Roman legal texts of this era, this work did not consider *servi ecclesiarum* separately from other *servi*. However, the traditional Roman provisions for *manumissio in ecclesia* included here, as well as the prohibition of marriage between slaves and free persons and the provision for the degradation of *liberti* (freedmen) who did not follow the conditions set upon their freedom, provided the context from which a number of ecclesiastical canons were later derived. This last, based on the fact that freedom came with certain conditions, usually involving certain obligations on the freed person and his descendants to serve their former master and his descendants, was also found in Frankish law. But, unlike the laws of the Franks, the Visigoths' secular laws did not carry the idea to the extent that those freed *in ecclesia* subsequently were under obligation to that church.[129]

The *Leges Visigothorum*, also known as the *Liber Iudiciorum* (Book of the Judges), was revised at least three times, in 654, 681, and 692. As we saw in the Frankish laws, clergy had a preferred status in Visigothic society, although not as high as the king's status, and they were held to very high standards of personal conduct.[130] Unlike what we saw in Frankish law, there is no indication that there were various levels of unfreedom in Visigothic society. The *Liber Iudiciorum* devoted an entire title to ecclesiastical affairs. In Book V (*Concerning Transactions*), Title 1, we find several provisions about financial transactions that made the inalienability of church property very clear. Some versions of the *Liber Iudiciorum* included a circa 672 decree of King Wamba that dealt directly with *servi ecclesiarum*.[131] The text's intention was to forbid marriage between freeborn persons and former *servi ecclesiarum* who continued to retain obligations to their church patron. Before this decree, the children of such a forbidden pairing would have become *servi ecclesiarum* themselves, but Wamba said that if the couple continued to cohabit even after having been scourged, their children would become slaves of the Crown. This was a very clever move on Wamba's part, finding a way to pry loose some ecclesiastical property to his own benefit. And even if this was mostly wishful thinking, it illustrates the amount of power that the Crown exerted in ecclesiastical affairs. However, for our purposes it is important because the text

---

[129] *Lex Romana Visigothorum* VI.

[130] *L. Vis.* III.iv.18.

[131] This text, cited as *L. Vis.* V.1.7, was included in Scott's translation and is discussed in King, *Law and Society* 67–68 n. 59. However, it was not included in the MGH edition of the *L. Vis.*, as edited by K. Zeumer, a circumstance that certainly raises questions about the authenticity of this provision.

states very clearly that some *servi ecclesiarum* remained under the dominion of the church after they had been manumitted and some did not.

It is, however, in the canonical documents that we find the vast majority of Visigothic texts concerned with ecclesiastical dominion over unfree persons. From the Visigothic secular law, we learn little about the situation of *servi ecclesiarum* except that they received their share of the general revulsion directed by the Goths toward those in servitude. The Visigothic laws also preserved the inalienability of church property, explaining this in much more detail than we found in the Frankish secular law.

Canon Law

Visigothic Ecclesiastical Law

There were several councils held by the church in territory occupied by the Visigoths, including the 506 Council of Agde, over which Caesarius of Arles presided.[132] Although Agde is geographically in Gaul, at that time the region was under Visigothic control, and the council proceedings show strong Visigothic influence. Canon 7 of this council, according to its heading in a later collection, was concerned with "Church property: how it is to be held by the bishops and how *servi ecclesiae* can be set free by a bishop."[133] In short, this canon said that church property could not be alienated by the bishop or other clergy except in cases of grave necessity, and then only with the approval of two or three neighboring bishops. This was in accord with Caesarius's position as discussed earlier. The canon also stated that if any deserving *servi ecclesiae* were given their liberty by the bishop, they had to be paid for properly. After such a former church *servus* died, any property that he had received from the church at the time of his manumission, in excess of stated minimums, had to be returned to the church from which he had been freed.[134] The inalienability of church property was reinforced by canon

---

[132] *Concilia Galliae A.314–A.506*, ed. C. Munier (Turnholt 1963).

[133] This heading was added to the canon from 506, when it was included in a collection of ecclesiastical canons that was compiled in the seventh century by Isidore of Seville, *La Coleccion Canonica Hispana*, vol. 4, *Concilios Gallos, Concilios Hispanos Primira Parte*, ed. G. Martinez Díez and F. Rodriguez (Madrid 1984). Also see Lotte Kéry, *Canonical Collections in the Early Middle Ages (ca. 400–1140)* (HMCL 1) 60–67. A note about vocabulary: The phrase *servi/ancillae ecclesiae* (slaves of the church or ecclesiastical slaves) was commonly used in the early medieval period. However, in the later texts, the canonists preferred the term *servi ecclesiarum* (slaves of the churches).

[134] *Concilia Galliae A.314–A.506*, 195–96.

48, which called for the bishop's own property to be kept separate from the *res ecclesiae*, and canon 33, which stated explicitly that the bishop's family was not to inherit anything that belonged to the church. A number of canons from Agde were concerned with clerical sexual misbehavior. Among the most interesting of these are canon 11, "Slave women or freedwomen are to be removed from the storerooms or from private duties and likewise from any accommodations where a clergyman is staying"; and canon 28, requiring that a monastery's slave girls be kept well away from the monks.[135] From canon 39, which addressed clerical marital relations, we learn that the concern was not merely a question of preventing illicit sexual relations, but also an issue of ritual purity. This canon stated that clergy should not have relations with their wives or even sing love songs, lest the sacred mysteries be "polluted [by contact with] indecent spectacles or words."[136]

The Visigothic church in what is now Spain held a number of general councils, usually under at least the nominal sponsorship of the king, as well as quite a few synods of regional importance. There were also at least eight councils held before the conversion of the Visigoths from Arian to Roman Christianity, but the proceedings of these earliest councils do not yield much information for our purposes.[137] But four of the major councils or synods of the Catholic Visigothic kingdom—III Toledo (589), I Seville (590), IV Toledo (633) and IX Toledo (655)—provided more than two dozen canons that detailed the special position of *servi*, *ancillae*, and *liberti ecclesiae*. Relevant to our topic, there were an additional dozen or so canons from the remaining synods as well as several passages in Isidore of Seville's *Regula monachorum*.[138] The texts about *servi ecclesiae* addressed the same two major issues we found in the canons from the Council of Agde. First, maintaining the resources of the church: it was unlawful to alienate any church property. The second issue was upholding the authority of the clergy, largely through the prohibition of behavior that would have been likely to cause scandal and the concomitant loss of respect that would have weakened clerical authority.

By far, the issue that seems to have caused the greatest concern to the Visigothic church was the preservation of ecclesiastical resources. The Third Council of Toledo (589) was convened to sort out how the newly converted

[135] *Concilia Galliae A.314–A.506*, 200, 205.
[136] *Concilia Galliae A.314–A.506*, 209–10.
[137] For a discussion of these councils see Rachel L. Stocking, *Bishops, Councils, and Consensus in the Visigothic Kingdom, 589–633* (Ann Arbor 2000), especially 15–16.
[138] Isidore of Seville, *Regula monachorum*, PL 83.867–94.

Visigothic King Reccared and the Orthodox bishops could mutually uphold one another's authority. Reccared, who had been advised by Gregory I,
bishop of Rome, to look toward the biblical King David as a model of good
kingship, seems to have taken seriously his role in coordinating the smooth
function of the church as well as of the state.[139] And canon 3, referring to
"ancient canonical tradition"—perhaps the Council of Agde just discussed—
said explicitly that "no bishop has the right to alienate the *res ecclesiae*" except
in cases of grave necessity.[140] Just as in the ancient world, in Visigothic Iberia
servi and *ancillae* continued to be a normal part of one's property. Thus, unfree persons under ecclesiastical *dominium* could not be set free because to
do so would have been to liberate (alienate) church property.

On the other hand, manumission had long been considered a pious act.
There was something inherently unsatisfactory in a state of affairs where everyone except the "men of God" were in a position to perform such a virtuous
act. Isidore of Seville's circa 600 CE *Monastic Rules* explained that the reason
that clergy could not free the *servi ecclesiae* was that they were not the actual
owners.[141] Since monks and other clergy were often referred to as God's *servi*,
the church property that was available for their use would have been akin to
a Roman slave's *peculium*. Although a slave would have had relatively unfet-
tered use of such resources, he was not generally allowed to alienate them
without the master's consent since the *peculium*, as well as the slave, were really the property of the master.[142] Analogously, the resources of ecclesiastical
institutions were the property of God and could not be alienated by those
who served him.

Along with their reiteration of the prohibition against alienating church
property, the bishops of III Toledo managed to provide a loophole that permitted a bishop, with the agreement of his peers, to manumit *servi ecclesiae*
who wished to be ordained or to enter the local monastery. The bishops said
in canon 4 that, since the *res ecclesiae* in question (the former *servus*) would
be given back to the local church, such transactions would actually not be to
the detriment of the church. However, the bishops declared in canon 6 that
any *liberti ecclesiae*, former *servi* who had been manumitted by the bishop,
and their progeny could not "vanish from the patronage of the church"
in any way. This ensured that former *servi ecclesiae* and their descendants

---

[139] For more about this see Peter Sarris, *Empires of Faith* (Oxford 2011) 326–29.
[140] This sentiment was echoed at almost every council that followed.
[141] Isidore of Seville, *Regula monachorum* 19.4, PL 83.889.
[142] See W. W. Buckland, *The Roman Law of Slavery* (Cambridge 1908) 201–5.

would continue to be of economic benefit to the church in perpetuity. Since the former owner, God (through the church), could not die, the relationship would never be terminated. In 638, VI Toledo canon 9 called for the ecclesiastical *liberti* to make a formal, written profession of their dependent status every time a new bishop was installed. The details of this arrangement between a church and its freedmen were not spelled out in full by the bishops at Toledo in 589. But they were clarified and expanded upon many times over the next century in the Visigothic kingdom as they also were in Francia.[143] The Fourth Council of Toledo in 633 said that *servi ecclesiae* could be fully freed contingent upon the payment of compensation to the church out of the bishop's own property, but this seems to have occurred infrequently.[144] Former *servi ecclesiae* (or their progeny) who tried to escape from ecclesiastical control were to be returned to full servitude. This principle endured for many centuries, and a number of these Visigothic canons, along with those from Frankish synods, were included in Gratian of Bologna's twelfth-century *Decretum*, whence they were able to exert an even wider influence when this legal treatise spread throughout western Christendom.

The second issue of interest for our inquiry that was discussed in these Visigothic councils and synods was the preservation of clerical authority by trying to ensure that the clergy would not offer grounds for scandal, especially sexual scandal. The bishops at III Toledo said merely that clergy should be faithful to their wives and must avoid any association with questionable women.[145] But, apparently this cautionary canon was not heeded because the next year (590), I Seville said that such women would be removed from a cleric's household, and in 633, IV Toledo called for the woman to be sold into slavery while the guilty cleric was obliged to do penance.[146] Then in 655, IX Toledo, lamenting the rampant clerical incontinence, called for the *children* "born of such pollution" to be condemned to slavery.[147]

This scandal question is of interest for our purposes for two reasons. From the wording of the canons it seems that the woman involved in an

---

[143] I Seville, c.1; II Seville, c.8; IV Toledo, c.67–71; VI Toledo, c.9–10; IX Toledo, c.11–16; X Toledo; Mérida, c.20–21; and III Zaragoza, c.4. For a discussion of this question see Dietrich Claude, "Freedmen in the Visigothic Kingdom," *Visigothic Spain: New Approaches*, ed. E. James (Oxford 1980) 159–88.

[144] IV Toledo, c.69.

[145] Canon 5.

[146] I Seville, c.3; IV Toledo, c.43.

[147] Canon 10. The early Visigoths were also concerned with mixed marriages between Goths and Romans. See Wolf Liebeschuetz, "Citizen Status and Law in the Roman Empire and the Visigothic Kingdom," in *Strategies of Distinction* 131–52.

illicit relationship with a cleric was often his own *ancilla*. It should then come as no surprise that harsh punishment of the woman did not put a stop to the problem. Punishing her would not necessarily have resulted in her master no longer ordering her to satisfy his desires. However, the enslavement of any offspring as the punishment for such an illicit union, irrespective of the mother's legal status, seems to have been somewhat of a deterrent. After this canon was proclaimed in 655, this issue received less attention in the conciliar records. Presumably, no father would want to see his children, legitimate or not, taken into slavery.

A couple of additional examples will serve to provide further illustrations of the curious nature of the Visigothic ecclesiastical mind when it came to their unfree dependents. In 675, XI Toledo forbade harsh punishments for ecclesiastical *servi*, such as the amputation of a limb.[148] This often-cited canon causes the modern mind to wonder what could have been happening that made it necessary for the bishops of the church to have to tell their clergy that such behavior was not acceptable. Interestingly, the reason given was not about cruelty, but rather that clergy were not to engage in bloodshed. Another frequently quoted passage is from the records of XVI Toledo (693), which explained that a "poor church" could be defined as one that had fewer than ten slaves. This certainly suggests that the circa 700 CE Iberian clerical household continued to retain the servile complement of the old Roman villa society, or at least the ideal of such a household.

The limited data available about the issue of *servi ecclesiarum* in the Visigothic kingdom precludes our making any comprehensive conclusive statements. However, we can begin to piece together some ideas about the Visigothic clergy and their *servi*. First, there were a number of similarities with the ancient Roman customs: the Visigothic church had quite a number of *servi*, and some of the language in both secular and canonical texts, along with the apparent tendencies toward mistreatment, suggests that these *servi* were held in great contempt. Second, the Visigothic canonical obsession with keeping clergy under control and with preserving ecclesiastical wealth suggests that the ecclesiastical authorities had little confidence in the clergy's ability—or willingness—to preserve the resources and reputation of the church.

---

[148] Canon 6.

These Visigothic texts describe a world unlike that of the church in Francia, where people seem to have been more concerned with the proper attribution and use of authority.

Frankish Church Councils

As we saw in Visigothic society, the Merovingian kings were eager to give the appearance of ecclesiastical cooperation to aid them in establishing the lawfulness of their reigns.[149] Thus when King Clovis and the Gallo-Roman bishops met at Orleans in 511, they reached a broad and fairly comprehensive agreement that both sides should respect the ancient principles.[150] Of interest to our inquiry, this agreement confirmed the practice of sanctuary (canons 1 and 3), the permanence of gifts bestowed upon the church (canon 15), and the proper conduct of clergy with women (canon 29). There were, however, no provisions that particularly concerned *servi ecclesiarum*, except as a part of the *res ecclesiae* in general. This omnibus agreement was reiterated and refined frequently during the course of Merovingian history. After a new treaty or when a new ruler came to power, both ecclesiastical and royal proclamations were issued.[151] The ecclesiastical canons were the church's way of agreeing to the new order, just as the royal decrees were a statement of the same agreement made by the other side. In this society, where a written text was really only a confirmation of a spoken declaration made by one person to another, the mutuality of these legal texts mirrors the back and forth of the negotiations that took place, even when these negotiations said merely that both parties would continue to uphold previously established customs. On some issues however, just as we saw with the problem of incontinence among Visigothic clergy, gradual refinement of the legal material continued until a satisfactory solution had been achieved.[152]

[149] On this question, see Moore, *Sacred Kingdom*, especially 122–60. Also see Gregory I. Halfond, *Archaeology of Frankish Church Councils, AD 511–768* (Leiden 2010).

[150] *Concilia Galliae A.511—A.695.* Later conciliar decrees can be found in *Concilia Aevi Merovingici.* Royal proclamations can be found in *Capitularia regum Francorum 1,* ed. Alfred Boretius, MGH, *Legum,* vol. 2 (Hanover 1883).

[151] For example, the councils held 538 at Orleans with Childebert; 573 at Paris with Guntram and Sigebert, the sons of Chlothar I; 614 at Paris with Chlothar II; at Bordeaux in the mid-seventh century with Childeric II; and nearby in the Burgundian kingdom with Sigismund in 517 at Epona. For more on these councils see, e.g., Odette Pontal, *Die Synoden im Merowingerreich* (Paderborn 1986) and Herrin, *The Formation of Christendom,* especially 90–127.

[152] It could also be that they stopped talking about it because they just gave up on trying to fix the problem.

Along with pastoral and sacramental questions, the main concerns of the Frankish councils were the social order and the maintenance of a stable social hierarchy, as in their secular law codes. And, like the Visigothic church, the regulatory concerns of the Frankish church revolved around two major issues: the retention of ecclesiastical property and the behavior of the clergy. However, the tone and direction of the laws make it clear that the Frankish approach was conceived mostly as an attempt to enforce the behavior that was proper for a person's social rank. Slaves' behavior was more constricted because that was fitting for their station, and church *servi* had to be mindful of the special relationship to God that arose from their association with holy things. However, the language chosen for the various regulations concerned with servile behavior did not convey contempt for the unfree in the manner of the Visigothic texts. At the other end of the scale, the clergy, who enjoyed a relatively high rank, had to be careful not to do anything improper for a person of such exalted status. Sexual misconduct on the part of the clergy was, of course, forbidden: many of the Frankish councils repeated the provisions of 511 that clergy were not to associate with inappropriate women. However, the canons of the Frankish church did not mention enslavement of clerical concubines or offspring: the worst-case scenario was that if a child were born to such a union, a high-ranking cleric would be demoted.[153] In Francia, unlike in the Visigothic kingdom, the burden of sexual misconduct was on the sinful cleric himself, as he was generally the one who had misbehaved.

Church property, on the other hand, was another matter. The Franks made it very clear that slaves remained slaves, even when their master was the church. An unusual canon from the synod held in Yenne in 517, upholding the need to respect status, said that the reason slaves of a monastery could not be sold was that it was not right for monks to be doing hard agricultural work when slaves were available to release the monks from these difficult tasks.[154] Also, as we have seen elsewhere, permanent obligations to the church were the inherited burden of the progeny of ecclesiastical *liberti*. The 541 Council of Orleans, during the reign of Childebert, said that if a bishop did make church *servi* free, they would remain free but would not be free of obligations to the church (canon 9). However, the council also made it clear that it was unbecoming the status of ecclesiastical personnel to benefit from

---

[153] Council of Macon (581), c.11; Council of Laon (583), c.1.

[154] C. Epaonense, c.8. Also see Patrick Geary, *Before France and Germany: The Creation and Transformation of the Merovingian World* (Oxford 1988) 96–97.

the suffering of newly captured slaves (canon 23).[155] The old dividing line between those who were already slaves and those in transition to the slave state was still in effect. While clergy were to refrain from making the situation of captives any worse, once someone had become an ecclesiastical slave, complete freedom from the power of the church would not ever be possible.

In 549 the bishops gathered at Orleans made a number of pronouncements that seem to have been intended to shed light on the boundaries between secular and church law.[156] Some of these canons are of interest to our study. The prohibition of contact between clergy and inappropriate women was reiterated by canon 3; and canons 13, 14, and 15 detailed the inalienability of church property. Canon 7 raised an issue that we have not yet seen in ecclesiastical law, but that echoes some of the provisions of the Frankish secular law that were outlined earlier. This canon about the efficacy and permanence of *manumissio in ecclesia* pointed out that it would be especially impious to violate these principles given that such a manumission had been effected in the sight of God. And, along with canon 23 from the 541 council, it expressed the Frankish bishops' belief that certain behaviors were not seemly in those associated with the church.

These standards were reiterated frequently in the canons from synods that met in Gaul during the remainder of the sixth and seventh centuries, major concerns continuing to be the nonalienation of church property and the proper sexual conduct of the clergy. In addition, although the church upheld a slave owner's property rights, that did not mean that the church condoned cruel treatment of one's *servi*. Gregory, a sixth-century bishop of Tours, recorded in his *History of the Franks* the story of a Frankish lord named Rauching as a cautionary tale about mistreating one's slaves. It seems that two of his slaves fell in love and were married in a local church, where they remained, seeking protection from their master. Rauching demanded their return, and the priest complied as required by law, but only on the condition that their master would not separate them. Rauching swore that he would not do so and the slaves were returned. Then Rauching immediately ordered them buried in each other's arms—alive. A rescue attempt was able to save only the groom. Gregory's judgment of Rauching, a man whose "savage brutality went far beyond the bounds of human cruelty and folly," was that his brutal murder sometime later at the hands of King Childebert's men was well

---

[155] See the discussion in Nehlsen *Sklavnrecht* 263–64 n. 1.
[156] *Concilia Galliae A.511–A.695.*

deserved.[157] This story also documents that unfree persons could be married in a church ceremony, although the canon law had apparently not yet caught up with the custom.

Thus, in general it can be said that the Frankish canons called for the same basic principles of church order as did the canons of the Visigothic church but did so with gentler language that seems to reflect customs that were somewhat less harsh than those faced by ecclesiastical *servi* in the early medieval Gothic kingdoms. While the Franks were to some extent obsessed with the proper ranking of all members of society and with the exact penalties for all sorts of offenses, the Visigothic law, especially their canon law, seems to have been less concerned with the details of the overall social hierarchy than with the harsh enforcement of the regulations for a few particularly offensive infractions and with the severe repression of certain groups, especially the unfree.

Summary

One cannot help but wonder at these differences in how the Lombards, the Franks, and the Visigoths interpreted and preserved the tradition of Roman law that they had inherited.[158] In contrast to the Visigothic and Frankish societies, where kings and church councils often issued complementary legal decrees, the Lombard royal legal traditions were not intimately connected with the ecclesiastical legislation, and the Lombards remained adversarial toward the bishops of their conquered peoples. These societies all seem to have had large numbers of slaves. Were the differences in their various legal texts simply cultural manifestations of the accidents of geography? Were they a reflection of how deeply a given group had engaged with and absorbed the norms of late antique Roman society? Were they deeply rooted in the ancient origins of the various northern peoples? It is hard to say—one can only speculate. And such speculation is made more difficult when one considers the Franks' long, slow acquisition of control over areas in southern Gaul that had previously been held by the Visigoths.

---

[157] *Historia Francorum* 5.3 and 9.9.
[158] An interesting discussion of this question can be found in Ian Wood, "The Code in Merovingian Gaul," in *The Theodosian Code*, ed. J. Harries and I. Wood (Ithaca 1993) 161–77. Also see Ubl, *Sinnstiftungen eines Rechtsbuchs* 37–66.

What is quite clear from this examination of the early medieval Germanic kingdoms' secular and ecclesiastical laws is that slavery was an unremarkable and nearly universal feature of these societies. Further, we have seen that, despite their regional differences, in a given region the institutions and personnel of the Christian church did not differ much from their lay neighbors in the way they exercised *dominium* over their servile dependents. But one provision found in the laws of both Francia and the Visigothic kingdom did set the *servi ecclesiarum* apart from their fellow *servi* who had lay masters. Since ecclesiastical property could never be alienated, in most cases manumission did not completely sever the ties of obligation between ecclesiastical *servi* and their former masters. Also, *servi* who received their freedom— from lay as well as from ecclesiastical masters—in a church ceremony usually found themselves bound by nonservile obligations to the church where the ceremony had taken place. And the weight of this service was inherited by their descendants. Although the burden of these ties extended in both directions, often providing needed protection for those under ecclesiastical hegemony, as long as such burdens remained, church *servi* could never really achieve complete freedom. Whatever the situation of ecclesiastical servile dependents became throughout the rest of the early medieval period, this did not change. As we shall see in subsequent chapters, canons from this period were incorporated into ecclesiastical legal collections for many centuries.

6

Carolingians and Ecclesiastical Servitude

Hincmar of Reims and Monastic Estates

Hincmar was the archbishop of Reims, a city located about eighty miles northeast of Paris, from 845 to 882.[1] Born to a minor noble Frankish family in around 806, he began his ecclesiastical career as a monk of Saint-Denis, near Paris, becoming abbot in 835. Hincmar was also a protégé of Charlemagne's son, Emperor Louis "the Pious," and then of his son, King Charles the Bald. As archbishop of Reims, Hincmar became not only one of the most important churchmen in the West Frankish kingdom, but also a major royal counselor. When Hincmar succeeded to the see of Reims, it was a time of great political turmoil, and there was controversy about the legitimacy of his episcopate because of charges that Hincmar's predecessor had been unjustly deposed. The fact that these uncertainties continued to dog him for many years may well help to explain the often harsh tone of his writings. Archbishop Hincmar was also at the same time the abbot of the nearby monastery of Saint-Remi. In both capacities, as abbot and as archbishop, Hincmar, with the help of his *oeconomus*, or economic administrator, was required to manage considerable ecclesiastical property. This included not only the vast agricultural estates that he found upon his accession to office, but also the many church holdings lost during the years of civil strife that he was able to restore to ecclesiastical hands.

In this chapter we continue the story of how the church regulated ecclesiastical slavery, especially in what is now France and Germany. The Merovingian Franks, whom we met in the last chapter, continued to enjoy nominal kingship over Gaul in the early eighth century. But in 741 things began to change when Pepin III (Pepin the Short) took office as the "Mayor of

---

[1] This biographical information has been compiled from several excellent studies of Hincmar, his life and times: Martina Stratmann, *Hinkmar von Reims als Verwalter von Bistum und Kirchenprovinz* (Sigmaringen 1991); Jean Devisse, *Hincmar: Archevêque de Reims 845–882*, 3 vols. (Geneva 1975–76) and his *Hincmar et la loi* (Dakar 1962); and Heinrich Schrörs, *Hinkmar: Erzbischof von Reims* (Freiburg 1884).

The Slaves of the Churches. Mary E. Sommar, Oxford University Press (2020). © Oxford University Press.
DOI: 10.1093/oso/9780190073268.001.0001

the Palace." This title referred to a job that was part chief of staff and part general of the armies. Pepin had big ambitions. After ensuring that his brothers could not provide competition, Pepin, according to legend, got papal support by asking whether it was the royal bloodline or the wielding of power that made a man a king. And the legend goes on to say that Pope Zacharias answered in Pepin's favor.[2] In 751 Pepin usurped the throne, imprisoning the last Merovingian, King Chilperic III, in a monastery. In 754 Pepin and his two sons, Charles and Carloman, were anointed by Pope Stephen II as the ruling family in Francia, the land of the Franks. The new "Carolingian" dynasty was named for Pepin's father, Charles Martel, who had been the Mayor of the Palace before his son. When Pepin died in 768, his throne was shared by his two sons. But Carloman's untimely—and suspicious—death in 771 left the entire kingdom to Charles, who has been remembered in history as Charlemagne, Charles the Great. Charlemagne spent a large part of his reign expanding the area of Carolingian hegemony, gradually absorbing territory from the Mediterranean to the Baltic seas and from the Atlantic Ocean to the Slavic border territories in the East. But he did not rest on his conquests. Charlemagne's program of administrative and ecclesiastical reforms established a flourishing culture supported by a thriving economy. The mutually beneficial alliance between the Frankish ruling house and the bishop of Rome helped the church gain effective control over considerable territory in central Italy, known as the Papal States, in addition to their many agricultural holdings elsewhere. At the same time, papal support for Pepin and his successors increased the legitimacy and prestige of the Carolingians' reign. Charlemagne continued many of his father's policies with regard to the Roman church. While Charlemagne's legal pronouncements superseded the old Germanic laws, as we shall see, some of the old customs lingered.

In December 800, Charlemagne was given an imperial crown by Pope Leo III. This was theoretically the re-establishment of the old Roman Empire in the West, and for years Charlemagne strove to achieve recognition of his status from the Byzantine or Eastern Roman Empire in Constantinople. The Carolingian "Holy Roman Empire," as historians have called it, extended to limits that were matched only by the conquests of Napoleon Bonaparte and Adolf Hitler a thousand years later. Although the Carolingian dynasty

---

[2] *Royal Frankish Annals* 749 (*Annales Regni Francorum*), ed. G. H. Pertz and F. Kurze, MGH, *Scriptores rerum Germanicarum* (Hanover 1895), translated as *Carolingian Chronicles* by B. W. Scholz (Ann Arbor 1970).

collapsed around the year 900, the idea of the Holy Roman Empire was renewed under German leadership in the new millennium and lasted for a very long time.[3]

Hincmar had many roles to fill, bishop, abbot, royal adviser, and champion of the church, but it is from his administration of the many agricultural properties in his care that we can learn about the position of ecclesiastical *servi* in Carolingian Europe. At this time the majority of the agricultural workers on ecclesiastical and lay estates were not free, or at least not fully free. However, some of the burdens of their daily circumstances seem to have occasionally been a bit easier than had usually been the case in earlier centuries. Hincmar seems to have viewed himself as the successor to the fourth-century bishops, whose *servi* and *mancipia* were slaves like those of any Roman. We can see this in an argument Hincmar directed against Charles the Bald, king of West Francia. Hincmar quoted from a Roman law issued by Emperor Constantius saying that "no one could impose obligations on ecclesiastical estates or *mancipia*."[4] And Hincmar's correspondence referred to these people in a way that clearly shows that he viewed them as property rather than as persons. As we saw in the story about Ignatius of Antioch's letter to Polycarp, interesting evidence about someone's real attitude toward a given subject can often be found when that person is talking about something completely different and their real opinions on, e.g., slavery, slip in unconsciously. We shall see from a close reading of letters, testaments, and other documents from the Carolingian era that many agricultural workers who lived on the land, whatever they were called, were frequently regarded as chattel and treated no differently than were the slaves we saw in earlier periods.

In 852, as western Europe was reeling from the civil wars and Scandinavian incursions that marked the beginning of the collapse of Charlemagne's

---

[3] A firsthand account of Charlemagne's life can be found in the rather hagiographical *Life* written by Einhard, a Carolingian courtier: Einhardus, *Vita Caroli Magni*, ed. O. Holder-Egger, MGH, *Scriptores rerum Germanicarum in usum scholarum separatim editi* (Hanover 1911). This is available in a number of modern translations as well. Some helpful, recent scholarly literature about the Carolingians includes Rosamond McKitterick, *Charlemagne: The Formation of a European Identity* (Cambridge 2008); Peter Sarris, *Empires of Faith: The Fall of Rome to the Rise of Islam, 500–700* (Oxford 2011); *The Long Morning of Medieval Europe*, ed. J. R. Davis and M. McCormick (Burlington, VT 2008); Janet Nelson, *The Frankish World* (London 1996); and also the collected essays in CMH 2.

[4] *Expositiones Hincmari Rhemensis ad Carolum Regem: Pro Ecclesiae Libertatum Defensione* 1, PL 125.1038. Simon Corcoran pointed out that Hincmar updated Constantius's version that said "on the clergy and their *mancipia*" by replacing "clergy" with "ecclesiastical estates." "Hincmar and His Roman Legal Sources," in *Hincmar of Rheims: Life and Work*, ed. R. Stone and C. West (Manchester 2016) 129–55, here 143–44. This makes the point even more strongly that these *mancipia* were owned by the church; they were part of the *res ecclesiae* and were not family retainers.

empire, Archbishop Hincmar wrote a letter to Wulfing, a minister of Emperor Lothar, about a revenue dispute between Lothar and his brother, King Charles the Bald. The dispute concerned the *census* payments (payments due from certain workers) for the Villa Douzy, an estate belonging to the monastery of Saint-Remi.[5] Hincmar, as abbot, was responsible for all of the Saint-Remi holdings, and he was concerned that further delay in resolving the matter might cause "the villa to fall into ruin and revert to allods [smallholds] and the ecclesiastical *mancipia* would be scattered around as *servi* and *ancillae*, just as has happened with much of the *res* and *mancipia* of this church."[6]

This passage is very helpful. While it is clear that the archbishop/abbot did not want this to happen, his words evidenced no compassion for any of the poor souls who would be "scattered around." Hincmar compared the Douzy *mancipia* to the *res* (things, possessions) as well as the *mancipia* of other church estates, and he expressed concern only about the property losses. His choice of the word *dispergo* (scatter or disperse) to describe the disposition of these *mancipia* indicates that little thought would be given to their relocation. We have no reason to assume that Hincmar mistreated his servile dependents, but this letter seems to make it clear that he did think of them in very much the same way as had the owners of the great Roman estates. *Mancipia* were anonymous sources of manpower, to be deployed to maximum advantage.

A few years earlier, Hincmar had also written to Lady Irminsinde about a property dispute involving one of his deacons, who had previously been in her service. This letter, whose contents were preserved in Flodoard's *History of Reims*, spoke of the difference between a "*servus . . .* who did not have liberty" and a "*colonus ecclesiasticus* who is not a *servus* but has been made legally free."[7] Hincmar's distinction between the two statuses shows clearly that he was aware of the differences between unfree peasants and those who were technically free even though they had obligations to their lords.[8] But we

---

[5] According to Flodoard (3.20), it was Saint Remigius himself who had received this property from King Chlodovald in the sixth century. Flodoard of Reims, *Historia Remensis Ecclesiae*, ed. M. Stratmann, MGH, *Scriptores*, vol. 36 (Hanover 1998).

[6] *Die Briefe des Erzbischofs Hinkmar von Reims*, vol. 1, ed. E. Perels, MGH, *Epistolae*, vol. 8.1 (Munich 1985) #63. Also found in Flodoard, *Historia Remensis Ecclesiae* III.26 (p. 332).

[7] The discussion is about a deacon who had been freed upon ordination. Flodoard, *Historia Remensis Ecclesiae* III.27. On the accuracy of Flodoard's tenth-century account see Walter Goffart, "From Roman Taxation to Mediaeval Seigneurie: Three Notes (Part II) 3. Flodoard and the Frankish Polyptichs," *Speculum* 47 (1972) 165–87.

[8] Throughout his correspondence, Archbishop Hincmar was customarily very careful about his choice of words. He usually used words based on the root *servare* to refer to people who were in the "service" of God, i.e., the clergy and those in monastic profession, and preferred the word *mancipium* when referring to unfree workers in households on the great estates, both those in the possession of

cannot read too much into this. Hincmar's interests lay in his being able to retain the services of the deacon whose freedom was in question, not in the deacon's personal liberty. While ordination may have occasioned the dissolution of the deacon's servile bond to Irminsinde, it created a new bond of service to the church.

Extensive records of the agricultural workers resident on the estates of the monastery of Saint-Remi in the ninth and tenth centuries have been preserved.[9] These records, known as the Reims polyptichs, give us a picture of a social order in transition. Barbier discovered marginal annotations in one polyptich that called attention to the case of slaves at Cortisols, an estate belonging to Saint-Remi, who had been living and behaving as though they were free.[10] These annotations seem to have been made by Hincmar himself and highlight the forty-two "*servi* and *ancillae* recently repressed" by a legal proceeding intended to re-establish the rights of their lord. If, indeed, these were Hincmar's notations, they constitute fairly strong evidence for his views on ecclesiastical servitude.

But the question remains: was Hincmar's attitude typical? Hypotheses about the land management policies followed by the Carolingian church have ranged from a reactionary adherence to the system used in ancient Rome, to an exemplary and progressive application of Christian teachings to the treatment of and the possibilities for freedom of church *servi*.[11] Whatever the case, it is impossible to ignore the fact that the institutional church was by far the largest landholder in Carolingian Europe. Scholars have generally accepted the estimate that about one-third of the arable land in Europe at that time was owned by ecclesiastical persons or institutions.[12] The majority of the church records that have been preserved are those dealing with other matters, theological, liturgical, or political, but there are many documents

---

the church of Reims and those belonging to others, noble or common, in the Carolingian Empire. Since we have the text of this letter only secondhand, it is only fair to note that the use here of *servi* or *mancipia* might well reflect Flodoard's choices, not Hincmar's.

[9] *Le polyptyque et les listes de cens de l'Abbaye de Saint-Remi de Reims (IXe-Xe siècles)*, ed. J.-P. Devroey (Reims 1984).

[10] Josiane Barbier, "'The Praetor Does Concern Himself with Trifles': Hincmar, the Polyptichs of St-Remi and the Slaves of Courtisols," in Stone and West, *Hincmar of Rheims* 211–27.

[11] See, for example, Pierre Boucaud, "Tous libres devant Dieu: Société carolingienne, église et esclavage d'apres l'exégèse de Claude de Turin," *Revue de l'histoire des religions* 228 (2011) 349–87; as well as the earlier works of Hartmut Hoffmann, "Kirche und Sklaverei im frühen Mittelalter," *Deutsches Archiv für Erforschung des Mittelalters* 42 (1986) 1–24 and David Herlihy, "Church Property on the European Continent, 701–1200," *Speculum* 36 (1961) 81–105.

[12] See, e.g., Herlihy, "Church Property"; and Julia M. H. Smith, "Religion and Lay Society," CMH 2.654–78.

that deal with property issues, including transfers from lay to ecclesiastical ownership or with conflicts between church and lay property owners.

In the Reims polyptichs it is clear that three main variables determined the agricultural workers' situation: the status (free or servile) of the land they worked; the status (free or unfree) of the workers themselves; and the nature of the "services" due the lord, in labor, in kind, or in money payments. Free persons often worked on "servile" plots of land and servile workers on "free" plots.[13] While, generally, the less servile the conditions, the less intrusive the burden of services due (in labor or in kind), there seems to have been no set system for determining this. Concerning the number of people who were in servile or quasi-servile relationships with the monastery of Saint-Remi, we can only estimate, since the records do not follow any standard pattern. Devroey calculated that circa 848, the population of Viel-Saint-Remi was 1,202 persons.[14] Roughly half of these were servile and half free, and their relationship to the land varied from near-proprietary status to that of the casual day laborer. And since Viel was only one of the monastery's more than two dozen estates, we can safely say that the monastery of Saint-Remi controlled thousands of workers, probably half of whom were not free.

The data shows that the situation of the laboring population was even more complex than we could see in the archbishop's correspondence. And this complexity shows up in similar records from other areas in the Carolingian realms. Yoshiki Morimoto's analysis of the polyptichs of the monastery of Prüm, in modern Germany, suggests that the labor services there varied according to the status of the land being worked, more than the status of the worker.[15]

There is a registry of the deeds from various property transactions, sales and gifts, made in the eighth to the thirteenth centuries to the ecclesiastical institutions managed by the bishop of Freising, a diocese in Bavaria.[16] This extensive compilation of deeds of gift provides a great deal of information about the situation of unfree agricultural workers and includes evidence about the views of the lay owners who were donating their property to the church. There are ten very early documents that are relevant to our study. The

---

[13] A "servile" plot of land was one whose workers had particular obligations to the landlord that those who worked "free" land did not have, such as a greater demand for the fruits of their labor.

[14] Jean-Pierre Devroey, "La démogaphie du polyptique de Saint-Remi de Reims," in *Compter les Champenois*, ed. P. Demouy and C. Culliez (Reims 1997) 81–94.

[15] Yoshiki Morimoto, "Aspects of the Early Medieval Peasant Economy as Revealed in the Polyptich of Prüm," in *The Medieval World*, ed. P. Linehan and J. Nelson (London 2002) 605–19.

[16] *Die Traditionen des Hochstifts Freising*, 2 vols., ed. T. Bitterauf (Aalen 1967).

language used in these oldest texts to refer to unfree agricultural workers' status, as well as to other items, is varied and somewhat ambiguous. Yet there is a clear distinction drawn between those who had certain legal rights and those who did not. For example, a parcel of land was excluded from the sale of some property to Bishop Arbeo of Freising circa 780 "because the *colonus* there held the legal rights to this homestead."[17] This eighth-century peasant, although his daily life may have been little different from the lives of other peasants, had legal rights that excluded him from the consequences of the landlord's actions that had affected the others.

Later deeds showed much more consistent terminology, probably because of the arrival of the imperial bureaucracy.[18] The people bound to the Freising land were called either *mancipia* or *coloni*. *Mancipia* were not free and were usually referred to in such a way as to suggest that they were viewed as chattel, whatever their exact legal circumstances may have been. In a gift they were often listed by name and included in with the buildings and fields that were being donated, frequently listed along with the cattle. Sometimes *mancipia*, along with the other livestock, were used in trade. In 861, a man named Kegio transferred all of the property in Gsiessbach that he had received from his lord, Katto, to the cathedral of St. Mary. In return, "he received the amount of three hundred solidi from the bishop in the form of slaves, cattle, and also clothing and other property."[19] Quite a number of the deeds listed in the register included only *mancipia*, with no mention of land at all. As goods that could be sold or given away independent of any land or services due, these *mancipia* were most likely to have been seen as chattel. *Coloni*, on the other hand, were somewhat different. In the Freising texts, they were mentioned only in connection with a homestead or *colonia* and a list of the services due the landlord from those who worked this land that was being transferred to the church. This suggests that in Freising, *coloni* were probably legally free, although their obligations to their landlord may still have been onerous. On a given homestead, the workers could be free or unfree, or a combination of both statuses. In the majority of the deeds in the Freising sample *mancipium*

---

[17] *Freising* #81.

[18] Tassilo, the (Agilolfing dynasty) Frankish duke of Bavaria, had sworn loyalty to his (Pippinid dynasty) Frankish relative, Pepin III, in 757. But before long, Charlemagne decided to bring Bavaria directly under his own control. In 788 he was successful and forced Tassilo and his family into monastic confinement. For more detail see McKitterick, *Charlemagne* 118–27.

[19] *Freising* #888. Also see Carl I. Hammer, *A Large-Scale Slave Society of the Early Middle Ages* (Burlington, VT 2002) 111–12.

was the most frequently used term to describe these workers, suggesting that they were not free—at least not on these lands given to the church.

A Freising deed from 805 provides clear evidence that ordinary laypeople recognized the inalienability of the *res ecclesiae*. In this document, a woman called Erchana declared that she was giving her land in Dachau to the church in view of the future of her soul, and so that "the *mancipia* that [she had] inherited from her father . . . would not be sold off to another location . . . but would be able to grow and prosper under the church's care."[20] Deeds like this, written for the less affluent men and women who gave (or sold) their property to ecclesiastical foundations, show that the donors often seem to have had a clear personal connection to their people, even if as *mancipia* they were seen as property subject to donation. In 809, when Irminperht and her brother gave seven (named) *mancipia* along with lands and woods and orchards to the service of St. Michael's in Gauting, Irminpehrt said that it would please her if Adolhart and Bernhilt were not assigned to operate the mill. They were, she said, "well able to perform other tasks."[21] We learn a couple of things from this document. First of all, since no mill was mentioned in the details of the gift, it seems likely that the *mancipia* were not given because of some special relationship to the land and its improvements but could be assigned to any task that the clergy of St. Michael's thought appropriate. And we can see that Irminpehrt knew her people well. It may have been that she knew that Adolhart and Bernhilt were not competent to operate such an expensive piece of equipment. But more likely, since she assured the recipients that they were well able to serve in other ways, Irminpehrt wanted to spare her people. Perhaps they were getting older, and she knew that it would be hard on them to have to perform such arduous labor.

Similar records are available from many different ecclesiastical institutions, across the empire. The first volume of the *Mainzer Urkundenbuch* lists 173 donations made in the diocese of Mainz from the seventh through the ninth centuries.[22] Although the phrasing of these documents from the Frankish heartland varies somewhat from the formulas used in Bavaria, the ideas expressed are very similar. Many records listed the names of the *mancipia* being donated. One such document provided an explanation for this specificity: in case someone should be tempted to make changes at a later time.[23]

---

[20] *Freising* #218.
[21] *Freising* #292.
[22] *Mainzer Urkundenbuch*, vol. 1, ed. M. Stimmung (Darmstadt 1932).
[23] *Mainzer Urkundenbuch* #77.

And a number of these deeds made it fairly clear that the named *mancipia* were viewed as chattel. Gebhard and his wife, Duda, made a donation to the monastery at Lorsch in 774 consisting of "a farmstead in the city of Mainz, including all of the buildings erected on the land and twenty-five beasts of burden, and, in the city of Worms, also twelve *mancipia*."[24] Here, as we saw in Bavaria, *mancipia* were donated without any connection to land or other particular assets, suggesting that they were probably viewed as chattel. Yet other documents show that there was often some ambiguity about the exact legal status of these individuals. A deed from 802 named a number of *mancipia*, identifying some of their spouses as *uxor* (wife), while another deed from 801 called the spouse of a named *mancipium* a *coniux*, an ambiguous term used to refer to anything from a wife to a female animal recognized as the male animal's mate.[25] In the Mainz documents we can also find evidence of the custom of lay-owned ecclesiastical foundations. Several of the deeds describe laypersons making gifts of churches and their associated property— including *mancipia*—to large ecclesiastical institutions, such as monasteries or the Mainz archbishopric.[26]

The monastery of Fulda was one of the most revered ecclesiastical foundations in Charlemagne's kingdom. It was founded in 744 by St. Sturm, who was a follower of St. Boniface, the "apostle to the Germans." This Benedictine house soon became an important center of Carolingian affairs, both ecclesiastical and political.[27] The first volume of Fulda's extensive register of deeds includes 529 gifts from the founding up to 802, records of gifts from major donors, as well as those from people of more modest circumstances.[28] As we saw elsewhere, in the Fulda texts the language used to describe agricultural and other workers is often unclear about the details of their status. In 796 Griuzing gave the monastery, among other gifts, his *mancipium*, Ruadmunt, along with Ruadmunt's *servus*, Theotbirg.[29] That same year, Reginswind gave the monastery his *servus*, Wolfold, along with Wolfold's own *mancipia*. Clearly there was some confusion about the legal terminology, since is it unlikely that a slave would have owned a non-slave

---

[24] *Mainzer Urkundenbuch* #40.
[25] *Mainzer Urkundenbuch* #91 and #87. The marriage of servile persons was not yet universally recognized.
[26] E.g., *Mainzer Urkundenbuch* #83, #91, #94.
[27] For more details about Fulda, see Janneke Raaijmakers, *The Making of the Monastery of Fulda: C. 744–c. 900* (Cambridge 2012).
[28] *Urkundenbuch des Klosters Fulda*, vol. 1, ed. E. E. Stengel (Marburg 1958).
[29] *Fulda* #244.

worker, although the opposite arrangement was quite common and slaves often had slaves of their own.

The sheer size of the Fulda register, along with the royal connections that made Fulda so prominent, makes it possible for us to see patterns of difference between the deeds of modest gifts made to the monastery and those accompanying substantial gifts made by the emperor or other magnates. The smaller donors usually visited a notary, who drew up the deed from a formulary book, such as the *Andegavensis* discussed in the previous chapter.[30] That they did so is clear because the text of many of the smaller deeds is identical, except for the details of a specific gift. Often the notaries stated explicitly that they were the ones who had drawn up the paperwork on behalf of their clients. However, the deeds recording large gifts were apparently drawn up individually, probably by the imperial chancery, or the equivalent. A more interesting difference between these two classes of documents is that the documents recording smaller gifts frequently listed the *mancipia* by name, often excluding a few, presumably favorites, from the gift.[31] But in this register, as a rule the records of larger gifts did not. These differences hold true for gifts made by ecclesiastical personnel of property that they (or their family) owned, or that they managed in their ecclesiastical office, as well as for lay donors.

Ermhild, the founder and abbess of Milz Abbey, was a blood relation of Emperor Charlemagne. In around 800, she gave the abbey's extensive lands, goods, and *mancipia* to the monastery of Fulda, reserving life tenure.[32] Shortly thereafter, Charlemagne ratified the gift.[33] Neither document mentioned any *servi* or *mancipia* by name. But the record of a more modest donation given by a nun named Mima listed nine *mancipia*, eight of whom were named, with the ninth listed as "his brother."[34] Mima may not have remembered Number Nine by name, but she knew the family relationships among her workers. There is also a document detailing a gift from Charlemagne's grandson, the emperor Lothar, to the Lady Chapel in Aachen in 855, shortly before his death. Here, although this was a large gift, some of the donated *mancipia* were mentioned by name.[35] Perhaps they were particularly beloved

---

[30] For more on these early legal handbooks see Alice Rio, *Legal Practice and the Written Word in the Early Middle Ages: Frankish Formulae, c. 500–1000* (Cambridge 2009).

[31] For example, *Fulda* #526 records that Ernust and his wife, Waltrun, gave Fulda all that they possessed, except for one *servus casatus* (a *servus* with a house).

[32] *Fulda* #264.

[33] *Fulda* #274.

[34] *Fulda* #212.

[35] MGH, *Diplomatum Karolinorum*, vol. 3, ed. E. Mühlbacher et al. (Berlin 1966) #136.

servants, as the others given to the chapel were called merely "other *mancipia* of both sexes." At any rate, this document shows that there were exceptions to the general patterns shown in the Fulda and Freising texts.

The sense of intimacy that is evident between those of modest means and their workers, both in the Fulda documents and in the Freising and Mainz texts, did not often occur with large landholders and their unfree personnel, whether the lords were ecclesiastical or lay. But this is understandable. The vast holdings of large ecclesiastical institutions or lay magnates were peopled by thousands of workers, and the administrators of these huge estates cannot be expected to have known all of their laborers on a personal basis. The sheer size of these estates and the sheer numbers of their *mancipia* made impersonal human resource management a given. Once property (real or human or otherwise) belonged to the church, it fell under the ban against alienating the *res ecclesiae*, and thus the size and impersonal nature of the ecclesiastical estates increased with the passage of time. In a way, they came to resemble the vast estates of late Roman aristocrats. A generation ago, Georges Duby noted that the great monastic estates were even "more consciously Roman" than their lay counterparts.[36] The church also continued to follow the old Roman law. Despite changes in the way personnel were managed on smaller landholdings, the agricultural workers of most ecclesiastical estates became numbers in a ledger, no longer cherished, their quirks no longer accommodated. Hincmar, whose episcopal and abbatial duties made him ultimately responsible for the vast holdings of both his diocese and his monastery, treated his labor force no differently than we can have expected him to have done. Over time, the increasing size of the estates belonging to the church seems to have resulted in increasing impersonalization of the relationships between these workers and their ecclesiastical masters. The greatest difference was not found between lay and ecclesiastical estates, but between great estates and smallholdings.

It is important at this point to say something about the changing vocabulary of the Carolingian era in connection with dependent labor. As early as the late Roman Empire, traditional chattel slavery was supplemented by *servi casati*, "hutted slaves," who lived relatively independently on the land they worked. However, they were not free to leave and often had no legal rights. The Carolingian sources show that the estate laborers were of varying

---

[36] Georges Duby, *The Early Growth of the European Economy: Warriors and Peasants from the Seventh to the Twelfth Century*, trans. H. B. Clarke (Ithaca 1974).

legal status: free, "half-free," unfree agricultural workers housed separately, and unfree workers housed centrally. By the ninth century, as we have seen, the documents used the words *servus* (plural *servi*, feminine, *ancilla/ae*), *mancipium* (plural *mancipia*), and *colonus* (plural *coloni*) in a number of situations where the meanings of these words had definitely evolved, although their exact meanings are still not clear to the modern reader. In the proceedings of a council held at Douzy in 871, the "Bishops' Reply" considered someone who, "having armed men, free, or *coloni*, or *servi*, with him, puts up resistance against the power of the king [as embodied in] his legates."[37] If these *servi* could bear arms in 871, their situation was certainly not the same as it had been in earlier centuries. Yet these *servi* who could bear arms were still referred to in a way that indicates that their masters still viewed them as chattel. This was also the era when words like *sclavus* and its cognates entered the European vocabulary, referring to the Slavs who had been captured on the eastern fringes of the Carolingian Empire and then marched to the Mediterranean port cities for sale to the East. At some point the term was generalized to include all slaves, whatever their ethnicity.[38]

The monastic records found in the polyptichs and other documents and registers reveal the idiosyncratic terminology in use at the various estates. Hans-Werner Goetz has provided an elegant summary of the Carolingian-era legal sources that also makes it clear that for the modern reader there is no clarity about the position of the many *servi*, *coloni*, *mancipia*, and others listed as workers on estates of lay and ecclesiastical owners in the eighth and ninth centuries.[39] Confirming what we shall discuss in the following section, Goetz noted that there seemed to be a more humane treatment of the unfree, in that they were granted some rights, and occasionally granted personhood, however limited. Goetz's sources were limited to "official" documents that were composed to address issues of legal status in particular cases, and reflected only what their composers wanted to include in the official records, not what people always thought or did. Yet we can still conclude that, no matter how they may have treated their servile dependents, people wanted the record to show their dependents' situation in this relatively positive light.

---

[37] *Die Konzilien der Karolingischen Teilreiche 860–874*, ed. W. Hartmann, MGH *Concilia* 4 (Hanover 1998) #37, p. 499. The bishops were talking about Bishop Hincmar of Laon's resistance against King Charles the Bald.

[38] A classic article on this question is Charles Verlinden, "L'origine de sclavus = esclave," *Bulletin du Cange* 17 (1943) 97–128.

[39] Hans-Werner Goetz, "Serfdom and the Beginnings of a 'Seigneurial System' in the Carolingian Period: A Survey of the Evidence," *Early Medieval Europe* 2 (1993) 29–51.

It is also important to point out here that our study does not attempt to discuss the overall Carolingian economy or the slave trade that seems to have formed such a large part of the Carolingians' relationships with those outside the empire. These are of course important questions and deserve careful consideration, but they are simply outside the scope of the present investigation. Neither shall we extend our inquiry to the enslavement of Slavs or their transport through the empire on the way to eastern markets. Michael McCormick's magisterial study, *The Origins of the European Economy: Communication and Commerce, A.D. 300–900,* has refreshed this exciting area of inquiry about the role of slaving in the Carolingians' success.[40] But here we are concentrating on ecclesiastical regulation of the church institutions and personnel in their roles as slave owners. We are looking at lay slave ownership only as needed to provide the context of the ecclesiastical behavior. And in doing so we need to respect the fact that the customs and vocabulary choices varied a great deal in various locations and over time. At this point, all we can do is to try to understand each situation in its own environment and according to its own particular circumstances. We can, of course, note possible patterns and any reasonable explanations that might present themselves. But we are not going to be able to establish general principles about anything other than what we find in the canon law.[41]

Carolingian Church Councils and Royal Proclamations

Let us now return to our central question: how did the church regulate its own relationship with its unfree dependents? In the last chapter we saw that the main concerns that were discussed in connection with our question in the church councils of the early Germanic kingdoms were the morality of the clergy, especially their sexual morality, and retaining control over the *res ecclesiae*. While Carolingian era councils continued the prohibition of extraneous women in clerical households, it had become somewhat pro forma. From here on, we shall focus our attention more on the *res ecclesiae*, especially ecclesiastical *servi*. The earlier Franks had emphasized the proper conduct for a given individual's rank and status. The Visigoths were more

---

[40] (Cambridge 2001). See especially 733–77.
[41] For a wonderful discussion of this problem see Alice Rio, "'Half-Free' Categories in the Early Middle Ages: Fine Status Distinctions before Professional Lawyers," in *Legalism: Rules and Categories,* ed. P. Dresch and J. Scheele (Oxford 2015) 129–52.

concerned with stringent enforcement of their often harsh regulations, while clearly repressing their Jewish and unfree populations. And perhaps most significant for our purposes, the church had also found that one way to limit the alienation of the *res ecclesiae* was to insist on a continuing bond between freed *servi ecclesiae* and their former masters.

Most of the legal material from the seventh through the ninth centuries was concerned with the epic question of the age: the establishment of a secure Carolingian realm, including, often depending on, a working alliance with the bishops.[42] Carolingian secular law ranged from formal public proclamations from the king's court to local unwritten, yet unbreakable, customs. The canon law of this time was, as Janet Nelson put it, "a disparate and lumpy mix" of papal and episcopal letters, local and regional synodal decrees, and local bishops' capitularies (summaries of legal pronouncements).[43] Church councils were often held in the presence of the ruler, and kings frequently issued capitularies of their own after a council, summarizing the important legal points that had been discussed. This was a way to show agreement with the ecclesiastical decisions as well as an attempt to demonstrate royal power over the church, power that rulers coveted. In turn, the bishops issued a catalog of the various canons or regulations that had been agreed upon by the assembly, tacitly demonstrating their agreement with the king's proclamation as well as their ideas about the independence of church law. In the ninth century, much of this legislation dealt with the problems that arose during the conflicts between Louis the Pious and his sons, and then later, the problems among those sons, as well as trying to normalize life in the wake of invasions from the Norsemen and the Magyars.

It is not surprising that there is relatively little conciliar material from this period that directly addressed the affairs of the church's unfree agricultural and domestic workers. They weren't the cause of the Carolingians' major difficulties. The question of the inalienability of church property was, however, quite frequently discussed in the Carolingian synods.[44] These discussions were complicated by attitudes toward church property that had not often been seen in the earlier centuries we have examined. In the fourth century, Constantine had supported the fledgling church as it emerged from the

---

[42] On this see Michael Edward Moore, *A Sacred Kingdom: Bishops and the Rise of Frankish Kingship, 300–850* (Washington, DC 2011).

[43] Janet L. Nelson, "Law and Its Applications," CHC 3.299–326.

[44] On this question see Wilfried Hartmann, *Die Synoden der Karolingerzeit im Frankenreich und in Italien* (Paderborn 1989) 458–62.

shadows, and soon the community of Christians was able to establish corporate ownership of considerable property. In time, the idea of corporate ownership under the administrative oversight of the bishop was challenged by
the idea of local churches owning their own resources, distancing them from
episcopal control.[45] When individual Romans had organized and paid for
the establishment of local places of worship, they sometimes felt a proprietary interest, but the bulk of church property continued to be under the control of the bishops. Most of the earliest legislation about controlling the *res
ecclesiae* had been intended to make clear the line between a bishop's personal
resources and the church property managed by the bishop. In later centuries,
lay intervention in ecclesiastical affairs increased. New rulers regularly issued
proclamations of their support of the church, and this secular protection of
the *res ecclesiae* gave rise to new challenges with the Christianization of the
Germanic aristocracy. As they settled down and became more accepted by
their subjects, these newly arrived lords and ladies began to endow churches
for the convenience of the people on their estates, and they saw themselves
as having authority over these properties. The nobles' proprietary attitude toward these estate churches can clearly be seen in the fact that often the priest
who served such a church had been one of the slaves on the estate. As far back
as Gregory I of Rome, the church had declared that ordained men must be
free. But the continuing need to remind people of this rule suggests that this
was not always the case. A council held in the northern Frankish territories at
Hohenaltheim in 916 felt the need to make it clear that any freedom granted
as a result of ordination was contingent on continuing service to the intended
church.[46] This is the same issue that we saw in Hincmar's letter to Irminsinde
about the status of her former deacon. In the next chapter we shall see that
the problem continued in later centuries.

Ecclesiastical lords and lay lords may have struggled for dominance, but
neither group sought to exterminate the other. In the Carolingian era, the
idea of a fundamental church-state opposition would have been inconceiv-
able. The church comprised all of the people of God, fighting together against
a world of sin and heresy and heathens.[47] Yet there was no question that

---

[45] A fascinating and comprehensive discussion of the privatization of church property can be
found in Susan Wood, *The Proprietary Church in the Medieval West* (Oxford 2006).

[46] *Die Konzilien Deutschlands und Reichsitaliens. Teil 1 916–1001*, ed. E.-D. Hehl, MGH *Concilia* 6,
#1, c.38. On this see Wood, *Proprietary Church* 525.

[47] For an interesting point of view on this issue, see Stefan Esders and Steffen Patzold, "From
Justinian to Louis the Pious: Inalienability of Church Property and the Sovereignty of a Ruler in the
Ninth Century," in *Religious Franks: Religion and Power in the Frankish Kingdoms: Studies in Honor of
Mayke de Jong*, ed. R. Meens et al. (Manchester 2016) 368–408.

ecclesiastical property was up for grabs in the struggle for political control. Bishops now came from an elite who were no longer seen as Gallo-Roman (or Hispano-Roman) but as Frankish aristocrats.[48] They were no longer Roman gentlemen. They held Frankish ideas, often blurring the line between legitimate authority and raw power and usually following Germanic traditions about law and society and the limits of royal authority.[49] The ancient Salic law as well as Visigothic Alaric's *Breviary* of Roman law were reconfirmed by Charlemagne early in his reign.[50] Carolingian rulers had no reservations about exploiting the possibilities of Roman law or ancient Germanic law when it came to questions of imperial privilege.

Misuse or misappropriation of the *res ecclesiae*, including human assets, seems to have been a major problem and came up for discussion in some way at most of the Carolingian councils and synods. The 756 synod in Ascheim, Bavaria (at the time, still a Carolingian satellite) cited the 325 Council of Nicaea as the authority for the rule that "all of the *res ecclesiae* are to be controlled by the bishop."[51] But it seems that invoking the normative authority of the Council of Nicaea was not sufficient persuasion, since later councils repeatedly felt it necessary to provide a justification for the need to restore the confiscated *res ecclesiae*. For example, at a council held in Austrasia (Pepin's brother Carloman's territory) in 743, it was explained that the property needed to be returned "lest the churches or monasteries suffer poverty and want."[52] This principle was emphasized again later in 822 at a council in Attigny under Louis the Pious.[53]

In Soissons in 744 the bishops simply declared that monks and nuns were to have what material goods they needed, and the bishops at Paris in 846/7 reminded the faithful that monks were the impoverished *servi* of God and that as such, their belongings should be protected.[54] Although these

---

[48] Rudolf Schieffer pointed out that the newer dioceses in the Frankish empire were much more susceptible to the royal demands than was the case for their brother bishops in areas where the church hierarchy enjoyed more ancient roots. "Über Bischofssitz und Fiskalgut im 8. Jahrhundert," *Historisches Jahrbuch* 95 (1975) 18–32.

[49] Wood, *Proprietary Church* 76. See Thomas F. X. Noble, "The Papacy in the Eighth and Ninth Centuries," in CMH 2.563–86, for a discussion of how this had created difficulties between popes and secular rulers as far back as Gelasius I, bishop of Rome 492–496. Ninth-century popes were still quoting Gelasius in their attempts to explain that while the secular authorities had the raw power to exert control, they lacked the God-given authority of the church.

[50] There is an excellent discussion of Charlemagne and "the mystical authority of law" in Karl Ubl, *Sinnstiftungen eines Rechtsbuchs: Die Lex Salica im Frankenreich* (Ostfildern 2017) 165–91.

[51] Ascheim 756, c.3. MGH, *Concilia*, vol. 2.1, ed. A. Werminghof (Hanover 1906).

[52] Ascheim, c.2. In MGH, *Concilia* 2.1, ed. A. Werminghof (Hanover 1906).

[53] Austrasia, c.4. In MGH, *Concilia* 2.2, ed. A. Werminghof (Hanover 1908).

[54] Soissons 744, c.3. In MGH, *Concilia* 2.1. Also see Paris 846/7, MGH, *Concilia* 3, ed. W. Hartmann (Hanover 1984). This idea of monks as God's *servi*, although widespread in the early medieval period,

somewhat emotional appeals may have exaggerated the suffering of the monks and nuns in order to bolster their demands for restitution, we must remember that the early Carolingians were no respecters of ownership in their grab for power. Plunder was plunder.[55] In an attempt to allay the church's concerns, the council in Ingelheim held in 826 under Charlemagne's son Louis (the Pious) quoted the sixth-century Byzantine emperor Justinian's law forbidding the alienation of church property.[56] Then the next canon in the text explained the circumstances in which it was legitimate for the *res ecclesiae* to be transferred to the imperial fisc: "si princeps voluerit"—if the prince wishes![57] This, too came from Justinian, apparently someone whom Louis found it advantageous to emulate. The king supported the idea that it was never acceptable to alienate church property, unless the king wanted to do so. Efforts on the part of church leaders to preserve their control over the *res ecclesiae* continued. For example, the council in Paris in 829 devoted several very long canons to this issue, including the provision that charitable use of church property was acceptable only in real emergencies and not for the clergy's personal gain.[58] And Louis continued to press his point of view as well.[59] Most of the councils of this period reiterated the need to protect the *res ecclesiae*; many of the canons from the synods at Meaux/Paris in 845–46 and Soissons in 853 evidence the bishops' worries.[60] Archbishop Hincmar's solution to the problem was based in scripture as well as in pragmatism. Citing the well-known "Render to Caesar that which is Caesar's and to God, that which is God's" (Matt. 22:21), Hincmar allowed that as long as enough church assets were devoted to providing for the poor, some could be diverted to supporting the military service necessary to the protection of the realm in which those poor lived.[61]

---

does not seem to have much affected the church's relationship to its servile dependents and thus will not be considered here.

[55] See Timothy Reuter, "Plunder and Tribute in the Carolingian Empire," *Transactions of the Royal Historical Society*, 5th series 35 (1985) 75–94; reprinted in Timothy Reuter, *Medieval Polities and Modern Mentalities*, ed. J. L. Nelson (Cambridge 2006) 231–50.

[56] MGH, *Concilia* 2.2 #45, c.1. Also *Epitome Iuliani Const.* VII c.1 (32). This sixth-century condensed version of Justinian's *Novellae* was very influential in Europe until the twelfth century. The standard edition is Gustav Hänel, *Iuliani Epitome Latina Novellarum Iustiniani* (Leipzig 1873).

[57] MGH, *Concilia* 2.2 #45, c.2. *Epitome Iuliani Const.* VII c.2 (33).

[58] MGH, *Concilia* 2.2 #50, c.15–18.

[59] E.g., the *Capitulare ad Missorum*, MGH, *Capitularia regum Francorum* 2 #188, from the year 829, ed. V. Kravse (Hanover 1897).

[60] MGH, *Concilia* 3 #11 and #27.

[61] Moore, *Sacred Kingdom* 374–75.

These ninth-century kings and churchmen had a good deal of Roman law at their disposal. The *Epitome Iuliani*, mentioned earlier, was in fairly wide circulation by this time. But in the ninth century a new, even more useful collection appeared, the *Lex romana canonice compta*, a compendium of Roman law that was relevant to ecclesiastical interests and may well have been the collection used by the Ingelheim council. It was widely understood in the Carolingian era that "the church lived by the Roman law."[62]

As the ninth century wore on, civil wars between Louis and his sons, and then among his sons, engulfed the empire, and the Carolingians never really recovered from this strife.[63] At the same time, the Scandinavians had begun to plague the Frankish lands from the North and West. None of the contending parties in the Frankish realm shrank from manipulating the church—and the church's wealth—to their own advantage. By now most of the leading churchmen were also great men in their own right, indeed many of them lay magnates who had received church properties as "honors," as royal rewards.[64] Kings and lay magnates saw land grants to lay or ecclesiastical recipients as temporarily expedient, while most ecclesiastical lords, embracing the principle of the nonalienability of church property, considered all gifts to the church to be permanent.[65] A capitulary from Charles the Bald, issued in 857 "in consideration of your needs and the excessive disruptions occurring in the realm," began with a reiteration of the principle of ecclesiastical immunity and explicitly forbade the violation of church property or personnel, as well as attacks on virgins or widows.[66] Such royal proclamations declaring the *res ecclesiae* to be sacrosanct did not, however, stop many Carolingian lords, lay or ecclesiastical, from using the church resources at their disposal to further their own aims. The ecclesiastical lords usually found that their personal ambitions were best achieved when the property

---

[62] *Lex Ribvaria* 61(58) 1, ed. F. Beyerle and R. Buchner, MGH, *Leges nationum Germanicarum*, vol. 3.2 (Hanover 1954).

[63] There are a number of good, recent scholarly summaries of the complex political history of this period. See, e.g., Stuart Airlie's collected essays in *Power and Its Problems in Carolingian Europe* (New York 2012); *Religious Franks: Religion and Power in the Frankish Kingdoms*, ed. R. Meens (Manchester 2016); Mayke de Jong, *The Penitential State: Authority and Atonement in the Age of Louis the Pious* (Cambridge 2009); and *Charlemagne: Empire and Society*, ed. J. Story (Manchester 2000).

[64] On this see Reuter, "Plunder." Also, Janet Nelson, "Making Ends Meet: Wealth and Poverty in the Carolingian Church," in *The Church and Wealth*, ed. W. J. Sheils and D. Wood (Oxford 1987) 25–35.

[65] On this see Matthew J. Innes, "Practices of Property in the Carolingian Empire," in Davis and McCormick, *Long Morning* 247–66. Also: Janet L. Nelson, "'Not Bishops' Bailiffs but Lords of the Earth': Charles the Bald and the Problem of Sovereignty," in *The Church and Sovereignty: Essays in Honor of Michael Wilks*, ed. D. Wood (Oxford 1991) 23–34.

[66] MGH, *Capitularia regum Francorum* #267.

under their control did not leave the church. Ninth-century nobles were not so different from those of Charlemagne's generation in this respect. However, Charlemagne's actions had served largely to unify the church, building up its power in support of his own.[67] The later Carolingians' actions resulted in strife within the church that did not shore up the power of anyone—except that of the bishop of Rome, as he eventually became the favored arbiter in such disputes.[68]

These conflicts that played out on the greater political stage had a very real effect on the predicaments of ecclesiastical *servi*. From the evidence provided by letters and deeds of gift, we have already seen how the administrators of large ecclesiastical estates do not seem to have had a personal connection to their workers in the way that was common on smaller properties. Large ecclesiastical estates were no longer seen primarily as sacred land, but suffered as casualties of war and ambition, in the same way as the estates of lay magnates. When the workers on church estates were no longer seen as valued and beloved brothers and sisters working together with their ecclesiastical masters in doing God's work, it is easy to see how their masters' attitudes might have changed. Just as in ancient Rome, *servi* or *mancipia* on large estates, ecclesiastical and lay, were simply livestock who were essential to the functioning of a valuable property. On a large, impersonal scale of operations, these *servi* would have easily become commodified. Nevertheless, pious churchmen still argued for decent treatment of these *servi*. Abbot Smaragdus of St. Mihiel (near Verdun) wrote a treatise called *Via Regia* (*The Way of a King*) in which, among other things, he urged Louis the Pious to treat his *servi* and *liberti* with justice and solicitude.[69]

---

[67] On this see Mayke de Jong, "Charlemagne's Church," in *Charlemagne: Empire and Society*, ed. J. Story (Manchester 2005) 103–35.

[68] One of the most fascinating areas of inquiry in church history today is the story of the "Pseudo-Isidorean" workshop that produced several collections of ancient legal material, both genuine and fabricated. Their aim seems to have been to advance the cause of certain bishops and monasteries that had suffered at the hands of various Carolingian rulers. The solution that was often provided in the Pseudo-Isidorean material was to appeal to the bishop of Rome to adjudicate in a dispute, at the time an impractical suggestion given the realities of travel and communication. However, once the Romans became aware of texts purporting to offer ancient authorities in support of papal power, they were quick to take advantage of the possibilities they afforded. (I shall not discuss these works further as they do not contain material relevant to our question.) For a brief account see Mary E. Sommar, "The Pseudo-Isidorean Decretals and Church-State Conflict," in *Politics and Theology*, ed. G. Ricci (New Brunswick, NJ 2012). For the latest developments in this ongoing effort see *The Pseudo-Isidore Project* at www.mgh.de/datenbanken/pseudoisidor/; also see *Fälschung als Mittel der Politik? Pseudoisidor im Licht der neuen Forschung: Gedenkschrift für Klaus Zechiel-Eckes*, ed. K. Ubl and D. Ziemann, MGH, *Studien und Texte*, vol. 57 (Wiesbaden 2015).

[69] Smaragdus Abbatis, *Via Regia* 30, in PL 102.967–69.

There are a few canonical texts that shed light explicitly on our question about ecclesiastical slaves. The discussions about the unfree workers under ecclesiastical dominion developed slowly over a long time, and they help to illuminate the Carolingians' attempts to weave together the Roman, the Gothic, and the Frankish traditions into a coherent whole that expressed their new ways of doing things.[70]

Many councils made it clear that the church leaders wanted it clearly documented that "*servi* and their *peculia*," or "*mancipia*, along with the fields and houses," formed a part, a necessary part, of the *res ecclesiae*.[71] In a capitulary presented in Paderborn sometime between 775 and 790, Charlemagne reaffirmed an earlier regulation that each and every church should be supplied with a small plot of land and that the members of the parish should furnish the church one male and one female slave for every 120 parishioners.[72] His son Louis, and Louis's son Lothar, repeated similar requirements, as did later ninth-century church leaders.[73]

The nature of the relationship between the church and manumitted ecclesiastical slaves was another question of concern to these councils. As we have seen in earlier chapters, the old Roman custom that a personal bond remained between a freed slave and his or her former master or mistress had led the church to say that this should be the case between the church and freed ecclesiastical slaves. However, since the ancient Roman law said that such a patronal bond was to continue through their descendants until the death of both parties to the original transaction, and since the church by definition could never die, theoretically the descendants of former ecclesiastical slaves would be forever under obligation to the church. In Carolingian Europe, however, this was not yet a universally recognized practice, although the basic theory had been established in several earlier councils. The Carolingian texts recorded the continuing discussion about this principle.

There was also a continuing question about the relationship between the church and former slaves who had received their freedom in the *manumissio in ecclesia* ceremony. The seventh-century *Lex Ribvaria* had said that

---

[70] On Carolingian innovation through continuity see Wilfried Hartmann, *Kirche und Kirchenrecht um 900: Die Bedeutung der spätkarolingischen Zeit für Tradition und Innovation im kirchlichen Recht*, MGH, *Schriften*, vol. 58 (Hanover 2008).

[71] For example, synods meeting in Rome (761, c.2, *servi* and *peculium* part of *res ecclesiae*) in Ingelheim (826, c.29, *res ecclesiae* include *rusticum mancipium*), and in Meaux/Paris (845–46, c.63, *mancipia* along with fields and houses were *res ecclesiae*).

[72] *Capitulatio de partibus Saxoniae* c.15. ed. A. Boretius, MGH, *Capitularia regum Francorum* 1 #26 (Hanover 1883).

[73] See Wood, *Proprietary Church* 439–41.

unfree persons who received their freedom by means of the *manumissio in ecclesia* would remain under obligation to that particular church. Not only would these *tabularii*, as they were called, live under the bishop's jurisdiction, but he would continue to have a say in their financial dealings.[74] Other Merovingian-era conciliar canons had made it clear that bishops had jurisdiction over ecclesiastical freedmen, who would presumably have been freed in a church ceremony.[75] But the 772 council held under Duke Tassilo in Neuching, Bavaria, said that those freed in a church—and their posterity—were "permanently in secure freedom."[76] While not exactly a repudiation of the Ripuarian custom, this provision does highlight the lack of uniformity in the Carolingian-era church's attitudes toward freed slaves. Not long after this, Charlemagne, himself the scion of a Ripuarian family, said in his 779 *Capitulary of Heristal* (a town in Ripuarian Francia, now in the vicinity of Liège, Belgium), "concerning the *tabularii* the [old customs] are to be observed.[77]" Presumably, he was referring to the continuing obligations the freed person owed to the church where the manumission ceremony had taken place. After Charlemagne deposed his Bavarian cousin Tassilo in 778, presumably this ruling extended to the Bavarian church as well. The *Capitulary of Heristal* also reinforced the magisterial power of the bishops (and thus also the practice of *manumissio in ecclesia*) by declaring that bishops could serve as representatives of the Crown in any transactions involving slaves and that slaves could be sold only in the presence of a bishop or of the count, and not in the marketplace.[78] This capitulary was a proclamation of his royal authority throughout the recently consolidated Frankish realms and it was endorsed by an assembly of bishops and other nobles. The provision that slaves could no longer be sold in the marketplace was intended to regulate commerce, and it was certainly to the economic advantage of the counts and bishops, which would in turn have increased their gratitude toward the king. But such episcopal or comital oversight of the markets may well have served to ease some of the worst abuses suffered by those on an unregulated slave block. The capitulary also repeated the prohibition against the sale of slaves to foreign parts, advantageous to the slave population as well as protecting valuable assets of the realm.

---

[74] *Lex Ribvaria* 58, 1.
[75] Macon (585), c.7; Paris (614), c.7. MGH, *Concilia* 2.1.
[76] Neuching, c.9. MGH, *Concilia* 2.1.
[77] MGH, *Capitularia regum Francorum* 1, c.6.
[78] MGH, *Capitularia regum Francorum* 1, c.19, 20.

In 853, at a council in Soissons, King Charles the Bald reversed his grandfather's policy that had supported the old Ripuarian custom and said that a freed *mancipium ecclesiae* was completely free.[79] Also, recalling Justinian's *Novellae*, Charles's proclamation said that the king must authorize any alienation of the *res ecclesiae*, including *mancipia*.[80] While not specifically eliminating the bonds of service between the church and its freedmen, it seems to establish a position in favor of freedom. But at the same time, this new policy also showed that for ecclesiastical *mancipia*, obtaining their freedom was a more complicated matter than it was for those belonging to lay masters.

This series of laws, zigzagging back and forth, makes it clear that the Carolingians did not have a consistent policy about the question of manumitted slaves. One might well ask why this continued to be an issue. It seems to us moderns reasonable to say that free is free and that is the end of it. However, more than a millennium ago, the ancient customs from the Carolingian ancestral lands were very hard to give up. The question of servitude involving the church was more complicated than a simple business relationship. Apart from the custom of *manumissio in ecclesia*, there was also the tradition that the *res ecclesiae* could never be alienated. And the manumission of a slave, by implication, was the alienation of human property, giving to the freed slave the legal rights over his or her own person. A practical solution—from the church's point of view—that would not deprive the church of its valuable labor force, yet still provide a way for ecclesiastical *servi* to get at least some freedom, was for them and their descendants to retain obligations of service to the church that had formerly held dominion over them. In this era when the inviolability of church property was under assault from both domestic and foreign enemies, allowing any chink in the legal wall of protection would have been intolerable. The church was determined to maintain control over church resources, both property and personnel, sometimes, as it might seem to us, in contradiction of common sense. And, as we have seen, any number of solutions were proposed, from limiting manumissions, to imposing permanent service obligations on the freed and their descendants, with the result that conditions were more difficult for servile persons dependent on the church than for those with lay masters.

---

[79] Ch. 12 of his capitulary, which was recorded in the council proceedings found in MGH, *Concilia* 3 #27.

[80] *Epitome Iuliani* Const. CXI.8.

A number of Carolingian era conciliar texts were concerned with protecting the well-being of the community, which sometimes had the effect of alleviating some of the onerous nature of the burdens of the unfree. For example, in 770 the bishops gathered in Dingolfing, Bavaria, declared that if a *servus* unknowingly married a noblewoman, he would become free and could not subsequently be re-enslaved.[81] This Bavarian rule was a good deal more lenient than the old Roman law that had called for capital punishment for both partners in such a union. A few years later a council in Neuching forbade the sale of slaves outside of the borders of the province (of Bavaria).[82] This would have helped keep slave families, if not intact, at least not separated by thousands of miles. However, it is important to realize that this law arose out of concern for the protection of Bavaria's valuable assets: military equipment and horses were also frequently listed among items whose sale was prohibited. It was only by chance that this law may have improved the lot of slave families. The ecclesiastical proceedings of the synod of Heristal, the assembled bishops' record of the event, repeated the ideas found in Charlemagne's renowned capitulary.[83]

A number of councils declared that "servile work" was not to be performed on Sundays.[84] While the canons do not specify that this extended to the unfree, the laws did not exclude them either, so one might be justified in seeing this as a lessening of their workload, however unintentional this result may have been. But again, we must not conclude that the Carolingians thought highly of their unfree workers. A late Carolingian preacher exhorted his listeners: "May your *servi* and your *ancillae* and your oxen and asses and horses have rest on the Lord's day and on saints' days, in the same way that you do."[85] To this man, *servi* were merely two-legged beasts of burden.

<hr />

[81] Dingolfing, c.10. MGH, *Concilia* 2.1. Note: The *Lex Baiuvariorum*, discussed in the previous chapter, was a summary of the Bavarian legal thinking up to no later than 756, the date of the first church council recorded in Bavaria. In 756 Tassilo, or more likely his father, Odilo, had been responsible for the compilation of the text. And, as we saw earlier, the Bavarian laws were generally concerned with common-sense solutions to maintaining the social order. See Peter Landau, *Lex Baiuvariorum Entstehungszeit, Entstehungsort und Charakter von bayerns ältester Rechts- und Geschichtequelle* (Munich 2004).

[82] Neuching 772, c.1, 2.

[83] MGH, *Capitularia* 2.1 #17. This idea was repeated in later councils, e.g., Meaux/Paris (845–46), c.76. MGH, *Concilia* 3 #11.

[84] Reims 813, c.35. MGH, *Concilia* 2.1. See also: Rome 853, c.30; Meaux/Paris 845/6, c.80; Mainz 852; all found in MGH, *Concilia* 2.2.

[85] From an anonymous eighth- or ninth-century sermon, quoted in Smith, "Religion and Lay Society" 662.

Perhaps the most important change in the legal position of *servi* can be seen in a canon from the 813 Council of Chalons that declared the marriage of two *servi* to be valid as long as both masters had given their consent.[86] Marriage is a legal contract, and this canon seems to have assumed that *servi* were able to enter into such a contract. Since ancient Roman times, it had been a fundamental principle that only a legally recognized person could enter into a binding contract. Thus, by implication this canon treated *servi* as legally recognized persons, effectively eliminating one of the fundamental elements of slavery: the lack of legal recognition of a slave's personhood. We should not conclude too much from this concerning the continuation of slavery or of the meaning of the word *servus*. However, the fact that *servi* were able to enter into a legal marriage contract on their own behalf does represent a difference, no matter how subtle, in the legal situation of the unfree. In the last chapter we saw that the Visigoths severely punished free-servile unions.[87] Frankish legal texts also dealt with mixed marriages between a free person and a slave, particularly in regard to the status of their offspring.[88] And the horrendous story about the priest Rauching in the previous chapter confirms that servile marriages did sometimes occur in sixth-century Francia. In the faraway Byzantine Empire, as we mentioned in the previous chapter, Emperor Justinian had declared that when a free person was captured and enslaved, that person's Christian marriage continued to be in effect, making it clear that he was not talking about a *contubernium*, a lower-status "slave marriage." However, it is not likely that this was widely known in the West.[89] But the Chalons canon is the first western law suggesting that servile persons could contract proper marriages as opposed to a mere *contubernium*. We shall continue to explore the evolving question of slave marriages in the next chapter.

The canons we have just discussed show no hint of increasing the workers' freedom, merely of making their bondage perhaps a little less unpleasant. And of course, the continuing concern with treating human chattel well—even if only to maximize their utility—suggests that even such marginally decent treatment was probably not the norm. However, in comparison with the conciliar texts from earlier centuries, it is evident that the ruling classes had begun

---

[86] Council of Chalons 813, c.30. MGH, *Concilia* 2.1. This canon was included in many later canonical collections.

[87] *L. Rom. Visig.* VI, *L. Vis.* V.17.

[88] *L.Rib.* 61 and *L.Al.* 17.

[89] Justinian, *Novella* 22.7. This law does not seem to have been included in the western abbreviations.

to recognize a bit of humanity in their *servi*, at least some of the time. And the church's efforts to regulate marriage seem to have produced the consequence of treating *servi* as legal persons when it came to their familial relationships, possibly unintentional but certainly significant. Nonetheless, ecclesiastical slave ownership continued without any fundamental changes. As we saw earlier, in Paderborn in around 785, Charlemagne made it very clear that every church needed to have slaves: "For every one hundred men, noble, *ingenuus* (freeborn peasant), or *litus* (freed or half-free), they are to provide a male and a female slave to their [parish] church."[90] Also, showing the special importance attached to things and people with ecclesiastical connections, a canon from a Bavarian council during Duke Tassilo's reign declared that the homicide of a *servus* who had been freed in church as well as at the king's court occasioned double the penalty of a *servus* who had been freed in a lower (lay) lord's court.[91]

By this time, eastern (Byzantine) and western Christians had drifted far apart, and most of the activity in the eastern church at that time seems not to have had any effect in the West. However, an ecumenical council held in Nicaea in 786/87 included representatives sent from Rome on behalf of Pope Hadrian I. Hadrian, however, never officially accepted the proceedings from that council. Given that the council had rejected his demand that they restore the principle of the Roman bishop's primacy over all Christian people, this is no surprise. However, a letter Hadrian wrote to Charlemagne in 794 makes it clear that the pope did support most of the canons from Nicaea II.[92] While the council did not explicitly consider the *servi ecclesiastici*, a few of these canons are of interest to our question.[93] Canon 8 reiterated the old provision that Jews might not own slaves (but there was no mention that this applied only to Christian slaves, as there had been in earlier centuries). Canon 18 reinforced the ancient prohibition of bishops and monks coming into unnecessary contact with women (at this time bishops as well as monks were expected to be celibate). The most interesting material is in canons 4, 5, and 12, which dealt with the bishop and money and the *res ecclesiae*. Canons 4 and 5 stated that a bishop may not accept or demand money (bribes) from any of his clergy or from anyone hoping to be ordained. Apparently, corruption was a major concern in late seventh-century Byzantium, and the council

---

[90] MGH, *Capitularia regum Francorum* 1 #26, ed. G. H. Pertz, MGH, *Legum* 1 (Hanover 1835).

[91] The 772 council at Neuching, c.10, called for an eighty-solidus *wergild* for slaves freed in a church or at the king's court, while the *wergild* for slaves set free by a lower authority was only forty solidi. MGH, *Concilia* 2.1 #16.

[92] See Heinz Ohme, "Sources of the Greek Canon Law to the Quinisext Council (691/2)," in HMCL 4, 77–84.

[93] These canons can be found in Greek, Latin, and English versions in *Decrees of the Ecumenical Councils*, ed., trans., N. P. Tanner (London 1990).

wanted to preserve the purity of the *res ecclesiae*. Canon 12 dealt with alienation of church property. It forbade a bishop or an abbot from transferring any
of the church's estates into the "hands of the ruler" or conveying it to another
person. Further, it was not permitted for the bishop "to appropriate any of
these things, nor to make a present of the things of God to his own relatives."
However, if the bishop operated under the legal fiction that the land was
worthless, he could give it to clergy or to those who worked the land. This last
provision does not seem to have affected western canon law. Nevertheless,
one cannot but wonder if perhaps the spirit of this last provision may have
been on occasion an inspiration to beleaguered European churchmen.

In the ninth century, Louis the Pious called two councils in Aachen (in 816
and again in 817), in which the king and the bishops laid out a program of
reform for monasteries and convents, based on the teachings of the fathers
of the church.[94] Several of the reform canons discussed how to handle family
slaves whom the monks and nuns had brought with them to their monastic
houses.[95] As we saw with Augustine of Hippo and Gregory of Nyssa, this had
been a problem for the church for a long while. Somewhat later, Archbishop
Hincmar of Reims, King Charles the Bald's right-hand man, said that each
priest should be provided with a house with about forty acres of land and
four *mancipia*.[96] Similarly, far to the south in Rome, Pope John VIII wrote
to Bishop Adelhard of Tours in August 878 that "every church ought to have
its own farmstead (manse) with four *mancipia*," as well as vines, land, and
other agricultural necessities.[97] As we have said, given that most of the ancient fathers were Roman aristocrats, it is not surprising that slavery was considered unremarkable in the early church. The later evidence shows that the
Carolingian viewpoint did not stray far from the fathers' teachings.

Nearly a hundred years after the second council at Nicaea, Nicholas I, the
bishop of Rome called for another council to be held in Constantinople in 869
(Constantinople IV). By the time of the meeting, Nicholas had died, so his successor, Hadrian II, sent two representatives (who were not permitted to preside over the assembly in his stead). Subsequently, although the western church
recognized the edicts of the council, it did not recognize them in their Greek
format, but only in the Latin version of the proceedings.[98] Canon 15 declared
that precious objects owned by the church were not to be sold and church lands

---

[94] MGH, *Concilia* 2.1 #39.
[95] Aachen 816, c.21, 22, 23. MGH, *Concilia* 2.1.
[96] Hincmar of Reims, "Inquiry," c.2.2, PL 125.777. On this also see Nelson, "Making Ends Meet."
[97] John VII, *Epistola* 112. MGH, *Epistolae Karolini Aevi* 5 #104 (Berlin 1928).
[98] *Decrees of the Ecumenical Councils*, 157–59.

could not be alienated, not even temporarily by means of a long-term lease arrangement. Canon 18 repeated the old precept that the *res ecclesiae* were not to be confiscated or violated in any way by the laity. Interestingly, the rule specified only those properties that the church had held for at least thirty years. Another canon, number 23, said that a bishop was not permitted to alienate the property of other churches, usurping the authority of their own bishops. These three canons show clearly that the council was concerned about the continuing lack of respect and order both within and without the ranks of the clergy when it came to handling the property of the church.

By the late ninth century, there seems still to have been no clear resolution of the slavery issue. Especially in the later texts, the terminology is inconsistent. Royal capitularies generally seem to have paid less attention to personal status and more attention to the duties and functions of the various personnel under the king's direction—all of his subjects being, as it were, slaves to the royal will. On the other hand, ecclesiastical documents, including correspondence, and property records, as well as conciliar legislation, all provide us with abundant evidence that personal status—free or unfree, or something in between—was of considerable concern to the church as a property owner. Those whose status merited their inclusion in the *res ecclesiae* were under strict control and faced little prospect of total freedom. While the church's attempts to regulate its worldly affairs and to have the society as a whole conform more closely to Christian norms may have had the effect of lessening some of the burdens of servitude, that does not seem to have been their purpose. Only when it came to the marriage of unfree persons was there any real change from ancient customs regarding slavery. Instead of the old Roman idea of *contubernium*, the Council of Chalons's canon implied that unfree dependents were legal persons capable of entering into a contract. However, this implication does not seem to have changed anything much for these workers, at least not in the Carolingian Empire.

Summary

The Carolingian church was not sure what to do about its dependents, except to hold them fast. Still at odds in choosing between the ancient Frankish customs and the customs of ancient Rome, tempered by the teachings of Christianity, and under the subtle influence of folk customs, the Carolingian church seems to have had no clear and consistent position on the treatment of unfree persons under ecclesiastical dominion by the end of the ninth century. However, it is quite useful to consider these texts because from the juxtaposition of the different strains of thought that can be seen in the corpus of Carolingian material, we can see the outlines of the church's eventual position on the treatment of *servi ecclesiarum*—that they could never become truly free. And we can begin to understand the evolution of this difficult principle.

The data discussed here is by no means sufficient to allow us to make broad generalizations about the nature of ecclesiastical versus lay lords with dominion over unfree workers. Indeed, with the exception of the nonalienability of the *res ecclesiae*, I have found no data to suggest that there were any legal or practical differences in their conditions. Unfree agricultural workers in these samples were clearly treated as chattel on the estates of the laity as well as those of the church. But the size of many ecclesiastical estates had increased greatly as a result of the principle that the *res ecclesiae* were never to be alienated. The majority of the ecclesiastical estates grew so large that they resorted to practices in the management of their servile workers that resembled the old Roman practices in many ways. As we saw in Archbishop Hincmar's letters, this resulted in a less personal and caring relationship between masters and the workers on large church estates than seems to have been the norm on those holdings that were not on such a vast scale. The church was not reactionarily clinging to old Roman land management practices. Indeed, small churches that were not closely affiliated with great foundations seem to have had the same kind of relationship with their *servi* as did most small-scale lay owners—except, of course, for the inalienability issue. However, the canon law that repeatedly insisted on the inalienability of the *res ecclesiae*, and the fact that human assets also fell under the nonalienation principle, made it nearly impossible for those in servitude to the church ever to escape the bonds of that servitude. Despite attempts to treat captives and others with Christian charity, to baptize the *mancipia*, and to allow them to form stable marriages, the catch-22 of the canon law on inalienability resulted in the condition of most unfree ecclesiastical personnel being much less favorable than that of unfree personnel on most lay estates.

The story of Willefrid, a priest in the diocese of Mainz, sums up the question of Carolingian ecclesiastical slavery rather nicely. Lull, the powerful archbishop of Mainz, wrote to Pope Stephen in about 755 complaining about Willefrid: "He took Faegenolph, our *servus*, and his two sons, Raegenolph and Amanolph, and his wife Leobthuthe and his daughter Amaltruthe, and sold them in Saxony to a man named Huelp in exchange for a horse."[99] The letter went on to detail

---

[99]   Lullus, *Epistola* 10, PL 96.827.

the subsequent unpleasant fates of these unfortunates and listed six other ecclesiastical *servi* whom Willefrid had "stolen away" and sold, along with four oxen, eight cows, seven bulls, and many horses, as well as gold, vestments, and armaments. Much of this property went to foreign buyers. The letter also explained why Lull thought that Stephen should intervene: these actions were "in contempt of [the pope's] decrees" about unauthorized alienation of church property and also in contempt of the king's laws about selling slaves, horses, and armaments beyond the boundaries of the realm. The letter listed the names of the donors whose pious intentions had been frustrated. There is nothing at all in this letter about the evils of engaging in the slave trade, or about the probable suffering of the *servi* who had been "stolen away" in such a manner. The issue was that Willefrid had acted without the proper authority. The slaves were simply the valuable property of the church, just like oxen, cows, horses, and armaments. And, like all ecclesiastical property, they were inalienable.

Two hundred years later, near the end of the Carolingian era, when the old political structures were collapsing and the European mainland was again in chaos, not much had changed in the church's views on slavery. There was little difference in this regard from the days of the New Testament writers at the height of the Roman Empire. An important voice from this period was Ratherius, who had become the bishop of Verona in 926. He was ostracized when his excessive zeal led him to make the wrong political choice and his unfortunate personality failed to win him any champions. Nonetheless, Ratherius was widely recognized for his great learning. In Book I of his *Praeloquia* (*Prefaces*), he discussed the duties of a Christian in each of nineteen different positions in society. Positions number 13 and 14 were master and slave, respectively. Rather's advice to the master was to "remember that you and your slave have one Lord and that therefore you are a fellow-slave."[100] A master should not be cruel but should definitely punish wrongdoing. The slave should remember that "if you serve your lord faithfully, you will be the freedman of the Lord of all." Slavery, after all, was created by God as a punishment for original sin, said Ratherius, and God has justly chosen those who are to be slaves. At about this same time, Regino, abbot of Prüm (near the western border of modern Germany), composed his two-volume work *On Synodal Cases and Ecclesiastical Discipline*. And in the section relevant to our issue, he listed regulations of the sale and keeping of *servi* that came right out of the *Theodosian Code*, that is, out of the old Roman law.[101]

What really mattered was the preservation of the *res ecclesiae*.

---

[100] Ratherius of Verona, *Praeloquia* I.13, 14, PL 136.174–76. An English translation can be found in *The Complete Works of Rather of Verona*, trans. P. L. D. Reid (Binghamton, NY 1991).

[101] Regino Abbatis Prumensis, *Libri Duo: De Synodalibus causis et Disciplinis Ecclesiasticis*, ed. F. G. A. Wasserschleben (Leipzig 1840) 2.100.119–23.

Ecclesiastical Slavery in the British Isles

In discussing ecclesiastical servitude in the British Isles, we cannot make unqualified comparisons to the developments on the Continent. The old Roman Empire in continental Europe had been transformed by the arrival of new ruling classes from the North. Before long the alliance of the Frankish rulers with the Christian bishops, especially the bishops of Rome, established a central nexus from which ideas and customs arose over the course of the next thousand years. The British Isles also experienced cultural shock when the Angles and Saxons arrived from the northern rim of Europe in the early fifth century. In the British Isles, the Roman culture—and its version of the Christian religion—seems not to have exerted as great an influence on subsequent cultures as it did on the Continent. Roman Christianity in Britain, which dated back before 200 CE, declined in the areas conquered by the Angles and Saxons until new missionaries arrived from Rome at the end of the sixth century to re-establish Roman Christian customs and order. In Ireland and Scotland and Wales, the ancient Celts and Picts had never fully succumbed to Roman domination. Neither were these regions controlled by the Anglo-Saxons. The Celtic church, including those in Britain who had been converted by Irish missionaries, clung to their ancient order in the tradition of St. Patrick. These very different styles of church organization were not reconciled until after the Synod of Whitby in 664, where all agreed to adhere to Roman customs, especially the criteria for determining the date of the Easter feast. The insular church was now, gradually, coming together and following most of the customs of the church on the Continent.[102]

In early medieval England the use of written law (as opposed to royal proclamations) as a way to regulate society grew very slowly. The new rulers on the Continent had rather quickly embraced the idea of a written law as a means of gaining acceptance and control over a subject population that had lived for centuries under the law of Rome.[103] But the Anglo-Saxon kingdoms, of which there were a number, seem not to have acquired much appreciation

---

[102] The best-known contemporary source for the early history of Christianity in England is Bede, *Historiam Ecclesiasticam Gentis Anglorum* (PL 95); a good English translation, *Ecclesiastical History of the English People*, done by Leo Sherley-Price, has been published by Penguin Books (1955). There are a number of specialized studies, such as Margaret Deansley, *The Pre-Conquest Church in England* (New York 1961) and Nicholas Brooks, *The Early History of the Church of Canterbury* (London 1984). John R. H. Moorman, *A History of the Church in England*, 3rd ed. (London 1973) remains a classic for its insight and lyrical prose.

[103] On this question see Patrick Wormald, *The Making of English Law: King Alfred to the Twelfth Century* (Oxford 1999) and Tom Lambert, *Law and Order in Anglo-Saxon England* (Oxford 2017).

for the usefulness of written law until after the arrival of the new Roman Christian missionaries. The evidence about earlier nonwritten law, both royal proclamations and legal custom, is scant. But it is clear that early on, along with the inconsistency in law from one kingdom to another, there was also no legal consistency from one reign to the next in a given kingdom.

David Pelteret's masterful study, *Slavery in Early Mediaeval England*, has examined in great detail the various factors that influenced the nature of servitude in England.[104] And he concluded that it was the principle of nonalienation of ecclesiastical property that restrained pious wishes to free ecclesiastical slaves. This accords with what we have seen in continental European society and in the Roman, Byzantine East. Here we shall examine for ourselves the records of the insular churches to see what, if anything, was different in their treatment of unfree ecclesiastical dependents.

As was the secular legal landscape, church law in England was relatively disorganized in the Anglo-Saxon era. However, there was also not yet much uniformity in the church on the Continent, except during the period of Charlemagne's reign. The canons from the Anglo-Saxon church councils reveal a church that seems to have been more concerned with eradicating undesirable pagan sexual and dietary customs and magic than with the details of stewardship over the *res ecclesiae* and the management of unfree dependents.[105]

After the Whitby synod, there was a flurry of organizational regulations that continued through the 670s. For example, a council held in Hertford in September 673 confirmed the long-observed, traditional Christian canonical material, but also issued a number of canons about how to organize monasteries, dioceses, and synods and about how to properly and effectively deploy clerical personnel. Ensuring the stability of the clergy—i.e., that they would remain in one place—seems to have been of paramount importance.[106] In contrast, the Council of Hatfield in 680 merely adopted canons issued by a council that had met in the Lateran Palace in Rome in 649. And it adopted only the canons about theological

Concerning ecclesiastical law, see Richard Helmholz, *The Canon Law and Ecclesiastical Jurisdiction from 597 to the 1640s* (Oxford 2004).

[104] (Woodbridge, Suffolk 1995), especially 255–56.
[105] For more depth about these councils see C. R. E. Cuthbert, *Anglo-Saxon Church Councils, 650–850* (London 1995).
[106] Arthur W. Haddon and William S. Stubbs, *Councils and Ecclesiastical Documents Relating to Great Britain and Ireland*, 3 vols. (Oxford 1869–78) 1.118–21.

issues, not the canons that addressed the practicalities of running a large organization.[107] Many church councils of the eighth and ninth centuries were concerned about clergy behavior: public drunkenness, murders, living in lay households, engaging in business ventures. And they clearly struggled with trying to change to a society that was more Christian than pagan: for example, one text commanded priests to refrain from using fresh blood or animal horns in celebrating the Mass.[108] Pagan customs in the Isles seem to have been hard to eradicate. The 747 English Council of Clovesho was concerned about priests who were adopting the presentation style of "worldly poets"—pagan bards?—in leading Christian worship.[109]

The relationship between the church and the various Anglo-Saxon kings varied greatly. King Ethelbert of Mercia exempted monasteries and churches from most, if not quite all, taxes and services due.[110] But most of the Anglo-Saxon kings, despite declarations of protection of the *res ecclesiae*, seem not to have wanted to allow the church full control over its considerable holdings. In 781, the proceedings of the Synod of Brentford recorded that the Monastery of Bath was given to King Offa of Mercia in return for his "confirmation" of the church's ownership of other properties.[111] However, as time went on, royal legislation showed more and more the influence of ecclesiastical advisers in its composition.[112]

As in continental Europe, manumission of one's slaves was regarded as a pious act in Anglo-Saxon England. St. Wilfrid, in the late seventh century while he was bishop of Selsey, received a grant of land and its associated chattels and personnel from King Ethelwalh of the West Saxons. According to Bede, Wilfrid instructed the 250 slaves in Christianity and "released all [of them] from the slavery of Satan by Baptism and by granting their freedom released them from the yoke of human slavery as well."[113]

A rather astonishing canon from the 816 Synod of Chelsea said that when a bishop died, "any Englishman who had been enslaved during his tenure should be set free . . . so that he could reap the fruits of his labors and the

---

[107] Haddon and Stubbs, *Councils and Ecclesiastical Documents* 1.141–59.

[108] Haddon and Stubbs, *Councils and Ecclesiastical Documents* 3.451.

[109] Haddon and Stubbs, *Councils and Ecclesiastical Documents* 3.360–86, c.12.

[110] Haddon and Stubbs, *Councils and Ecclesiastical Documents* 3.386–7, Charter of 749.

[111] Haddon and Stubbs *Councils and Ecclesiastical Documents* 3.438–48.

[112] Helmholz, *Canon Law* 36–37; Pelteret, *Slavery* 80–81.

[113] Bede, *History* IV.13, trans. Sherley-Price 227. Concerning manumission in the British Isles, see David Wyatt, *Slaves and Warriors in Medieval Britain and Ireland, 800–1200* (Leiden 2009).

forgiveness of sins."[114] This sounds as though all of the slaves in the land should be set free. However, as the canon went on to add that lower clergy in the diocese who were mourning the bishop should also each free three slaves, it is more likely that it meant for all those whom the decedent had enslaved (most likely in penal slavery) to be freed upon his demise. Pelteret pointed out a connection between this canon and King Alfred's legislation that referred to the commemorative manumission customs of the ancient Hebrews that were detailed in the book of Exodus.[115] Later legislation continued to provide for manumission on various occasions, although the requirement for all of those in penal servitude to be set free upon the death of their episcopal judge seems to have soon been lost. These regulations indicate the continued belief that freeing slaves was a virtuous act, just as we have seen in stories going back to the Roman Stoics. They also document the fact that clergy and ecclesiastical institutions in the ninth century owned quite a number of slaves. Significantly there is a complete absence of any concern that such manumissions might alienate valuable church property.

Anglo-Saxon manumission documents from before the tenth century are quite scarce, but we have a text from 925 that recorded King Ethelstan's manumission of a slave named Eadhelm and of his children upon Ethelstan's taking the coronation oath.[116] This text and others show that manumissions, by the tenth century at least, usually took place before the clergy and before the altar. In other words, the Anglo-Saxons practiced *manumissio in ecclesia*. But there is no mention in any of these records of any continuing obligation to the church that served as the venue for manumission. The 696 laws of King Wihtred of Kent referred to *manumissio in ecclesia* as well, stating explicitly that anyone who gave someone his freedom "at the altar" would continue to have guardianship over his former slave and his family, no matter where they might be.[117] This post-manumission connection was to the former master, not to the church, as was the continental practice.[118]

---

[114] Chelsea, c.10. Haddon and Stubbs, *Councils and Ecclesiastical Documents* 3.583–4.

[115] Pelteret, *Slavery* 81–85.

[116] *English Historical Documents, c. 500–1042*, ed. D. Whitelock, 2nd ed. (London 1979) #140.

[117] *Laws of King Wihtred of Kent* §8. Haddon & Stubbs, *Councils and Ecclesiastical Documents* 2.235. An interesting study of the laws of King Wihtred and of his contemporary, Archbishop Theodore of Canterbury, can be found in Lisi Oliver, "Royal and Ecclesiastical Law in Seventh-Century Kent," in *Early Medieval Studies in Memory of Patrick Wormald*, ed. S. Baxter et al. (Burlington, VT 2009) 97–112.

[118] A peculiar canon from the Welsh church circa 600 does connect the church with master-slave relationships. Canon 60 states that if a man wanted to marry his female slave, it was allowable, but then he could not sell her. If he did, subsequently, want to sell his slave-wife, he would be punished

Church canons were augmented by another source of ecclesiastical norms called "penitentials."[119] These lists of various sins and their associated penalties—or penances—seem to have originated in the Irish monasteries, whence they spread throughout Europe.[120] The penitential books were quite popular in the Isles and very influential, apparently more so than on the Continent. However, they provide only limited help for our inquiry. Manumission of one's slave(s) was a frequently recommended penance, but it seems to have been more of a financial penalty than anything else. The price of a female slave was commonly used as a unit of value.

The late seventh-century *Penitential of Theodore* said very clearly: "Greek monks do not have slaves; Roman monks have them."[121] Nothing was said, however, about what the Anglo-Saxon church should do in this regard. Provision for slave marriages is found in 13.4. If one of the couple was subsequently set free while the other had to remain in slavery, the free partner was allowed to marry a freeborn person. It is clear that at this point at least, slave marriages were still seen as something analogous to the Roman *contubernium* and had not yet achieved recognition as permanent marriages in the Christian sense. Late Roman church law also appears in the penitential books. In connection with a case where a woman beat her slave, causing the subsequent death of that slave, the *Old English Penitential* prescribed seven years of penance, three if the death had been accidental.[122] A seven-year penance in this situation (five for an accident) had been imposed by canon 5 from the early fourth-century Synod of Elvira. Jurasinski suggested that this penitential may have been a re-casting of the ninth-century Frankish penitential of Halitgar that called for a seven-year/five-year penance in this same situation.[123] However, most of the scholarship about this penitential literature argues that the continental tradition developed under the influence of Anglo/Irish missionaries to the

and the slave woman would be "placed at the disposal of the priest" (Haddon and Stubbs, *Councils and Ecclesiastical Documents* 1.137). I am reluctant to attempt an analysis of this provision other than to note that the Welsh church was not well integrated into European Christendom at that time.

[119] The most well-known collection of these documents is *Medieval Handbooks of Penance*, trans. J. T. McNeill and H. M. Gamer (New York 1938). A standard work on these penitentials is A. J. Frantzen, *The Literature of Penance in Anglo-Saxon England* (New Brunswick, NJ 1993).

[120] Helmholz, *Canon Law* 30.

[121] *Penitential of Theodore* 2.8.4, *Medieval Handbooks of Penance* 3.173–213.

[122] Stefan Jurasinski, "The Old English Penitentials and the Law of Slavery," in *English Law before Magna Carta: Felix Lieberman and Die Gesetze der Angelsachsen*, ed. S. Juranski, L. Oliver, and A. Rabin (Leiden 2010) 97–118.

[123] Jurasinski, "Old English Penitentials" 106–7. His suggestion that the Halitgar text derived from the 506 Council of Agde is inaccurate.

Continent, such as Boniface. And thus, given the old Irish and Anglo-Saxon familiarity with synodal canons, it seems more likely that the Elvira synod was the source for both penitentials, with the Irish church opting for less severe treatment of accidental death than that recommended at Elvira or by the Frankish church. However, these questions of marriage and slave-beating do not necessarily relate to ecclesiastical *servi* and thus do little to answer our primary question. What we have learned about English ecclesiastical *servi* is that *manumissio in ecclesia* does not seem to have resulted in any obligation to the church. And while there was some concern about preserving the *res ecclesiae*, there seems not to have been any idea of a permanent bond between a former slave and the church that had owned him.

In what are now Ireland, Scotland, and Wales, the ancient social structures continued for some time after the Anglo-Saxon church had begun to join the mainstream of Roman Christianity. The eighth-century canonical collection known as the *Hibernensis* included several canons that echo the scriptural commands for slaves to obey their masters and for masters to treat their slaves well. A canon from the Council of Neocaesarea explained that religious piety was no excuse for a slave to neglect his duty.[124] Another important issue was addressed by a canon from the Council of Antioch, saying that when a bishop died it was necessary to separate his personal property from the *res ecclesiae*, which the bishop was forbidden to bequeath to anyone.[125] However, a new Irish canon clarified that a *princeps*, probably meaning an abbot, might bequeath property from the *res ecclesiae* worth the price of a female slave, or up to twenty silver solidi.[126] His successor ought to confirm the gift, but if the gift were more than twenty solidi in value, later "church princes" should revoke it.[127] Augmenting what was clearly an insular custom (a female slave as a unit of value), the canon referred to the Synod of Agde concerning the need for confirmation of a gift. Canon 7 from the 506 Council of Agde included a provision that anything that a bishop might alienate from the *res ecclesiae* had to be approved by two or three other bishops, although nothing about an abbot's bequests. An abbot, frequently referred to as a prince (*princeps*) in early Irish texts, ruled the monastery and all of its lands and dependencies in the same way that a secular ruler would have

---

[124] *The Hibernensis*, ed. R. Flechner (Washington DC 2019) c.23.2, 23.3, 23.4. Also see James F. Kenney, *The Sources for the Early History of Ireland: Ecclesiastical* (New York 1966).

[125] *Hibernensis* 40.5.

[126] *Hibernensis* 40.4.

[127] Fletchner (p. 702) suggested that such a bequest may have been the gift of freedom to the slave.

done.[128] Bishops were usually monks, and as such were subject to the abbot. The position of abbots in the early medieval continental church was different in many respects. But it is interesting to see how the authors of the *Hibernensis* canon tried to legitimate what they must have realized was an unusual provision in their customs by connecting it with a prestigious Gallic synod.[129] And it is interesting that they clearly realized that the role of an Irish abbot was roughly equivalent to that of a continental bishop when it came to church property. The Irish penitential books, as well as a number of the *Hibernensis* canons show that the Irish church shared the same concerns about clerical behavior and safeguarding church property that we have seen elsewhere.

In sum, the insular church of the Early Middle Ages was only beginning to join the mainstream of western Christianity. Its main concerns were still directed toward establishing a Christian culture, and the finer points of church order seem not to have been as urgent as they were in the Carolingian church. In terms of our inquiry, a few things can be noted. First of all, the insular church and its leaders owned a considerable number of slaves. The Irish documents show a careful effort to keep personal property separate from the *res ecclesiae*. The Anglo-Saxon texts were more interested in royal infringements upon the *res ecclesiae* than they were about episcopal improprieties of this sort. And while the insular church was well aware of continental church law, in the early years at least it chose to absorb only those canons that it found useful.[130] Most significant for our purposes is the fact that the Anglo-Saxon church, while practicing *manumissio in ecclesia*, does not seem to have bound the freed person to the church where the ceremony took place, not even if the freed person had been a slave of the church.

---

[128] On this see Maurice Sheehy, "Influences of Ancient Irish Law on the Collectio Canonum Hibernensis," *Proceedings of the Third International Congress of Medieval Canon Law: Strasbourg, 3–6 September 1968*, ed. S. Kuttner Monumenta Iurus Canonici C.4 (Vatican City 1971) 31–42.

[129] Wasserschleben (*Kanonessammlung* 184) noted that the reference to Agde did not appear in all of the manuscript versions of the *Hibernensis*; however, he must have thought that the reference was genuine, given that he included it in the text.

[130] For more on this see Michael D. Elliot, "New Evidence of Gallic Canon Law in Anglo-Saxon England," *Journal of Ecclesiastical History* 6 (2013) 700–730.

7

The Classical Canon Law

The previous chapter introduced a ninth-century canon that said slaves could contract a valid marriage as long as both masters gave their consent.[1] This possibility rested on the implied assumption that slaves were legally recognized as human persons capable of entering into a contractual relationship. The 813 canon from the council in Chalons stated that the marriage of two *servi* was valid and permanent: "A legitimate marriage of *servi* cannot in any way be torn apart . . . 'What God hath joined together, let no man put asunder.' " There was no mention of any qualifications or limitations on the marriage, except for the consent of their master(s). The long debate about the possibility of and the nature of servile marriage continued, and the Chalons canon was included in a number of influential canonical collections over the next few centuries.[2] Most of the earlier discussion about slaves' conjugal relationships had focused on whether or not it was possible—or fitting—for a free person to contract a marriage with an unfree spouse, contamination of the free partner being the main issue. In chapter 3, for example, we saw the strong reaction to Pope Callistus saying that it was better for a free Christian woman to marry a Christian slave than to marry a free pagan. A Christian master who wanted to marry his slave woman had to free her first. Fear of defilement from contact with a servile person continued through the early medieval period. In the absence of any general consensus through these centuries, local customs prevailed, and there was

---

[1] Council of Chalons 813, c.30, MGH, *Concilia*, vol. 2.1, ed. A. Werminghof (Hanover 1906). It is not crucial to our investigation to discuss the motivations for this law. Whether or not it was intended to further the interests of the elite and/or of the institutional church, it still made a difference in the lives of unfree persons.

[2] These collections include, among others, Burchard of Worms's tenth-century *Decretum* IX.2.9; Ivo's eleventh-century *Decretum* 8.167 and 16.335; the eleventh-century *Panormia* 6.40; and Gratian's twelfth-century *Decretum* C.29 q.2 c.8.

Burchard of Worms, *Decretorum libri XX*, ed. G. Franzen and T. Kölzer (Aalen 1992); new editions of Ivo of Chartres and of the *Panormia* can be found at https://ivo-of-chartres.github.io/. (For Gratian's work see note 7.)

For an overview of the debate, see Michael M. Sheehan, "Theory and Practice: Marriage of the Unfree and the Poor in Medieval Society," *Mediaeval Studies* 50 (1988) 457–87.

The Slaves of the Churches. Mary E. Sommar, Oxford University Press (2020). © Oxford University Press.
DOI: 10.1093/oso/9780190073268.001.0001

no resolution of the question of servile marriage, whether with another of servile status or with a free person.

But, by the early twelfth century, the general consensus about the canon law concerning marriage of the unfree was that, as baptized persons, they should indeed be permitted to marry and to receive the sacrament of marriage, especially since the alternatives were either abstinence (unlikely) or fornication (undesirable). Hiding one's servile status in a marriage to a free person was generally considered grounds for annulment. Marriage between unfree persons having different masters, sometimes called *formariage*, was encouraged. This would decrease the likelihood of incestuous unions, but such a marriage generally required the masters' consent the same as for marriages contracted locally. Once a marriage had been made, however, the spousal duty seems to have rivaled or even superseded the duty to one's master. For example, a master could not prevent a *servus* from visiting his spouse who lived on another estate. As an illustration of this we have two letters written by Pope Alexander III (1159–1181) about the abbot of Saint-Remi in Reims, Peter Cellensis. Peter had apparently caused difficulties for at least three "men of Saint-Remi" who were married to women tied to other masters. Peter's actions could be interpreted as an attempt to preserve the *res ecclesiae*. However, the pope said that such behavior on the part of the abbot was improper. These were legitimate marriages that could not be dissolved, and Peter was neither to pursue these men if they were visiting their wives nor to impose any undue burdens upon them.[3] However, not all ecclesiastical masters were so difficult. In many cases the solution was for the masters to exchange *servi* so that spouses could live together.[4]

A groundbreaking legal treatise of the early twelfth century provided a thorough analysis of marriage in all of its forms and provided solutions that supported the church's desire to regulate the pairing of all European Christians, no matter their legal status.[5] And, as with the Reims case, spousal

---

[3] *Perlatum est* (JL 11957) and *Significauit nobis* (JL 11826) reprinted in Antonina Nina Sahaydachny, *De coniugio servorum: A Study of the Legal Debate about the Marriage of Unfree Persons among Decretists and Decretalists from A.D. 1140–1215* (Columbia University dissertation 1994) 59–60.

[4] See Robert F. Berkhofer III, "Marriage, Lordship and the 'Greater Unfree' in Twelfth-Century France," *Past & Present* 173 (2001) 3–27.

[5] There have been a good number of scholarly discussions of the medieval canon law of marriage, especially the law from the twelfth and later centuries. These include Peter Landau, "Die Eheschliessung von Freien mit Unfreien bei Burchard von Worms und Gratian: Ein Beitrag zur Textkritik der Quellen des kanonischen Rechts und zur Geschichte christlicher Umformung des Eherechts," in *Christianità ed Europa: Miscellanea di studi in onore di Luigi Prosdocimi*, ed. C. Alzati (Rome 1994) I.453–61;

rights could sometimes conflict with the principle of the nonalienation of church property.

Master Gratian of Bologna

In the twelfth century, when the church began to concern itself with a more comprehensive approach to church law, including regulations for Christian marriages, the canon from Chalons was included in a new analytic compendium of canon law *Concordia discordantium canonum*, better known today as Gratian's *Decretum*. Although this treatise was not officially promulgated as the law of the church until the late sixteenth century, from its first appearance in around the 1130s it enjoyed considerable authority.[6] In a number of texts written shortly after the appearance of this otherwise anonymous work, scholars attributed it to a "Master Gratian."

Master Gratian of Bologna is the central figure of this chapter. However, for Gratian even more than for the people who were the exemplars in earlier chapters, we have almost no reliable biographical information. Over the centuries, scholars have attempted to establish his life story and the circumstances that gave rise to the *Concordia discordantium canonum* that so revolutionized the study of church law.[7] But, while there is little certainty of

Peter Landau, "Hadrians IV. Dekretale 'Dignum est' (X.4.9.1) und die Eheschliessung Unfreier in der Diskussion von Kanonisten und Theologen des 12. und 13. Jahrhunderts," *Studia Gratiana* 12 (1967) 512–53; John T. Noonan, "Speech at Catholic Law School on *Causa* 29," *Catholic University Law Review* 47(1998) 1189–98; Sheehan, "Theory and Practice"; Anders Winroth, "Neither Slave nor Free: Theology and Law in Gratian's Thoughts on the Definition of Marriage and Unfree Persons," in *Medieval Church Law and the Origins of the Western Legal Tradition*, ed. W. P. Müller and M. E. Sommar (Washington, DC 2006) 97–109; and Charles de Miramon, "Guillaume de Champagne et la règle de droit des personnes," in *Der Einfluss der Kanonistik auf die europäische Rechtskultur*, ed. O. Condorelli et al. (Cologne 2009) 33–66.

See also Christopher N. L. Brooke, "Aspects of Marriage Law in the Eleventh and Twelfth Centuries," in *Proceedings of the Fifth International Congress of Medieval Canon Law, Salamanca, 21–25 September, 1976*, ed. S. Kuttner and K. Pennington, MIC, Series C: Subsidia, 6 (Vatican City 1980) 333–44; James A. Brundage, *Law, Sex, and Christian Society in Medieval Europe* (Chicago 1987); James A. Brundage, "E Pluribus Unum: Custom, the Professionalization of Medieval Law, and Regional Variations in Marriage Formation," in *Regional Variations in Matrimonial Law and Custom in Europe, 1150–1600*, ed. M. Korpiola (Boston 2011) 21–44; and R. H. Helmholz, *Marriage Litigation in Medieval England* (London 1976).

[6] The dating of this work is unclear; estimates range from as early as 1129 to as late as the 1140s. The recent insight that there was more than one recension of the *Decretum* was the subject of Anders Winroth, *The Making of Gratian's Decretum* (Cambridge 2000). On the eventual promulgation of this text as the official law of the church see Mary E. Sommar, *The Correctores Romani: Gratian's Decretum and the Counter-Reformation Humanists* (Vienna 2009).

[7] This *Harmony of Discordant Canons* was soon referred to simply as the *Decretum*.

the accuracy of our reconstructions of Gratian's story, it is fairly certain that the *Decretum* was produced in Bologna, Italy, in the first half of the twelfth century.[8] The University of Bologna had begun as a law school, soon outshining the school of law in the nearby city of Pavia, and it was in Bologna that the new science of jurisprudence began to flourish. A large body of written legal decisions as well as learned commentary was soon produced.[9] Learned in theology as well as in both the secular and the ecclesiastical legal traditions, Gratian produced a work that, to my professorial imagination, most resembles a collection of lecture notes for a course covering all aspects of canon law, with the later versions, or recensions, reflecting his developing thought on various legal questions over the years. The work was used by generations of students as a textbook. This *Decretum* was organized into thirty-six *causae* (cases) and 101 *distinctiones* (individual or "distinct" items to be discussed), as well as two treatises, "On Penance" and "On Consecration."[10] The *causae* were further organized into *quaestiones* (questions). Pertinent material, legal and theological, from the previous thousand years of ecclesiastical tradition was gathered for each question. Then each aspect of a question or distinction was analyzed from all sides, listing ancient and recent texts (*capitula* or "little chapters") pro and con. As well as supplying explanations for obscure or difficult texts, Gratian also provided his own commentary (*dicta*), showing how logic and basic legal and theological principles could resolve apparent conflicts in the material. What Scholastics like Thomas Aquinas did for the study of theology by using Aristotle's dialectic method to resolve difficulties by means of logic and reason, Gratian of Bologna did for the study of law.

The most recent full edition of this work is that of Emil Richter, revised by Emil Friedberg (*Corpus iuris canonici*, 2 vols. [Leipzig 1879]). It can be accessed online at https://searchworks.stanford.edu/.

[8] Some scholars claim that "Gratian" is a composite of several different people because of the considerable inconsistencies in the final version of the *Decretum*, while others think that these variations stem from Gratian's maturing ideas over the course of his lifetime. Some think Gratian was a monk, and interesting evidence has been produced for the idea that he was the bishop of Chiusi, Italy, in the mid-twelfth century. But there is no doubt that Gratian was a law professor at the newly established university in Bologna, Italy in the early twelfth century. Examples of the considerable scholarly debate on these questions can be found in Anders Winroth, "Recent Work on the Making of Gratian's *Decretum*," *Bulletin of Medieval Canon Law* 26 (2004) 1–29 and Anders Winroth, "Where Gratian Slept: The Life and Death of the Father of Canon Law," *ZRG.KA* 99 (2013) 105–28, and in Kenneth Pennington, "The Biography of Gratian, the Father of Canon Law," *Villanova Law Review* 59 (2014) 679–706.

[9] For more about the schools of law see James Brundage, *Medieval Canon Law* (New York 1995) 44–69.

[10] John Dillon's interesting article, "Case Statements (Themata) and the Composition of Gratian's Cases," *ZRG.KA* 92 (2006) 306–39 explored how Gratian's cases resemble modern legal teaching.

Historical Context

Before we analyze Gratian's handling of the *servi ecclesiarum*, as he called them, it would be helpful to review the relevant social and political as well as legal changes that had taken place in western Europe since the Carolingian period.[11]

After the waning of the Carolingian kingdoms at the end of the ninth century, a long time passed before stable monarchies with strong leaders emerged to reshape the map of Europe. Throughout much of that interval, Europe was threatened on all sides: by the Vikings in the North and in the West; by the Arabs, often called Saracens, from the South; and by the Magyars and others from the East. Under pressures from without and within, politics became very local, and the nobility gained in power and in the ability to act on their own. Chris Wickham has put this very well: the Carolingian duke *in* a region had been the king's man; his descendants saw themselves as the dukes *of* a region, rulers in their own right.[12] After the turn of the millennium, although the press of foreign invasion lessened, these powerful noble families' continuing struggles also required the efforts of their dependent people, sometimes in battle, but always in producing food and other necessities. Whether these peasants were servile or free made little difference in their living conditions: nearly everyone was forced into supporting their lord in one way or another.[13] The chronicles lament the nobles' regular violation of long-held social and moral norms concerning power and the maintenance of public order. However, as Susan Reynolds pointed out, in the absence of strong kings, local lords had no choice but to maintain order in their own

---

[11] Recent scholarship has enjoyed a lively debate about just what was going on during this era. In the last decade or so before the year 2000, a number of people talked about the "revolution" of the year 1000. See, e.g., Thomas Bisson's 1994 article, "The 'Feudal Revolution,'" *Past & Present* 142: 6–42), which became the focus of a series of responses: in #152 (1996) from Dominique Barthélemy (196–205) and Stephen White (205–23); in #155 (1997) from Timothy Reuter (177–95) and Chris Wickham (196–208), as well as Bisson's reply to his critics (208–25). Since then, a number of scholars have argued for a more nuanced approach that takes into account enormous variability from place to place and over time. Helpful works include R. I. Moore, *The First European Revolution, c. 970–1215* (Oxford 2000); Susan Reynolds, *Kingdoms and Communities in Western Europe, 900–1300*, 2nd ed. (Oxford 1997); Chris Wickham, *The Inheritance of Rome* (New York 2009); Chris Wickham, *Medieval Europe* (New Haven 2016); and Alice Rio, *Slavery after Rome* (Oxford 2017). Charles West, *Reframing the Feudal Revolution* (Cambridge 2013), added to the discussion with his appeal to the Carolingian roots of what changes did occur.

[12] Wickham, *The Inheritance of Rome* 430.

[13] On the idea of enslavement as a common metaphor for the peasants' "radical dependency" in this period, see Thomas Bisson, *The Crisis of the Twelfth Century: Power, Lordship, and the Origins of European Government* (Princeton 2009).

lands.[14] Many of these men took seriously the idea that they had a God-given duty to provide justice and to behave honorably as well as to respect those over whom they ruled and to honor their customs. Reynolds also reminded us that, in medieval Europe, unlike the situation in most modern societies, those who were under these lords' control generally seem to have believed in the idea of a society where all men were most definitely not created equal. Being subject to another was acceptable—as long as one's betters followed the rules. By the twelfth century, relatively stable kingdoms began to emerge in France and England. The Holy Roman Empire was now reconstituted as a collection of smaller political entities (kingdoms, duchies, and principalities) centered in what later became Germany and Italy. In England and France, the king was theoretically supreme, although the effectiveness of the royal efforts varied. In the empire, the rulers of the smaller polities pledged loyalty to one imperial leader, chosen from among their own number for a life tenure. But the fervor of that loyalty often waivered.

The church's position in this unsettled period was complex. The papacy, which had not had much independent political power in the late Carolingian period, was able to benefit from the relative power vacuum caused by the absence of powerful kings and began slowly to establish itself as a pan-European authority.[15] The bishop of Rome was transformed from a bishop who commanded local authority and enjoyed a measure of influence throughout Europe into the "Vicar of Christ" who could negotiate with kings and princes. These changes began with local monastic reforms in the tenth century that were eventually extended to include the whole church, non-monastic clergy as well as the papacy. Secular rulers' influence over their local clergy was often viewed as unacceptable interference with the more centralized control that Rome tried to implement along with the new reform standards. But the

---

[14] Susan Reynolds, *Kingdoms and Communities*. Also very helpful is Reynolds's preface to her collected articles in *The Middle Ages without Feudalism: Essays in Criticism and Comparison on the Medieval West* (Surry 2012).

[15] This period is sometimes called the "Gregorian Reform" after Pope Gregory VII, who was a powerful proponent of these changes. And the church-state struggle is also known as the "Investiture Controversy" (named for a dispute over who had the right to invest a new bishop in a vacant see). There are several classic discussions from the late twentieth century: Ute-Renate Blumenthal, *The Investiture Controversy: Church and Monarchy from the Ninth to the Twelfth Century* (Philadelphia 1988); Kenneth Pennington, *Pope and Bishops: The Papal Monarchy in the Twelfth and Thirteenth Centuries* (Philadelphia 1984); I. S. Robinson, *The Papacy, 1073–1198* (Cambridge 1990); and Gerd Tellenbach, *Die Westliche Kirche vom 10. Bis zum frühen 12. Jahrhundert* (Göttingen 1988). Recently a number of scholars have revisited these conclusions, but a new consensus has not yet emerged. See Conrad Leyser's review article, "Church Reform—Full of Sound and Fury, Signifying Nothing?," *Early Medieval Europe* 24 (2016) 478–99 and Claudia Zey, *Der Investiturstreit* (Munich 2017), for an overview of the most recent understandings.

secular rulers' desire to control their ecclesiastical aristocracy was hard to overcome.[16] Nevertheless, the Roman papal bureaucracy grew in time into an administrative center for an international church hierarchy of bishops and their priests. The local churches, as well as the monasteries, had to compete against the local secular lords for both power and resources, and it was the competing goals of these various groups that resulted in the numerous clashes between ecclesiastical and secular power. These clashes occasionally involved armed men, but more often were expressed through legal and diplomatic battles.

Not surprisingly, the situation of the laboring population experienced many changes as well in this period of adjustment. Although the process varied enormously throughout the various regions of western Europe, by the later medieval period, the phenomena of servility and dependence were no longer the same as they had been in earlier centuries. By Gratian's time, although the vast *latifundia* of the ancient world were long gone, unfree labor was still a staple of everyday economic life. Agricultural workers no longer labored in gangs but instead lived in family units who worked a particular parcel of the lord's land. Yet many of them were still unfree *servi*, despite their somewhat better everyday circumstances. According to Wickham, only in Italy and Spain was there a significant population of free landowning peasants at this time.[17] Domestic slavery continued as well, especially in southern urban areas, little changed over the centuries. And the international slave trade, especially with the caliphate in the East and with Scandinavia, continued to prosper.[18]

Towns had become more influential in social, economic, and political life, but the laboring population was not treated the same in all towns. Modern scholars have described the customs in the North with the cliché: *Stadtluft macht frei!* (City air makes one free). But this was not universally the case. Especially in the South, where the urban centers of the ancient Romans had never totally disappeared, there was considerable slavery in nonrural settings. Port cities such as Venice, Genoa, Marseille, and Barcelona were entrepôts

---

[16] On this see, e.g., T. Reuter, "The 'Imperial Church System' of the Ottonian and Salian Rulers: A Reconsideration," *Journal of Ecclesiastical History* 33 (1982) 347–74.

[17] Wickham, *Medieval Europe* 125.

[18] See, for example,Iris Origo's fascinating study, *The Merchant of Prato: Francesco di Marco Datini, 1335–1410* (New York 1957) and also Olivia Remie Constable, *Medieval Trade in the Mediterranean World* (New York 2001). Charles Verlinden, *L'esclavage dans l'Europe médiéval* (Bruges 1955) provided a good deal of documentary evidence showing that the Mediterranean slave trade continued strong into the fifteenth century.

for the slave trade with other Mediterranean areas, as well as with the Black Sea region.[19] In the southern cities, slaves, usually with non-European and thus non-Christian origins, worked mostly as domestics (predominantly women) and as laborers and in the trades (predominantly men).[20] As in ancient Rome, in late medieval southern Europe the very fact that someone was willing to perform such dishonorable labor was seen to confirm their inherent servility.[21]

In the last chapter we saw some gradual changes in peasants' lives during the course of the Carolingian Empire. The political changes of the post-Carolingian era resulted in more changes for the agricultural labor force. Europe had more free and semifree peasants than had been the case in earlier centuries, but they were often worse off.[22] There has recently been a great deal of scholarship about these changes: what were they and why did they come about? For our purposes it is necessary to understand only the general situation of the workers and their relationships with their masters, in particular, their ecclesiastical masters. Property owners needed profitable estates to fund their efforts to amass power and territory. Peasants were responsible for producing the profits. And their lords, lay or ecclesiastical, used whatever means were at hand to maximize these profits. While some chattel slaves were useful for household tasks, for the most part it was easier and cheaper to let the laborers fend for themselves, whether free or unfree. Instead of outright legal ownership of the labor force, the lords gradually instituted new systems of control over the peasants' lives that included far more than the exorbitant

---

[19] On the question of urban slavery see Sally McKee, "Inherited Status and Slavery in Late Medieval Italy and Venetian Crete," *Past & Present* 182 (2002) 31–53; Olivia Remie Constable, "Muslim Spain and Mediterranean Slavery: The Medieval Slave Trade as an Aspect of Muslim-Christian Relations," in *Christendom and Its Discontents*, ed. S. L. Waugh and P. D. Diehl (Cambridge 1996) 264–84; Stephen P. Bensch, "From Prizes of War to Domestic Merchandise: The Changing Face of Slavery in Catalonia and Aragon, 1000–1300," *Viator* 25 (1994) 63–94; William D. Phillips Jr., *Slavery from Roman Times to the Early Transatlantic Trade* (Minneapolis 1985) 88–113; Susan Mosher Stuard, "Urban Domestic Slavery in Medieval Ragusa," *Journal of Medieval History* 9 (1983) 155–71; Jacques Heers, *Esclaves et domestiques au Moyen Age dans le monde méditerranéen* (Paris 1981); Iris Origo, "The Domestic Enemy: The Eastern Slaves in Tuscany in the Fourteenth and Fifteenth Centuries," *Speculum* 30 (1955) 321–66; and Neven Budak, "Slavery in Late Medieval Dalmatia/Croatia: Labour, Legal Status, Integration," *Mélanges de L'École française de Rome* 112 (2000) 745–60.

[20] Steven Epstein's *Speaking of Slavery: Color, Ethnicity, & Human Bondage in Italy* (Ithaca 2001) is exceptionally helpful on this. Susan Mosher Stuard investigated the lives of female domestic workers in "Ancillary Evidence for the Decline of Medieval Slavery," *Past and Present* 149 (1995) 3–28, as did David Herlihy, *Opera Muliebria: Women and Work in Medieval Europe* (New York 1990).

[21] William Chester Jordan pointed out that tradesmen were seen as performing duties just as dishonorable as those of agricultural workers. *From Servitude to Freedom* (Philadelphia 1986) 12.

[22] This has been a particularly rich area of scholarship in the past couple of decades, and here only a superficial summary is possible if we are to continue on topic. See the appendix for a somewhat more detailed overview of the scholarly trends of the past few decades.

rents that were charged for the privilege of farming the land. This has sometimes been called "banal lordship." The lord's *bannum*, his coercive and/or sovereign powers, forced the peasants to use the lord's ovens, to buy the lord's beer or wine, to use his mill, and to cut their wood from his forest—all for a fee—and to pay for the use of roads and bridges and ports and even market facilities. Additionally, since the lord had control over the local administration of justice, he controlled the application of penalties and then received all of the fines that were levied. The difference between free and unfree peasants became blurred: aristocrats had so much control over their peasants' lives and behavior that legal status of servility or freedom no longer seems to have mattered very much. Indeed, as time went on, many lords found that encouraging the peasants to buy their freedom, either individually or as a group or as a town, was a convenient source of funds.[23] These "banal" rights were a major asset for whoever held them. The cartulary of the monastery of Saint-Nicaise in Reims has a number of entries that documented this *bannum*.[24] For example, in August 1160, Archbishop Samson of Reims confirmed that on one of the numerous property holdings of this monastery the monks held assets in the form of *servi* and *ancillae* and also land with tenants, mills, and so on, some "with ban and justice" and some without.[25] Early in the twelfth century, the revenue from such lordship, as well as from the courts, was a major factor in the monastery's wealth. In a deed of August 3, 1135, the archbishop confirmed Saint-Nicaise's acquisition of various properties "with ban and justice" as well as various other real estate and personnel.[26] When real estate was sold, by the mid-thirteenth century, banal rights were included along with the right of dominion over the associated free as well as unfree personnel.[27]

In the last chapter we looked at the records of a number of different monasteries to see what they could tell us about the unfree population. We saw that, indeed, there were many gifts of servile persons given to ecclesiastical institutions and that in many circumstances it was clear that these individuals were very much like chattel slaves and that the *res ecclesiae* were clearly respected as inalienable. A somewhat surprising discovery was the variability in the language used to describe the servile persons who were being

---

[23] One of the best recent explanations of these developments can be found in Wickham, *The Inheritance of Rome*, in the chapter titled "The Caging of the Peasantry" 529–51.

[24] *Cartulaire de Saint-Nicase de Reims*, ed. J. Cossé-Durlin (Paris 1991).

[25] *Saint-Nicaise #27*.

[26] *Saint-Nicaise #48*.

[27] *Saint-Nicaise #261* (August 13, 1249).

given to the church. In the records of smaller gifts from those who did not have great wealth, the donated *mancipia* were often named and their personal traits described. But in the deeds of larger gifts from the very wealthy, this was not the case, perhaps because masters of more modest means may have had a more personal connection to their servile dependents, thinking of them as individuals who had the misfortune of servile status rather than merely as resources to be deployed for maximum efficiency.

Arguably the major landowners in the late medieval world, ecclesiastical institutions held *dominium* over thousands of agricultural workers, free and unfree.[28] The Cistercians attempted to reform the monastic exploitation of their laborers by making them *conversi*, members of the Cistercian religious community who were not regular monks, but lay brothers. But the attempt was not very successful.[29] Before long, the Cistercians were acquiring and exploiting servile laborers as much as any other monastic community.[30] Monastic records like the polyptichs of Saint-Pierre de Lobbes detail the workings of their vast estates.[31] There are fewer such records about the ecclesiastical domestic *servi*. However, we do see reference to them, especially to priests' *ancillae*. With the growing emphasis on legal documentation, the later medieval period also produced innumerable registers of gifts and other transactions.

In addition to a continuing interest in the inalienability of church property, these later gift registers show something new.

The cartulary of the Abbey of Saint Père near Chartres is very extensive, but it has been extremely well organized according to the category of gift, making it amenable to analysis. Among the 185 charters from the twelfth century that discussed subservience, we find several interesting items.[32] On November 2, 1107, Gaufridus and Gausleno de Leugis gave the abbey their *servus* "Godescaldum and his wife, M." and "all their children, those born

---

[28] For some statistics see David Herlihy, "Church Property on the European Continent, 710–1200," *Speculum* 36 (1961) 81–105.

[29] On the *Rule* establishing this "lay brotherhood," see Constance H. Berman, *The Cistercian Evolution: The Invention of a Religious Order in Twelfth-Century Europe* (Philadelphia 2000) 20–21. On the difficulties of the reform see Coburn V. Graves, "The Economic Activities of the Cistercians in Medieval England (1128–1307)," *Analecta Sacri Ordinis Cisterciensis* 13 (1957) 3–54.

[30] There are a number of records of these transactions in numerous Cistercian inventories. See G. G. Coulton, *The Medieval Village* (Cambridge 1925) 331 n. 3, 147 n. 2 for citations.

[31] *Le polyptique et les listes de biens de l'abbaye Saint-Pierre de Lobbes (IXe–XIe siècles): Edition critique*, ed. J.-P. Devroey (Brussels 1986).

[32] *Cartulaire do L'Abbaye de Saint-Père de Chartres*, ed. M. Guérard, *Collection des Cartulaires de France*, vol. 2 (Paris, 1840) part II. *Codex Argenteus*, Book 1: De rebus ad cellarium pertinentes (257–399).

and those yet to come," and all of the family's belongings.[33] This simple gift of a servile family was made "to save [the donors'] souls." A number of entries mentioned manumission, including purchasing one's own freedom. In the early twelfth century, Radulf Conduit bought his own freedom and that of his wife in exchange for "a stall at the city gate" and for a "portion" in his will. The deed stated that he and his wife were "fully free forever."[34] The "stall" that he gave probably meant at least a portion of its revenue, and without any stipulated amount or period of time, we can probably assume that this meant in perpetuity. At about the same time, when a certain Guarinus was freed in exchange for a parcel of land, he also had to make continuing payments.[35]

By mid-century, there were a number of documents mentioning such payments to the abbey, frequently using the word *census* to describe the kind of payment needed; beginning in the second half of the twelfth century, the word *feudum* was often used instead, at least in this particular register. However, instead of the *census* being post-manumission obligations, it was usually the obligations resulting from various ways that individuals gave themselves or other persons to the ecclesiastical institution. Sometimes the exchanges were simple gifts or simple sales; sometimes there was no gift except for the annual payments due. One deed made it clear that labor and services were two very different things.[36] The *census* payment was often taken over by the heirs of the original party: when Gaufridus died, his brother Robert took over the *census*; in another deed, it was the sons who assumed responsibility for the annual payment of fifteen solidi.[37] In these deeds, the use of personal names does not particularly suggest fondness for the workers, but rather that the abbey wanted to be clear about who bore legal responsibility for the payments.

The register of gifts for the diocese of Regensburg in Bavaria, including the monastery of St. Emmeram, recorded a number of these *censuales*, as those who had to pay the *census* were called.[38] Indeed, most of the register's deeds of exchange for the tenth, eleventh, and twelfth centuries discussed the arrangements for *census* due to the imperial monastery of St. Emmeram. The rights of the *censuales* were clearly delimited as well. In 1174, Abbot Adalbert

---

[33] *Saint-Père de Chartres* #17.
[34] *Saint-Père de Chartres* #36.
[35] *Saint-Père de Chartres* #43.
[36] *Saint-Père de Chartres* #47.
[37] *Saint-Père de Chartres* #45 and #44, respectively.
[38] *Die Traditionen des Hochstifts Regensburg und des Klosters S. Emmeram*, ed. J. Widemanns (Munich 1943).

of St. Emmeram confirmed that a certain group of *censuales* were "men of the most free condition."[39] Other *censuales* remained *servi*. In the late twelfth century, one man gave his *servus* to the monastery as a *censual* but retained ownership of the *servus* and his agricultural labor services, and the donor made the annual *census* payment to the monks.[40] Not all *censuales* were farmers. Ulrich the furrier bought his freedom from his mistress Gertrude and gave himself to St. Emmeram, stipulating that as a freedman as well as a *censual* he was "not under [their] *dominium*.[41]

The records of the monastery of Saint-Aubin of Angers contain similar cases about those who paid a *census* to the monastery.[42] Here these persons were referred to as *colliberti*. In around the year 1100, the monks promised to give up their claim on Gortrud's house if she would give up any rights over Drogo and his siblings, former *servi* who were now *colliberti*.[43] In the late eleventh century, Martinus Chabot was apparently unhappy to have been declared a *collibertus* and part of the *familia* of Saint-Aubin's daughter house, Saint-Remy-la-Varenne. But it seems that Martinus's relative, Giraldus, had received land and other considerations in return for forcing Martinus into this situation.[44] And in about 1165, another unfortunate soul, Guillaume de Beaumex, was forced to give a parcel of land to the Saint-Aubin daughter house of Fresnay-le-Vicomte in exchange for the *census* payments he owed.[45] In 903, Norduin, a man of some means, gave substantial gifts to the abbey in Flavigny for the salvation of his soul and the souls of his family.[46] The gifts included the *mancipia* Stephan, his wife Raginelde, and their daughters Araginelda and Palsinna, along with another family group of *mancipia*, Arembald, his wife Armelda, and their sons Arembert and Archivis and his two sons. The *census* payments for the females was half that for the males. And it was to be paid unless the *mancipia* returned to the land that Norduin had donated for the general use of the monks. There was no clear statement that the *mancipia* had been freed, but this last provision, that they had to pay the *census* only if they chose not to work the land, suggests that if they paid the annual amount, no labor services were required.

---

[39] *Regensburg #906.*
[40] *Regensburg #985.*
[41] *Regensburg #908.*
[42] *Cartulaire de Saint-Aubin D'Angers*, ed. E. De Long (Paris 1903).
[43] *Saint-Aubin D'Angers* #65.
[44] *Saint-Aubin D'Angers* #194.
[45] *Saint-Aubin D'Angers* #357.
[46] *The Cartulary of Flavigny*, ed. C. B. Bouchard (Cambridge, MA 1991) #26.

This data demonstrates that this post-Carolingian period had seen a large increase of another group of unfree persons called, variously, *censuales* (German *Zensualen*), *tributarii*, or *colliberti* (French, *culvert*) or *tributarii* (Flanders).[47] In the last chapter we saw that in 852, Hincmar had been concerned about census payments due the Villa Douzy of Saint-Rémy. And earlier we saw references to similar situations in the law of the Alamans and in the *Formulae* of Angers. By the end of the millennium, the practice had increased considerably.

While their condition varied considerably over time and from place to place, these individuals had a few things in common. First, they all acknowledged that they owed their lords or masters some form of service (often referred to as *census*). Also, while their situation allowed them a good deal of control over their lives, they clearly did not enjoy full legal freedom. In return for the services and the lowered status, they received some kind of protection. Most of these relationships were between an unfree person and the church, but some *censuales* were managed by a lay lord whose estate chapel's patron saint was the recipient of the pledge of service. And some enjoyed free legal status despite their obligations to the church.

There were two principal ways of becoming a *censual*. The most common way was in cases where a person donated his or her *servus* to a local monastery, the deed of transfer stating that a *census*, a money payment or some other relatively light annual obligation, was due to the monastery from the donated person. As early as 855, Charlemagne's grandson, Emperor Lothar, made a generous gift to the Chapel of Our Lady in Aachen including "*mancipia* and *censuales* and their fees."[48] Sometimes people would simply give or bequeath their *servi* to the church. But frequently, the deed of gift would say that the

---

[47] There is quite a bit of scholarship on this practice. Knut Schulz, "Zum Problem der Zensualität im Hochmittelalter," in his collected essays, *Die Freiheit des Bürgers: Städtische Gesellschaft im Hoch- und Spätmittelalter* (Darmstadt 2008), is an excellent introduction. See also Stefan Esders, *Die Formierung der Zensualität: Zur kirchlichen Transformation des spätrömischen Patronatswesens im früheren Mittelalter* (Ostfildern 2010); P. C. Boeren, *Etude sur les tributaires d'église dans le comté de Flandre du IXe au XIVe siècle* (Amsterdam 1936); and Michael Borgolte, "Freigelassene im Dienst der Memoria: Kulttradition und Kultwandel zwischen Antike und Mittelalter," *Frühmittelalterliche Studien* 17 (1983) 234–50. Marc Bloch's article "Les 'colliberti': Etude sur la formation de la classe servile," *Revue Historique* 157 (1928) 1–48, still remains very helpful. See also, among others, Michael Matheus, "Forms of Social Mobility: The Example of *Zensualität*," in *England and Germany in the High Middle Ages*, ed. A. V. Haverkamp and H. Vollrath (Oxford 1996) 357–69; Dominique Barthélemy, *The Serf, the Knight, and the Historian*, trans. G. R. Edwards (Ithaca 2009) 126–36 (originally *La mutation de l'an mil a-t-elle eu lieu? Servage et chevalrie dans la France du Xe et XIe siècles* [Paris 1997]); and Francesco Panero, "Il tema dei colliberti medievali," in *Uomini paesaggi storie: Studie di storia medievale per Giovanni Cherubini* (Siena 2012).

[48] MGH, *Diplomata Karolinorum*, vol. 3, ed. E. Mühlbacher et al. (Berlin 1996) #136.

owner first freed the *servus* and then gave the freedman to the church, with the requirement that the freedman pay a *census* to the church, in lieu of the customary obligations that a freedman would owe a former owner. This led Stefan Esders to conclude that the *censuales* were a later form of those obligated to the church after being freed by means of *manumissio in ecclesia*.[49] The other possibility for entering into such a relationship was when those who had formerly been fully free gave themselves voluntarily into the service of the church. More exactly, they were given into the service of the patron saint of that particular church as *censuales*. Alice Rio pointed out that sometimes this seems to have been a way for the non-noble class to retire to a monastery at the end of their lives without having to take the monastic vows.[50] And it was certainly a good way for anyone who felt vulnerable to gain the protection, legal as well as physical, of a powerful monastery.

The most striking feature of the *censuales* is that they were almost always classified as servile, even those whose occupations gave them high status in the community. Many *censuales* were estate administrators or even knights. Eventually, in some areas it became customary to pledge oneself as a *censual* in order to gain a position as an administrator or an artisan or a skilled tradesman. For such persons, the spiritual motivation may well have been rather insignificant, the *census* being viewed as a sort of licensing fee. At the same time, it was of considerable value to the ecclesiastical institution (or other recipient) to have the services of these skilled *censuales* available, as well as any annual *census* payments in cash or in kind.

The records almost always state that this person was given to a particular saint and that the *census* would be paid to "the altar of St. X." Numerous records of such donations indicate that this gift (of oneself or of one's *servi*) was made for spiritual reasons, "for the good of my soul," or "so that God will forgive my sins." Although the anticipated countergift was expected from a heavenly source, it was the very earthly agent who cared for the saint's tomb who actually managed the disposition of the *census* payments. The *censuales* and their *census* payments were included among the assets of the church, among the *res ecclesiae*, and thus they are of interest for this study of how the church dealt with its unfree dependents. However, the *censuales* were not the same as *servi*; this was not exactly enslavement, but a contractual relationship between the donor and the respective saint.

---

[49] Esders, *Die Formierung der Zensualität*.
[50] Rio, *Slavery after Rome* 60, 101–2. Page 55 n. 2 presents a number of examples of such donations.

It is hard for post-Enlightenment minds to understand this. The modern Western heaven is not a very businesslike place. But it is this experience of the immediacy of God and the saints in medieval people's lives that probably explains why they so easily went along with the principle that the *res ecclesiae* were not to be alienated. It was not so much the stated legal reasons or the need to keep church personnel in the circumstances to which they had become accustomed, or even that people were afraid of the power of some of the larger ecclesiastical institutions. It is much more likely to have been that many if not most medieval people would never have taken away what belonged to God or to one of the saints. We saw that in earlier centuries, donors believed that their salvation was on the line. Alienation of the *res ecclesiae* required a very serious reason because of the majesty of their supernatural owner and because of the potentially eternal consequences of noncompliance with the terms of the original agreement.

Recently much interest has been paid to the "gift economy" of medieval Europe. In societies without a universal, stable monetary system, giving gifts, with the expectation of countergifts, is quite common. In gifts made to a church or to a monastery "for the good of my soul," a person gave something to God or the local saint, expecting salvation as the countergift. This of course was nothing new. Since the most ancient times people had been sacrificing to the gods with the hope of receiving divine favor in return, and these ideas did not disappear with the arrival of Christianity. The circa 600 *Vetus Gallica* collection of early canon law, mentioned in an earlier chapter, presented the possibilities for gifts given in atonement for various sins.[51] The gifts discussed in the *Vetus Gallica* were not animals to be immolated as in pre-Christian ceremonies. Instead the gifts were pious acts like the manumission of several slaves or a donation of some sort to the poor or to the local church or monastery. Such an act was performed in the expectation that God would view generosity to the church or to the downtrodden as a gift to Him and would respond with a countergift of some kind, forgiveness of a particular sin or some other favor, or, especially in bequests, the countergift of eternal salvation.[52] Gifts made to one of the saints were made with the

---

[51] *Die* Collectio Vetus Gallica: *Die älteste systematische Kanonessammlung des Fränkischen Gallien*, ed. H. Mordek (Berlin 1975).

[52] See Arnold Angenendt, "Donationes pro anima: Gift and Countergift in the Early Medieval Liturgy," in *The Long Morning of Medieval Europe*, ed. J. R. David and M. McCormick (Burlington, VT 2008) 131–54. Also, Wendy Davies, *Acts of Giving: Individual, Community, and Church in Tenth-Century Christian Spain* (Oxford 2007); Patrick Geary, *Phantoms of Remembrance* (Princeton 1994), especially 165–75.

expectation that the saint would use his or her special position to ask God to provide the desired countergift. And, as we have seen in earlier chapters, there were a number of canons about the policy that bishops exercised authority over such gifts received by the church.

As time went on, the custom arose of giving one's own self to a particular saint, with a subsequent annual gift, known as a *census*, "to the altar of Saint X." These annual gifts were reminders to the saint of the original gift of this person, the *censual*. The expected countergift was that the saint would intercede with God, ensuring the donor's eventual salvation. Occasionally the gifts were made to the monastery directly, and the expected countergift was that the monks would pray for the donor. As we have seen, sometimes instead of, or in addition to the donor himself, the gifts were *servi* who were often first manumitted and then commended to the institution in question as *censuales*, they and their descendants in perpetuity.

Some scholars have dismissed this situation as a purely financial arrangement with the local church, saying that the stated desire for salvation of one's soul was mere window dressing. Enriching the local ecclesiastical institution would prompt them to perform favors in return, such as protection, legal or otherwise, or economic rewards, and it would also enhance the status of the donor. Another motive suggested is the perpetuation of the donor's memory, with the annual payment ceremony detailing the circumstances of the gift. However, these suggestions fail to recognize how intensely most people of that era felt the presence of the holy ones in their daily lives.[53] Still, the skeptics do make a good point: from a practical point of view, the annual services of the *censuales* was indeed a serious factor in the economic life of the ecclesiastical institution in question.

From the eleventh century to at least the end of the thirteenth in German lands there was an additional kind of servility, the *ministeriales*. These ministerials, both men and women, were members of the nobility, but they were not legally classed as free. Typically, the men in these families were high-ranking vassals and courtiers of the great magnates, the kings, counts, and archbishops. They were not "knights" (*miles*); knights were vassals of the ministerials.[54] However, the *ministeriales* were very different from the

---

[53] On the medieval experience of the numinous see Davies, *Acts of Giving*, as well as Peter Brown, *The Cult of the Saints*, 2nd ed. (Chicago 2015).

[54] The literature about the ministerials is not very extensive. A useful overview can be found in Werner Hechberger, *Adel, Ministerialität und Rittertum in Mittelalter* (Munich 2004). More detailed considerations are provided by Benjamin Arnold, *German Knighthood, 1050–1300* (Oxford 1985). John B. Freed did an in-depth analysis of this phenomenon in the Salzburg area in *Noble*

censuales as well as from the ordinary unfree laborers. The *censuales* were able to live as they pleased and owed no services to their lords except for the payment of their *census*. The ministerials, on the other hand, owed no monetary payments, but were not free to do as they pleased. They were not free to leave their lord's lands without his permission and could be relocated without giving their consent. They were not free to marry without the lord's permission, which was generally given only for marriages between the families of a lord's own ministerials. They were not free even to alienate their property because, in theory, it actually belonged to their lord, rather like the *peculium* of an ancient Roman slave. And ministerial status was hereditary through the female line, as servitude generally was. The ministerials' unfreedom was not like that of the peasants at the lower levels of society who, even if legally free, were forced to pay a head tax and other fees for using their lord's facilities, as well as to render services. Ministerials were the aristocracy, the nobility, living in castles and enjoying great privilege, wealth, and comfort. A person's good character might be attested to by the fact that he was "a very noble ministerial."[55] In some areas, the ministerials had real political power. They were among the electors of the prince-archbishops of Salzburg, and, along with the princes and other free nobles, they were among those who gave their consent to imperial legislation.[56] In theory, the ministerials had no choice in certain areas of their lives, but given that the ministerial families were the upper nobility, often possessing great wealth and commanding the fealty of many military vassals of their own, the German magnates did not always find it easy to control them.[57]

The origin of the *ministeriales* is not entirely clear. They do not seem to have been common before the eleventh century and seem to have disappeared almost completely by the end of the thirteenth. They were not in evidence outside the German lands.[58] It is possible that this custom

---

Bondsmen: Ministerial Marriages in the Archdiocese of Salzburg, 1100–1343 (Ithaca 1995); see also Thomas Zotz, "Die Formierung der Ministerialität," in *Die Salier und das Reich*, ed. S. Weinfurter (Sigmaringen 1991) 3.1–50.

[55] E.g., concerning Oteno of Rotensi: "erat de nobilioribus ministerialibus." *Historiae Monasterii Marchtelanensis*, ed. G. Waitz, MGH, *Scriptores* 24; (Hanover 1879) 666.11.

[56] Arnold, *German Knighthood* 71.

[57] One is reminded of the Ottoman janissaries, slave soldiers who eventually became one of the most powerful elite groups in the empire.

[58] The fact that the *ministeriales* were limited to German lands may help explain why I have been unable to find any consideration of this custom in the canon law. Practical considerations have limited our sample to the most widely used works of the classical canon law. These were meant to apply to the universal church and were largely the product of Italian, or Italian-educated, jurists.

may have been no more than a way of ensuring the loyalty of the higher ranks of a great lord's military. These German ministerials did not always take an oath of fealty, as was common practice for vassals elsewhere; they were simply under their lord's *dominium*. The ministerial was a part of the lord's *familia* and was sometimes called a *homo proprius*, a man whom one owned.[59] Whatever the origins of the ministerial class, from the eleventh to the thirteenth centuries the *ministeriales* apparently saw legal unfreedom as an acceptable price to pay for their noble status and privileges. Knighthood and vassalage were honorable states in which the ministerials took great pride.

The phenomenon of the ministerials is of interest to our question in two ways; first, because they were frequently the property of ecclesiastical lords—although these bishops sometimes found that their powerful vassals did not share their bishops' ideas about what this servile relationship should entail; and second, because they often enjoyed high ecclesiastical rank themselves.[60] As we shall see later, ordination of an unfree person was forbidden. However, since many if not most of the ministerials seem to have belonged to ecclesiastical lords or institutions, their ordination for service to that lord or institution would not have resulted in any conflict of interest or alienation of ecclesiastical property. In 1072, Liemar of Bavaria, who had begun as one of King Henry IV's ministerials, became the archbishop of Hamburg-Bremen.[61] Pope Alexander II sent Liemar the pallium, a sign of papal support. The chronicle does not mention anything about a manumission, but perhaps the future emperor's close connection with the church put Liemar in the same situation as that of an ecclesiastical ministerial.[62]

---

[59] See Arnold, *German Knighthood* 58. This phrase reminds one of the Ripuarian class of *homo/femina regius/a* or *ecclesiasticus/a* that was discussed in chapter 4. However, without any data to support it, such a connection is only speculative. Hechberger suggested that there may be a connection to the Merovingian status of *puer regius* (*Adel, Ministerialität und Rittertum* 27).

[60] A fascinating case involving such a dispute has been analyzed in Zotz, "Die Formierung der Ministerialität."

[61] Albert of Stade, *Annales Stadensis*, ed. G. H. Pertz MGH, *Scriptores* 16 (Hanover 1859) 316.

[62] Medieval European kings everywhere had a close connection with the institutional church. However, there has been a lot of scholarly speculation about the connection between the Holy Roman (i.e., German) Empire and the church. For a good analysis see Reuter, "The 'Imperial Church System.'"

Most of the literature on the subject of the ministerials has concentrated on them as they functioned as the German knighthood and nobility. Their ordination and any associated canonical exemptions are undoubtedly deserving of study, but as yet I have not been able to find anything about this in the literature or in the canonical sources.

Law

One of the consequences of consolidating ecclesiastical authority in the Roman bureaucracy was the emergence of a generally accepted body of canon law that took its place beside Roman law and local custom as normative for society.[63] The Latin church had become strong enough to stand on its own against many secular interests, and it had become a pan-European organization centered in Rome under the guidance if not yet the total authority of the Roman bishop. It is not surprising that such a large and powerful organization would find it useful to establish uniform guidelines about the behavior of its officials and about how to conduct its affairs. And having such influence over ecclesiastical legal affairs helped to consolidate papal authority.

In the previous chapters we looked at many different sources of legal and normative information in an attempt to construct a "big picture" about ecclesiastical servitude. And what we found was that there were many regional and temporal variations in the rules for dealing with servile persons, especially those under ecclesiastical control. Other than the inalienability of the *res ecclesiae*, there were no universally acknowledged rules concerning ecclesiastically owned slaves and other unfree dependents. Local customs seem to have varied a good deal. Diocesan records from the turn of the millennium demonstrate that this variability of regional customs continued into the later centuries. In the bishops' frequent correspondence with their clergy and other major figures in their dioceses there was little said about the servile ecclesiastical dependents other than to caution the clergy about their own behavior.[64] However, a few of these letters do give us a glimpse into everyday life. In the registers of the archbishops of Canterbury from the 1170s and 1180s there are four documents confirming land grants to lay tenants.[65] The tenants had to pay various annual amounts in rent as the "services due for free, undisturbed tenancy on the land. One text confirmed that William, son of Richard, had purchased the land from the previous tenant.[66] Another

---

[63] For the earlier period, see Lotte Kéry's *Canonical Collections of the Early Middle Ages* (HMCL 1). Also see Linda Fowler-Magerl, *Clavis Canonum: Selected Canon Law Collections before 1140* (Hanover 2005), which includes a searchable database of the canons. An in-depth survey of the "classical" period is provided by the essays collected in *The History of Medieval Canon Law in the Classical Period, 1140–1234*, ed. W. Hartmann and K. Pennington (HMCL 6).

[64] A number of such letters have been preserved in the MGH *Capitula Episcoporum* series and in the *English Episcopal Acta* series from the British Academy. On these see Peter Brommer, "*Capitula Episcoporum*": *Die bischöflichen Kapitularien des 9. und 10. Jahrhunderts* (Turnholt 1985).

[65] *English Episcopal Acta II: Canterbury 1162–1190*, ed. C. R. Cheney (London 1986) #67–#70.

[66] *English Episcopal Acta II* #68.

made it clear that although Adam of Charing, son of Ivo, held his land in free tenancy, he was still obliged to render "two solid weeks' work" along with his rents.[67] When two churches in the Canterbury diocese swapped parcels of land, the tenants on those lands were part of the swap and were listed by name.[68] At about the same time in the nearby diocese of Lincoln, Hugh Malet donated his land, including the tithes, to the monastery of St. Hilda in Whitby and kept the unnamed *villeins* (English unfree persons) and their tenure to himself.[69] Land management practices varied so widely that universal norms were simply not helpful.

Gratian of Bologna's twelfth-century *Decretum* proved to be the first major step in a new legal direction, and by the end of the Middle Ages, the canon law of the church was well established and was held to be binding on all of western Christendom—which, of course, is not to say that there did not continue to be enormous variation in people's behavior and in how the canon law was actually applied and enforced. A large number of legal compendia and treatises were produced, along with arrangements to preserve the written documentation needed to support one's position in a culture now dependent on written law instead of unwritten local custom. To continue our investigation of all of the various avenues of thought and custom through the late medieval centuries would not only be overwhelming, it would be nearly impossible to comprehend. And it probably would not be very helpful in answering the central question of this study: how did the institutional church think it should deal with its servile dependents? So from here on the analysis will focus on the emerging consensus about the canon law relevant to this investigation. These brilliant medieval jurists managed to consolidate a thousand years' worth of material into a relatively useful body of law.[70] The first stage in these developments had been compiling collections of conciliar and synodal canons. At first these collections had a somewhat idiosyncratic organizational system, but in time the compilers found it helpful to organize the canonical material into various topics. The ultimate collection was Gratian's

---

[67] *English Episcopal Acta II* #67.
[68] *English Episcopal Acta II* #78.
[69] *English Episcopal Acta I: Lincoln, 1067–1185*, ed. D. M. Smith (London 1980) #280.
[70] Recently the scholarship has produced several fairly accessible surveys of the development of what is called "the classical canon law." Brundage, *Medieval Canon Law* is both comprehensive and comprehensible. Peter Landau's chapter "The Development of Law" in *The New Cambridge Medieval History*, vol. 4, ed. D. Luscombe (Cambridge 2004) 13–47, is extremely erudite and extremely readable. And Susan Reynolds, "Medieval Law," in *The Medieval World*, ed. P. Linehan and J. Nelson (London 2001) is an excellent survey written from the perspective of a medieval historian, rather than that of a canonist.

Decretum, which for the first time provided a fairly comprehensive analysis of many of the major questions. This analysis rested on a well-organized presentation of supporting material. As Gratian's work found wide acceptance, a number of commentaries and analyses of his *Decretum* emerged—just like what happens when a modern scholar proposes a groundbreaking new theory and the other scholars all publish their analysis of the work. The "Decretists" continued their work for several centuries, but the intellectually fertile twelfth century also gave rise to an increase in another kind of canon law, the papal "decretals." We saw earlier that a decretal is a formal letter written in answer to a legal question. As the head of the church, the pope had the right and the responsibility to respond to appeals from local jurisdictions. In many cases the bishop of Rome would reply to an appeal in the same way that the ancient Roman emperors had done, by means of a formal rescript that discussed the relevant questions and prescribed the appropriate remedy for such a situation. These papal letters were preserved and soon formed a considerable body of case law that could be used in later legal discussions.

During the period between the height of the Carolingian Empire and the consolidation of canon law in Gratian's *Decretum*, a copious amount of legal material about *servi* in general and about the servile dependents of the church had continued to be produced. A few examples will illustrate the sorts of questions being considered by local bishops and secular rulers: A local council held in Koblenz in 922 said that anyone who sold a Christian into slavery was guilty of homicide (canon 7) and also that the bishop had sole power over the *res ecclesiae* (canon 5).[71] In 998 a synod was held in Pavia that seems to have been concerned mainly with repairing the relationship between the bishops of northern Italy and the emperor. Emperor Otto III, who attended the synod, issued a formal prohibition of the alienation of the *res ecclesiae*.[72] In line with what we have seen earlier, conflicts about the substantial wealth of the church continued in the later medieval centuries. At times, it also suited the purposes of secular rulers to uphold the principle of the inalienability of church property, which, of course, included the servile ecclesiastical dependents. In 1000, only two years after the Pavia synod, Otto III elaborated on his earlier prohibition. He declared that although *servi* were "panting for liberty," for the *servi ecclesiarum* manumission was strictly

---

[71] MGH, *Concilia* 6.1, ed. E.-D. Hehl (Hanover 1987) #4.
[72] MGH, *Concilia* 6.2, ed. E.-D. Hehl (Hanover 2007) #58.

forbidden.[73] And concerning any ecclesiastical *liberti* who had been given full freedom (i.e., the status of freeborn with no obligations to the church), their freedom was to be revoked and they were to be returned to ecclesiastical servitude. Similar edicts about the protection of church property were issued in about 1027 by Emperor Conrad II, in 1111 by Henry V, and in 1153 and 1157 by Frederick I.[74] Whether the emperors were deeply concerned about the integrity of ecclesiastical resources or whether they simply needed ecclesiastical political support is another question. Nonetheless, the principle of nonalienation of the *res ecclesiae* was on the books.

Interestingly, in 960, a synod held under Patriarch Bonus of Grado (Venice) and Doge Petrus Candianus IV of Venice issued a strong condemnation of the slave trade that was being pursued through the Venetian port.[75] This was confirmed by an accompanying statement condemning the commerce in Christian *mancipia* with the rival port of Constantinople. Given the context of Venice's on-again, off-again treaties with the Byzantine capital, it is again hard to tell whether these regulations were inspired by theoretical considerations about slavery or by the doge's concerns about the lucrative slave trade with non-Christians in the eastern and southern Mediterranean.

Although only a modest sampling is possible from the vast amount of local legal material that was produced during this era, a more thorough survey of the canon law produced by the ecumenical or general councils that were acknowledged by the western church is feasible. As we discussed in chapter 6, two of the general councils held in Constantinople before the east-west schism addressed our issues. The 787 council, II Nicaea, declared that bishops were not to alienate the church's suburban properties.[76] And the late ninth-century IV Constantinople passed three canons protecting the *res ecclesiae* from lay and episcopal predation. The first two councils held in the Lateran Palace in Rome (1123 and 1139) also included material protecting the *res ecclesiae* from lay interests.[77] Neither these nor the other general councils produced any material specifically about ecclesiastical *servi*, however. Unfree dependents were apparently considered to be an unremarkable component

[73] MGH, *Constitutiones* 1, ed. L. Weiland et al. (Hanover 1893) #21.

[74] MGH, *Constitutiones* 1 #39 and #89, #146, and #169, respectively.

[75] MGH, *Concilia* 6.1 #21. The "doge," or duke of Venice, was the head of state who had been elected by the republic's leading citizens to a life term.

[76] II Nicaea, c.12, *Decrees of the Ecumenical Councils*, ed., trans., N. P. Tanner (London 1990) 147–48.

[77] I Lateran, c.8, 12; II Lateran, c.5, 10, *Decrees of the Ecumenical Councils*, 191–92, 197, 199.

of the church's movable property, and the canonical material seems to have been concerned with land more than with what went along with the land.

During this era quite a large number of canonical collections were compiled, for private use or to be shared with others. Some of these collections were influential enough that we still have copies of them today. For example, as mentioned in the previous chapter, Regino of Prüm's circa 906 collection, *Libri duo de synodalibis causis et disciplinis ecclesiae*, included some rather old-fashioned ideas about *servi*. In connection with the marital affairs of servile persons, Regino presented canons that went back to Roman law about slaves, and, despite the trends we have discussed, he clearly seems to have thought that servile marriages were not valid.[78]

Many of the eleventh-century collections were explicitly part of a church reform movement of that period that has often been associated with Pope Gregory VII. The anonymous collection from about 1050 known as *The Collection in 74 Titles* presented a number of earlier canons and papal letters in a well-organized fashion.[79] Relevant to our purposes is Title 42, "That no one should presume to hold as a clerk the *servus* of another." Particularly interesting for our question are 42.230 and 231, saying that neither a bishop nor a monastery could accept a *servus* without his master's consent. There are also several canons that forbade the ordination of *servi*, including Gregory I's statement from a 595 synod that a *servus ecclesiae* who wanted to be ordained should first prove himself worthy as a free layman (42.232).[80] There were also two entire titles (eleven canons) devoted to preserving the *res ecclesiae* from lay interference.[81] The question of preserving church property and of not ordaining an unfree man continued to be of great interest to canonists for several centuries. However, how the church ought to deal with its servile dependents was rarely an issue; these canons were about the preservation of property rights.

Another aspect of the reform movement can be seen in the work of Bishop Ivo of Chartres (1090–1115). He and his circle produced three major collections of canonical material that continued to be influential.[82] A treatise

---

[78] Regino of Prüm, *Libri duo de synodalibis causis et disciplinis ecclesiae*, ed. F. W. Wasserschlebin (Leipzig 1840) 2.118–22. On this see Rio, *Slavery after Rome* 220 and Kéry, *Canonical Collections* 128–33.

[79] *Diversorum partum sententie siue Collectio in LXXIV titulus digesta*, ed. J. Gilchrist, MIC Series B, vol. 1 (Vatican City 1973); Eng. trans. *The Collection in Seventy-Four Titles: A Canon Law Manual of the Gregorian Reform*, ed., trans. J. Gilchrist (Toronto 1980).

[80] Including Titles 5.55; 16.155, 156; and 42.232.

[81] Title 160: "The resources of the church should not be entrusted to the laity" and Title 61: "On the condemnation of the invaders of ecclesiastical estates."

[82] See https://ivo-of-chartres.github.io/ for the in-progress Latin edition of these works.

known as Ivo's "Prologue" was arguably his greatest contribution to the development of ecclesiastical jurisprudence.[83] Ivo was not content merely to gather material together. He also wanted to address the challenges that arose when implementing the frequently contradictory canonical principles. It would be his successor, Gratian of Bologna, who was able actually to reconcile the contradictory advice of the various canons in a collection. But Ivo came up with a way of dealing with these problems that combined giving a "dispensation" from the law when circumstances warranted and allowing the judge to find a merciful solution in cases where such was needed.[84] Ivo was a superb jurist, but he seems to have been a pastor at heart. A thorough catalog of all of the material in the three massive Ivonian collections that might be relevant to our question would not be practical here, but a quick look at the Ivonian *Decretum*'s handling of servitude is informative. Of the more than 350 canons in Book XVI, where we find the material concerning the laity, many addressed various problems in connection with *servi* and *liberti*. Here we can clearly see evidence of pastoral concern. God made some people slaves and some masters, said canon 45, because that is one of the consequences of original sin. However, as most of the canons that follow made clear, the church was expected to protect these vulnerable people from excessive exploitation by their masters. Ivo's work did not stray from the goals and teachings of the reformers. Indeed, much of this work described how best to protect the *res ecclesiae* in all kinds of situations. Nonetheless, in Ivo's mind *servi*, of lay or ecclesiastical masters, were first of all human beings whom God had given life. And it was the duty of the church to care for them when they were in need of help.

The *74 Titles* and the Ivonian work both proved extremely influential in the long run. Also important were collections compiled by Anselm of Lucca and Burchard of Worms, and there were dozens of less well-known collections that documented questions of local concern.[85] In general, these collections all contained pretty much the same canonical material, but they were organized according to the particular interests of their compilers.

---

[83] A recent English translation of the "Prologue" is included in Robert Somerville and Bruce Brasington, *Prefaces to Canon Law Books in Latin Christianity* (New Haven 1998) 132–58. For more on the influence of Ivo's "Prologue" see Bruce Brasington, "Studies on the *Nachleben* of Ivo of Chartres: The Influence of his Prologue on Several Panormia-Derivative Collections," *Proceedings of the Ninth International Congress of Medieval Canon Law, Munich, 13–18 July 1982* (Vatican City 1997) 63–85.

[84] Somerville and Brasington, *Prefaces* 115. On this also see Christof Rolker, "Ivo of Chartres' Pastoral Canon Law," *Bulletin of Medieval Canon Law* 25 (2006) 114–45.

[85] Kéry, *Canonical Collections*, listed more than seventy collections from this "reform era" alone.

Despite occasional examples of a change in attitude in regard to servile persons, by the twelfth century, the idea that freedom was the right of every individual had not yet caught fire. The church not only upheld existing servile relationships, but even prescribed enslavement as the punishment for certain offenses. In 1179 the third general council that was held in the Lateran Palace in Rome called for the enslavement of those who "provide the Saracens with arms . . . to attack Christians . . . and act as captains or pilots" on Saracen vessels. Such men were to be "excommunicated for their wickedness." Their possessions were to be confiscated by the "Catholic princes and civil magistrates." They themselves, if captured, "should become the slaves of their captors."[86] The council also called for the same fate to befall any heretics or rebels who took up arms against the Catholics.[87] And the council repeated the ancient principle that forbade Jews or Saracens to have Christian *mancipia* in their households. Recognizing that excommunication would not deter Jews or Muslims from anything, the canon called for punishment of the Christian *mancipia* in question: "Let those be excommunicated who presume to live with them."[88] But it is hard to imagine how anyone thought it just to punish the poor Christian slaves who found themselves in the service of non-Christian masters. Since the slaves had not had much say in the matter, one is led to assume that this canon is meant to express negative feelings about the non-Christians more than it is meant as a practical legal principle. General councils in Lyons in 1245 and 1274 reiterated the importance of protecting the *res ecclesiae* as well as calling for the enslavement of those who aided the enemies of Christendom.[89]

Gratian on Ecclesiastical *Servi*

In Gratian's work *servi* continued to be deprived of almost all legal rights: the right to bring suit against their lords, to bear witness, to claim injury, or to

---

[86] III Lateran Council, c.24, trans. N. P. Tanner, *Decrees of the Ecumenical Councils*.
Also see John Gilchrist, *The Church and Economic Activity in the Middle Ages* (London 1969).
[87] III Lateran Council, c.27.
[88] III Lateran Council, c.26. This was repeated by the IV Lateran Council in 1215, Constitution 71, and the Council of Basel in session 19, held in 1434.
[89] *Decrees of the Ecumenical Councils:* I Council of Lyons, session 2, c.1, session 11, c.5; II Council of Lyons, session 6, c.22.

make a will.[90] And penalties for killing or injuring a *servus* were often different from those for the same offenses committed against a free person.[91]

For the most part, the servile persons who are the focus of this study fell under the general provisions having to do with *servi* and *liberti*. In the twelfth century, there continued to be little difference between *servi* under ecclesiastical dominion and *servi* with lay masters. However, in a few situations, especially in connection with manumission, the position of the ecclesiastical *servus* was very different. The following overview of texts from Gratian's *Decretum* that particularly addressed our question will highlight those differences that made the circumstances of the unfree in ecclesiastical service both better and worse than those of their servile brothers and sisters. I will examine the most relevant topics one by one, and then offer some general remarks at the end.

In Gratian's *Decretum*, the problems of servile marriage were handled mainly in *Causa* 29.[92] The problem posed for discussion was whether or not a mixed (free/servile) marriage was dissoluble. After listing a half-dozen citations on both sides of the question, the *Decretum* came back to the canon from Chalons that referred to the New Testament where Jesus is recorded as having said, "What God has joined together, let no man put asunder."[93] As we have already seen, this canon said that the precept applied when the

---

[90] This section is a revised and expanded version of ideas that appeared in "Gratian and the *Servi ecclesiarum*," in *Proceedings of the XIII International Congress of Medieval Canon Law, Esztergom, August 3–9, 2004*, ed. P. Erdö, MIC Series C 14 (Vatican City 2010).

[91] In 1976 John Gilchrist wrote an important article summarizing some of the basic teachings of Gratian and the Decretists concerning unfree persons: "The Medieval Canon Law on Unfree Persons: Gratian and the Decretist Doctrines c. 1141–1234," in *Melanges G. Fransen*, vol. 1, ed. S. Kuttner and A. M. Stickler, *Studia Gratiana* 19 (1976) 273–301. This was soon followed by the companion article, "St. Raymond of Peñafort and the Decretalist Doctrines of Serfdom," *Escritos del Vedat* 7 (1977) 299–327. Using tools that were not available forty years ago, I have been able to identify even more texts where Gratian mentioned these issues, but even with this greatly enlarged database, Gilchrist's conclusions hold. *Wortkonkordanz zum Decretum Gratiani*, 5 vols., ed. T. Reuter and G. Silagi, MGH, *Hilfsmittel* 10 (Munich 1990).

The concordance was searched for the following words and their cognates: *servus* (the most frequent, used 226 times) as well as *ancilla, servitus, libertus, mancipium, famulus, servilis, colonus*, and *originarius*. The word *rusticus* was not considered in the analysis, as this does not seem to have been used as a status indicator, but merely as a geographical description. Several other common words did not appear at all: *adscriptus, ministerialus, villanus/villeinus*, as well as *collibertus, lidus/litus, tributarius, aldius, censuales*, and *ministeriales*. The word *census* was used often, but not in situations relevant to our inquiry. Occasional additional texts that do not contain any of these words were added to the sample when relevant.

[92] An English translation of this *causa* can be found in *European Legal History*, ed. O. F. Robinson, T. D. Fergus, and W. M. Gordon (London 1994) 318–20.

[93] *Causa* 29 *quaestio* 2 *capitulum* 7 (C.29 q.2 c.7). Matt 19:6. Anders Winroth ("Neither Slave nor Free," 107–8) noted that this canon was not included in the earliest version of the *Decretum* but was added, perhaps twenty years later, by the compiler of a second recension of this work. See also Landau, "Die Eheschliessung."

marriage of two servile persons had been legal and permitted by their masters. It is interesting that all of the discussion and analysis that had taken
place during the intervening three hundred years had not changed this principle. However, in another part of the *Decretum* Gratian included a passage
from the sixth-century archbishop Isidore of Seville saying that inherent in
the natural law was the right for a man and a woman to come together.[94]
Connecting these two ideas, the jurists after Gratian soon moved the discussion in new directions. For example, in the late twelfth century, Sicard of
Cremona expanded on the Isidore passage in his analysis of C.29 q.2. He said:

> All humans are free according to the natural law, even these [*servi*]. So they
> can do whatever the natural law says that they can do. The union of man
> and woman is also from natural law. Therefore they [*servi*] can enter into a
> marriage.[95]

But *servi* were in fact not free. And physical union is not the same as a marriage.

Some Decretists, as the late medieval scholars who wrote about Gratian's
work are called, developed Sicard's line of thought even further. For example,
Huguccio of Pisa, writing about the same chapter of the *Decretum* a few years
after Sicard, emphasized the biblical support for this principle. But he also
emphasized that the right to marry did not dissolve the obligations that servile persons had toward their lords.[96] Just as we saw in earlier centuries, the
importance of upholding the ancient principles that supported a person's
right to own property overcame any scruples that one might have had concerning the issue of slavery.[97] The thirteenth-century *Glossa Ordinaria* to the
Decretum on D.1 c.7 took pains to make clear that the definition of natural
law described by Isidore and cited by Gratian referred only to the kind of
coupling that was also found in animals.[98] And indeed, the word "marriage"

---

[94] D.1 c.7. This is part of Gratian's introduction on the nature of law and on the various kinds of law.

[95] Sicard on C.29 q.2 c.8 (MS Bamberg 38, fol. 106r): Latin text printed in Landau, "Hadrians
IV. Dekretale" 532 n. 99. See also Charles Reid, *Power over the Body, Equality in the Family* (Grand
Rapids, MI 2004) 232 n. 203. For more about Sicard and other less well-known medieval canonists,
see the encyclopedic database at http://amesfoundation.law.harvard.edu/BioBibCanonists/Report_
Biobib2.php?record_id=a494.

[96] Huguccio, *Summa* at C.29 q.2 c.8 (MS *Admont* 7 fol. 355). Reprinted in Landau, "Hadrians IV.
Dekretale" 534–36.

[97] These questions of natural law and private property, slavery, and the right to marry appeared
again and again in legal discussions in subsequent centuries, up to our own. We will look at this again
later in the chapter.

[98] Almost immediately after the first version of the *Decretum* appeared, scholars began writing
commentary (glosses) in the margins of their manuscript copies, the way we still do in our books

did not appear in the Isidore text, although some canonists, like Sicard and Huguccio, clearly understood the word *conjunctio* (come together) as a synonym for marriage (*matrimonio*). The twelfth- and thirteenth-century jurists agreed that there were times when the "natural law" could be ignored, or "limited" because circumstances warranted it, particularly in connection with private property and servitude. But when and how the law of nature could be limited was a question on which the canonists could not agree.

There do not seem to have been any special provisions concerning the marriage of unfree persons subject to ecclesiastical persons or institutions. Alexander III's letters, mentioned earlier, did not say anything about special regulations for ecclesiastical *servi*, but only that Abbot Peter's conduct was unbecoming someone of his status. The pope had been called in, not because of any special provisions applying to the *servi* in question, but rather as the ultimate overlord of the parties involved in the dispute. In a related issue, the canonist Peter Cantor's remarks on C.29 q.2 of Gratian's *Decretum* discussed the case of a bishop's *servus* who fled to a town in order to secure his own freedom.[99] The question was whether or not his servile wife could join him and abandon her servile duties. Any special circumstances surrounding the manumission of ecclesiastical dependents do not seem to have been considered, only whether or not the wife's duty to follow her husband trumped her duties toward her master.

Another frequent issue in the twelfth-century church was that the lack of free status was an impediment to ordination or to monastic profession.[100] Various chapters of the *Decretum*, principally in D.54, suggest that the reason for this resistance against ordaining the unfree was an unwillingness to interfere with the property rights of those who owned or held patronal rights over one who sought orders or profession. Gratian's *Decretum* included the sixth-century Byzantine law that if the master had consented, ordination itself

today. In the early thirteenth century, Johannes Teutonicus edited a compilation of all of the most important glosses that had been produced in the previous century. This *Glossa Ordinaria* (Standard Gloss) was provided in the margins of many later editions of the *Decretum*. For more on this see Rudolf Weigand, "The *Glossa Ordinaria*," in *History of Medieval Canon Law in the Classical Period, 1140–1234: From Gratian to the Decretals of Pope Gregory IX*, ed. W. Hartmann and K. Pennington (HMCL 6) 55–97.

[99] Petrus Cantor, *Summa de Sacramentis et animae consiliis*, Pars. III, cap. XXIX, §274 (pre-1200). Reprinted in Landau, "Hadrians IV. Dekretale" 536 n. 121.

[100] The most important scholarship in this much less researched area can be found in Peter Landau, "Frei und Unfrei in der Kanonistik des 12. und 13. Jahrhunderts am Beispiel der Ordination der Unfreien," in *Die abendländische Freiheit vom 10. zum 14. Jahrhundert: Der Wirkungszusammenhang von Idee und Wirklichkeit im europäischen Vergleich*, ed. J. Fried (Sigmaringen 1991) 177–96; and Richard H. Helmholz, *The Spirit of Classical Canon Law* (Athens, GA 1996) 61–87.

could constitute manumission. Thus, even a *servus* who was ordained or professed without the knowledge and consent of his master might be considered a free man after the passage of time, leaving the master only the ability to claim financial compensation for his loss.[101] On the question of ordaining the unfree, Gratian made several provisions that applied particularly to the *servi ecclesiarum*, but we shall wait a bit to discuss them.

There are also a number of chapters forbidding relations between a cleric and his *ancilla*, some originating as late as the eleventh century.[102] A text from the XI Council of Toledo in 655 that we discussed earlier said that children born of such an illicit union would become church *servi*.[103] This canon was included in many of the reform-era canonical collections, and Gratian thought it worthy of being included in his own analysis as well. Later twelfth-century scholars who glossed Gratian's work reminded the reader that it had long been the custom that children should inherit the status of their mother. In other words, they saw nothing untoward in a situation where the church enslaved the illegitimate children of the clergy, no matter how shocking it may seem to us moderns.

A few texts in Gratian's *Decretum* suggest that the medieval understanding about lordship over unfree persons was sometimes more complicated than simple property law. The first example is the long-standing rule that Jews could not keep Christian *servi*, a rule that was later extended to Muslims and others as well.[104] While Christians continued to exercise *dominium* over their fellows, the fact that religion could make non-Christians ineligible to do so in some situations suggests that even at this relatively late date, servitude was not purely a matter of economics. Another example of the complex nature of servitude is the question of sanctuary on sacred ground. This practice, which goes back to pre-Christian Rome, was quickly extended to Christian sacred places as well, offering safety and protection to those fleeing the law, especially runaway *servi*.[105] This protection was so inviolate that even clergy were not permitted to remove runaway *servi ecclesiarum* who had claimed shelter.[106] However, this safe haven was not intended to last forever. The

---

[101] D.54 c.20 (*Novella Justiniani* 123 c.26.)

[102] E.g., D.32 c.10; D.34 c.7, 15; D.81 c.30.

[103] C.15 q.8 c.3.

[104] D.54 c.13–18. There is also C.17 q.4 c.34 saying that a Christian *servus* who was circumcised by his Jewish master was thereby granted his freedom.

[105] See, e.g., D.87 c.6–8 and several *capitula* in C.17 q.4.

[106] C.17 q.4 c.19, a *palea*, or later addition to the text, whose inclusion may have been merely an extreme example used to beef up the case for the general inviolability of sanctuary rather than evidence that incidents of this sort were common in the twelfth century.

owner's property rights were inviolate as well, and sanctuary served mainly to provide a cooling-off period during which an equitable solution to the problem could be negotiated.[107]

As we have seen in earlier texts, in Gratian's *Decretum* practically all questions about *servi ecclesiarum* turn out to be questions about church property. In the twelfth century, the natural law's idea of individual freedom presented little challenge to the natural law right to property ownership. And our *servi ecclesiarum* were the property of the church. A *servus* was an asset, to be protected and used for the master's—the church's—benefit. *Servi* were still an important part of the assets needed for economic survival in the twelfth-century world. In a letter written in 1127 to Bernard of Clairvaux, Abbot Peter the Venerable of Cluny made this very clear. Responding to Bernard's criticism of the abbey's worldly possessions, Peter said in effect that the *Rule of Saint Benedict* had provided for monasteries to own the land they needed to produce food. And since people to work the land were a necessary part of this process, it made sense that the *Rule* had also forbidden the monks to grant these peasants freedom.[108] In other words: if God had given them the land to own, they also needed to own people to work the land. This was not a case of greedy clerics looking for loopholes to their own advantage, but a real case of conflicting values, as we have seen so often before.[109] On the one hand, the church needed substantial resources if it were going to be able to do God's work in the world. But on the other hand, according to natural law, slavery was considered to be contrary to nature, the result of human error or sin. Yet the church did need material resources to carry out its mission.

Since the beginning of this study we have seen that the church leaders wrote again and again limiting the alienation of the *res ecclesiae* by sale, gift, or manumission. Only bishops (or sometimes abbots) were permitted to dispose of church property. And we have seen attempts to deal with the problems that arose when bishops were sometimes tempted to satisfy their desire to care for the poor, or to care for their own comfort, at the expense of the essential material resources of the institution. In Gratian's *Decretum*, there is quite a lot of material about the *res ecclesiae*. Gratian considered the acquisition and management of property, and also its disposal, as well as the need for separation of property belonging to the institutional church

---

[107] E.g., C.17 q.4 c.32.
[108] Peter the Venerable, "Epistola ad Dominum Bernardum Abbatem Claraevallis," *The Letters of Peter the Venerable*, ed. G. Constable (Cambridge, MA 1967) Ep. 28.
[109] On this see Helmholz, *Spirit*, 79–83.

from that belonging to those who act on its behalf.[110] Of particular interest for our question about the *servi ecclesiarum* is the second question of *Causa* 12.[111] Here, after a long list of canonical sources, Gratian summed up in his comments:

> Through this examination of all [of these] authorities it has been demonstrated that no clergyman may hand over church property to anyone or sell gifts that they have been given as the church's representatives. Someone who receives such property illicitly must return it.[112]

But then he went on to say, "It must be noted that in certain pressing situations, the *res ecclesiae* may be alienated."[113] For example, it was quite all right to sell *servi ecclesiarum* who persisted in running away.[114] There is also evidence that a *servus ecclesiae* might be freed if the manumitter provided financial compensation for the *servus* out of his own means.[115]

It is in this continued attachment to their former ecclesiastical master, further detailed in *capitula* 58–66, that we can see the second feature of ecclesiastical servitude that put such persons at a distinct disadvantage when compared to their fellows.[116] These *capitula* and Gratian's accompanying *dicta* detailed the inviolable nature of this ecclesiastical *patrocinium*, which extended even to the descendants of manumitted *servi ecclesiarum*. Failure to abide by the regulations governing the patronal relationship resulted in immediate return to servitude. This freed—as opposed to free—status would continue to bind the descendants of the former *servi ecclesiarum* as well.[117] It is not clear for how many generations this patronal relationship was supposed to continue, although the words *progeniti* and *posteritas*, used here in several *capitula* taken from councils held in sixth- and seventh-century

---

[110] For more discussion on this see Gilchrist, "Medieval Canon Law" 297–98.

[111] Other texts that discuss the inalienability of the church's human assets include C.16 q.3 c.12 and C.17 q.4 c.40. Also see D.54 c.22; D.87 c.6; and C.10 q.1 c.7.

[112] C.12 q.2 d.p.c.49. This *dictum* as well as the chapters from 32 to 72 discussing the details of this problem all date to the earliest versions of the *Decretum*.

[113] In Friedberg's edition a continuation of the same d.p.c.49 but really an introduction to c.50, this idea is in accordance with the general custom found in canon law that most of the administrative canonical regulations could be altered in cases of necessity or for the *utilitas ecclesiae*.

[114] C.12 q.2 c.54. This was later supplemented by c.55, inserted as a *palea* (literally, "a bit of fluff") that pointed out the unfairness inherent in the fact that runaway *servi ecclesiarum* could be sold (and eventually find their way to freedom under another master) but the well-behaved *servi ecclesiarum* could not follow that path.

[115] C.12 q.2 d.a.c.56, c.56, d.a.c.57, c.57.

[116] Also see Gilchrist, "Medieval Canon Law" 281, 299–300.

[117] C.12 q.2 c.63. This principle was repeated in c.64 and c.65.

Toledo, normally would be taken to indicate many generations. The complexities of such a perpetual bond suggest that this may not have been enforceable over long periods. However, further *capitula* and their *dicta* make it clear that a freedman's release from this bond could be achieved by compensating the church with appropriate generosity.

> *Servi ecclesiarum* may not be set free if the church does not retain patronal rights over them unless, perhaps, if the manumitter wishes to give the church both their price and the worth of any possessions they take with them (i.e., their *peculium*).[118]

Nonetheless the attention that Gratian paid to preserving the patronal relationship makes it very clear that this was an important principle and that it had been so for a long time. For example, *capitulum* 65, from the IV Council of Toledo in 633, saying that neither freedmen nor their posterity might be released from the church's patrimony, had been included in at least twenty-five of the pre-Gratian canonical collections.[119] Interestingly, Gratian does not seem to have considered this problem in terms of the old regulations surrounding *manumissio in ecclesia*. In earlier chapters we saw that, no matter who the former owner had been, someone who received their freedom in a church ceremony was then bound to the church where that had taken place. Since the manumission of ecclesiastical *servi*, even in later centuries, certainly must have involved some sort of church ceremony, it is unsurprising that the conditions imposed would have resembled the conditions for early medieval freedmen after *manumissio in ecclesia*. But Gratian did not mention this. The medieval jurists often cited the ancient canons out of context, so it is probably to be expected that Gratian and later scholars were sometimes not aware of all of the earlier customs.

The rest of C.12 q.2 considered a number of special situations where ecclesiastical resources might or might not be alienated. Feeding the poor or for the good of the church, for example, were acceptable motives, but business considerations were not.[120] The fact that Gratian's *Decretum* included so many canons on both sides of the question—inalienability and how to avoid it—suggests that in the twelfth century there were differing opinions about the permanency of ecclesiastical servitude. But for a century thereafter

---

[118] C.12 q.2 d.p.c.57.
[119] Frequency data from Fowler-Magerl, *Clavis Canonum*.
[120] C.122 q.2 c.66–75.

there seems to have been a relative lack of interest about this question. In other words, the scholars apparently accepted the *Decretum*'s presentation as sufficient. The bottom line was clear: although *servi ecclesiarum* could be manumitted in certain situations, the longevity of the *patrocinium ecclesiae* ensured that these human assets would continue to benefit the church in practically every circumstance.

Earlier, while discussing ordination, I said that I wanted to postpone discussion of certain questions. D.54 discussed the ordination of servile persons. It was not permitted.[121] The obligations of the ordained state would trespass upon the proprietary rights of a servile person's master.[122] But there was a remedy via manumission, and the canons emphasized that this freedom must be a public matter.[123] After evidence had been examined about how such potential ordinands conducted their lives as free men, they might be accepted for ordination. Anyone who did not lead an honorable life was to be returned to servitude. This followed the ancient Roman ideas of what to do with an "ungrateful freedman," as the *Glossa Ordinaria* on this passage reminded the reader.[124] However, there was a catch. If a slave had been ordained without his master's consent, the master had a certain period of time in which he might claim his runaway property and have it (him) returned. But, as Helmholz pointed out, any other stolen property that had been consecrated for the use of the church would not be returned to its former owner.[125] Apparently, the return of a runaway *servus* was seen as proper because presenting himself for ordination had, in effect, been a fraud and thereby the ordination might not have been valid.

The question of ordaining ecclesiastical *servi* was something else. There was an argument to be made that, as church property, *servi ecclesiarum* should not easily obtain freedom, even for the purposes of ordination.[126] D.54 c.22 was a reminder that *servi* attached to a monastery who wished to be ordained could not be set free. As we saw in an earlier chapter, this text from around the turn of the seventh century explained that neither the abbot nor any of the monks might set free any of the *servi* of their monastery, because

---

[121] D.54 c.1.

[122] However, one commentary known as the *Summa Parisiensis* noted in connection with D.54 c.20 that ordination would not necessarily prevent a *servus* from performing his agricultural duties. Cited in Gilchrist, "Medieval Canon Law" 296.

[123] D.54 c.2, a canon from a council held in 895 in the German imperial city of Tribur.

[124] *Gl. Ord.* to D.54 c.4, *religet.*

[125] Helmholz, *Spirit* 76–77.

[126] For more discussion on this topic also see Gilchrist, "Medieval Canon Law" 295–97.

"you can't alienate something that does not belong to you."[127] The *res ecclesiae* belonged to God and his church, not to the monks and clerics who were the earthly stewards of God's property. But D.54 C.4, sometimes attributed to the IX Council of Toledo in the seventh century, repeated a principle of Pope Gregory I, who had said that *servi ecclesiarum* ought to be freed for this purpose. Gratian addressed the contradiction inherent in all of these canons and the seeming unfairness of the situation of ecclesiastical *servi*. He added a *dictum* saying that the *servi* of a monastery could be legally freed in order for them to be ordained because as ordained clergy they could still serve the monastery as they had before and thus there would really have been no loss.[128] Elsewhere, in a *dictum* post-C.12 q.2 c.63, devoted to the alienation of the *res ecclesiae*, Gratian clarified that although in most cases when *servi* were manumitted in order to make them eligible for ordination there was no thought of the former master retaining *patrocinium*, it was different for former *servi ecclesiarum*.[129] They "would never be free of duties to their ecclesiastical masters." The main point of forbidding the ordination of a slave was not, as one might have expected, difficulty with an unfree person's lack of "honor" making him unfit for ordination. The problem was that ordination obliged one to serve the church, resulting in a conflict with the rights of the master.[130] The Decretist commentaries on this text reinforced the principle of the need to respect an owner's rights, and also emphasized the differences that pertained to *servi ecclesiarum*.[131]

These last texts had the effect of allowing the church to free its *servi* while still retaining their services, albeit in a different form. Ecclesiastical *servi* who wished to be ordained or to take monastic vows could be given provisional freedom to enable them to do so on the grounds that they would merely be changing the status of their service to the church. If things didn't work out, such persons would revert to their servile status. For *servi* of lay masters,

---

[127] Isidore of Seville, *Regula monachorum* 19.4, PL 83.867–94.

[128] D.54 d.p.c.22. See Peter Landau, "Slavery and Semifreedom in the High Middle Ages," in *Slavery across Time and Space: Studies in Slavery in Medieval Europe and Africa*, ed. P. Hernaes and T. Iversen (Trondheim 2002) 97–104.

[129] Recall the correspondence between Archbishop Hincmar and the woman whose freed slave had become a deacon.

[130] For a survey of the history of this question, see Landau, "Frei und Unfrei" and Helmholz, *Spirit* 66–67.

[131] Huguccio of Pisa, perhaps the most important of the Decretists, said that the priesthood liberated a man from servitude no matter what, but even he agreed that an ordained monastic *servus* could be called back to do agricultural work. (Huguccio's aberrant views were not included in the *Glossa Ordinaria* on the *Decretum*.) Landau, "Frei und Unfrei," 191.

ordination meant permanent freedom; for *servi* of ecclesiastical masters, there was no such way out.

It is pretty clear that in the canon law of the *Decretum* the fundamental difference between *servi ecclesiarum* and *servi* under the control of lay masters was the fact that the *res ecclesiae* should never be alienated. While on the one hand, this principle prevented the sale of such *servi* and any accompanying familial disruptions, on the other hand it also hampered any attempt to achieve complete freedom. Services due a former master were valuable assets and, like any church assets, they could not easily be alienated. Compared to their fellows, *servi ecclesiarum* would face a much harder, if not an insurmountable, path to eventual independent, legal freedom. Gratian does not seem to have considered the difficulties that might arise if a freedman who wished to be ordained had obligations to his former lay owner. The 305 Council of Elvira, as we saw in chapter 4, had forbidden the ordination of a freedman because of this very problem.[132] However, something seems to have changed by the twelfth century, perhaps having to do with donating the freedman's services to the church, as we saw earlier in *manumissio in ecclesia* and in the situation of the *censuales*.

As I mentioned briefly before, there are a few texts that show that the early twelfth-century view of the unfree, especially those intimately connected with the church, was complicated and seems to have involved more than purely economic factors. First of all, the protections and immunities offered to the clergy were also extended to their *servi*, including immunity from certain taxation and public services; and their persons were inviolate—in the same way that any church property was protected.[133] This may have been simply to shield these *servi* against those who wanted to harm their ecclesiastical masters, but there may have been more to it than that. We can see a hint of this in D.37 c.15, which has to do with forbidden reading material. It is followed by a *dictum* that excuses a cleric from responsibility when his *servus* knowingly read what was forbidden a layperson. Priests were enjoined to take care that dangerous materials, suitable for clerical eyes only, were not accessible to the laity. However, Gratian acknowledged that domestic servants would, by the very nature of their duties, have relatively easy access to forbidden or holy things. And therein lies what could be an important difference between *servi ecclesiarum* and the rest of the unfree, the implications

---

[132] Elvira c.80. *Concilios visigoticos e hispano-Romanos*, ed. J. Vives et al. (Barcelona 1963).
[133] C.16 q.1 c.40 and C.23 q.8 c.24.

of which clearly present an opportunity for further investigation. The ecclesiastical *servi* had access to, were in some way connected to, the holy things and thus sometimes seem to have had a faintly religious aura along with their economic function.

The *Decretum* often discussed questions concerning the *res ecclesiae* in contexts that did not explicitly mention *servi*. *Distinctio* 89 and *Causa* 10 considered the difficulties that arose when laypersons were in control of ecclesiastical property. For example, a bishop needed to have a clergyman as his *oeconomus*, essentially a sort of chief financial officer who oversaw the handling of the *res ecclesiae*, because a layperson was not allowed to dispose of church property. Several other *capitula* discussed what happened when a bishop left his diocese, or a monk left the monastery to whom he had given his worldly goods.[134] As had been the case in the earliest centuries of the church, in the twelfth century it seems that it wasn't easy to unravel the property of an individual clergyman from that of the institutional church. *Causa* 23, about how to deal with heretics, included a discussion of what to do with any ecclesiastical property that might have been under a heretic's control. There were also the many *capitula* about many different topics that mentioned the *res ecclesiae* in passing. And in every instance that I have found, the principle of inalienability was mentioned.[135]

To sum up: according to Gratian's *Decretum*, the outstanding characteristic of ecclesiastical *servi* was the comparative difficulty they faced in breaking free of their servitude. Even after manumission, the ties binding them to the institutional church were still very strong. We might, rather cynically, judge this to be evidence of avarice so great that even the compassion and piety that might move one to free these *servi* from bondage could not prevail against the church's protective devices. However, such a judgment might not be fair. While the large amount of material devoted to questions about the preservation of church property certainly attests to the idea that preserving the church's patrimony, its wealth, was of paramount importance, we have also seen that there were other factors to be considered in an analysis of the church's attitude toward its unfree dependents.

We might also question whether the *Decretum* was representative of twelfth-century thinking. After all, most of the texts of these *capitula* were from earlier centuries. Nevertheless, the answer is clearly yes. The bulk of

---

[134] See especially C.17 q.3 and 4.

[135] For example, C.1 q.3 c.12; C.3 q.2 c.2, 8, 9; C.7 q.1 c.14; C.8 q.3 c.1; as well as most of C.16 q.7 and C.17 q.4.

Gratian's argument on the question of servile persons is found in his *dicta*, and this was elaborated upon in the Decretist glosses. These *were* twelfth-century ideas. Of course, they were the ideas of a small group of legal scholars with, arguably, a relatively narrow view of the world.[136] But these writings were carefully preserved and used for several centuries as the best possible guidelines to church law and to the church's teachings on legal questions about its servile dependents. The very fact that they were so widely used shows that they were accepted. And these discussions were not limited to the Christian community. Twelfth-century Jewish scholars discussed similar traditions about slavery. The *Mishneh Torah* of Moshe ben Maimon empha-sized that Jews could not sell a slave to a nonbeliever (8.1) or the slave would automatically receive his freedom after having been repurchased (at ten times the value) and then manumitted by the former Jewish master. However, rec-ognizing the realities of life, there were certain situations where this ideal might not apply. Similar regulations applied to a slave who was sold to one of the king's men (8.3) or if a "resident of the Land of Israel" sold his slave to a foreign land (8.6). Also, one might not emancipate a heathen slave un-less it was in order to do a good work (9.6). Reminiscent of the justifications for the permanence of ecclesiastical servitude, the underlying assumption in Maimonides's collection seems to have been that being in a good, believing Jewish household was such a positive thing that one shouldn't deprive a slave, even a "heathen," of this opportunity.[137] Analogously, Gratian's presentation of the canon law as it pertained to ecclesiastical *servi* represented the view that serving God in any way, even in legal servitude, was a good thing.

Decretals and the Decretalists

Before long, another group of texts became even more influential as sources of church law. While Gratian's work continued to be widely known, as were the numerous commentaries on the *Decretum*, papal "decretal" letters be-came even more important in the day-to-day legal activities of the church. The jurists produced collections of the decretals that they thought were the

---

[136] For a discussion of this point see Epstein, *Speaking of Slavery* 175–83.

[137] Moshe ben Maimon, *The Code of Maimonides: Book 12. The Book of Acquisition* (New Haven 1955), chapters 8 and 9. Maimonides, a twelfth-century Jewish scholar, was born in Spain, but as a boy was forced to flee for his life. He composed this work, a compilation of Jewish law reaching back to the book of Deuteronomy, while he was living in Egypt.

best representations of various legal principles and soon produced a very large body of commentary on them. Important papal letters had been collected since the late Roman Empire and, as we have seen, had often proved useful in deciding legal questions over the early medieval centuries. Gratian had included a lot of this early material in his *Decretum*. From the eleventh century on, the number of these papal letters increased considerably, as did their influence. The most long-lasting and authoritative decretal collection was the *Decretales Gregorii IX* (*The Decretals of Gregory IX*), better known as the *Liber extra*.[138] In 1234, Pope Gregory IX sent the *Liber extra*, whose compilation had been supervised by Raymond of Peñafort, to the law schools at Bologna to be taught to students of the canon law. This was the definitive collection of decretal law, and over the course of the next hundred years, new sections were appended to this corpus to include more recent material.[139] Commentaries on these decretal letters began to appear almost immediately and continued over the next centuries. Since these commentaries were the product of learned jurists, their opinions carried considerable weight in the courts.

Detailed letters about problems that involved unfree persons can be found in a number of places in these collections, which were organized systematically according to long held juristic tradition. The most important letters for our question of ecclesiastical *servi* can be found in the material about ordination. But papal responses to other sorts of questions can also provide us with some useful insights, especially about the changing ideas that people held about their unfree dependents.

In earlier chapters we noted how the attitudes of Christian society seemed to change a little over time in connection with servitude, becoming servile, and becoming free. In the later medieval period, as we have seen, while some servile persons were real chattel slaves, there were many different types of unfreedom and dependence, although the language used by legal scholars tended to ignore many of these differences. In addition, by the turn of the millennium even slaves were generally seen as human persons, whether or not they possessed "juridical personality."[140]

---

[138] In other words, the book in addition to Gratian's *Decretum*.

[139] The decretal collections grew to include several important compilations of later letters: in 1298, the *Liber Sextus*, and again in 1317 and 1325 the *Constitutiones Clementinae* and the *Extravagantes* of John XXII, respectively. The most well-known edition of this *Corpus iuris canonici* is that of Emil Richter, revised by E. Friedberg (Leipzig 1879–1881).

[140] The reasons for these changes lie primarily in the domain of the theologians and thus far outside the scope of this inquiry. But the law and other records document that change had occurred. For an interesting discussion on this see Helmholz, *Spirit* 65–87.

In the law of the *Decretales*, often called the *ius novum* (new law), there were limitations on who could be enslaved. For example, in ancient times, it had been common for exposed children to become the slaves of their rescuers. But an 1136 letter of Pope Gregory IX stated that children who had been exposed were not to become the slaves of their rescuers and were to be independent of their fathers' power as well. Such a child born to a freedman would gain the status of freeborn, but a servile child who was rescued would be classified only as freed.[141] The *Liber extra* also included the material that we mentioned earlier about any persons who had been giving aid to the Saracen enemy. If captured, they were to be enslaved.[142] It is interesting to note that the commentary on this was focused on various issues of commercial law and did not mention the question of slavery.[143] While in general it was not lawful to enslave Christians at this time, it was still a valid punishment for certain offenses, so the jurists of the time saw no reason to discuss that aspect of the decretal.

Book V, Title 6 addressed the question of "Jews, Saracens, and their *Servi.*" Most of the chapters that are of interest for our purposes were taken from the Lateran council of 1179 mentioned earlier.[144] It was forbidden for non-Christians to have Christians serving them. Any Christians who did so would be excommunicated. And, as suggested earlier, it is likely that this excommunication threat was not meant to deter Christians from serving such masters, but rather as an expression of contempt for the Jews and Saracens.[145]

Marriage law comprised a large part of the decretal material. And the issue of servile marriage continued to produce a good deal of discussion. Book IV, Title 9 of the Decretals is *De coniugio servorum* (Concerning the marriage

---

[141] *Liber extra* book 5, title 11, chapter 1. Or X 5.11.1, according to the standard scholarly citation format for the Decretals.

[142] X 5.6.17, also known as *Ad liberandum* after the opening words of the letter as was—and still is—the custom when referring to papal decretals or encyclicals.

[143] A lot of scholarly attention has been directed toward this letter. See, especially Ute-Renate Blumenthal, "A Gloss of Hostiensis to X 5.6.17 (*Ad liberandum*)," *Bulletin of Medieval Canon Law* 30 (2013) 89–122.

[144] Especially X 5.6.1, 2, 5, 8, 13, and 19.

[145] It is also interesting that this material was considered important enough to be included in the *Decretales* at all. The *Decretum* and the *Decretales* did not include all of the canonical material from the previous thousand years, only what was considered particularly important to the compilers. So the fact that an entire title—consisting of nineteen chapters from the Lateran council as well as recent papal letters and miscellaneous other texts—was devoted to this question is significant. The thirteenth-century concerns about the "Saracens" is understandable. The Crusades and the Turks continued to be of considerable importance to the Europeans. And anti-Jewish feeling had a very long history and very deep roots. This title is evidence that these feelings continued to be very strong in the later medieval period.

of *servi*). X 4.9.1 is Pope Hadrian IV's letter from the late 1150s that began, "Dignum est . . ." (It is fitting . . .). Hadrian said, "In no way may [masters] prevent the marriage of their *servi*"; and further, that if *servi* did marry after their masters had refused consent, there was no way that this lack of consent could be considered grounds for the church to dissolve such a marriage. This represented a real departure from the position taken by the ninth-century Council of Chalons that valid servile marriages required the masters' consent.[146] Another thing to consider, as Landau noted, is that by the twelfth century, consent for the marriage of servile person, including *censuales*, usually required payment to the master.[147] Thus Hadrian's decretal had major financial implications as well. It seems to have taken a while for this decretal letter to gain acceptance, as it was apparently not cited by the Decretist scholars in Bologna until the late 1170s, when Sicard's comments on the *Decretum* C.29 q.2 c.7 could no longer be ignored.[148] If *servi* were indeed human beings, then, according to the natural law, they did have a right to marry as did anyone else, marriage being the only acceptable way for a Christian couple to join together. After the *Liber extra* was promulgated, many commentators wrote at length discussing and confirming this basic principle, the right to marry. However, if a servile person married a free person without disclosing his or her servile state, that was considered grounds for annulment, so long as the marriage was not consummated after the free person discovered the deception.[149]

Thus far, the decretal materials we have seen did not include anything special pertaining to ecclesiastical *servi*. The church's servile dependents seem to have been considered as being no different than the *servi* of lay masters in most situations and, like the rest of the *res ecclesiae*, they were inalienable property. But as in the *Decretum*, in the *Decretales*, and in the *summae* and commentaries written after 1234 there was some discussion about the regulations for an ordinand who was unfree, especially an ecclesiastical dependent.

According to the *Decretum*, the difficulty with ordaining a servile person was that he would have obligations to his master that conflicted with his duties to the church.[150] Manumission was the remedy, and ordination would override any obligations of service to the former master—except those to an

---

146 Discussed previously as C.29 q.2 c.8 of the *Decretum*.
147 Landau, "Hadrians IV. Dekretale."
148 See Gilchrist, "Medieval Canon Law" 291 n. 80.
149 X 4.9.2.
150 Mostly in D.54 and C.12 q.2, as discussed earlier.

ecclesiastical master. The *Decretum*, careful to protect ecclesiastical property rights, had said that in the case of a new priest the customary right of a layperson to the services of his freedman was not upheld. He could be required to provide the patron with spiritual services, but the new priest's obligations to the church superseded any other obligations to the former master. There was of course no conflict of interest if both obligations, those of an ordinand and those of a freedman, were to the same church.

The *Liber extra*, throughout, took the principle of the inalienability of church property very seriously. Book III, Title 13, "On the Alienation of the *Res Ecclesiae*," included twelve letters on this issue, and dozens more were scattered throughout the rest of Book III as well as in other parts of the collection. The decretals upheld the ancient theories saying that church property was not to be alienated in any way, except to ransom captives, to feed the poor, and in other cases where the needs of the church demanded it. X 3.13.3 and 4 repeated the seventh-century canons from Toledo saying that priests could not free ecclesiastical *servi* and that the manumission of *servi ecclesiarum* effected by a bishop, even if he had paid for them, could be reversed by that bishop's successor if he believed the manumission to have been unlawful.[151] An interesting idea about the needs of the church was introduced by Pope Alexander III's letter of 1180 saying that unproductive land might be leased out to someone who would cultivate it. In earlier centuries, leasing church lands had been forbidden.[152] But this situation was not exactly alienation of the unproductive land because when the term of the lease expired, the church would have land that was now more valuable, thanks to the lessee's improvements. And instead of having to pay for the land to be improved, the church would actually have profited from the exchange. Other decretals as well as the jurists' commentary worked out the details of such an arrangement.

The collection of chapters in Book I, Title 18, "Concerning the fact that *servi* are not to be ordained and about their manumission," demonstrates the thirteenth-century position on the ordination of servile men. Chapters 1, 2, and 3 repeated the early medieval Toledo canons about ordination requiring full freedom and the master's consent saying that a *servus ecclesiae* could be

---

[151] Bishops could recover land that had been improperly alienated as well. See Mary Cheyney, "Inalienability in Mid-Twelfth Century England: Enforcement and Consequences," *in Proceedings of the Sixth International Congress of Medieval Canon Law: Berkeley, California, 28 July–2 August 1980*, ed. S. Kuttner and K. Pennington MIC, Series C, Subsidia 7 (Vatican City 1985) 467–77.

[152] X 3.13.7.

freed for ordination. But the church would retain some patronal rights in the new priest: the church would be his eventual heir and, if he did not conduct himself properly, he might be forced back into servile status, conditions that had been common in ancient Roman law as well. X 1.18.7 is a letter from Pope Alexander II that provided for a master to retain the right to demand spiritual services from a priest whom he had freed in order to make ordination possible. X 1.18.6 is a letter from Pope Innocent III (1198–1216) saying that a *servus ecclesiae* who had been freed in order that he might be ordained could not be transferred to another ecclesiastical position, as that would violate the principle of nonalienation. Remaining chapters detailed particular circumstances. But the weakness of a decretal letter collection becomes apparent when considering X 1.18. Since these letters were primarily the popes' responses to particular situations, sometimes the general principles to be upheld are not immediately obvious to the modern reader. And there were no helpful *dicta* like the ones Gratian had provided. For a discussion of the underlying principles of decretal law, we need to turn to the jurists' separate analyses.

While working on the compilation of the *Decretales* for Pope Gregory IX, Raymond of Peñafort also produced his own treatise, known as the *Summa de Poenitentia*.[153] Raymond was a Spanish canonist who had been trained in Bologna as well as in Barcelona. His argument was similar to that of Augustine of Hippo. Raymond said "servitude was introduced by God's law" since in the Bible, Canaan (Ham) had been cursed to be the slave of his own brother.[154] This went against the teachings of a number of Raymond's contemporaries, who still held to the principles of Roman law: according to natural law, all persons were free and slavery was the product of human laws (*ius gentium*). But Raymond explained that human laws had merely "approved" the divine law of slavery, and that the canon law had "confirmed" it.[155] Nonetheless, as Gilchrist found, in most situations Raymond did come down on the side of freedom.[156]

In the section "Concerning the fact that *servi* are not to be ordained and about their manumission," Raymond made the complex treatments of these

[153] Raymond of Peñfort, *Summa de poenitentia et matrimonio* (Rome 1603, rp. Turin 1969).

[154] *Summa de poenitentia* 1.4.7.

[155] In support of these statements, Raymond cited D.1 c.9 (which said that the *ius gentium* covered, among other things, weapons, war, captives, and slaves). And the approval of the canon law, said Raymond, could be found in C.12 q.2 c.69 (a chapter among the many in that *quaestio* that discuss the importance and inalienability of church *servi*).

[156] Gilchrist, "St. Raymond."

issues found in the *Decretum* and even in his own collection of the *Decretales* much easier to understand. He followed the other canonists in ruling out the ordination of unfree persons, saying that there were two reasons for this, referring the reader to Gratian's D.54: the *utilitas* of the *servus* (i.e., the owner's proprietary rights in his services) as well as the unseemliness of a lowly *servus* holding the exalted rank of a clergyman.[157] If the *servus* who wished to be ordained had a lay master, he would first have to be given the fullest possible freedom without any patronal ties at all to his former master.[158] However, for a *libertus ecclesiae*, certain patronal obligations to the church would continue. Why was it acceptable to free a church *servus* in this context? Because, said Raymond, ordination restored to God a *servus ecclesiae* who had been alienated through his manumission. And thus the *res ecclesiae* had not been alienated after all.[159] When considering whether or not *servi ecclesiarum* could be set free, Raymond reiterated Gratian's teaching that when a bishop manumitted a *servus ecclesiae* who was particularly deserving (*benemeritus*), the church would retain patronal rights. However, he said that in other situations the bishop could free a *servus* without retaining patronal rights and compensate the church with double the value of that *servus*. In neither case would the *res ecclesiae* actually be diminished.[160] Double the value of the undesirable slave improved the church's bottom line and manumission of someone who was not *benemeritus* might well eliminate a personnel problem. A deserving slave could be rewarded with legally free status, but the church's retention of patronal rights kept the value of his services as part of the *res ecclesiae* in perpetuity.

Raymond then listed three ways in which *liberti ecclesiarum* were different from *liberti* with lay masters. First, *liberti ecclesiarum* could be recalled into servitude for not performing their obligations. Second, their children, even if they had been born after their parent's manumission, remained *liberti* bound to the service of the church. The children of non-ecclesiastical *liberti* became *ingenui*, that is, the same as freeborn. And finally, *liberti ecclesiarum* were bound to serve the church even if no particular services had been included in the manumission agreements, as was usually required when a lay master

---

[157] *Summa de poenitentia* 3.17.1. and 3.17.5.
[158] *Summa de poenitentia* 3.17.2. Gilchrist held that Raymond seems not to have agreed with other canonists who held that a lay patron could demand the right to have his former freedman provide "spiritual services" ("St. Raymond" 311–13). On the other hand, perhaps Raymond thought that such spiritual services didn't count as patronal obligations.
[159] *Summa de poenitentia* 3.17.3.
[160] C.12 q.2 d.p.c.57 and *Summa de poenitentia* 3.17 (part 2) 2.

wanted to retain a freed person's services.[161] None of these concepts was new, but the fact that Raymond thought it worthwhile to pull them together into a clear and concise list seems significant. This is the first time that we have seen much attention paid to the idea that *servi* and *liberti ecclesiarum* were not like the others. It is the aggregation of the differences that is important for our investigation, even more so than the differences themselves. By the thirteenth century, a new consciousness about servitude was emerging, and the differences between lay and ecclesiastical masters were seen as important in ways that we have not seen since the era of the Germanic kingdoms, centuries earlier.

We should also look at Henricus de Segusio on the question of ordaining *servi ecclesiarum*. Henricus de Segusio, or as he is better known, Hostiensis, was one of the most brilliant canonists of the classical period of canon law. Born around 1200, Henricus studied law at Bologna and then followed an ecclesiastical career, including many years of service to the papacy, especially to Pope Innocent IV, whom he had met during their student days in Bologna. Henricus de Segusio ended his career as cardinal bishop of Ostia, whence the name, Hostiensis. Perhaps the most well known of his works is his 1253 *Summa* on the *Decretales* of Gregory IX, soon known as the *Summa aurea*, or *Golden Summa*.[162]

In his discussion of X.1.18, on the ordination and manumission of *servi*, Hostiensis said several things of interest to our inquiry.[163] Regarding the origins of servitude, he agreed with most of his predecessors that servitude was part of human laws (*ius gentium*) and that it was against nature. And, like Raymond, Hostiensis said that slavery had begun with the Noah incident when Noah was "inspired by God" to consign his sons to servitude. Subsequently the idea of slavery was "approved" by the *ius gentium*.[164] Revealing his familiarity with ancient Roman law, Hostiensis listed a number of different ways in which a *servus* could be given his liberty, including *manumissio in ecclesia*. This is the first time that we have seen the old custom of *manumissio in ecclesia* referenced explicitly in the classical canon law. Concerning this, Hostiensis declared that it was appropriate that a bishop have the power to set *servi* free because, after all, he had the power to grant

---

[161] *Summa de poenitentia* 3.17 (part 2) 4. On this see Gilchrist, "St. Raymond" 317–18.

[162] Hostiensis, *Summa Aurea* (Venice 1574) available on line at the Medieval Canon Law Virtual Library (http://web.colby.edu/canonlaw/2009/10/01/resources/).

[163] On this also see Landau, "Frei und Unfrei" and Helmholz, *Spirit* 61–87.

[164] *Summa aurea* I, tit. *De servis non ordinandis & eorum manimussione*, no. 2.

the remission of sins.[165] If servitude was the result of human sin, manumission was, in a way, the remission of that sin. This idea, which we have not seen elsewhere, gives rise to questions about what Hostiensis thought of slavery. Although he did not say so explicitly, this statement certainly implies that Hostiensis saw servitude as analogous in some way to sin.[166] Interestingly, he added that while a bishop could give a *servus ecclesiae* full liberty, an abbot did not have quite the same power concerning a *servus* of his monastery. Full manumission in that circumstance required the consent of the bishop as well as that of the monks of the monastery.[167] Presumably, the bishop was needed for the remission of the sin of slavery and the monks' consent for the alienation of a major asset of the monastery community. While Hostiensis provided an interesting justification for why a bishop could preside over a manumission ceremony, he did not provide us with any information about how frequently *manumissio in ecclesia* occurred in connection with lay masters in the later medieval period.

A little further on in this same title, Hostiensis revealed his softer side. If you sell an *ancilla* (female servile dependent), he said, you may not sell her to someone who will use her for prostitution. And if you give an *ancilla* in marriage, you must provide her with a dowry. Despite all of the concern to preserve the church's patrimony, there were limits on how servile dependents should be treated. A female servile dependent had to be cared for. It was not acceptable to sell her into sin or to let her marry without the customary dignity. As we have seen, by the mid-thirteenth century there was no confusion about the fact that *servi* were human beings. Yet, although Hostiensis may have believed that *servi* should be treated with a modicum of neighborly love, this was not true of everyone. In 1355 in England, a bishop named Grandisson freed one of his *servi* saying: Now that you are in your fifties and have no family and no real skills, "we cannot hold it unprofitable to us or to our church of Exeter to restore to you your natural liberty [so that you will have more opportunities to support yourself, given the circumstances] and moved by piety."[168] In other words, this poor man had become a burden to the church of Exeter, so Grandisson set him free to starve on his own.

[165] *Summa aurea* I, tit. *De servis non ordinandis*, no. 5.

[166] It is not within the scope of this study—nor within the scope of my competence—to pursue the theological implications here. But it is an interesting question.

[167] *Summa aurea* I, tit. *De servis non ordinandis*, no. 10.

[168] *The Register of John de Grandisson, 1327–69*, ed. F. C. Hingeston-Randolph (London 1894–99) #1159; reprinted in H. S. Bennett, *Life on the English Manor* (Cambridge 1937) 283.

In Hostiensis's work we find an even longer discussion than Raymond's about how *servi* or *liberti ecclesiarum* were different from those with lay masters or patrons, especially concerning the terms of their manumission. In this same section of the *Summa*, Hostiensis listed five ways in which church freedmen and freedmen with lay patrons were different from one another. First, a freedman with a lay patron might not be ordained unless he was given full liberty because the rights of the church to its priest would conflict with the rights of a freedman's lay patron. A church freedman, who could not be given full freedom because of the need to preserve the church's property, could nevertheless be ordained because the patron retaining rights over the freedman would be the same church that had the right to the services of the ordained person. Second, former church *servi* who were ordained could be recalled into servitude for "ingratitude," as might have happened to any freedman in ancient Rome or the earlier medieval period who did not perform the services required by his patron. In the later Middle Ages this does not seem to have applied to former *servi* of lay masters because lay masters no longer seemed to have patronal rights of that sort, especially not when the freed *servus* was ordained. Since a freedman was likely to become a tenant, the purposes of the traditional post-manumission connection would have been met by the landlord-tenant relationship. But, as we have seen, ordination required full freedom; a former master could claim only spiritual services from his freed slave. Third, the offspring of any church freedman would retain their parent's freed status and the accompanying obligations. Fourth, church freedmen could be required to render (unspecified) services to their former master (the church), even if that had not been mentioned at the time of the manumission procedures. And finally, church freedmen who were ordained could not give their possessions to anyone else. Their property, unlike that of ordinary freedmen, was not their own. It was still church property and thus could not be alienated. None of these provisions is unique to Hostiensis's treatise. But, as we said about Raymond of Peñafort, the even greater length and specificity of Hostiensis's discussion of the differences between ecclesiastical and ordinary freedmen is noteworthy in itself.

The *Ius Commune*

By the end of the thirteenth century, European law had become a great deal more complicated. While the canon law generally applied to the entire Latin

Christian church, this was balanced by local, secular law that varied greatly. Not only did the *ius proprium* (local laws and customs) have provisions and regulations that were specific to a particular people or territory, but also each local culture had its own ancient ideas about the role of law in a society. Nevertheless, throughout Europe, jurists relied on an underlying theoretical understanding of law and legal science that ultimately derived from ancient Roman jurisprudence. An earlier chapter mentioned the Byzantine Emperor Justinian's massive attempt to bring some order to the thousand years of Roman law that had accumulated by his day. But for the most part, this work had not been very well known in Europe. In the eleventh and twelfth centuries, European legal scholars rediscovered the Justinian corpus and began to use the basic principles behind Roman law in their discussion of medieval European law.[169]

A thousand years earlier, the ancient Roman scholars had begun to think of law as a set of principles that could be applied in any situation, rather than as a set of precedents to be used when the right circumstances presented themselves. These men, especially Gaius, Ulpian, and a few other second-century legal analysts, had seen the records of imperial decrees and judicial pronouncements as the application of basic ideas of what could or could not be done and discussed the implications of these principles at some length. In the sixth century, Emperor Justinian's project had updated the earlier collection made under the direction of Emperor Theodosius II and sorted through the legal documentation and commentary that had accumulated in the long centuries of Roman history. There was simply too much material for any one person to master, and the Byzantine scholars distilled it down to a manageable size. This new legal compendium consisted of several volumes containing Roman laws up to the reign of Justinian as well as commentary from the ancient jurists. As noted in earlier chapters, several collections of Roman law had circulated earlier in medieval Europe, and the church courts had long followed Roman legal procedural rules. But it was not until around the turn of the millennium that the Justinian corpus was rediscovered, or "received," in western Europe and began to be the object of serious scholarly attention. Thus, in his twelfth-century *Decretum*, Master Gratian said that

---

[169] For more detail on this see Wolfgang P. Müller, "The Recovery of Justinian's Digest in the Middle Ages," *Bulletin of Medieval Canon Law* n.s. 19 (1989) 1–29. Also see Peter Stein, *Roman Law in European History* (Cambridge 1999). Paul Vinogradoff, *Roman Law in Medieval Europe* (New York 1909) still remains very helpful.

civil law was to be used when it did not contradict the canons.[170] And the old principle that we saw in the *Lex Ribvaria*, that the church followed the Roman law, received new energy.[171]

The international community of university-educated legal scholars talked about the common legal ideas, the *ius commune*, of late medieval European culture.[172] The *ius commune* was not a code of laws. While the canon law did provide universally applicable regulations, the body of canonical jurisprudence also provided theoretical principles and analytical possibilities. Roman law contributed mostly theory, with some general regulations that seemed helpful. And the local laws and customs provided ideas and examples that enriched everyone's understanding of law in general as well as of their own legal system.[173] The *ius commune* was the law as it was discussed by the legal scholars, the theorists and the most learned judges and legal advocates. Law students studied the *ius commune* at universities throughout Europe. Beginning in Bologna, but soon in Salamanca, Orleans, and Oxford as well, students learned how to be better judges and better advocates for their future clients.[174]

Regrettably, a full consideration of all that the *ius commune* had to say on our question is beyond the scope of this analysis, and this sea change in the European legal world marks an endpoint to our inquiries. There were no new "official" canonical pronouncements on issues related to how the church should deal with ecclesiastical *servi*. And in the analyses of these late medieval jurists one thing did not change: *servi ecclesiarum*, as the inalienable

---

[170] D.10 d.p.c.6.

[171] On this principle see Dafydd Walters, "From Benedict to Gratian: The Code in Medieval Ecclesiastical Authors," in *The Theodosian Code*, ed. J. Harries and I. Wood (Ithaca 1993) 200–216.

[172] There has been much scholarly discussion of the *ius commune* in recent years. A classic work is Manlio Bellomo, *The Common Legal Past of Europe: 1000–1800*, trans. L. Cochrane (Washington, DC 1995) originally published as *L'Europa del diritto commune* (Rome 1994). Also helpful are Harald J. Berman, *Law and Revolution: The Formation of the Western Legal Tradition* (Cambridge, MA 1983) and Richard Helmholz, *The Ius Commune in England* (Oxford 2001). Very short and readable introductions have been provided by Kenneth Pennington in "Learned Law, Droit Savant, Gelehrtes Recht: The Tyranny of a Concept," *Rivista internazionale di diritto commune* 5 (1994) 197–209 and Peter Stein, "The *Ius Commune* and Its Demise," *Journal of Legal History* 25 (2004) 161–67. The collected articles in *The Creation of the Ius Commune: From Casus to Regula*, ed. J. W. Cairns and P. J. du Plessis (Edinburgh 2010), provide interesting discussions about the application of the legal principles.

[173] Jean Birrell, "Manorial Custumals Reconsidered," *Past & Present* 224 (August 2014) 3–37, presented an interesting consideration of some of these local laws.

[174] A good overview can be found in Thomas Rüfner, "Die Rezeption des römischen Sklavenrechts im Gelehrten Recht des Mittalalters," in *Sklaverei und Freilassung im römischen Recht*, ed. T. Finkenauer (Heidelberg 2006) 201–21.

property of the church, remained in a difficult situation that unfree persons with lay masters did not have to deal with.

Conclusions

By the thirteenth century, differences between free and unfree laborers had frequently become irrelevant. Peasants, free or servile, were rarely able to leave the land they worked and had little control over their lives. And workers generally resided in individual dwellings, in family units. Traditional chattel slavery continued as well, largely in the Mediterranean port cities where the slave trade provided many non-Christian *servi*. Economically, the vast majority of workers were inextricably tied to their lords, but as time went on, the slow rise of a money economy and the success of some of the peasants' revolts made it harder for their lords to control them. Peasants and urban slaves gained access to money and even sometimes to the courts.[175] And the society at large had generally recognized that servile dependents were not the same as cattle or other movable property. They were encouraged to enter into Christian marriages, even when that resulted in inconveniences to their masters.

Unfree ecclesiastical dependents were mostly treated no differently than were those with lay masters. However, the fact that it was forbidden to alienate church property meant that ecclesiastical dependents, even if they managed to achieve free legal status, still found it nearly impossible to escape their obligations to the church. Although ecclesiastical lords were subject to the same pressures from below as were the lay lords, the church did not loosen its grip on the canon law. Ecclesiastical law, found in Gratian's *Decretum* and the *Decretals* of Gregory IX, was not much changed in response to these late medieval social pressures. Scholarly commentary, although it had begun to recognize the humanity of servile persons, continued to uphold the principle of the inalienability of church property, including the services of ecclesiastical freedmen, especially when such a person wanted to be ordained.

---

[175] For developments in court procedures relating to the use of unfree persons as litigants and as witnesses, see the essays in *The History of Courts and Procedure in Medieval Canon Law*, ed. W. Hartmann and K. Pennington (HMCL 7).

A new kind of legal thinking, known as the *ius commune*, spread throughout the European scholarly community by the end of the thirteenth century. This was also the time when the Europeans' use of slave labor began to undergo significant changes. Our study must end here, bounded not only by the beginning of the new kind of legal scholarship in late medieval Europe, but also by the thirteenth-century beginnings of the Europeans' ventures into the Atlantic World and the new understandings about slavery that emerged.

8

Conclusions

This book has been an investigation of the Christian church as a slave owner. More specifically, it has been a survey of the church's own regulations about how to deal with its own unfree dependents and with those of ecclesiastical personnel, from the earliest Christian centuries until the beginnings of the Atlantic World. There are no big surprises here, no breakthrough theories, although this study has been able to shed new light on a few smaller, related questions. Instead, what has emerged is a new and clear picture of the slow evolution of the church law concerning ecclesiastical slave ownership, law that reached its apex in the classical canon law of the twelfth and thirteenth centuries. As with biological evolutionary processes, the evolution of the canon law about the slaves of the churches experienced a number of branches that died out. But the "main branch" continued to be normative for the Catholic Church until the twentieth century.

Such a comprehensive longitudinal study of canon law naturally began with first-century Palestine, at the beginning of Christianity. At that time, Palestinian society was a mixture of two different cultures, the Greco-Roman conquerors and the indigenous Jewish population. Greco-Roman society was the archetypical slave society, where slaves were things, not persons, and had no legal standing. This was held to be acceptable because most people, following Aristotle, believed that slaves were inherently inferior beings. The Stoic philosophers, however, taught that slavery of the body was unimportant and that the condition of one's soul was much more significant. They also believed that one should treat one's slaves well, not only because they were fellow human beings, but also because such good treatment was beneficial for the master's soul. By the second century CE, Roman legal philosophers taught that slavery was not a natural phenomenon, as Aristotle had taught. Rather, slavery was something that had been instituted by human customs. The Jews also had a long tradition of slave ownership, although their laws demanded preferred treatment of one's co-religionists.

The earliest records of the Christian community are in the New Testament. Here we found that Jesus—or at least the late first-century

The Slaves of the Churches. Mary E. Sommar, Oxford University Press (2020). © Oxford University Press.
DOI: 10.1093/oso/9780190073268.001.0001

writers of the gospel stories—accepted the prevailing customs about slavery without comment. By the turn of the second century, Christians were cautioned to go along with the social norms of the greater society in such matters. Slaves were commanded to obey their masters. Christian masters, in line with the Stoic tradition, were exhorted to treat their slaves decently because all people were equal in the eyes of God. Those with sufficient means, including bishops and other leaders of the Christian community, owned slaves, but there is no clear evidence of corporate ownership of slaves by the Christians as a group at that time. As time went on, there were few changes. Many Christians did own slaves, and, despite continued appeals for masters to treat their slaves well, there is a good deal of evidence that slaves were still held in considerable contempt by many Christians. But Christians also observed positive Roman customs concerning the unfree. Great efforts were made to rescue fellow Christians who had been captured in order to save them from enslavement. And a freed slave could rise to very high status in the Christian community: the former slave Callistus became the bishop of Rome in around 200 CE. In addition, forcing one's Christian slave to fulfill the Roman requirement that every household sacrifice to the Roman gods was condemned as a serious sin, worse than making such a sacrifice oneself. And in line with ancient Jewish tradition, Christian men were urged to allow female captives a period of adjustment before demanding their rights to her person. However, the frequency and the specificity of these exhortations suggest that such negative treatment was rather common. The third-century *Apostolic Tradition* said that a Christian's slaves needed their master's permission to convert to the new faith. And those with pagan masters were to be rejected out of hand. It is clear that there was no generally held Christian position about slaves and slavery. The early Christians' ideas and behavior varied as did those of the rest of the people throughout the empire.

For much of the third century the Christians were persecuted by the secular authorities, and those enslaved as a result of these persecutions were venerated as martyrs for their faith. Some people even considered self-sale into slavery to be a pious act. Yet Christians who could afford to own slaves usually had slaves. Bishops were given no special regulations to follow in regard to their servile dependents. And while there is still no concrete evidence that the Christians owned slaves as a community, there are indications that the bishops' slaves would have been assigned to render the services required by the local churches.

With Constantine's acceptance of the Christian faith in the early fourth century, the church was absorbed into the general culture of the empire, and Christian churches were treated like any other corporate body. The churches now customarily owned the slaves needed to support their functioning and to support the needs of their personnel. Regulations were issued by the emperor and by councils of bishops about how the church as an institution should conduct its affairs. In our survey of this earliest legal material, there emerged three issues that are of interest to our question. First, slaves were part of the *res ecclesiae*, and the bishop was to be in control of all ecclesiastical property. Second, bishops and other clergy were to be morally pure and thus were not to engage in sexual relations with their female slaves, even though this was tolerated from laymen. And third, the *res ecclesiae* received considerable protection under Roman law, as did all private property. The traditional Roman customs about slavery continued in the Christian community and in the treatment of ecclesiastical slaves, subject to these minor limitations. Among the many changes Constantine instituted in his empire, Christian bishops were now given certain magisterial powers, including the power to preside over a manumission ceremony. This *manumissio in ecclesia*, as it was called, seems eventually to have produced what were the most significant characteristics of ecclesiastical lordship over servile dependents.

From Augustine in Africa to the Cappadocian fathers in what is now Turkey, the old Roman attitudes, tempered by the Christian/Stoic attitude of benevolence toward one's inferiors, continued largely unchanged throughout the fourth and fifth centuries. Imperial legislation and conciliar canons continued to uphold the Roman customs and the inviolability of the *res ecclesiae*. Even Bishop Gregory of Nyssa, whom many have mistaken for a proto-abolitionist, held to the old traditions about slaves and the right to private property. However, like any good Stoic, Gregory inveighed against unhealthily lavish displays of wealth, including excessive numbers of slaves. Augustine said that slavery was God's punishment for sin. The Christian leaders of the late empire were still Romans at heart, and their Christian faith did not require anything specific in connection with their *servi*.

The next few centuries saw the transformation of Europe by the emergence of regional kingdoms under the leadership of Germanic groups whose southwestern migrations had destabilized the institutions of the Western Roman Empire. These new rulers brought with them new understandings about social structures. The old Roman culture had seen slaves as property, and the Christian command to love one's neighbor had not done much to change that. The Visigoths, who ended up in Spain, exhibited an especially low regard for their slaves. They seem to have thought that inappropriate contact with one's servile dependents would contaminate the master. Inappropriate relations between a priest and his slave woman could render him unfit to preside over worship. The Franks in Gaul were more matter of fact. Social status was crucial to them, as was maintaining the behaviors and receiving the treatment that was appropriate to one's status. Since slaves' status depended on the status of their owner, ecclesiastical slaves and royal slaves were of relatively high social status despite their servility.

Several new things concerning the church's relationship to servile persons emerged during this period. In addition to the generally harsh treatment of slaves, a late sixth-century Visigothic council held that if an ecclesiastical slave were set free, he and his descendants would forever be bound in obligation to the church where he had been a slave. It had long been the Roman custom for a master to continue as the former slave's patron in return for certain services, but this did not continue into future generations. In some parts of Gaul, particularly in Ripuaria, this perpetual obligation to the church was also applied to slaves who had been set free in a church ceremony, no matter who their former master had been. Since *manumissio in ecclesia* was becoming very common, this meant that the church acquired the right to perpetual services from countless numbers of freedmen and their free descendants. The data does not permit us to judge with any accuracy just how universally this law was accepted in practice. However, it is very clear that a significant number of people, ecclesiastical and lay, took it very seriously. And the custom spread.

In Lombard-ruled Italy there was no mention at this time of a post-manumission relationship with the church. Neither was there anything about this in the British Isles. At that time, European Christian leaders were struggling to establish a stable presence on the western side of the Channel, and local royal support was not always forthcoming. The English church often had to fight against royal usurpation of church property. While it is clear that church leaders were usually aware of canonical developments on the continent, their implementation was not a priority. It would be several centuries before the insular church joined the European mainstream.

In the eastern, "Byzantine" half of the Roman Empire, there were few changes to ecclesiastical law during this time and the emperors continued to uphold the nonalienation of church property. However, the sixth-century Emperor Justinian proclaimed two laws that are relevant to our question.

First of all, a master whose slave had been ordained without his consent had only a limited period of time in which to claim his lost property. After this, while the former master might receive some financial compensation, the former slave was henceforth considered fully free. Another of Justinian's laws had long-lasting philosophical implications. If a married person was captured and enslaved, the marriage continued to be valid. The implication is that the captured and enslaved partner continued to enjoy legal personhood. Earlier considerations of the equality of all before God were of a theological nature. But in this instance the concept had legal support.

By the end of the eighth century, one of the Germanic groups, the Franks, had established political dominance in most of western Europe. Charlemagne and his descendants ruled over a new "Roman Empire" that controlled most of western Europe. Thus, despite some adherence to old local customs, there was a body of secular and ecclesiastical regulations that applied to most of the western, Latin church. The two main issues that this study found in the Carolingian era legislation were questions that had already emerged in the sixth century: slaves' ability to marry and the permanence of the bond between the church and ecclesiastical freedmen. In the ninth century, a council meeting at Chalons declared that the marriage of two servile persons was valid, as long as their master(s) had agreed. And there was considerable discussion back and forth during these years about the post-manumission situation of ecclesiastical *servi*. Both of these questions proved problematical because of the need to respect the right to private property. If a master did not consent to his slave's marriage, any time spent with the spouse was in effect stolen from the master. And no matter the rationale for the church's right to perpetual services from ecclesiastical freedmen, once that right had been acknowledged, terminating those services would have been alienating something of value from the church. The question of a relationship between a freedman and the church where he had received his freedom was debated back and forth without any resolution at this point.

From our examination of economic records there emerged a new picture of ecclesiastical institutions as owners of unfree laborers. In the changing economic structures of Carolingian Europe, churches became the owners of vast agricultural estates that employed thousands of unfree workers. And the ecclesiastical lords behaved no differently toward their servile personnel than did the secular owners of similarly large establishments. Smallholders, lay or ecclesiastical, frequently mentioned the names of those individuals who were included in their donation to a monastery or a church foundation, suggesting that there was a personal connection to their workers. But the impersonality of "big agriculture" overcame any such inclinations that ecclesiastics may have had toward their servile personnel on larger estates.

The intellectual resurgence of twelfth-century Europe brought about a formalization of church law as well as a deeper understanding of jurisprudence in general following the rediscovery of ancient Roman legal scholarship. The twelfth and thirteenth centuries are often called the "Classical" period of canon law because the major analytical compendia of church law that were produced at that time remained the foundations of church law until the twentieth century.

European society had gone through another period of upheaval around the turn of the millennium due in part to the collapse of the Carolingian Empire and in part to the pressures of other cultures from all directions. These centuries had transformed the social, political, economic, and intellectual world, and the church had become an international hierarchy guided by the Roman papal bureaucracy. In this new society, the laborers were very much dominated by their lords—to the point where free or servile status ceased to make much difference in the lives of the workers. A legally free peasant owed rent and other services to his landlord that were little different from the obligations of a servile peasant. Domestic slavery also continued, especially in urban areas. Two new types of unfree status became common. *Censuales*, also known as *colliberti*, were unfree dependents of ecclesiastical institutions who were obliged to pay an annual *census* but otherwise were pretty much free to do as they liked. In German-speaking areas there were also *ministeriales*, unfree dependents, ecclesiastical or otherwise, whose only obligations were to render services but not to make any payments. These new institutions may have been later iterations of the practices associated with *manumissio in ecclesia* in the early medieval period. The various obligations to a particular church were clearly viewed as part of that church's assets.

The canon law that is relevant to our question primarily dealt with managing the *res ecclesiae*. There was still no real freedom for ecclesiastical slaves. Gratian of Bologna's *Decretum*, an analytical treatise on the canon law, soon became widely influential. This twelfth-century text reinforced the inalienability of church property, including church slaves and freedmen. But if an ecclesiastical *servus* or freedman wanted to be ordained, he could be set free. Ordination of anyone required freedom because the obligations of the ordained state would conflict with the obligations to a master. Ecclesiastical personnel would only be changing the category of their services to the church, thus maintaining the integrity

of the *res ecclesiae*. The question of servile marriage that had occasionally sur-
faced in earlier centuries received a thorough analysis in Gratian's work and that
of his commentators. According to ancient Roman and Christian traditions,
freedom was the natural state of a human being, slavery having been introduced
because of human weakness or sin. Men and women coming together was
also part of the law of nature, and twelfth-century scholars agreed that unfree
status did not imply an incapacity for contracting a proper Christian marriage.
However, although in theory marital obligations superseded the obligations to
one's lord, lay or ecclesiastical, this did not mean that the masters' rights could
be ignored. A century after Gratian, his *Decretum* was supplemented by a compendium of recent papal "decretals," authoritative letters about canonical cases,
that was sponsored by Pope Gregory IX. The questions of church property, servile ordination, and servile marriage that were found in Gratian's work were expanded and clarified in this *Liber extra*, but not substantially changed.

After the mid-thirteenth-century publication of the decretals, there was
relatively little new in the canon law that relates to our question. Canonists
like Raymond of Peñafort and Hostiensis provided explicit discussions of
the differences between unfree persons who had lay or ecclesiastical masters. However, recognizing the disabilities of ecclesiastical *servi* does not seem
to have produced any changes in their situation. In most discussions, church
servi were not differentiated from those with lay masters. And, in most of the
canonists' discussions, the issue of the right to own property, whether the *res
ecclesiae* or the private property of a layperson, trumped the question of individual liberty. In the following centuries a Europe-wide common jurisprudence
of canon law and Roman law would emerge and enhance the study of many
legal issues at the local as well as the international levels. But this did not change
the laws that pertained to unfree ecclesiastical personnel.

Canon Law after the Classical Period

An ecumenical council took place in the Lateran Palace in Rome from 1512
to 1517, just before Martin Luther's formal break with the papacy. In a circle-
the-wagons maneuver, the council forbade "anyone to presume to make
glosses or commentaries" on the official corpus of canon law.[1] The Council

---

[1] V Lateran Council, Session 9, May 5, 1514, *Decrees of the Ecumenical Councils*, ed., trans., N. P.
Tanner (London 1990) 625.

of Trent (1545–1563) expanded the scope of such restrictions to include new editions and commentaries on the Scriptures and "apostolic traditions" unless they had received formal approval from church authorities.[2] Then in 1582, Pope Gregory XII promulgated a new *Corpus Iuris Canonici,* which was a re-presentation of the *Decretum* and the decretals after they had been thoroughly edited and corrected by some of the best Humanist legal scholars of Europe, working under papal direction. However, following in the spirit of the Lateran decree, the commentary on the texts concerning slavery, as on the majority of the *Corpus,* were limited to source-critical explanations. This 1582 edition would continue for some time to be the definitive authority on the canon law.[3] Canon law scholars now had to work differently. After the emergence of Protestant legal scholarship, eventually the Catholic canon law was largely consigned to the theologians.[4] Later canonists, in their encyclopedic surveys of church law, continued to uphold the traditional principles that apply to our question about ecclesiastical slave ownership, especially the inalienability of the *res ecclesiae* and the ineligibility of a servile person for ordination.[5] In Giovanni Paolo Lancelotti's 1588 *Institutiones Iuris Canonici,* for example, his consideration of the principle of the enduring relationship between the church and ecclesiastical servile personnel was brief and clear: "If someone of the church *familia* is manumitted, the freedman and his possessions and his posterity remain under the patronage of the church."[6] The basic principles of the classical period of canon law remained unchanged.

These discussions were informed by the ideas of Thomas Aquinas. In the late thirteenth century, Thomas had argued that, while freedom was the natural state of a human being, Aristotle's theory of "natural slaves" was equally valid. Further, he argued, even the great St. Augustine had said that slavery was a consequence of sin. Thomas said that although before Adam's Fall some would have ruled over others, as Adam over Eve, it would not have been slavery because slavery involved pain. Such was the

---

[2] Council of Trent, Session 4, April 4, 1546, trans. N. P. Tanner, *Decrees of the Ecumenical Councils* 663–64.

[3] For more about this work see Mary E. Sommar, *The Correctores Romani* (Vienna 2009).

[4] On this see Christoph Strohm, "Religion und Recht in der Frühen Neuzeit," *ZRG.KA* 102 (2016) 283–316 and Kenneth Pennington, "Protestant Ecclesiastical Law and the *Ius Commune,*" *Rivista Internazionale di Diritto Comune* 26 (2015) 9–36.

[5] Emanuele Conte's brilliant analysis in *Servi Medievali: Dinamiche del diritto comune* (Rome 1996) concluded that while servitude was a serious issue in written law, the degree of dependency that servitude required was negotiated according to local customs (254–56).

[6] Johannus Paulus Lancelottus, *Institutiones Iuris Canonice* IV.xxvii (Lyons 1588) 299.

freedom of the natural law. Slavery, as the result of sin, existed only after the First Sin, explained Thomas.[7] Like so many before him, Thomas recognized the evils of slavery. But since servitude was such an integral part of every society that he knew, he believed that it somehow must be part of God's plan. It was, he said, an unfortunate consequence of the human disobedience of God's law. But by the time of the European settlement of the Americas, some scholars had begun to question the Thomistic explanation of the servile institutions.[8] Francisco de Vitoria (d. 1546) and Bartolomé de las Casas (d. 1566) used references from Roman and canon law to expand Thomas's ideas that nature (i.e., God) had made all human beings equally free. They held that liberty was a fundamental human right.[9] The other side of the slavery question was argued by, among others, Juan de Sepúlveda, a contemporary of Las Casas who held that the inhabitants of the New World were barbarians and, thus, examples of Aristotle's "natural slaves."

Helmholz concluded that when the jurists of late medieval Europe considered the many different legal questions where servitude was an issue, they generally came down on the side of freedom.[10] Nonetheless, servitude continued to exist in European society while the scholars continued the debate. The right to liberty was an important principle of the natural law, they argued, but so too was the right to private property. These two rights were in conflict when it came to servitude. The jurists of the *ius commune* continued to support both of these "natural rights"—but mostly only in theory.

---

[7] *Summa Theologiae* Q.4 Art.4 For more on Thomas and our questions see Brian Tierney, *Liberty and Law: The Idea of Permissive Natural Law, 1100–1800* (Washington, DC 2014) 69–91.

[8] Recently, there has been a renewed scholarly interest in these discussions. Most recently, the work of Richard Helmholz has focused slavery and the canon law. See *Natural Law in Court: A History of Legal Theory in Practice* (Cambridge, MA 2015); "The Law of Slavery and the European Ius Commune," in *The Legal Understanding of Slavery*, ed. J. Allain (Oxford 2012) 17–39; and "Human Rights in the Canon Law," in *Christianity and Human Rights: An Introduction*, ed. J. Witte and F. S. Alexander (Cambridge 2010) 99–112. Also see John T. Noonan, *A Church That Can and Cannot Change* (Notre Dame, IN 2005) and "Experience and the Development of Moral Doctrine," *Catholic Theological Society of America Proceedings* 54 (1999) 43–56; John B. Killoran, "Aquinas and Vitoria: Two Perspectives on Slavery," in *The Medieval Tradition of Natural Law*, ed. Harold J. Johnson (Kalamazoo, MI 1987) 87–101; Brian Tierney, *The Idea of Natural Rights: Studies on Natural Rights, Natural Law and Church Law, 1150–1625* (Atlanta 1997) and his *Liberty and Law*, as well as his *Medieval Poor Law* (Berkeley 1959); Kenneth Pennington, "*Lex Naturalis* and *Ius Naturale*," *The Jurist* 68 (2008) 569–91; and Rudolf Weigand, *Die Naturrechtslehre der Legisten und Dekretisten von Irnerius bis Accursius und von Gratian bis Johannes Teutonicus* (Munich 1967).

[9] Tierney, *Idea of Natural Rights* 272–87. Las Casas took this idea far beyond the issue of slavery, even to the extent of arguing that a ruler requires the consent of the governed. On Las Casas, see Kenneth Pennington, "Bartolomé de Las Casas," in *Great Christian Jurists in Spanish History*, ed. R. Domingo and J. Martínez-Torrón (Cambridge 2018) 98–114.

[10] Helmholz, "The Law of Slavery."

Although Gratian of Bologna had argued in the early twelfth century that since God ultimately owns everything, there were limits on humans' rights to "their" property, in practice an individual's property rights were generally upheld.[11] The *Liber extra* had repeated Isidore of Seville's ancient precept that such natural rights must be just in order for them to be upheld.[12] But the lack of clarity about how to determine what was just made the jurists' arguments in favor of the right to freedom impossibly complex.[13] The canonists were torn between the traditional teachings of the church and their own new insights into the natural law.

Discussions about the immorality of slavery continued through the next few centuries, but nothing changed in the Catholic Church's official position until modern times.[14] Popes occasionally condemned the evils of slavery, they did not act to change it. And during these centuries, the idea of the church as slave owner does not seem to have been at issue. Nevertheless, there are many indications that some individuals, lay and ecclesiastical, were against slavery, even though the church had not forbidden the practice. At the end of the seventeenth century, a former Brazilian slave named Lourenço da Silva brought a petition to Rome asking that the church condemn unjust enslavement and the excessive mistreatment of slaves. The cause was taken up by the leader of the Capuchin monks as part of the Capuchin order's ministry to slaves in Congo. While no such declaration ever appeared, perhaps because of pressure from the Spanish Crown, the case did make it at least as far as the Congregation for the Propagation of the Faith in the papal court.[15] Yet the canon law remained unchanged, and the institutional church as well as individual ecclesiastical personnel continued to own slaves. Even the popes still had slaves: records show that thousands of Muslim slaves were used to man the galleys of the papal navy from 1600 to 1800.[16]

---

[11] *Decretum* D.8 c.1.

[12] X 5.40.12.

[13] For more discussion of this issue see Helmholz, "Human Rights."

[14] As the scope of this book ends before the beginning of the Protestant Reformation, it does not address slavery in these other Christian denominations. However, it is appropriate to note that although a number of individual Protestant thinkers spoke out against slavery, until later centuries, the institutional churches do not seem to have condemned the practice outright, with the exception of the Religious Society of Friends, the Quakers.

[15] On this see Richard Gray, "The Papacy and the Atlantic Slave Trade," *Past & Present* 115 (1987) 52–68.

[16] See Giulia Bonazza, *Abolitionism and the Persistence of Slavery in Italian States, 1750–1850* (Cham 2019) 116–29.

Modern Issues

This brings us back to the Jesuits: In 1838, the Jesuits of Maryland decided that a mass sell-off of their African-descent slaves would provide the funds they needed to minister to the needs of European Catholic immigrants.[17] In June 1838, 272 slaves were sold to landowners in Louisiana. Most of the money received was earmarked for training new priests to minister to the recent European immigrant population, but about 22 percent went to support Georgetown University and take care of other financial obligations.[18]

The Jesuits had long been major slaveholders in the Americas. Jesuit scholars in South America wrote a number of tracts about the New World applicability of Greco-Roman ideas about slavery, particularly the Aristotelian ideas about slaves' natural inferiority.[19] So it is not surprising that in the days after the American Revolution, the Maryland Jesuits saw their African slave population as inherently inferior. They believed, in accordance with the later New Testament epistles, that it was their duty as Christian slave owners to care for their slaves.[20] Manumission, many believed, would only have loosed these helpless persons into a world where they would have a very hard time competing against an inherently superior labor force of recent European immigrants. In return, it was the Christian duty of the Jesuits' slaves to obey and serve their masters well.

For the most part, the nineteenth-century Maryland Jesuits behaved in much the same way as anyone else in their society. Slaveholding was permitted by secular and, as we have seen, by ecclesiastical law. And the social customs of nineteenth-century Maryland supported slave owners disposing of their workers however they saw fit. Of course, according to canon law, the alienation of church property was generally not permitted, except in cases

---

[17] Thomas Murphy, S.J., has written a comprehensive and candid account of Jesuit slaveholding in Maryland. He concluded that the American Jesuits were no more immune to racism than were others of European descent in the southern US states. *Jesuit Slaveholding in Maryland, 1717–1838* (New York 2001). Also very helpful is Robert Emmett Curran, "'Splendid Poverty,' Jesuit Slaveholding in Maryland," in his book *Shaping American Catholicism: Maryland and New York, 1805–1915* (Washington, DC 2012) 30–51.

[18] Curran, "Splendid Poverty" 46–50. Of the $115,000 sale price, $8,000 was used to retire the Jesuits' debt to the archbishop, another $17,000 to Georgetown University for partial payment of obligations incurred in the course of a building project, and the remaining $90,000 was put in a fund to be used for the "formation" of new Jesuits.

[19] See Rafael de Bivar Marquese and Fábio Duarte Joly, "*Panis, disciplina, et opus servo*: The Jesuit Ideology in Portuguese America and Greco-Roman Ideas of Slavery," in *Slave Systems Ancient and Modern*, ed. E. Dal Lago and C. Katsari (Cambridge 2008) 214–30.

[20] On this see Murphy, *Jesuit Slaveholding in Maryland* 101, 121, and *passim*.

where it would be to the greater benefit of the church or its mission, like the rescue of ancient captives. In this case, it was seen to be of great benefit to support the church's ministry to European Catholic immigrants. Correspondence among the leaders of the Jesuit order at that time concerning the Maryland slaves confirms that the potential impropriety of alienating their "patrimony" was one of the issues to be considered, although canon law was not explicitly invoked.[21]

A number of nineteenth-century Jesuits had doubts about slavery, on both moral and economic grounds. But, as had been the case when some late Roman church leaders preached against cruelty and excess in connection with slave owning, nothing was changed in the behavior of the larger institution. The Jesuit order on the whole was opposed to abolitionist ideas, to some extent because the abolitionist cause was championed by so many Protestant thinkers.[22] This echoed the larger church's resistance to Protestant Humanist and Enlightenment ideas in general and also probably reflects the Jesuits' anxieties after they had been "suppressed" by the church authorities in Rome between 1773 and 1814.

So a mass sell-off of the Maryland slaves was a compromise. It more or less ended the Jesuits' slave-owning activities in a way that did not make them "dangerous abolitionists." And at the same time, it raised money to support their new mission to the European immigrants. Using the revenues obtained by the sale of their slaves to support a more urgent ministry was viewed in a positive light. And while the manner in which these poor unfortunates were "sold South" was seen by some as unnecessarily cruel, the man ultimately responsible for the sale, Thomas Mulledy, was back in charge of the Maryland Jesuit province within a few years.[23] In short, the nineteenth-century Jesuits were, like just about all of the people we have seen in this study, men of their time. And they behaved accordingly, in what David Collins has called "enculturation gone awry."[24]

In 1888, after most of the secular regimes in the Western world had abolished slavery, Pope Leo XIII wrote a letter known as *Ineffabilis* to the bishops of Brazil on May 5 saying that the Catholic Church had always wanted slavery to be

---

[21] Letter from Francis Dzierozynski to Luigi Fortis (both high-ranking Jesuit superiors) April 12, 1822. Quoted in Curran, "Splendid Poverty" 44.

[22] Murphy, *Jesuit Slaveholding in Maryland* 129–62.

[23] Curran, "Splendid Poverty" 49–51.

[24] The Georgetown *Hoya*, February 9, 2015, at www.thehoya.com. David Collins, S.J., is the chair of the Georgetown Working Group on Slavery, Memory and Reconciliation.

abolished.[25] He may genuinely have thought that conversion to the Catholic faith would cause people to abandon slaveholding voluntarily. However, Leo was not a historian, and his arguments were based on very bad history.[26] Less than two weeks after this letter was written, Princess Isabel of Brazil legally ended slavery in that country. Since the timing makes it nearly impossible for Leo's letter of May 5 to have influenced Isabel's proclamation of May 15, we can probably conclude that Leo was aware of her antislavery sentiments and wanted his sentiments in that direction to be on record.

Leo's letter of 1890, *Catholicae Ecclesiae*, was a summary of the arguments in *Ineffabilis* as a justification of his appeal for money to be sent to Rome for the purpose of sending more missionaries to Africa.[27] Many of these missionaries were freed slaves who had returned to Africa to spread the Christian faith.[28]

Leo's 1891 encyclical letter, *Rerum Novarum*, has frequently been presented as evidence of papal disapproval of slavery. It said: "A man's labor . . . is personal, inasmuch as the force which acts is bound up with the personality and is the exclusive property of him who acts, and, further, was given to him for his advantage."[29] While this was a landmark statement, it was not made in connection with unfree servitude. The letter went on to say that it is for this reason that a worker is entitled to earn a living wage. Indeed, the letter as a whole is about the proper treatment of labor in a capitalist society. Taken together, Leo's letters do suggest that he, personally, may have held an antislavery position, but they are in no way an expression of any change in the official church position, much less in the canon law concerning slavery. The nations of the West or controlled by Western powers had all outlawed slavery by the end of the nineteenth century, but that was not everywhere the case. Whether ecclesiastical persons or institutions still owned slaves in these non-Western areas has yet to be investigated.

The canon law of the classical period was not significantly changed until a new *Code of Canon Law* was promulgated in 1917 under the authority of Pope Benedict XV. Along with considerable concern for the nonalienation of the *res*

---

[25] Leo's letter is available at www.vatican.va. An English translation can be found at papalencyclicals. net.

[26] For more discussion on this see John Francis Maxwell, *Slavery and the Catholic Church: The History of Catholic Teaching Concerning the Moral Legitimacy of the Institution of Slavery* (London 1975) 115–20.

[27] This letter is available as in note 23.

[28] David Maxwell, "Freed Slaves, Missionaries, and Respectability: The Expansion of the Christian Frontier from Angola to Belgian Congo," *Journal of African History* 54 (2013) 79–102.

[29] *Rerum Novarum*, par. 44. Trans. www.vatican.va.

ecclesiae, this new *Code* upheld the prohibition against the ordination of servile persons, "those who are strictly speaking slaves before receiving liberty."[30] The canon upheld, or at least acknowledged, the rights of slave owners, even in the twentieth century. It is clear from the context that the reason servile status was an impediment to ordination was because of the conflicting obligations a slave would have to the church and to his master. The same canon also forbade the ordination of men "bound to ordinary military service until they have completed it." Likewise, canon 1083 reiterated the old provision that the marriage of a free person with someone who misrepresented themselves as free was not valid. One suspects that the reticence of the Roman church authorities to condemn slavery outright, even at this late date, may have stemmed in part from their desire to support missionary efforts in a number of places where slavery was still legal. Encouraging slaves to leave their legal masters would have been a significant deterrent to conversions. But such speculation is not useful to our purpose here.

The church officially and explicitly condemned slavery for the first time in the documents of the Second Vatican Council (1962–1965). In the pastoral constitution "The Church and the World," the council condemned all forms of slavery:

> Whatever is hostile to life itself . . . whatever violates the integrity of the human person, is offensive to human dignity, such as subhuman living conditions, arbitrary imprisonment, deportation, slavery, prostitution and trafficking in women and children . . . all these and the like are a disgrace, and so long as they infect human civilization they contaminate those who inflict them more than those who suffer injustice, and they are a negation of the honor due to the creator.[31]

The new *Code of Canon Law* promulgated in 1983 followed in the spirit of the Vatican council by condemning "Offenses against Human Life and Freedom," saying, "One . . . who forcibly kidnaps, detains, mutilates or seriously wounds is to be punished [appropriately]."[32] But the 1983 code also stated, "In order

---

[30] §§1528–43 on ecclesiastical property; §987 on the ordination of servile persons. *The 1917 or Pio-Benedictine Code of Canon Law* (Latin and English), ed. E. N. Peters (San Francisco 2001). Also available online at vatican.va.

[31] *The Church in the World* II.27, "Respect for the Human Person," in Tanner, *Decrees of the Ecumenical Councils* 1085–86 or at vatican.va. On this see John T. Noonan's cogent analysis in *A Church That Can* 119–23.

[32] *Codex Iuris Canonici: Auctoritate Ioannis Pauli PP. I Promulgatus* §1397 Latin / English translation, published at Washington, DC 1983. Also at vatican.va.

for one to be ordained he ought to possess the required freedom."[33] While one can infer that this meant freedom from marital or military obligations, it seems a bit odd that these were not specified as they had been in the 1917 code. Then the new *Catechism of the Catholic Church*, whose composition was overseen by Josef Cardinal Ratzinger (later Pope Benedict XVI) and was approved by Pope John Paul II in 1992, explicitly said that enslaving another human being is a sin against the seventh commandment: "Thou shalt not steal."[34]

None of these late twentieth-century documents mentioned ecclesiastical servile dependents. By this time, slavery had been outlawed by just about every recognized civil government, although illegal human trafficking does still occur in many places at the time of this writing. Once slavery was illegal according to secular law, there was no question of the church continuing to own servile dependents. And the sinfulness of mistreating one's workforce had been made abundantly clear, with no exceptions made for ecclesiastical employers. So we are probably safe in assuming that ecclesiastical slave-holding had finally come to a complete end. It didn't end with a bang, or even with a whimper. It merely ceased to exist.

From all of this long analysis, several points have emerged: First, societies from the Roman Empire to the European colonies of the New World all saw that slavery was an inherently undesirable practice. Freedom, they said, was the rule of "nature's law" or the law of God. However, abolishing slavery does not seem to have been considered. They simply justified their use of slaves by declaring that the slaves "deserved" it somehow. Aristotle had said that there was a class of "natural slaves" who were inherently inferior. Foreigners were inferior, as were prisoners of war. Soon these were joined by those who followed a different religion, criminals, sinners, and so on. More than seven hundred years after Aristotle, Augustine, the bishop of Hippo, taught that God had instituted slavery as the just punishment for human sin. Nevertheless, theologians and philosophers, Jews, Christians, and pagan Stoics, all taught that slavery is bad because a slave is a human being. But they concentrated on the slavery of the spirit, slavery to sin, saying that the slavery of the body did not matter very much. They seem not to have been able to conceive of a society without slave labor. As late as the sixteenth century CE, jurists and theologians continued to hold these same ideas in

---

[33] §1026.
[34] *Catechism of the Catholic Church* 3.2.2.7.2, available at vatican.va.

connection with the New World colonies, even though servile labor had waned in much of Europe. In short: ecclesiastical slave owners throughout nearly two millennia had a strong body of support for their position.

Second, the need to protect the rights of individual property owners provided a strong counterweight to arguments in favor of human freedom. A powerful example of this principle is the fact that an unfree person could not be ordained or enter a monastery unless his lay master consented and relinquished all rights in and to the slave and the slave's services. The church respected the master's property rights. The property of the church was inviolate as well. But ordination or monastic profession did not take away the slave's services to the church, to God. It merely changed their nature. The only exception to the rights of an ecclesiastical slave owner occurred in connection with married slaves. By the twelfth century, the church's concern to prevent the sin of fornication had resulted in slaves being able to contract proper Christian marriages. And, according to the jurists, the natural right to marry superseded the aberration of natural law that had given rise to slavery. Thus, the property rights of the slave owner could be challenged by the rights of a slave's spouse.

Third, the situation of ecclesiastical *servi* was different from that of those with lay masters. It was almost impossible for ecclesiastical servile dependents ever to achieve freedom from their ecclesiastical masters. Slaves and the services due from ecclesiastical freedmen were among the *res ecclesiae*, and the inalienability of church property, except for a very few pious purposes like ransoming Christians from captivity, was absolute.[35] The human stewards of God's property were not authorized to dispose of it casually. In the limited cases where ecclesiastical unfree persons were able to achieve free legal status, the ancient Roman custom of a former master retaining the right to certain services from the freed slave still applied. And the principle of the inalienability of church property resulted in the progeny of that freedman inheriting the burden of those services. Those services had value and were thus a part of the inalienable *res ecclesiae*. This continuing hold on the services of an ecclesiastical freedman was the loophole that permitted the church to liberate an unfree worker for the purpose of ordination or monastic vows. As long as the former *servus* continued to serve his old ecclesiastical masters, they reasoned, the church had not really lost anything. For many centuries, these regulations were extended to include those who had been manumitted

---

[35] The ancients do not seem to have recognized the irony that it was acceptable to sell away ecclesiastical *servi*, who had become *servi* by way of being captured, in order to rescue captive Christians from the threat of enslavement.

in a church ceremony and whose obligations had thus been transferred from their former master to the church, as well as to two other categories of ecclesiastical servile dependents, the *censuales* and the *ministeriales*, groups who later disappeared quietly from history. But as the burdens of ecclesiastical freedmen and other semifree dependents were inherited by subsequent generations, there was almost no way for someone to achieve real liberty from ecclesiastical servitude.

This one significant difference between slaves with ecclesiastical owners and those with with lay owners, the perpetual obligations resulting from ecclesiastical servitude, may not seem to be a very large result for so many pages of research. However, the gradual unfolding of the story, of how the slave-owning practices of the New Testament–era Roman world became such enduring customs, is enlightening. The early and medieval church did not preach abolition. It preached a proper relationship to one's slaves. More than a thousand years later, the "Second Scholasticism" of the sixteenth century redirected the question to begin a conversation about whether slavery was even permissible. But while the situation of unfree persons with lay masters had changed considerably, the new scholarly insights did not produce much change in the situation of ecclesiastical *servi*. The jurists of the *ius commune* (as well those in later eras) upheld the practice of slavery and the inalienability of the *res ecclesiae*. While the natural law did support human freedom, they wrote, it also supported the right to private property. John Henry Newman, an English cardinal, wrote in 1863 that slavery is not intrinsically evil, but only by the "accident" of particular circumstances. Only the body is enslaved and not the spirit, he said. And Christian teachings showed how to provide the proper circumstances to reduce those accidental evils.[36]

The Catholic Church continued to own unfree laborers until at least well into the nineteenth century. And the church continued to defend that right using the medieval canon law that safeguarded the inalienability of church property, as well as more modern notions about the duty for superior individuals to care for their inferiors who were unable to care for their own needs. The Catholic Church did not forbid slavery until the twentieth century. It was not until Pope John Paul II in the last decade of the twentieth century that the church officially proclaimed that slavery was intrinsically evil.

The canon law never did say that it was unlawful for the church or its personnel to own slaves. The church just continued to follow the dictates of the

---

[36] Noonan, *A Church That Can* 3–5.

local secular law concerning servile labor. And the need for any canon legal prohibitions became moot when slavery was declared to be a sin. In the late twentieth century, the irrelevancies of the old canon law lapsed through lack of use.

Some Final Thoughts

For the most part, there was little concern about the unfree dependents of the church. Yes, occasionally someone mentioned that slaves should be well treated, but fundamentally they were to be dealt with as any other part of the *res ecclesiae*—about which there was a great deal of concern. In the early centuries, the only significant issue involving ecclesiastical *servi* that was not about property rights was the concern that clergy would enjoy the sexual services of their slaves, as was generally agreed to be a master's right. Clergy, however, were held to higher standards of behavior. In fact, in some particularly status-conscious societies, ecclesiastical slaves enjoyed a somewhat higher status in society because of their connection to the clergy, just as royal slaves enjoyed higher status because of their connection to the king. By the turn of the millennium, however, these were no longer prominent concerns. What emerged instead were increasingly complicated regulations concerning the preservation of church property. These regulations included not only the church's unfree dependents, but also the services due from those, servile or otherwise, who were ecclesiastical dependents. This human bookkeeping was so detailed that even the transformation of an unfree worker's services to a given institution into the services of an ordained person was a matter for the jurists. The books had to be balanced and the ecclesiastical patrimony had to be protected. It is important to remember, however, that church leaders were not the owners of the *res ecclesiae*. They were merely the custodians of property that belonged, ultimately, to God.

Only one thing threatened the harmony of this system. In time, unfree persons were expected to enter into proper Christian marriages instead of the old custom of extralegal pair-bonding (known to the ancient Romans as *contubernium*). This presented challenges for the management of the *res ecclesiae*. The fact that servile persons could now enter into a legal contract meant that they could enjoy the rights of any married couple. But the exercise of their spousal rights sometimes inconvenienced the church's exercise of its property rights. With the beginning of the Europeans' involvement in the New World, the discussion of individual human rights took off in a new direction. Nonetheless, discussions about ecclesiastical unfree dependents continued to center on the issue of preserving the *res ecclesiae*.

In short: the church dealt with its unfree dependents in the same way that it dealt with all of its property. Ecclesiastical dependents were usually treated in the same way as were any servile dependents in a given society. Despite idealistic preaching about the importance of an individual's soul, the canon law continued to emphasize the church's property rights in its unfree dependents. When slavery was abolished in a given area, the church could no longer claim property rights in its people. But it was not until the twentieth century, when secular society almost everywhere had abolished slavery, that the canon law officially prohibited it as well.

Many modern people question how something that the twenty-first century sees as pure evil was not seen as such in earlier centuries. It would be easy simply to condemn the ancient church leaders as having been greedy and power hungry. And some may well have been so. But the historian's job is not to judge, merely to describe. What we have uncovered here is a picture of how ecclesiastical slave ownership developed. At times, using slave labor troubled the consciences of some individuals, clergy as well as lay. However, the need to preserve God's church from ruin was also an important value. A church that was not able to support itself could not take care of its people. God's economic resources had to be preserved so that God's work could be done—even if that meant that the human greed and ambition of some ec-clesiastical personnel were gratified in the process. Bishops and others often recognized the potential cruelties of slavery, and cautioned against them. And they often recognized their own unfree dependents as human beings. But they did not do much to change the situation. These ecclesiastical leaders had human weaknesses that generally resulted in their succumbing to the so-cial and economic pressures that supported slave ownership.

In a way, the church had painted itself into a corner, morally speaking, and it took a sea change in cultural as well as spiritual values for the church to see a way out. The wide-ranging abolitionist movements of the nineteenth cen-tury soon made the question of owning unfree labor moot, and the church could no longer legally retain its unfree workforce. Only then could the church law explicitly forbid slave ownership without violating what it saw as its custodial duty.

APPENDIX

Historiographical Overview of Ideas about Medieval Slavery

Although it is clear that by the end of the thirteenth century the situation of the unfree workers in Europe had changed a great deal from the way things had been in the Roman Empire, how and why things changed has long been the subject of scholarly debate. At the beginning of the first century CE, servile workers were chattel slaves. They were property, categorized with cattle, buildings, and other major assets, and had no say in their life circumstances. There were also other laborers, free or freed, who worked mostly as artisans or soldiers or shopkeepers, and there were agricultural workers known as *coloni* who lived apart from their masters and whose situation varied from actual slavery to near independence. By around 1300 CE, although the practice of chattel slavery had not disappeared, many, if not most, peasants lived in an arrangement that has had many names, including "serfdom" or "banal lordship." In this situation, the landholder exercised a great deal of coercive power over the peasants who worked his land, by means of restrictive laws and customs and burdensome payments for basic privileges and services. The legal status of these peasants, free or servile, does not seem to have made much difference in their lives. The rest of society paid little attention to their legal status as well. Those peasants who were legally free suffered under almost all of the same disabilities as those who were servile. Nevertheless, in many places, all peasants, no matter their ancestry, were classed as unfree. As Orlando Patterson said: "European serfdom was, in effect, recombinant slavery."[1] These new social and economic arrangements came about only after a long and gradual process of change from the pattern of chattel slaves and their owners to the relationships of lord and dependent peasantry. Fundamentally both of these kinds of arrangements exploited the less fortunate for the benefit of the lord/owner, and lord/owner offered something, however little, to the workers, both to protect his investment and status and to keep the peasants from fleeing. Slavery and "serfdom" served the same functions for both groups: for the lords, labor, revenue, and status; for the slaves and other dependents, protection and sustenance.

However, for the purposes of this study, it is not urgent that we determine exactly how and when and why "slavery" became "serfdom," as so many scholars have phrased their question over the years. It is sufficient to note that over the course of the centuries, the details of how the more powerful exercised control over the less powerful changed as circumstances required. These details varied greatly from place to place. And the data about the lord/dependent relationships was recorded rather idiosyncratically, making it difficult for the modern researcher to draw parallels from one group to another. But it is clear that by the later medieval period, legal freedom did not guarantee an individual's freedom to determine the circumstances of his or her life, nor did it significantly hinder the privileged class's exploitation of the less fortunate.

---

[1] *Freedom in the Making of Western Culture* (New York 1991) 351.

Most of the literature on this subject does not distinguish between lay and ecclesiastical property owners, a distinction that is crucial to the present study. Georges Duby did see some differences in the data from lay versus ecclesiastical landholders: his data showed that as the wealth of the lay aristocracy was diminishing at the end of the first millennium, the church seemed to have prospered and grown.[2] But Duby did not follow up much on these differences because, he said, of the likelihood that the contrast may have been an artifact of his sampling. As Duby found, there is much more data available about ecclesiastical institutions than about their lay counterparts, probably due to the superior education and literacy of the clergy. Chris Wickham, however, writing a good half-century later, thought that even taking these factors into account the data does show that ecclesiastical estates were more tightly organized than lay.[3]

In general, the scholarship agrees on several main points. Despite enormous regional variations, eventually virtually everywhere in western Europe the line between free and unfree became very blurred, and there were a number of ambiguous or half-free statuses. The idiosyncratic use of words like *servus*, *mancipium*, etc., makes it difficult to compare the conditions in one society to those of another. It is clear, however, that throughout the medieval period in Europe there were always some chattel slaves, especially in areas where the slave trade was still active, like the Mediterranean commercial centers and the insular trade with Scandinavia. The circumstances of agricultural laborers, who usually lived on their own in family units, was more complicated. It is clear, however, that the demands of their lords often resulted in oppression. The fact that the nobles could no longer depend on the relatively weaker kings of the post-Carolingian era may well have been a major factor in their looking to their peasants to provide more financial resources. And in many cases, exploiting tenant farmers for rents or "services" seems to have been more profitable than direct exploitation by means of slavery. A lord had to care for his slaves or face the loss of a profitable asset. Tenants, free or unfree, were responsible for their own well-being and could usually be replaced without much difficulty. The peasants paid rent in cash or in kind or in labor services, along with fees for such privileges as grinding their grain or baking their bread. Some managed to buy their way out of servile status. It is important to note that medieval peasants did not have any notions of modern freedoms and rights; they merely longed for an end to their oppression. However, although the lords could demand a lot of money for manumission, the peasants got little real freedom in return. And granting people's desire for legal freedom did not disadvantage the lords economically.[4] In addition to the payments received for their freedom, the lord continued to charge the free tenant rents and services pretty much as before. Indeed, as the political economist Pierre Dockès pointed out, giving a peasant his own land, whether as renter or as owner, actually made him weaker because now he had something to lose.[5]

In some places, the lords lived on their property and managed it directly. In other places, the lords controlled their peasants remotely, using the services of high-status overseers, often unfree themselves, to manage the estates and to collect what was due. The

---

[2] Georges Duby, *The Early Growth of the European Economy: Warriors and Peasants from the Seventh to the Twelfth Century*, trans. H. B. Clarke (Ithaca 1974; orig. Paris 1973). Also see his work *L'économie rurale et la vie campagnes dans l'Occident Médiéval* (Paris 1962), trans. C. Postan, *Rural Economy and Country Life in the Medieval West* (Columbia, SC 1968).

[3] Chris Wickham, *The Inheritance of Rome: Illuminating the Dark Ages, 400–1000* (New York 2009) 546.

[4] William Chester Jordan, *From Servitude to Freedom* (Philadelphia 1986) 99.

[5] Pierre Dockès, *Medieval Slavery and Liberation*, trans. A. Goldhammer (Chicago 1982).

overseers frequently received a percentage of what was paid and could grow quite wealthy from extorting money from the tenants. Some peasants found opportunities to escape this domination through assarting (clearing wilderness lands far away) and through the growth of urban areas where the local lords often exercised less control. However, towns, especially Mediterranean port cities, provided new opportunities for exploiting slave labor. In other areas, the social, political, and economic changes eventually did result in different patterns of labor by the end of the medieval period. [6] But agriculture continued to be at the center of the European economy for a long time, and the aristocrats, lay or ecclesiastical, continued to control most of the land. However, these later developments are well beyond the scope of this book.

Generally, modern scholars agree that it was a French scholar, Marc Bloch (killed by the Nazis in 1944), whose work most definitively redirected the scholarly conversation away from many earlier assumptions that the arrival of Christianity had been responsible for the end of chattel slavery in Europe.[7] Bloch posed the question: "How and why did ancient slavery come to an end?"[8] And the rest of the twentieth century produced innumerable studies dedicated to finding ever-better answers to that question.[9] By the turn of

---

[6] Chris Wickham pointed out that, in late medieval Italy, many landowners seem to have found it more profitable to sell the produce of their land themselves. *Medieval Europe* (New Haven 2016) 137–39. Also see the collected essays in *Forms of Servitude in Northern and Central Europe: Decline, Resistance, and Expansion*, ed. P. Freedman and M. Bourin (Turnhout 2005).

[7] However, in 1925, G. C. Coulton had argued that we might understand things better "if the public will accustom itself to require real documentary evidence throughout this necessarily contentious stage of social history." *The Medieval Village* (Cambridge 1925) 388. And as early as the mid-nineteenth century, Karl Marx had famously asserted that slavery, the dominant mode of production in only a few societies, had given way to serfdom in Europe on the way to the establishment of capitalism. In 1895, John Kells Ingram, *A History of Slavery and Serfdom* (London 1895), looked at these changes as a process of social, political, and economic development on the path toward universal freedom.

[8] Marc Bloch, "Comment et pourquoi finit l'esclavage antique?," *Annales* 2 (1947) 30–44, 161–70. A number of his essays have been translated into English by W. R. Beer in *Slavery and Serfdom in the Middle Ages: Selected Essays by Marc Bloch* (Berkeley 1975).

[9] There are far too many studies to list here, but, along with the work of Georges Duby mentioned above, some of the more important general works include Moses I. Finley, *Ancient Slavery and Modern Ideology* (New York 1980), expanded ed., ed. B. D. Shaw (Princeton 1998); Stanley L. Engerman, "Some Considerations Relating to Property Rights in Man," *Journal of Economic History* 33 (1973) 43–65; Joseph C. Miller, *The Problem of Slavery as History: A Global Approach* (New Haven 2012); and David Brion Davis, *The Problem of Slavery in Western Culture* (Ithaca 1966). *Serfdom and Slavery: Studies in Legal Bondage*, ed. M. L. Bush (London 1996), provides a good anthology of essays contributed by some of the most important scholars in this area.
A number of the most successful works focused on a particular region. Eliminating the confusion of geographical differences makes it easier to see the changes over time in a particular region. These regional studies include, for France, Duby, *Early Growth*; and Dominique Barthelemy, *La mutation de l'an mil a-t-elle eu lieu? Servage et chevalrie dans la France des Xe et XIe siècles* (Paris 1997), trans. G. R. Edwards, *The Serf, the Knight, and the Historian* (Ithaca 2009); for the Iberian Peninsula, the collected essays of Pierre Bonnassie in *From Slavery to Feudalism in South-Western Europe*, trans. J. Birrell (Cambridge 1999), Thomas Bisson, *Tormented Voices: Power, Crisis, and Humanity in Rural Catalonia, 1140–1200* (Cambridge, MA 1990), and Paul Freedman, *The Origins of Peasant Servitude in Medieval Catalonia* (Cambridge 1991) and *Images of the Medieval Peasant* (Stanford 1999); for Italy, Steven Epstein, *Speaking of Slavery: Color, Ethnicity and Human Bondage in Italy* (Ithaca 2001); for the British Isles, David Pelteret, *Slavery in Medieval England* (Woodbridge, Suffolk 1995) and Paul Hyams, *Kings, Lords, and Peasants in Medieval England* (Oxford 1980); for Scandinavia, Ruth Mazzo Karras, *Slavery and Society in Medieval Scandinavia* (New Haven 1988), and Tore Iversen et al., collected essays in *Trelldommen: Norsk slaveri I middelalderen*, ed. T. Iversen (Bergen 1997),

the twenty-first century, it had become clear that ancient slavery did not actually come to an end in the Middle Ages. As Dominique Barthélemy pointed out in 1997, a distinction between antique slavery and medieval "serfdom" has been an issue only relatively recently, only since the nineteenth century.[10] It was in the eighteenth and nineteenth centuries that effectively all Western cultures abolished slavery.[11] But they did not abolish mistreatment of those less fortunate. Neville, in her study of Scots history, put it succinctly: "Slavery as a distinct legal category may have been abolished ... at the behest of an enlightened ruler, but the personal and social disabilities associated with the lack of freedom endured."[12] Scholars' more recent question has been: what are the differences between the late antique, Carolingian, and successor schemes of peasant exploitation and those of the later medieval period?[13]

Susan Reynolds sparked a good deal of controversy by challenging previous notions of how the social structures of the old Carolingian Empire changed around the turn of the millennium.[14] She argued that the situation was much more fluid than had previously been thought to have been the case. There was no orderly structure of fiefs and vassals; the nobles did not all hold land from their liege lords in return for military service. Indeed, Reynolds argued that the line between nobles (the upper 10 percent) and the rest of society was actually rather fuzzy.[15] Thus, the earlier models of how the economic exploitation of the peasantry changed in response to "the feudal revolution" around the year 1000 would no longer hold up very well.[16] Reynolds also called for an end to using the term "serf" to describe the peasantry[17] Chris Wickham also argued that concept of "serfdom," where a peasant was tied to the land and to the lord's justice, was not really very different

---

German trans., *Knechtschaft im mittelalterlichen Norwegen* (Ebelsbach 2004); Cameron Sutt, *Slavery in Arpad-era Hungary in a Comparative Context* (Leiden 2015) for Hungary; and Youval Rotman, *Les esclaves et l'esclavage: De la Méditerranée antique à la Méditerranée médiévale Vie–XIe siècles* (Paris 2004), trans. J. M. Todd, *Byzantine Slavery and the Mediterranean World* (Cambridge, MA 2009) for the Eastern Roman Empire.

[10] Cynthia Neville, *Land, Law and People in Medieval Scotland* (Edinburgh 2010) 71.

[11] Although Hungary (1000) and Finland (1335) abolished slavery in the later medieval period, it took a long while for the rest of Europe to follow suit. (Although the king of Denmark ended the slave trade in the tenth century, Denmark-Norway was very active in the later slaving from the 1670s on.) In the eighteenth century, Portugal, England, Scotland, Wales, and France outlawed slavery at home, but waited fifty years or more to abolish slavery in their colonies abroad. Sweden, Denmark, Norway, Russia, and the Netherlands followed in the nineteenth century, as did most of the polities in the New World and the Ottoman Empire.

[12] Neville, *Land, Law and People* 155.

[13] *Serfdom and Slavery* provides a good anthology of essays contributed by some of the most important scholars in this area.

[14] Susan Reynolds, *Fiefs and Vassals: The Medieval Evidence Reinterpreted* (Oxford 1996). See also her work *Kingdoms and Communities in Western Europe*, 2nd. ed. (Oxford 1997).

[15] Susan Reynolds, *The Middle Ages without Feudalism: Essays in Criticism and Comparison on the Medieval West* (Surry 2012) xiv.

[16] On this see Dominique Barthélemy, *La mutation de l'an mil a-t-elle eu lieu? Servage et chevalerie dans la France des Xe et XIe siècles* (Paris 1997), trans. G. R. Edwards, *The Serf, the Knight, and the Historian* (Ithaca 2009). Thomas Bisson's ideas on this question sparked considerable controversy. His 1994 article "The 'Feudal Revolution,'" *Past & Present* 142: 6–2 became the focus of a series of responses: in #152 (1996) from Dominique Barthélemy (196–205) and Stephen White (205–23); in #155 (1997) from Timothy Reuter (177–95) and Chris Wickham (196–208), as well as Bisson's reply to his critics in #155 (1997) 208–25. Also see Charles West, *Reframing the Feudal Revolution* (Cambridge 2013).

[17] Reynolds, *Kingdoms and Communities.*

from the slavery of the earlier centuries.[18] He found that the Roman legacy was still important, although less so in the North than in Italy, southern France, and Spain. Jeffrey Fynn-Paul very effectively countered any lingering ideas that Christianity had ended slavery in Europe by pointing out that "any European aversion to slavery during the High Middle Ages was strongly aided by the economic reality of dirt-cheap labor."[19]

Other scholars have focused on social aspects of slavery, on the domination of one group over another and on the gender differences seen in such domination.[20] When the economic relation of slaves and lords changed into the situation that historians have often called "serfdom," the less powerful were, likely as not, still considered to be unfree. Given the nature of their tasks, servile women were more likely to be domestics or housed in common as factory laborers, giving rise to the impression that their lives were more slave-like. Servile men were more likely to be housed separately on the land that they farmed, or in the businesses they ran. The difficulty with this analysis is that these servile men were joined by the servile women when it was time to start a family. And then the women were viewed in the same way as their husbands. Some of these women remained in their earlier stations, but for many, it was only temporary work.[21]

Alice Rio's recent work has brought Bloch's question full circle.[22] She argued that the reason that no satisfactory answer to his question has been produced in the seventy years since his posthumously published essay is that the reality is too complex for a simple answer. The enormous regional variations make it impossible for any longitudinal models to have more than very local validity. While Rio's findings might at first glance seem discouraging, they recognize the fact that the data has never really fit with the earlier attempts to provide a generalized answer to Bloch's question. This provides an exciting challenge to future medievalists to explore what these regional variations in economic and social change can tell us.[23]

[18] Chris Wickham, *The Inheritance of Rome: Illuminating the Dark Ages, 400–1000* (New York 2009) 538.

[19] "Empire, Monotheism and Slavery in the Greater Mediterranean Region from Antiquity to the Early Modern Era," *Past & Present* 205 (2009) 3–40, here 32.

[20] For example, David Wyatt, *Slaves and Warriors in Medieval Britain and Ireland, 800–1200* (Leiden 2009), whose work built on the earlier gendered analyses of Karras, *Slavery and Society*, as well as Susan Mosher Stuard, "Ancillary Evidence for the Decline of Medieval Slavery," *Past and Present* 149 (1995) 3–28.

[21] This does not take into account the non-European, non-Christian female slaves who were so common in port cities. See Iris Origo, *The Merchant of Prato: Francesco di Marco Datini, 1335–1410* (New York 1957).

[22] Alice Rio, *Slavery after Rome, 500–1100* (Oxford 2017).

[23] Michael McCormick's essay "Slavery from Rome to Medieval Europe and Beyond," in *On Human Bondage: After Slavery and Social Death*, ed. J. Bodel and W. Scheidel (Chichester 2017) 249–64, looked at the possibilities offered by genomic analysis and linguistic meta-analysis as well as by more sophisticated archaeological techniques.

Latin Lexicon

ancilla. Female slave

bannum. Sovereign or jurisdictional power of the lord

beneficium. A favor

censual. Someone who owes a yearly amount to their patron, usually the church

census. Yearly reckoning

colonus. Tenant farmer (free/servile status varied)

contubernium. Servile equivalent to marriage

cursus honorum. Career ladder (literally, path of honors)

de. Concerned with, regarding

dominium. Dominion

ecclesiasticus. Related to the church

epistola (ep.). Letter

familia. Household

homo. Man (often used to indicate one's slave, as in "my man")

ius gentium. The law of nations (as opposed to the law of nature or of God)

latifundium. Large agricultural estate, usually run on slave labor

lex/legis. Law, statute

liber. Free

mancipium. Slave (either gender)

obsequium. Duties of a former slave to the former master

patrocinium. Patronage

peculium. Money for the use of a dependent person, technically the master's property

regius. Of the king

res. Thing, property

res ecclesiae. Church property

Romanitas. Roman-ness

servus. Male slave

utilitas. Usefulness

villa. Country estate

Index

For the benefit of digital users, indexed terms that span two pages (e.g., 52–53) may, on occasion, appear on only one of those pages.